D0899960

Revelations of a
Russian Diplomat

Dmitrii Ivanovich Abrikossow, circa 1910

Revelations of a Russian Diplomat

The Memoirs of Dmitrii I. Abrikossow

EDITED BY

George Alexander Lensen

University of Washington Press
Seattle, 1964

Other books by George Alexander Lensen

REPORT FROM HOKKAIDO

RUSSIA'S JAPAN EXPEDITION OF 1852 TO 1855

THE MEANING OF YALTA
(with John L. Snell, Charles F. Delzell, and Forrest C. Pogue)

THE RUSSIAN PUSH TOWARD JAPAN

THE WORLD BEYOND EUROPE

RUSSIA'S EASTWARD EXPANSION

FIRST EDITION
Copyright © 1964 by the University of Washington Press
Library of Congress Catalog Card Number 64–18426
Manufactured by Kingsport Press, Inc., Kingsport, Tennessee
Printed in the United States of America

To the memory of Serezha

Editor's Foreword

DMITRII IVANOVICH ABRIKOSSOW WAS A DIPLOMAT OF BOURGEOIS origin, as rare a phenomenon in Tsarist days as since the Revolution. An interloper in the world's oldest aristocratic profession, he brought to it a refreshingly different point of view. Independent in mind and means, he stood apart from the madding crowd, ridiculing monocled bureaucrats and unkempt radicals alike. A confirmed bachelor, Abrikossow lavished most of his time and affection on his work, notably on the sorting and putting into order of diplomatic archives. This made him exceptionally well-informed on Russian foreign policy. At the same time his own lack of family led him to take an unusual interest in the private lives of others. His memoirs thus are packed with comments about well-known historical figures. Although diplomats usually remain diplomatic in their reminiscences, since the people they mention are still active in public life, the shattering of Old Russia and its Foreign Service by the Revolution freed Abrikossow from such inhibitions. When a Russian ambassador runs off with a little Lolita or a grand duke deprives a subordinate officer of his spouse, he reports it with the air of "What fools these mortals be." Indeed, it was as a biography of someone else that his memoirs found their inception. Urged by a friend to write his recollections of Count Benckendorff, the Russian ambassador to England, he unwound a thread of thought that entangled his own existence.

Dmitrii Abrikossow was born into a wealthy and respected Moscow merchant family in 1876. He died in Palo Alto, California, seventy-five years later. His life spanned continents of time and change. The days of the wealthy Russian merchant class are no more; gone are capitalist Moscow and bureaucratic St. Petersburg; gone are Edwardian London, Manchu Peking, and the Tokyo of before the great earthquake of 1923. The Russian experience stands on the threshold of oblivion. It does not belong to history in the way that Edwardian England may be said to belong, for even history has been expropriated in the Soviet Union. The happy aspects of pre-Revolutionary life have been exorcised, the names of distinguished diplomats and historical figures deleted from encyclopedias. Abrikossow's descriptions of his childhood, university education, military service and diplomatic career bridge a variety of Russian backgrounds and ways. His reminiscences of travel and work abroad extend the horizon to the far corners of the world. The memoirs thus are more than the story of one man; they are the record of his time.

Abrikossow was not a key figure in history. He did not shape foreign policy. But in this there are advantages as well as disadvantages. In a position high enough to know international relations from the inside, he was yet low enough to be primarily an observer. He pens his impressions without the compulsion to defend or to justify either a particular policy or himself. Secure in place and position, Abrikossow viewed life with a detachment that gives his narrative a certain "truth" which would have been lacking had he been caught up in the usual struggle for power. Even after the deluge, when all the props of stability, livelihood, familiarity, and "belonging" had been swept from under him, Abrikossow remained uninvolved, finding strength and solace in the outlook of Spinoza, the favorite philosopher of his stepfather and himself. "How often have I overcome the irritation of endless little annoyances by looking on everything *sub specie aeternitatis*!" Abrikossow remarks.

Abrikossow was a man of the Imperial regime. He is straightforward and unequivocal in his political and social views and prejudices. Reactionary and occasionally naïve as these may appear to modern readers, Abrikossow was a man of principle, unwilling to make any "accommodations" for the sake of expedience. Making no attempt to retailor his habit in the fashion of our day, he emerges as himself, and portraying himself with remarkable fidelity, ranks well as a writer of memoirs. Armed with philosophical fortitude, a healthy sense of humor, and a flair for the dramatic, Abrikossow succeeded in breathing life into his reminiscences.

Abrikossow was intimately associated with historical events of importance. During the Russo-Japanese War he served as attaché in the Russian Embassy in London; during the Chinese Revolution of 1911-12 as second secretary of the Russian Legation in Peking; during World War I he worked in the Asian Section of the Foreign Office in St. Petersburg; from 1916 to 1925 he was first secretary and then chargé d'affaires of the Russian Embassy in Tokyo—which during the civil war and the Allied Intervention tried to support, if not coordinate, anti-Communist efforts in Siberia. His chatty, readable, and highly personal commentary, bulging with anecdotes and irreverent observations as well as deeply moving reflections, adds flesh to the skeleton of historical analysis.

Abrikossow wrote his memoirs to preserve the past, a past that to him seemed much better than the present. But he wrote them also as a warning to men of the free world, lest they be deceived and overcome by the forces of Communism. The present remains rooted in the past, and the recollections of Abrikossow are a seedbed of current events. The Far Eastern Republic of the 1920's was merely the first of the "People's Republics," the Allied Intervention in Siberia aroused the mistrust of friend and foe and bore a remarkable resemblance in lack of purpose, lack of planning, and ineffectiveness to later interventions elsewhere, and the student demonstrations and strikes in Tsarist Russia are not unlike the political agitation on university campuses in Latin America, Asia, and elsewhere. In the pages of the past are lessons for today.

Following the recognition of the Soviet government by Japan, Abrikossow remained in Tokyo as a private person. Stateless, since he refused to recognize the Communist regime, he was not an "enemy alien" upon the outbreak of the Pacific war and could not leave Japan on an exchange ship. Thus his years of hardship as a refugee were capped with the agonies and privations of wartime living. Only after the defeat of Japan did he succeed in coming to the United States. Tired of squalor, hunger, and mistrust, he longed for a life of plenty among people of his own race. Soviet efforts to persuade him to return to the fatherland, where his brother Aleksei Ivanovich had attained great honor as a member of the Academy of Sciences, prodded him to put more miles between himself and the U.S.S.R. But obsessed as he was to go to the United States, he faced his last day in Japan with heavy heart.

It was raining and the air was damp and misty. It was as if Japan were crying at the prospect of losing somebody who for thirty years had made of it his second fatherland, whose figure was quite familiar on the streets of Tokyo and who had shared the joys of its people in the days when Japan had been a country of happiness and smiles. If the steady rain really meant such sorrow, the feeling was mutual, because one cannot live in a country for thirty years without falling under its influence. . . .

On November 4, 1946, Abrikossow set foot in San Francisco. His old friend Admiral Boris Petrovich Dudorov, who had been Russian naval attaché in Tokyo and had helped him greatly after the departure of the Ambassador, lived in Palo Alto and it had been arranged that Abrikossow stay with him and his wife. The day after his arrival in Palo Alto Abrikossow wandered to the campus of Stanford University. Absorbed in thought he entered the beautiful Memorial Chapel and the peace, which for years had forsaken him, re-entered his tormented soul.

As I sat in the chapel all alone, my whole life seemed to pass before me [Abrikossow recorded]. I remembered my happy childhood in Moscow, the brilliant life abroad, the long exile in the Far East, the miseries and anxieties of the Revolution, the thousands of refugees with their stories of horror and death, the war and its privations, and finally peace in this strange and beautiful land. I realized how lucky I had been that all these misfortunes had passed near me without truly touching me personally, without destroying my faith in Providence, that I had preserved the ability, taught me by my father, to look on things and events *sub specie aeternitatis*. The Memorial Chapel reminded me of the Cathedral of the Holy Savior in Moscow, the gorgeous edifice built in memory of the liberation of Russia from Napoleon in 1812 and pulled down by the Bolsheviks in their struggle against religion, and as I sat there alone with my thoughts, I had the same religious feeling that I had experienced as a child when taken to the Cathedral of the Holy Savior. Forgetting my surroundings, I offered thanks to God for all the happiness of my past and for the peace I now felt.

Abrikossow died on November 4, 1951.

His brother Aleksei, who had finished medical school with honors and had remained at Moscow University to prepare himself for a professorship, weathered the Revolution. He made a brilliant career as a scientist, was summoned to embalm the body of Lenin, and participated in consultations when Stalin was ill. A member of the Academy of Sciences, he is listed in standard Soviet encyclopedias. In addition to Aleksei there had remained in Russia Uncle Nicholas [Nikolai Aleksandrovich] and Aunt Vera; cousin Vera, who had married a professor of chemistry; sister Anna, a Roman Catholic martyr; brother Boris, a lawyer; cousin Avgusta, wife of a lawyer; and cousin Nikolai, also a lawyer and member of the board of directors of the Abrikossow company. Brother Ivan, who had studied mathematics at Heidelberg University in Germany, transferred in 1904 to the Polytechnical Institute in Hanover, then moved to Winnipeg, Canada, and to Seattle, Washington; cousin Sergei, a mathematician by training and president of the Abrikossow company, emigrated to France; cousin Pavel [Paul] to whom the editor is indebted for this and other information not in the manuscript, spends his winters in Florida, otherwise resides in Canada, where brother Khrisanf had gone also. During the German occupation of the Ukraine cousin Nikolai, who had remained in the Soviet Union, obtained permission through the efforts of his brother Sergei to go to France, but when he received the visa he was so overjoyed that he had a heart attack and died. By 1964 all but Pavel and perhaps Ivan, Avgusta, and Khrisanf had passed away.

Requirements of publication dictated a cut in the original manuscript. The passages deleted from the text here and there were mostly unimportant digressions or repetitions that detracted from the narrative. The major amputation consisted in the total deletion of the last one hundred-odd pages, covering the period after Japanese recognition of the Soviet regime and Abrikossow's removal from the Embassy in Tokyo. The story of the Russian diplomat really ends here, and the subsequent pages contain more hearsay and secondhand information than personal observations. The blue pencil was not used to retouch Abrikossow's outlook, to eliminate his anti-Semitic barbs, or to rehabilitate the characters of some of the more idealistic revolutionaries whom he has lumped together with unsavory opportunists. To have done so would have meant altering the nature of the memoirs.

[xi]

It is not clear exactly when Abrikossow began to write his recollections. The idea seems to have germinated in the 1930's during a conversation with Mr. Bock, a colleague from his early days in the Foreign Office, who wound up in Japan as a language teacher at a commercial school in Takaoka. Bock had urged Abrikossow to record his impressions of Count Benckendorff, under whom he had served in London and who was greatly misunderstood in Russia.

"I did not take the suggestion seriously at the time," Abrikossow notes, "but later, as I began to realize that with all the changes brought by the Revolution future generations would soon know nothing about the past, the suggestion made by Mr. Bock one cozy evening in Takaoka came back to mind." When "later" was, we do not know. Abrikossow's preface suggests that the memoirs were begun in the "peaceful atmosphere" of Japan. If the idea did not germinate until sometime in the 1930's, this must have been in the late thirties or in 1940, for peace was soon shattered. The last date given in the manuscript is 1946, but the work seems to have been completed in about 1950, shortly before Abrikossow's death on November 4, 1951.

"As far as I know," Admiral Dudorov informed me in a personal letter in Russian, "he wrote the memoirs directly on a typewriter (which I believe he brought with him from Japan) in one copy only. He never gave me, nor probably anyone else, his work to read. . . . In his will, written shortly before his demise, he instructed me, as his executor, to transmit this work of his to his cousin Pavel Nikolaevich Abrikossoff, which was carried out by me. No other papers, notes, and drafts of this work were found in his estate. . . . I have no doubt that the late Dmitrii Ivanovich did not seek any publisher for the printing of his work. First of all, because the work, insofar as one can judge, was far from completed. And he did not talk about it at all to anyone, not even me, in spite of the fact that he was in our house at least twice a week. Probably he deemed it necessary to go over it again upon completion, which, alas, evil fate did not let him do. . . . He did not bring out any documents of the Russian Embassy in Tokyo and all secret documents and archives were destroyed by order of the former Ambassador V. N. Krupenskii, who left upon recognition of the Soviet Government by the Japanese Government."

[xii]

On June 2, 1954, Mr. Paul Abrikossoff deposited the manuscript in the Archive of Russian and East European History and Culture at Columbia University, where I came across it in the summer of 1960, shortly before visiting the former Russian capital for a period of research. There was no record of Mr. Paul Abrikossoff's current address in the Archive at Columbia, though it was believed that he was somewhere in Canada. It would have appealed to the author's sense of the ridiculous to know that the editor had traced his cousin through a Montreal phone book, only to have the correspondence forwarded to Florida, where the editor himself lived. The contact proved invaluable, however, for Mr. Paul Abrikossoff graciously supplied all the photographs in this book and clarified some unclear passages.

As Abrikossow tells in his preface, the memoirs were written in English. His English was often cumbersome and larded with phonetic misspellings and Anglicized Russian words. To footnote all corrections would have been sheer pedantry. The manuscript has been edited to the extent of tightening the sentences, changing the sentence structure, substituting synonyms, and occasionally eliminating duplication. In a sense, I have rewritten the entire memoirs. On the other hand, I have remained faithful to the author's meaning, and my "liberties" are no greater than those of a translator. My changes and eliminations are essentially grammatical and stylistic. Except for the cuts mentioned above, they do not extend to content. I do not share all of the author's sentiments and disagree with some of his interpretations. I did not deem it my prerogative, however, to delete what was personally objectionable to me or to engage in footnote polemics. If the style is mine, the story and thoughts are those of Abrikossow. I have made every effort from a variety of sources, printed and unpublished, to identify the various individuals mentioned in the manuscript by position only and to provide the given names and patronymics whenever possible. Such additions as well as pertinent dates are given in brackets. Footnote comments have been restricted to assist the reader rather than to take issue with the author, except to point out a number of inadvertent errors. The chapter divisions and headings are mine.

The transliteration of Russian names always poses a problem, particularly because there were men of various national origins in the Imperial service. As a rule, names have been given according to the Library of Congress system, which most readily permits retransliteration into the Cyrillic alphabet, and according to Webster's *Biographical Dictionary*. In the case of such well-known figures as Count Benckendorff the spelling commonly used (and found in Webster) has been retained. The most obvious problem arose with the transliteration of the author's name. Theoretically it should have been rendered as "Abrikosov." The original manuscript gives it variously as "Abrikossoff" and "Abrikossow." After receiving assurance from Paul Abrikossoff that his cousin generally used the latter spelling, I bowed to the author's preference. Chinese names are cited according to the Wade-Giles system, place names according to Webster's *Geographical Dictionary*. In Chinese and Japanese names the surname comes first.

I am deeply indebted to the Columbia University Archive of Russian and East European History and Culture for permission to edit the manuscript, which forms part of its collection; to Mr. Lev F. Magerovsky, Curator of the Archive, for bringing the manuscript to my attention; and to Professor Philip E. Mosely, Chairman of the Archive's Administrative Committee, for encouraging me to edit the memoirs. I am most grateful to Mr. Paul Abrikossoff for the photographs used in this book and for the light thrown on many questions in person and by mail. I appreciate likewise the informative letters of Admiral Boris Petrovich Dudorov.

I acknowledge with pleasure the helpful comments of my father, Mr. Alexander Lensen, who was personally acquainted with many of the leading Russian figures mentioned in the book, and the many suggestions made by Professors Hans Kohn, John A. White, and Donald W. Treadgold, readers of the edited manuscript. I am thankful to my old friend and classmate Mrs. Tomoe Arai who obtained for me a microfilm copy of the manuscript, and to the Florida State University Research Council for financing the duplication of the manuscript and the photographs.

I would like to take this opportunity to express my appreciation to the American Philosophical Society, the American Council of Learned Societies, the Social Science Research Council, and the Inter-

University Committee on Travel Grants for their encouragement and support of my research in the history of Russo-Japanese relations, of which this work is a byproduct. Needless to say their support does not constitute endorsement of the views expressed in the book.

GEORGE ALEXANDER LENSEN

June, 1964
Tallahassee, Florida

Author's Preface

IN MY EARLY YOUTH I TRIED SEVERAL TIMES TO KEEP A DIARY. AT THE outset I faithfully recorded daily events and my reactions thereto, but so ordinary and uneventful was my life at the time that my imagination began to encroach upon events and feelings. Disgusted with such insincerity, I soon put a stop to these literary efforts. When I found them years later, I was touched by their naïveté, but confirmed in my opinion that only those to whom fate has given an interesting and exciting life have the right to keep diaries. Otherwise a diary leads to egoism; one begins to consider oneself the center of the universe, attaches too much importance to one's own feelings, and becomes dissatisfied with real life and its simple joys. Thus I destroyed my early efforts to make myself interesting in my own eyes and decided to accept life as it came, without too much analysis. When, with no effort on my part, life did become interesting and eventful and I found myself face to face with prominent people, I had lost the habit of recording my observations and feelings. I did not realize that years later, as events would pass, as old age would come, and as life would turn ordinary and uneventful again, the desire to jot down my experiences would reassert itself, and I would regret the absence of a diary. Nor did I anticipate that revolution would cut me off from the past—from archives and letters, from relatives and friends—from all my possessions, indeed from my fatherland.

In exile the desire to recapture the past grew steadily, strengthened by the realization that the old way of life had gone forever and by the desire to leave a kind of testimony for those who had taken our place and in their arrogance thought that theirs was the only way of life worth living. Soviet assertions notwithstanding, the question remains whether a happy future for Russia might not have been attained more readily by evolution than by revolution. The old tradition, which revolution destroyed, had in its time created the Russia which was great not only in size and power, but also in the character of its people, in that humanity which we exiles seek in vain in those countries to which our destiny has taken us.

Japan, where I lived for nearly thirty years, was not a bad stepmother to Russians who there found asylum, however alien her customs, thoughts, and feelings. Japan offered the refugees true hospitality, in no way restricted their life and, grumble though they might from time to time, treated them well and with remarkably good sense. From the moment of my arrival in Japan in 1916 as First Secretary of the Old Russian Embassy, through the Russian Revolution and civil war, when in spite of the disappearance of the old Russian government the old Embassy continued to exist, as well as in the sad days of 1925 when I, as the last representative of Old Russia, was obliged to close the Embassy, I enjoyed great kindness on the part of the Japanese government and people. Though World War II in many ways changed the character of the Japanese, I feel that I must be thankful always that in the years of Russian ruin and suffering destiny brought me to Japan. Even after the end of my public life, until the boundless ambition of the Japanese military plunged the country into a senseless war, I found in Japan a peaceful existence among an amiable, smiling people.

It was in such a peaceful atmosphere that I decided to record my past and the events that I had witnessed, to relive once more before leaving this world the life that had so much happiness in it. I began to write in Russian, for myself, but later switched to English in the hope that my memoirs might be published after my death. So much nonsense has been written about life in Old Russia, that I felt it my duty to show that one could be happy in Old Russia and that I personally would not exchange my life in this Old Russia for all the so-called attractions of the U.S.S.R.—attractions which exist only on paper. Why else are Soviet citizens not allowed to travel abroad? Why else do few who have had the opportunity to escape from Russia desire to return?

Contents

Illustrations

Revelations of a
Russian Diplomat

1

Childhood

I was born on april 11, 1876, into the wealthy merchant family of Abrikossow, known throughout Russia for its confectionery, jams, biscuits, and preserved fruits. When I began my diplomatic career and mixed with the aristocracy, I was greatly embarrassed that my name was associated with sweets and caramels, and would have preferred a more obscure name. But now that the Revolution has leveled everyone and after I was forced during the Second World War to stand in line for hours to obtain a handful of sugar or a small jar of jam, I think of my name with special tenderness, and would give much for the restitution of all those factories which once distributed chocolates and candies throughout Russia.

I was born in Moscow, in a house whose windows looked on a boulevard called Clean Ponds,[1] probably because it led to a dirty little pond. My earliest recollections go back to the daily walks which we children—four brothers and one sister—took on this boulevard with our nurse Nastasia, who, like most Russian nurses, came from some forsaken village and was illiterate but full of self-invented knowledge and different superstitions, which impressed us children far more than all the teachings of our parents.[2] How well I remember the winter days, the snow-covered rows of trees and the sounds of orches-

---

[1] Chistye Prudy.

[2] The word "nurse" does not fully convey the position of the Russian "niania," really an institution in Old Russia.

tra music emanating from the skating ring into which the little pond was transformed every winter. So strong is this recollection that whenever I hear the strains of the Blue Danube waltz I am taken back to my childhood and see before me the snow-covered white pond and hear the angry voice of Nastasia, holding forth on the dangers of skating. Later my family moved to another part of town, where my grandfather, as his wealth increased, started to build houses, occupied mostly by members of his family. Thus there were two streets in Moscow, filled with my grandfather's houses, that formed a real nest of the Abrikossow family.

My grandfather [Aleksei Ivanovich] was a remarkable person. He was the creator of the large Abrikossow family and its fortune, which permitted different members of the family to figure prominently as businessmen, physicians, philosophers, country squires, lawyers, Catholic priests and, in my case, as diplomats. I have always marveled at the evolution of the Russian merchant families in Moscow, which until the transfer of the capital [1917] was solely a commercial city. Out of the general mass of small merchants, who did not differ substantially from the general mass of peasants, a clever man would emerge and succeed through sheer brainpower and initiative in amassing a great fortune. He would build factories employing thousands of workers, reside in Moscow but travel widely, and though without formal education, would begin to participate in the general cultural life, buy paintings and found picture galleries, hospitals, and clinics. Thus he would pass in one lifetime through the gamut of evolution from simple peasant to most-cultured person. His sons would not rest content with purely commercial endeavors; all would finish the university and patronize the sciences and arts, or buy old estates from the nobility and try to play the part of real landowners. Their wives would begin to be ashamed of their husbands' commercial activity and would become leaders in society, receiving artists and scientists in their salons. The third generation would go a step further, starting independent careers unconnected with commerce or leading a life of leisure, but generally supporting the most extreme movements in art or politics and usually squandering the inheritance received from its hardworking grandfathers and parents.

Our family passed through the same evolution. Though our business was founded in 1812, before the time of my grandfather, it did not stand out above ordinary concerns, its owners showing neither ability nor ambition to leave an imprint on history. Grandfather Aleksei Ivanovich was the first of the Abrikossow family to step out from comparative obscurity and become one of the most prominent businessmen of Moscow. He was a remarkable personality from many points of view. He lived until the ripe old age of eighty-five, and I clearly remember his tall figure with the long white beard. Though he had not received any special education and had been interested only in commerce throughout his active life, in old age he gave the impression of a highly cultivated person.

I distinctly recall how in my childhood we used to enter his book-lined study with fear and usually find him absorbed in reading some historical work. An enormous Danish dog, lying at his feet, would get up to sniff us and, after satisfying itself that we were members of the family, return majestically to its usual place. So solemn was the whole atmosphere of the room that we children were afraid to laugh or play inside and generally entered to announce that it was our birthday or name day, our grandfather insisting on being reminded thereof so as to give us a present. He would take from his desk a notebook, listing the birthdays of all his children, grandchildren, and eventually great-grandchildren; and after verifying the date and telling us the exact hour of our birth he would extract from his wallet a fresh banknote and give it to us with the exhortation to be sage, obey our parents, and not forget to go to church. Following this ceremony he would return to his book and we would leave the room with a feeling of relief. On the seventeenth birthday he would give us a gold watch, of which we were particularly proud as a sign of being regarded as grown up.

There was nothing small in my grandfather. In all his deeds he showed the greatest nobility and was very moderate in his personal tastes, never indulging in the loose habits of most Moscow merchants, especially those whose sole aim was to make money. The best proof of my grandfather's character lies in the fact that he lived with his wife for more than fifty years, celebrating his golden wedding anniversary in 1899, and that he had from her twenty-two children even though her tyrannical character, lack of education, and harsh treatment of the children did not suit him at all. In those days religious people—and my grandfather was deeply religious—believed in the sacredness of marriage and were strong enough to bear their cross in order to save the family from dissolution. I always feel that my grandfather could serve as an example of the support which the throne and the Orthodox Church could have found among the merchants, but to the great misfortune of Russia, the evolution of all classes of society progressed so quickly that the second generation was already indifferent to the old tradition; and the third generation, with few exceptions, joined the ranks of the intelligentsia, whose opposition to any sort of conservative authority and abnormal craving for change contributed to the destruction of Old Russia and to its transformation from a bulwark of world stability into a center of Communist revolution and destruction.

It is fortunate that grandfather did not live to see the Revolution. He believed firmly in the stability of the way of life which had given him the opportunity to rise to prominence in his native town; its destruction would have been an incomprehensible calamity for him. In his struggle for a better place in society he was favored by no privileges, achieving everything by his own efforts. I remember the significance he attached to the fact that he had refused to begin by following in his father's footsteps, and had become a clerk in a German firm, where he learned the foreign business methods which he then applied in his own enterprise. Not satisfied with the family business, he joined forces with another young man by the name of Popov, who had come from the north of Russia with only five rubles but with a great deal of energy, and created a tea business, which soon became one of the biggest concerns in Russia.[3] A great Moscow bank made its appearance then and my grandfather together with other Moscow merchants founded a big commercial school; he participated in many large concerns and was one of the most prominent men in Moscow. He also greatly expanded the Abrikossow family business and at the first opportunity passed it on to his two oldest sons.

But the eldest son, as so often happens, having inherited his father's brains and nobility of character, was not interested in making money. A graduate of Moscow University in the field of natural sciences, his mind was on scientific research. Not wishing to disappoint his father and obliged to support his increasing family, he did work in his father's concerns as a member of their boards, remaining in the

[3] It was on this tea business, rather than on the better known jam and confectionery line, that the Abrikossow fortune actually rested.

[6]

office the required number of hours, but the rest of the time he worked either in his library or in the laboratory of Moscow University. After his father's death, when his children were already independent, he retired from all business and went with his wife to Paris where, notwithstanding his advanced age, he attended lectures at the Sorbonne. Returning to Moscow before the First World War, my uncle and aunt were caught by the Revolution and lost everything; obliged to leave their home, they found refuge in one room with the only servant who remained faithful. My uncle never lost his courage and in one of the few letters to reach me from Moscow after the Revolution, there was a touching description of their golden wedding anniversary, with my aunt, paralyzed in bed, receiving a few oranges, which someone had brought as a present to remind them by their color of the golden gifts which it had been the custom to offer on this occasion before the Revolution.

Of all my grandfather's sons only the second one, Ivan, my father, inherited his business acumen. I remember him dimly, because I was only five years old when he died, but from everything that I have heard he was an exceptionally nice man. Full of life, ever gay and loved by everybody, he concentrated all his attention on business. When grandfather handed down the Abrikossow family business to his two oldest sons, my father, though quite young, became the leading spirit of the whole enterprise and sacrificed his all too short life to the development of the firm. The clerks and workers adored him, and I remember how later, when as an adult I visited the factory, the old workmen told me with tears in their eyes what a wonderful man my father had been. Those workers must have been very disappointed in my three brothers and me, for not one of us followed in the footsteps of our father.

Going back to my childhood, I recall how full of life and energy my father used to enter the dining room where we waited for him, and tell mother of his new business plans. Every summer he went to the Nizhni Novgorod mart, where merchants from all corners of Russia engaged in big transactions. In the autumn father took the whole family to the Crimea, to Simferopol, where the firm had a factory for making fresh fruit preserves. I vaguely remember the apricot-covered trees and a small river filled with bathing gypsies (the latter merely from the words of our old nurse, who would not let us out of the garden), and in the center of everything my father—young, nice-looking, and always gay. I recall the great beauty of the Black Sea, and dimly remember returning from somewhere late in the evening in a carriage along the shore, the perpetual sound of the waves, a white round pavilion on top of a hill, clear in the brilliant moonlight, and far away the blaze of a burning wood, like a red snake crawling on a mountain side.

I remember my mother even less than my father; she died ten days before him. Having four sons, my parents had always wanted to have also a daughter. Their wish was fulfilled, but my mother died during childbirth. My father, already on his deathbed never learned of her demise. The cause of father's death was consumption in the throat, contracted, the doctors said, by counting dirty paper money. A healthy man who had just reached the age of thirty, surrounded by a loving family and many friends, a brilliant future before him; and suddenly a bit of dirty paper, a slight pain in the throat, and a galloping consumption devoured his life.

As my father lay ill, silence fell over the house. The best doctors came, the famous holy icon of the Mother of Christ was brought from the Iverskii Monastery and the rooms were filled with the smell of incense. But to no avail. My father was dying. The old nurse insisted that we children must be led to the sickroom so that father could take leave of us. She dragged us to the door by force and pushed us inside, trembling with fright. But the white figure which sat on the bed coughing terribly made a sign that we be removed, and the old nurse who adored everything tragic was deprived of the scene of the dying father taking leave of his children with everybody weeping and herself making a hysterical declamation about orphans.

I remember my father's funeral—crowds of priests, a multitude of candles, and a wax figure in the coffin. I recall how somebody lifted me and told me to give a farewell kiss to my father and how I screamed because I could not admit that this wax figure was my father, whom I knew to be a gay and laughing man who would hold me up high in the air. Both of my parents were buried together in the Aleksei Cemetery near the tomb of one of my uncles who also had died quite young, on the eve of his marriage to a girl who remained faithful to his memory for the rest of her life. These deaths seemed so senseless and unjust that it was a great trial for my grandfather with his profound religious feeling, to reconcile them with the idea of divine justice, and he had the following inscription from Isaiah put on the grave of my parents: "My thoughts are not your thoughts; neither are your ways my ways. For as the heavens are higher than the earth, so are my ways higher than your ways, and my thoughts higher than your thoughts." Whenever I visited the grave in later years I was struck by these words, which contain such profound wisdom for every religious person.

After my parents passed away we were informed that our uncle Nicholas, the eldest brother of our father, had promised to him before his death to be our guardian and not to forsake us. Throughout their lives my uncle and aunt did everything to live up to this promise. Taken to my uncle's house right after the funeral, we became from that moment members of their family, which consisted at that time of three boys and two daughters of about our age. My uncle and my aunt, incredible as it may sound, did their best not to make any distinction between their own children and us, with the result that we at once began to treat them as our real father and mother. Because our recollection of our actual parents was not yet firmly fixed in our minds, we were able to begin a new life in new surroundings without the least feeling of being orphans. Only the old nurse, with the love for drama so often found in persons of her class, did not stop her lamentations and as she persisted in trying to persuade us that nobody would care for us, she was pensioned off to return to her village, where she probably found full scope among her neighbors for her tragic description of our fate. From time to time she would reappear in our house and annoy us with her lamentations over the sad lot which her imagination had bestowed on us. We were healthy children, quickly became friends with our new brothers and sisters, and filled the big house of our uncle with perpetual noise.

When I was older I often asked myself how my uncle and aunt, who were both young, loved to lead a social life and receive guests, could so readily have reconciled themselves to the doubling of their family. The answer lay, of course, in their wonderful character. My uncle, as mentioned already, had no interest in the innumerable businesses created by my grandfather and passed all his spare time in his library or the laboratory. The habit of meditating about higher matters made a real philosopher out of him; unperturbed by the little things of this life, he faced all difficulties with absolute calmness. He never regretted what might have been, and was always reconciled with the facts of life.

I remember the time when his mother, who could be a real fury, had discovered that he had given refuge to his sister after she had left her husband (to whom her tyrannical mother had married her against her will), and rushing to him had demanded angrily that he make a choice between her and his sister. He had calmly replied that he could not change the laws of nature, and that whatever choice he might make, she would always remain his mother and his sister his sister. The furious mother departed with the observation that ever since his study of science he had fallen into his second childhood. Another time, when I had already embarked on my diplomatic career and was in London and, having heard a rumor about the difficulties a firm from which I received the greater part of my income was having, sent him a telegram of inquiry, his consolation was typical: "It could be worse." The whole character and philosophy of my [step]father[4] was reflected in the reply: be thankful for what you have, because things could be worse. As long as he was there to regulate our lives, they were shaped by his ability to look on all events from the brighter side without exaggeration of the dark realities. This attitude helped him to withstand the horrors of the Revolution, as he and his wife, deprived of their entire fortune and separated from many of their children, were obliged to live in one room on the little money my aunt in Paris and I in Tokyo were able to send them.

His wife, my aunt Vera, with whom he lived for fifty-three years through all the vicissitudes of fortune, was his chief support in life. She was a wonderfully nice and exceptionally refined person, never angry and equally kind to everybody: to her relatives and friends, the ten (and after the birth of another boy eleven) children and the numerous nurses, housekeepers, governesses, and other servants rich Russian families employed in days past. As a result everybody thought only of pleasing her.

The story of my aunt's life is of interest; it shows how readily people in Russia brought up in one type of surroundings could adapt themselves to quite different circumstances. She came from faraway Siberia, from Kiakhta near the Chinese frontier, where her father, a rich

---

[4] "Father" and "uncle" are hereafter used interchangeably by the author.

Abrikossow's father, in Moscow, January, 1878

The Oaks

The Abrikossows. Seated from left to right: Ivan, youngest brother of the author; Vera, his third-oldest cousin; Anna, the author's only sister and youngest member of his immediate family; Aleksei, his eldest brother; Sergei, his second-oldest cousin; Boris, his younger brother; Aunt Vera and Uncle Nicholas (Nikolai Aleksandrovich); Pavel, his youngest cousin; Avgusta, his fifth-oldest cousin; Nikolai, his eldest cousin. Standing from left to right: Dmitrii and Khrisanf, his fourth-oldest cousin.

merchant engaged in the tea business with China, owned vast lands. In those days there was no Siberian railway and the inhabitants, except for a few months in summer, buried in snow, were separated from the rest of the world. And yet they had a very agreeable life: they were relatively independent and absorbed in their great enterprises, notably the camel caravans which carried their goods to China and returned with boxes of tea. They had many friends among the rich Chinese across the frontier and entertained each other royally. To us natives of Moscow the Siberian life that my aunt and her older relatives described seemed a fairytale. But everything must end. The father of my aunt contracted an eye disease, and as there was no specialist in Kiakhta he had to go to Moscow, a journey which in those days took several weeks, for treatment. His eyesight improved and he returned to Kiakhta, but soon he had a relapse and was obliged to travel to Moscow again. This time the doctors could do nothing and he went blind. It would have been madness to go out to Kiakhta in such a state, hence he liquidated his business and stayed in Moscow. Most of his relatives migrated with him; they took a large house, where they all lived together, talking and thinking of their life in Kiakhta.

The old blind man soon died and the young generation quickly adapted to the new surroundings and forgot about the pleasures of faraway Siberia, but the oldtimers clung to the past. I remember one of my aunt's uncles who visited us frequently. His hair was snow white, his face brown with Mongol features. He adored his niece and always brought presents for her. I began my piano lessons on an instrument which had been the gift of this quiet and nice old man. I think that the childhood passed among the snows of Siberia left a permanent imprint on my aunt's character and helped to develop the calmness and impartiality she displayed in her treatment of everybody and everything, qualities so alien to people raised in the hubbub of a large city.

Our childhood passed in an atmosphere of mutual confidence and love. We lived in a big house belonging to my grandfather, who was building a new house for himself. We had a large garden from which we could see a big church painted red and white. I remember this garden well, especially in spring, when the first window was opened and the air of spring, the noise of the street, and the sound of church bells rushed inside. The house had a fascinating history. Not only was it very old, having survived Napoleon's invasion and the burning of Moscow, but it had served as police headquarters and its cellar had contained cells for criminals. From these cells an underground passageway led to the church on the other side of the garden so that the prisoners could attend religious services without stepping into the street. When my grandfather bought the house, the walls of the cellar still contained remnants of the iron rings and chains.

We children lived in the innumerable, rather small rooms down-stairs, under the supervision of nurses and governesses. The walls were so thick that we could easily play on the windows without touching the floor. Our parents lived on the second story, which had been rebuilt by grandfather to contain reception rooms, a big dining room, a ballroom, and so forth. Like all old houses, especially those connected with murder stories, our house was supposedly haunted. Among its various ghosts the most famous one was that of Vanka-Kain or Johnny-Cain, who, centuries ago, according to tradition, had mur-dered a countless number of persons and had died chained to the wall in the cellar of our house. All these stories made a great impression in the servant quarters and in the evenings the maids avoided passing alone through the long corridors. We children were afraid too and tried to remain as long as possible in the upstairs rooms, whose modern decor dispelled all ideas of ghosts. Naturally nobody ever saw any ghosts except an old nurse who insisted that once, waking up at night, she had discovered a bearded old man in chains sitting on her bed. Realizing at once that it was the ghost of Vanka-Kain, she had fearlessly advised him to repent of his innumerable crimes. Allegedly the ghost had agreed and they had shed tears together. As children we excitedly believed the story and always asked the nurse to repeat it, which she did with great pleasure and endless variations.

I also remember autumn evenings when our parents were abroad, we boys having remained in Moscow to attend school. A certain Vasilii Ivanovich, whose duty it was to teach us painting, stayed with us. He was an original and most lovable person. I do not know whence he came and how he became part of our childhood. Probably father met him somewhere and took a liking to him, and when father liked anyone he trusted him completely. Thus in addition to his painting lessons, which were quite fruitless, none of us becoming an artist, he acted as a sort of guardian of the older boys in the family. We liked him immensely, because with his vivid imagination he himself appeared half child. During those lonely evenings we used to sit in the dining room upstairs, drinking tea and listening to his endless stories. There was no electricity and in the absence of our parents and the younger children the rest of the rooms were not illuminated. As bedtime approached and we would try to prolong the stories, Vasilii Ivanovich would suddenly make a frightened face, say that he had heard a strange noise in the dark room, quickly get to his feet and run downstairs, followed by all of us with Vanka-Kain seemingly in pursuit. Downstairs, in our cozy rooms and warm beds our fright would disappear in general laughter. The trick never failed, so that the old murderer did serve a certain educational purpose in our childhood. Vasilii Ivanovich was a passionate fisherman and in our free moments taught us how to make nets, soaking them to prevent rotting in some kind of oil that smelled so bad that people would come down to see what we were doing. Taken to task, Vasilii Ivanovich would usually reply that a good net was more important than fresh air. He would fetch us from school, and for the sake of exercise we would walk home, accompanied by other pupils who also liked his stories.

The walks were particularly pleasant on winter days. We had to pass through the main street, called Blacksmith Bridge[5] though there was no sign of any bridge (but then all Moscow streets had most astonishing and completely illogical names). The best shops were situated on Blacksmith Bridge. It was a beautiful sight. Everything was white with snow, the show windows with their displays of the city's riches—magnificent materials, furs, and priceless diamonds— were brilliantly illuminated. Sledges drawn by marvelous horses such as one could only see in Moscow, for wealthy Moscow merchants took pride in having the best horses money could buy and the most daring coachmen to drive them, sped down the streets. All this brilliance pleased me no end and from early childhood I had the secret hope of spending my life amid scenes of luxury and pomp. Thus the daily walks on Blacksmith Bridge may have drawn me toward diplomacy. Once we left the main street, we found ourselves in dark, crooked streets, the sight of which made me miserable. I particularly hated one corner, where a cheap eating place for droshky drivers was situated. When we passed it, the door would usually open to admit some new

5 Kuznetskii Most.

[13]

arrival and the smoke of cheap tobacco and the smell of cabbage soup would fill the whole street. It was the real Russia.

We usually walked in a file, one behind the other, the eldest son at the head, the youngest at the end, with Vasilii Ivanovich in his fur coat, the long beard half-covered with ice, bringing up the rear with a big stick in his hand. Once, as we were passing the corner eating place, a butcher boy ran out the door. The sight of the file of neatly dressed boys in school uniforms—at one time there were seven of us brothers going to the same school—was too strong for the mischievous boy, and running near us, he knocked off all our caps. We were so astonished we did not know what to do, but Vasilii Ivanovich ran after the boy and threw his stick at him. Just then the boy turned around the corner and the stick hit somebody else. Vasilii Ivanovich could not admit that he had failed in defending us and made up a story of how his stick came to the corner, hesitated an instant, then flew around the corner and hit the butcher boy in the back. I think that after telling the story Vasilii Ivanovich himself began to believe it; at any rate, it became a favorite yarn in his endless repertoire.

But my fondest recollections of Vasilii Ivanovich are connected with our early spring fishing expeditions on the river that flowed through our estate near Moscow. The oncoming darkness, the twitter of birds, the glimpse of the cigarette in the mouth of our tutor, the impatience with which we listened for the sound of the small bell attached to our rods, signaling that a fish had been caught on the hook, and the struggle to get the fish out of the water—these were exciting and the surroundings, with the trees bending over the river and the moon coming out, were beautiful. We would make a fire to cook the fish, have excellent fish soup, which tasted especially good because we had caught the fish, and listen to one of Vasilii Ivanovich's fish stories, the more mysterious in the flickering light of the dying fire.

Vasilii Ivanovich came from a peasant family in the Orel region. By his own efforts he finished art school in Moscow, but having no special talent never became a great artist and ended up as a primary schoolteacher and then somehow as our tutor. His only dream was to buy a bit of land in his native province; all his life he saved for it and in the end acquired a small parcel of land near his native village. I do not know what became of him during the Revolution. I hope he did not live to pass in his old age through all the sufferings and privations which the Revolution, with few exceptions, brought to all classes of Russian society.

Living with our new parents, we no longer spent the summers in dull Sokolniki, in the suburbs of Moscow, but on the estate my uncle had recently bought about forty miles from the city. He too had used to live in Sokolniki, where my grandfather had a big villa and where our factory was located. My late father, absorbed in business, had not minded living so close to town, but my uncle wished to get away from the city and my grandmother, one of those women who tried to rule all members of the family. The sons were able to acquire a certain amount of independence and could bear the peculiarities of their mother's character calmly, but the daughters, who formed the majority of the family, were quite dependent on her and suffered a great deal. For instance, my grandmother was obsessed with the fear that one of her daughters might become an old maid, and tried to marry all of them off as quickly as possible. As soon as a daughter attained the age of seventeen, she began to render her life unbearable by keeping after her (why she did not marry?) and by trying to find her a suitable husband. Some of the daughters did not have enough character to oppose the choice of their mother; others were rushed into making a hasty selection of their own, though actually, with only one exception, the results were not so bad, probably because in those days women were generally less independent and marriage was held more sacred. The independence of her sons was a source of constant irritation to my grandmother, and she used to say that when my grandfather, who was older than she, would die and leave her all his money, she would show them what it meant to rule with a strong hand. But fate decided otherwise; she got cancer and died three years before her husband.

It was when my grandmother was still alive that our new parents, their family doubled, decided to find a new place where they could spend the summer away from town, business anxieties, and family complications. They were looking for such a place when my father met one of his acquaintances, a rich German banker who, having made enough money in Russia, was returning to Germany and wanted to sell an estate he owned not far from Moscow. Believing that the best way out of difficulties was to trust in luck, father bought the place without delving into the details or even looking at the place. It created a sensation when he announced to us that the matter was settled and that we were leaving at once for the country; spending money on land for one's own pleasure was not in the family tradition and grandmother had the opportunity to say once more that since graduating from the university her son had lost all common sense. But we children were delighted. There was so little space where one could truly feel free in Moscow and its suburbs, and we knew the real country scarcely at all.

We called the new place The Oaks, for the house, on a hill at the shore of a river, was surrounded by magnificent oak trees. There was a large park and a field near the river that was covered with wild flowers in the summer. This marvelous place, where we spent all our summers, became part of our happy and carefree childhood. There were nicer places near Moscow, places with long traditions, with parks whose trees were centuries old. Our place was quite different. Created by a rich German who loved comfort, it was furnished to the last detail, and we found horses and cows in the stables, even two donkeys. Everything was young and fresh and as we all, including our parents, were young too, we felt at home in the new surroundings from the first day. I particularly remember our big, two-storied dining room with the enormous elk head mounted on the wall. This old elk witnessed the countless meals at which we ten children tried to speak at once to the great horror of our English governess, who vainly tried to impress on us that in England, in her family, when the parents spoke, the children had to be silent.

Coming to the place early in the spring, we would see how suddenly, after a few sunny days, the snow would begin to melt, the trees would burst forth with leaves, and the song of birds would fill the air. The melted snow would inundate the fields on the other side of the river, and our house with its oaks would seem to be standing on the shore of a big lake. This revival of nature after a long winter was a most marvelous and uniquely Russian experience. But the winters themselves were beautiful too as we skied across the white snow, brilliant in the sun, the majestic stillness of the woods broken by the sound of a frightened squirrel jumping from one tree to another. This communion with nature left a deep imprint on our childhood.

It was during summer vacation—from the end of May till the end of August—that we stayed at The Oaks longest. The size of the family, which consisted of my parents, ten children, French and English governesses, and the faithful Vasilii Ivanovich, made an addition to the original house necessary, and my father, meeting two peasants in search of carpentry work on one of his walks and liking their faces, brought them back home to construct it. All he told them was to build an addition that would not spoil the general style of the house and these two unknown peasants, without the help of an architect, constructed a new wing to accommodate several of us as well as my father's library and laboratory. Returning to their families in the winter, these two peasants would come back to our place every summer, my father always finding work for them. In those days there was no sign of any class hatred and the two peasants from somewhere far away in the interior of Russia accepted our life—which must have seemed the height of luxury to them—without envy, were grateful to become part of it and, I thought, grew quite attached to us. We learned a great deal about the life of common peasants from them, and as far as I can remember, their stories were without complaint.

My mother was fond of flowers and the lawn before the house was full of the most gorgeous roses. Our gardener, though uneducated, was a real artist and always wanted to surprise us with some new flower arrangement. From time to time he would disappear in a fit of drunkenness, resisting all efforts to cure him. But after such a fit he would apply himself with double energy and create new masterpieces. The little terrace where we usually sat in the evenings had been adorned by him with some climbing Australian vines which I have never seen anywhere else. In the spring they were covered with peculiar blossoms, whose strong aroma perfumed the whole terrace. Nearby was a low, tree-filled ravine to which the nightingales came every spring. I often recall how we used to sit on this terrace as the day drew to a close, breathe the perfume of the Australian blossoms, watch the slowly rising moon, and listen to the nightingales trying to excel each other. It was so beautiful and nobody talked; even we small children were impressed and did not want to go to bed. In later years my eldest brother would play the slow movement of one of the Schubert pieces; and now in old age, when I want to recapture these childhood sensations I play the same pieces on the phonograph and when I hear the slow movement the whole scene returns to me: the moonlight, the aroma of the flowers, the songs of the nightingales, and the family, together, ecstatic over the unsurpassed beauty of The Oaks. And to think that new people came and in their envy and hate cut down the trees, destroyed the home of the nightingales, and killed the beauty and happiness.

A young aunt stayed with us the first summers to help our parents look after the new members of the family. She was one of the victims of my grandmother's tyranny. When she reached the age of seventeen, grandmother found her a husband, a man much older than she, and ignoring all her pleas forced her to marry him. When the poor girl, accompanying her husband to the interior found his place not only dilapidated but occupied by another woman playing the role of hostess, she fled to a neighboring town and telegraphed her brothers to rescue her if they did not want her to die. The brothers, young and energetic fellows, came at once and took her back to Moscow, where she found asylum in the house of my father [uncle]. My grandmother was furious, and when the husband appeared to claim his wife, she supported him. They tried to make her go back with the help of the police; in those days the wife's name was inserted in the passport of the husband, and without a passport she could not stay alone. To counteract this, my father took his sister to the governor of Moscow, who was so touched by her story and by her tears that he issued her a special passport. After that neither her husband nor her mother could do anything, and he returned to his estate, keeping the dowry. Grandmother could never forgive her daughter, however. She used to say that we must stone her because Christ Himself had said that such women must be stoned. When people asked her when Christ had said such a monstrous thing, she replied that as they did not go to church often enough, they did not know what Christ had said; she who attended services regularly had heard the priest read how, when a woman sinner had been brought before Christ, He had taken the first stone and cast it at her. Thus my grandmother with her strong will twisted the teachings of Christ Himself to suit her inclinations.

Notwithstanding the protection of my father, the position of my aunt was difficult, and when one of her sisters, having lost the use of her legs as the result of hysteria, was sent to Paris to the famous Dr. [Jean Martin] Charcot, my aunt was asked to accompany her. The strong personality of Dr. Charcot, who cured the patient merely by approaching her bed, made such an impression on my aunt that she decided to remain in Paris and study medicine under him. But summers she would return to The Oaks to help my parents look after us.

It was then that she became my favorite aunt, and when I lived abroad I spent my holidays with her.[6]

After establishing herself in Paris my aunt initiated divorce proceedings through my father. At that time it was extremely difficult to obtain a divorce, and the case took nearly ten years during which she completed her medical studies and became a doctor. I remember how my father used to go to St. Petersburg every autumn to try to free my aunt from her husband.

Life in St. Petersburg was quite different from life in Moscow. Moscow was a commercial city, where the rich merchants played the most important parts. There was more freedom in Moscow, life was easier and more congenial. St. Petersburg, on the other hand, was the seat of government. There was the court and the countless officials who thought only of their careers; thus there were more uniforms, more envy, more flattery, and less independence. Moscow people did not like St. Petersburg and its inhabitants; the latter in turn regarded Moscow with contempt and could not understand how Moscovites could live without the glamour of the court, without all those generals, and without thinking of a brilliant career.

Though my father used to complain that these journeys to St. Petersburg upset his life, he was a man who took interest in everything and rather liked them, returning always full of new impressions of the city where, as he put it, people preferred an administrative career, in which everybody from the lowest to the highest rank depended on his superior, to independence. He made good friends in St. Petersburg, and I remember how A[natolii] F[edorovich] Koni, a well-known senator and later member of the State Council who took an interest in the case of my aunt, used to stay at The Oaks. Unaccustomed to the countryside and eager to pay my mother a compliment, he told her how on waking in the morning and hearing the birds, he could not decide whether he was still on earth or already in heaven. After looking about, the sunlit room and the song of the birds outside the window led him to conclude that the Almighty had taken pity on him, had sent him a painless death, forgiven all his sins, and taken him to Paradise.

When the Synod continued to make difficulties regarding the di-

[6] The manuscript jumps back and forth in the account of Aunt Vera's life. For the sake of clarity, this part has been rearranged in chronological order.

vorce, the Senator advised my family to send a petition directly to the Emperor. As luck had it, the petition was one of the few that came to the personal attention of Alexander III, who wrote on it that the divorce must be granted. At last my aunt was free to remarry. Shortly after becoming a doctor but before ever practicing, she married a distinguished French professor and had two charming daughters. When my grandmother died, grandfather invited my aunt and the girls to Moscow and everyone tried to show that the past was forgotten and made much fuss over our French relatives. The two daughters, my cousins, became great friends of mine, especially Lucette, the younger, with whom in spite of our difference in age I was to correspond regularly until the holocaust of the [Second World] War separated friends and families and made all communication impossible. After the War I learned that Lucette had died during the German occupation of Paris. A clever woman, she had followed in her mother's footsteps and become a doctor for children, whom she always adored; overworked and undernourished during the War, she succumbed to pernicious anemia.

I remember also a new nurse we had to look after my sister. She used to tell us endless stories about a certain Doña Dolores and her adventures. Later I discovered that these stories came from a Spanish novel, *The Mysteries of the Spanish Court*, but the greatest mystery remained from where our nurse, who had nothing to do with Spain and could not read, had gotten the material. When we started to learn to read, we tried to teach our nurse. She began to read herself, but found Russian books so stupid that she said it was not worth learning how to read, and returned to her adventures of Doña Dolores.

Thus our childhood passed in an atmosphere of love and unconcern. To simplify the education of such a crowd of children, father sent his two oldest boys [Nikolai and Sergei], though still quite young, to school. After such a carefree childhood, school seemed very frightening, and I remember how I cried in bed the night before my first school day. Finding me in tears, our nurse tried to calm me by demonstrating that there was nothing fearful to school. All that a teacher would demand, she assured me, was that I would read to him, and handing me a book that she had brought and making a stern face, she asked me to read from it. Her simplified idea of school restored my courage, but only for the moment. The next day, when my brother

[Aleksei] and I found ourselves surrounded by unknown children, who at once began to tease us newcomers, we started to howl and the teacher had to summon our cousins, whose uniform belts we grasped to their horror and simply refused to let go.

Before long I accustomed myself to the new life, however, and throughout the nine years of middle school was perfectly happy. It was a classical school, with Latin and Greek the most important subjects. The first year was merely preparatory, and we did not have to learn Latin and Greek yet, but from the second year on we were amply filled with classical languages. For some reason most of our Latin and Greek teachers were Czechs; almost all of them had peculiarities that promptly earned them nicknames. One, because of his strictness and red hair, was known as Red Devil, another, because of his thinness, Smoked Fish, and so forth. Every teacher regarded his subject as the most important, and took it as a personal offense if we did not do our homework well and gave us a low mark. When I think of my school days I am astonished at the amount of work schoolboys had to do in Old Russia: six hours a day of constant study with but an hour for lunch and walking in the yard, two hours of homework after dinner, not to mention various lessons in painting, music, and English, only German and French being taught in school. The innumerable examinations at the end of the year with the threat, in the event of failure, of having to repeat the entire year again, were a real nervous strain, unmitigated by the relaxation of sports common in foreign schools. But though my life as a schoolboy was strenuous, I recall my school days with great pleasure, much more so than my five years at the university, which are normally considered the best time of one's life.

Our school was in an old house which had formerly belonged to an old noble family. It contained a big hall, where we used to walk after lunch when the weather was bad, and a row of big rooms, which had once been the reception rooms and which still bore the remnants of magnificent decorations on the walls and ceilings. It was easy to imagine how in days gone by big receptions had been held here, how the whole nobility of Moscow had assembled, orchestras played, couples danced, and romances blossomed in secluded corners among palm trees and flowers. But all this glory had long passed, and the graceful figures had been supplanted by rows of schoolboys walking about the hall or sitting at their desks. In the summers we lived at The Oaks, but even there our French and English lessons continued.

The French governesses changed so quickly, I cannot remember any but one, a remarkable person by the name of Madame Besson. Our English governesses were more solid in character than the French ones. At first our lack of discipline and our comradely attitude toward elders made them think that we were half-mad, but as they grew attached to Russian ways and treated us like grown-ups we got along well. Miss Fleming, our last governess and a true friend of the family, remained with us even after we all had grown up; only the Revolution, during which she and all British subjects in Moscow were imprisoned for several months in reprisal for the arrest of several Communists in London, forced her to leave our family and return to England.

Another person who took part in our education and left some rather humorous recollections among my childhood impressions was our piano teacher, a stout lady with a red face who came twice a week from the nearest station in a big carriage. A relative of my late mother, she told everybody that my mother on her deathbed had expressed the wish that her children take piano lessons from her. Improbable as it may have been that my mother's last thoughts should have been concerned with piano lessons for us, when we reached the right age for such lessons, she appeared on the scene and insisted that the last wish of my mother be carried out. From that time she became part of our life. Years earlier she had studied in the St. Petersburg Conservatory, and claimed that, upon hearing her play, the famous professor of piano Anton Rubinstein had said that now he could die calmly for he had a successor. I am afraid that this story was the product of her imagination, because as a pianist she was strictly second rate. She played everything *fortissimo*, so that the strings would break, and after years and years of lessons only my eldest brother could play. But she was a kindhearted person, brought us sweets to make us play the scales, and amused us with stories about her brilliant life in St. Petersburg.

She had the opportunity to renew this brilliant life when on the advice of our family doctor some of us young boys were sent for treatment to mud baths near St. Petersburg and our parents, not wishing to accompany us, asked her to take us there. She did so with pleasure, because the best of St. Petersburg society used to come there during the summer and there was a good orchestra and a nice park. With her wonderful capacity to make friends, our piano teacher soon became the central figure in that society. She used to drag us to the park, where she sat surrounded by ladies. We had a box in the local theater where we saw some dreadful melodramas absolutely unsuitable for our age, and our house was full of different ladies who came to confide their love affairs and family sorrows to our teacher. Needless to say, our musical education did not make much progress that summer. In her old age this dear lady lost all her pupils and we had to support her, but she retained her optimism: I remember how she tried to persuade me, when I visited her in the two tiny rooms which we had rented for her, that I had never seen such a magnificent suite of rooms, and showing me a tiny potted palm tree on the table near her chair assured me that she felt as if she were in a winter garden. It is a great thing not to see things as they are, but as one wishes them to be. She tried to persuade my parents that one season in the mud baths was not enough for us, no doubt hoping to have another summer among the grand society of St. Petersburg, but my parents did not agree, and instead sent us to the Baltic Sea with our German schoolteacher and his family. It was quite another experience.

Herr Linde was a huge man with a red beard. Normally he was quite kind, but when he lost his temper he roared like a madman. He was a great butterfly collector and taught us how to collect butterflies. Each morning we used to go for long walks with our nets. I found this sport quite interesting and developed considerable skill in pursuing beautiful butterflies which I had barely noticed before. To this day I remember their German names. On the rare occasions that Herr Linde espied a butterfly not yet in his collection, he would go quite mad and rush after it with his net, shouting the name of the butterfly. As we followed with great noise, the frightened butterfly usually flew away, high above the trees, to the great chagrin of Herr Linde. He had a daughter, a fat girl of our age, whom we used to tease; this made her cry and caused Herr Linde to lose his temper.

Frau Linde was a kindhearted person. She was always afraid that we did not eat enough and filled us with different cakes and pies so that when our parents came to visit us they were horrified at how fat we had become. The picture of a virtuous German family was completed by two elderly sisters of Herr Linde: Tante[7] Berta and Tante Mary. Tante Berta was the widow of a German planter in Brazil. She used to tell us how in Brazil a huge snake hung from every tree and tried to catch passersby, and how she used to defend herself with an umbrella. These stories gave us nightmares and made my sister's nurse angry, partly because her own Doña Dolores stories were pushed into the background. The other Tante, having lived all her life in Germany, ridiculed the snake stories, thereby constantly offending her sister.

But the most memorable event of the summer was the visit of Tsar Alexander III with his family to a nearby town for the dedication of a new church. When plans for the visit were announced, Herr Linde decided that we must not lose the opportunity to see our Emperor. Tickets were obtained, and on the great day we were washed and dressed in our best suits. Frau Linde insisted that each of us must carry a basket of flowers to throw at the feet of the Emperor. We tried to protest that throwing flowers was for girls, but were told that such objections were unpatriotic. We were taken to the pier which the Imperial yacht approached, and at the signal of Herr Linde began throwing flowers. We did so very clumsily, but still earned a gracious smile from the Empress, who looked girlish next to her huge husband. We had to wait until the departure of the Imperial couple, and when the yacht began to move from the pier, our Herr Linde suddenly lost his head and, though he was German and Alexander not his sovereign, in a state of patriotic ecstasy rushed toward the yacht and began waving his hat and hurrahing at the top of his voice. With his tremendous size and red beard he presented a startling figure, and the Emperor pointed him out to the Empress and they both laughed. But the last salute of the Emperor went to Herr Linde and made him happy for the rest of his life.

Herr Linde was not only a butterfly collector but also a poet. He would write an endlessly long poem at night, then recite to himself in the wood. Once an old woman, picking mushrooms, came upon Herr Linde reciting his poem and got so frightened that she rushed home losing all her mushrooms, shouting that there was a devil with a red beard in the wood.

I remember another summer when our parents sent three of us on a

[7] "Tante" is German for "aunt"; "Herr" is "Mr." "Frau" is "Mrs."

journey along the Volga River, ostensibly to acquaint us better with our country but, I suspect, actually to diminish the noise that ten schoolboys made at their summer place. As we were too small to go alone, one of our recently married young aunts and her husband, who had been planning to make the same trip, consented to take us. This couple had always been cited as an example of marital happiness, but during our journey I realized how false reputations can be. The couple quarreled from morning until evening, and we did not know what to do during these encounters.

To tell the truth, there was plenty of time for quarreling. The boats were always late and when they started, got stuck in the middle of the shallow river. There was absolutely nothing to do except to eat fresh caviar; it was hot and the public was generally in a state of irritation. I remember how a lady shouted at me when she discovered that my tie had cost three rubles, her irritation only doubling when I tried to calm her with the gentle observation that it was not she who had spent the money on my tie. Things improved when we turned from the huge shallow Volga into the tributary Kama, with its wild and picturesque shores. At the stations we saw such strange people as the Kirghiz and Kalmucks, the remnants of different Mongol tribes which the famous Genghis Khan had collected in his march against Europe. For nearly two centuries they had been masters of Russia; now they were reduced to small groups of people who had found peace and, I hoped, happiness in the large bosom of Russia, which accepted and assimilated such a variety of tribes. We went as far as the town of Perm, where we stopped for the night.

Going ashore, we found the streets deserted and covered with dust. We entered a garden, where there was some sort of entertainment on an open stage. People sat at small tables and drank beer. Some clowns tried to be amusing, but nobody paid any attention except two or three persons who had imbibed too much and noisily showed their approval or disapproval—it was not clear which. But the program announced in bold letters the appearance of Isabella Orsini and though we did not know the star we decided to stay for her number, curious about this combination of a provincial Russian town and an Italian name with a glorious historical tradition. Following a chorus which sang Russian songs and danced Russian folk dances to the accompaniment of a concertina, it was time at last for the performance of the Italian prima donna. But the woman who appeared on the stage was undoubtedly Russian and absolutely drunk. She started to tell a story but in such a voice that nobody could hear her. When people began to shout that she must speak louder, she retorted with absolutely unprintable abuse. The public shouted back and Madame Orsini became more and more furious. Bottles and apple peels flew on the stage and the whole performance turned into a real battle until the police arrived to restore order.

To escape the melee we fled from the garden, and with difficulty found our way to the boat through the dark streets. Early the next morning our vessel left Perm; when we woke up we were already far away from the town. In later years, when Perm played a certain role in the struggle between Whites and Reds, all I could remember of the place was a drunk woman with the grand name of Isabella Orsini fighting singlehandedly with the audience of a small summer theater.

With what pleasure I returned to The Oaks, where everything was so clean and cultured. I vividly remember the celebration of St. Nicholas Day, my father's name day, on the twenty-second of May. The peasants of all the neighboring villages came to The Oaks to congratulate my father. The whole open space in front of the house was filled with bearded men and women and children in bright clothes to whom we distributed money and sweets. My father talked to older peasants with his usual kindness, and, slightly ashamed, shoved money into their hands. All these people had certainly not come out of love for us, but to receive the gifts they knew would be forthcoming. In the evening when we sat on our balcony, surrounded by flowers, and listened to the nightingales, the breeze carried to us from the big village across the river the drunken voices of our morning visitors, still celebrating Father's name day. This tradition was repeated every year until the Revolution made enemies out of all the simple and trusting people, and the whole place was taken from us and destroyed, including the big oak trees which had been the joy of our childhood. My French cousin, who spent several summers with us, wrote a small poem in which she described those oaks—how they had sheltered our children's games, how birds had nested in their branches, and how finally wicked people, filled with hatred for those who by their labor had made it possible for themselves and their children to enjoy the good things of this earth, had come and destroyed the trees. The poem

[26]

was naïve but very touching. When I read it in Japan, where I lived by then, it made me cry, for it reminded me so vividly of my happy childhood, which was forever lost not only to me but also to future generations; they may find a new happiness, but it will never be like the one with which our childhood was blessed.

• Next to our estate was a small village of about twenty houses. It had a rather interesting origin. Some sixty years before our acquisition of The Oaks, the government had decided to create a model village. Selecting about twenty young peasants, it had given them special agricultural training, built houses for them, and put them on the land. In those days there were no private homes in the neighborhood; the village was surrounded by a forest, and the peasants had plenty of land. I do not know how the experiment fared in its early stages, but when we arrived there was nothing left of the model character of the village. Except for two or three old men, who were the greatest drunkards of the village, all original inhabitants were dead, their children having retrogressed to the normal state of Russian peasants, tilling the land in the summer and spending the long winters in idleness. Some were attracted by Moscow and left their village; the third generation worked in nearby factories, looked smart on holidays, played the concertina, and flirted with local girls.

We knew all of the villagers. The old men in their sober moments came to our place and philosophized with father, complained about the young generation, and told stories about their youth, when they had studied in some agricultural institution in St. Petersburg. They were very skeptical of those studies, and considered everything that differed from their ways as nonsense. One of the old men was engaged by us to guard the house during the night. During the first hour he would usually make much noise, beating some sort of wooden gong, announcing to any thief, it seemed to me, on what side of the house he was standing guard; then he would go to sleep, repeating his performance early in the morning. But in those days there were no thieves, everything was peaceful, and the peasants did not hate us. Those truly were good old times.

My childhood happiness, which I felt extended to all around us, was due in large measure to the wonderful character of the man who replaced our late father. I have always pitied children who must live in an atmosphere of restrictions, punishment, and fear. We were for tunate in not having anything of the sort, and even when one of us acted not as expected of him, my parents tried to understand him and guard him from the dangers which his new path might entail. To illustrate: One of my cousins [Khrisanf], the favorite of mother, was unduly influenced in his adolescence by the teachings of [Leo] Tolstoi. He even wanted to seek refuge in a monastery when one of his tutors gave him one of Tolstoi's books on religion to read. The book was such a revelation that he decided to visit Tolstoi. Tolstoi was touched by my cousin's sincerity and showed him so much kindness that the latter began to visit Tolstoi's house more and more often, and entered the circle of his followers. Our easy life began to burden him, and during his summer vacations he used to spend most of his time on the estate of Tolstoi. His admiration for Tolstoi was so great that he did not notice that Tolstoi himself lived surrounded by the same contradictions he tried to avoid in our midst, Tolstoi's wife and most of his children not following his principles in their everyday lives. My father did not oppose his son and even began to study the teachings of Tolstoi; as for mother, she did everything to keep him on The Oaks. A small peasant house was specially constructed for him, with a garden where he grew excellent vegetables, killing animals and eating meat being against Tolstoi's teachings, and our whole life, which had never been particularly luxurious, was greatly simplified. But my cousin was too sincere to be satisfied with such child's play and dreamed of great acts to prove his devotion.

At that time Tolstoi took interest in the Dukhobors, a Russian sect which opposed the teachings of the established church and created their own faith, a mixture of high moral principles and superstition. What appealed to Tolstoi was the Dukhobors' refusal to take up arms against human beings. The government could not allow such opposition to military service and started to persecute the Dukhobors, exiling them to the Caucasus near the Turkish frontier in the expectation that there they would be obliged to take up arms in order to defend themselves against robbers who infested these parts, but the Dukhobors found other ways of dealing with the robbers and remained true to their principles. When the government thereupon resumed its persecution, Tolstoi, who saw in the Dukhobors followers of his basic teaching of nonresistance to evil, started a movement to permit their emigration to Canada. Though Tolstoi had already discarded as useless the writing of literature, on which his own fame primarily rested, he wrote one more literary work, *The Resurrection,* and sold its copyright to a magazine in order to obtain the funds for the Dukhobors' transportation to Canada.

Meanwhile my cousin announced that he was going to the Caucasus to share the sufferings of the Dukhobors. Realizing that his son was too young to play the role of martyr, that his views might change, but that the suspicion aroused in the mind of the Russian authorities would never be allayed and could well ruin his whole life, father asked Tolstoi to dissuade my cousin from this step. Tolstoi agreed with my father and advised my cousin, before taking the important step of self-sacrifice to undergo a certain amount of preparation. Some of his followers, including members of the highest society, exiled for their support of the Dukhobors against the government, had established a colony in England, where they tried to put his teachings into practice. He told my cousin to join this colony, and so instead of going to the Caucasus, he proceeded to England and for two years lived among those cranks. I visited him there and stayed in the colony for three weeks, trying to do whatever everyone else did. It was very amusing, but noble as the creation of a purely artificial life to apply certain principles may have been, in the current state of civilization it was absolutely impractical and did not appeal to me.

The experience with my cousin had a happy ending, for he later met a charming girl in Tolstoi's family, fell in love with her, and married her in church, to the great indignation of Tolstoi's other followers, who were opposed to the established Church. "What can I do if I love Natasha more than the Truth?" he retorted. Father bought the couple a small estate in the interior of Russia, where they lived modestly like well-to-do and cultured peasants, taking from the teachings of Tolstoi what was practical: life on the land, without luxury or class arrogance.

I shall never forget how once, when I came from Japan to Russia, my parents took me to visit my cousin on his estate. We arrived late in the evening; I was tired and went straight to bed. When I opened the window in the morning, the wonderful spring air, unique to the Russian countryside, filled my room. The typical farm noise made my heart jump with joy, because in my wanderings abroad I had begun to forget that such paradise existed in this world. My cousin came to greet me with his eldest son, a charming boy with a shock of dark hair

[29]

arranged to fall across his forehead in imitation of some Cossack hero, for the Great War was upon us. Yet in the calmness of country life the War seemed far away, and nobody could imagine what horrors were in store for us.

Later I learned that upon the outbreak of the Revolution, the peasants had at first tried to defend my cousin, but then, under the influence of agitators, had turned against him. He had to leave the place where I had had my last glimpse of happy Russian country life. I do not know what became of him after that, but once, while in a Tokyo theater, I saw a Soviet movie, a very rare thing in those days. I had already wanted to leave, because I simply cannot stomach Soviet propaganda, when I saw my own family name among the list of actors. I stayed. It was a dull film about virtuous workers struggling against saboteurs. The chief saboteur, who bore my name, was a very nice-looking young man with dark hair falling across his forehead. I recalled the beautiful spring morning when my cousin had brought his son to my room; it was the same face and the same name. Though the movie was stupid and the Soviet propaganda most irritating, I remained till the end, following with great tenderness all the movements of the young actor, who in spite of the Soviet backdrop seemed to me the same charming boy who had tried to imitate the exploits of a Cossack hero. Life is full of surprises. But I have strayed far from the general course of my story. I am afraid it is difficult to avoid such digression, for one recollection brings to mind another, until one is lost in memories.

2

University Years

OUR SCHOOL YEARS WERE PASSING QUICKLY. FROM CHILDREN WE GREW into adolescents, but our life remained the same, happy and carefree. Like most Russian youths we went through periods of searching for answers to life's problems, but living in a healthy atmosphere, untouched by the hard sides of life, these periods did not affect us profoundly, did not develop in us that deep pessimism and discontent with life, which were becoming so characteristic of prerevolutionary youths and making them future revolutionists.

At last came the final year of our middle school, when we had to present ourselves before the government commission for the final examination after which we obtained the diploma that gave us the right to enter the university. As often happens when life does not present any urgent claims which push one into a particular profession and if one is not endowed with special talents, as was my eldest brother [Aleksei] who from early childhood was determined to study medicine, I was quite undecided about my future career. When asked as a child what I wanted to be when I grew up, I used to reply that I would lead a luxurious and brilliant life. People would laugh and say there was no such career as a brilliant and luxurious life, but somehow this childish phrase unconsciously became the leading spirit of my life. I had to be more concrete when finishing school, however; I had to choose a specific field of study at Moscow University. Knowing that my father, notwithstanding his commercial activity, was fond of the natural sciences and passed all his spare time in the laboratory, I enrolled in the Faculty of Natural Sciences in the hope of pleasing my father, though I felt that I was making the mistake of my life.

As a graduation reward father took my brother and me to St. Petersburg [1894]. Though it was spring and the Neva River with its row of palaces looked magnificent and such neighboring places as Tsarskoe Selo[1] and Peterhof,[2] created by Peter the Great and Catherine II, were more beautiful than anything that Moscow had to offer, I did not like St. Petersburg. After a fortnight in the capital father put us both on a freighter which was leaving for England and with the advice not to return until autumn, when classes began at the university, sent us on our great adventure.

The first trip abroad made a strong impression on me, and I am afraid that I returned to Russia with a slightly diminished pride in my country. But not everything was smooth on our journey. When our ship entered the North Sea the weather became rough and we were seasick. As nobody had told us about the existence of such an illness, we seriously thought that we were dying and I desperately began to ring the bell. When a huge steward with a red face appeared, we started to implore him to save us. To our horror he gave a hearty laugh, and declared that no one had yet died from seasickness. This was poor consolation, and I began to think what a blessing it would be if our vessel went down and we would obtain release from our suffering at the bottom of the sea. But the ship did not sink and we safely reached Hull. At first sight, I thought there must be a fire in town with everybody rushing to see it. But there was no fire; it was simply the difference in tempo between English and Russian life. As we debarked, an old English lady who had been traveling with us told us that she liked us so much that she was sure our mother must be a very nice woman and would like to send her a present. The present consisted of an old teapot, which we obediently carried with us till we returned to Moscow, where mother was greatly touched but did not know what to do with it.

From Hull we went straight to London, where we felt quite lost. On the advice of our father, who had been in London some twenty years before, we stopped at the Golden Cross Hotel, a gloomy place

[1] Now called Pushkin.
[2] Now called Petrodvorets.

that was mentioned in one of Dickens' novels—with the same old waiters, judging by their age. But we did not spend much time in the hotel. We were mostly in the streets, running from museum to museum and picture gallery to picture gallery. We felt like small ants in a big anthill. Often we lost each other and returned to the hotel trembling with fright, lest we not find each other there. In those days London was quite different from what it was to become afterward. Most people wore frock coats and silk hats, there were no motorcars, and instead of ugly taxicabs elegant two-wheeled vehicles, with the coachman seated behind, filled the streets. The whole city looked extremely correct and gentlemanly. In the afternoon Hyde Park was a sight of wealth and luxury. Never before had we seen such splendid carriages with such proud ladies inside; in comparison Moscow was an old woman in an outmoded coat, moving slowly through dirt and poverty. The impression of richness increased when we started to visit the theaters, especially the opera, where we saw rows and rows of magnificently dressed ladies covered with precious stones. My craving for luxury and brilliance was satisfied, but alas, father did not spoil us and our traveling budget was limited, so that we had to admire all the splendor from the heights of the galleries. I did make it a point, however, to stand close by when the crowd departed, just to be near all those lucky people. How I longed to be one of them, to ride in their luxurious carriages and dine in their magnificent restaurants. Instead we tried to pretend that we were grown up and sat on high stools in a bar, eating sandwiches, terrified that one of the barmaids who wore such elaborate hairdresses might talk to us.

One of the purposes of our trip to London was to find out how well we had learned English. We were not very successful at first. In the streets, when we had to ask our way, nobody could understand us. We lost so much time in repeating "please" and "thank you" that our listeners lost patience before we came to the point. Once when we visited the family of our governess we were left in the company of an old lady. My brother was even shyer than I, so that it fell upon me to make conversation. Knowing that the English like to talk about the weather, I asked the old lady: "Do you have snow in the winter?" To my surprise she did not answer anything, and looked at me in astonishment. I repeated the question. Her astonishment changed to fear, and she rushed out of the room and came back with her daughter, who inquired what I had asked her mother. I repeated my question for the third time. The daughter laughed, and explained that her mother had understood me to ask if she snored in the winter. I understood the astonishment of the old lady; had I merely asked if she snored in general, it could have been passed off as the strange curiosity of a visitor from barbaric Russia, but the addition "in the winter" made the whole thing too absurd.

Our adventures were many. Once, at the hotel, a stranger came up to our table and said that he saw we were foreigners and that he wanted to be helpful, and invited us to the theater. We accepted the invitation, but when we found ourselves in the box, we became afraid of associating with a stranger and when our host left the box for a moment, ran out of the theater. The play had been very amusing, and it troubled me that we had not seen the ending. Twenty years later I was greatly relieved when watching an annual amateur performance in Tokyo, I recognized the comedy as the same one from which we had fled in London, and was able to see how it came out. It was called "Charley's Aunt."

After nearly a month in London, having exhausted all of Baedeker's suggestions, we wrote to our father that we longed to return home. He replied that it was too early and, sending us a newspaper clipping advertising Cook's conducted tours in Scotland, suggested that we go there before starting home. Dutifully we joined the next conducted tour. Ever since I have felt that conducted tours are terrible ordeals. A group of people, not knowing each other, tied together with a guide in command of their destiny, telling them where to go and what to see. In our case the guide was perpetually drunk because he insisted at every waterfall upon trying the water for his whiskey. He found special pleasure in tyrannizing two Russian boys, lost in the wilderness of Scotland. When he saw us looking somewhere other than indicated by him, he would shout that when he explained things we must watch what he was showing. Our fellow travelers were also strange. I remember an old man who suffered from some sort of rash and scratched himself on every pointed object he found, and an elderly lady who tried to kiss us because we reminded her of her nephews. I was not surprised when I overheard someone whisper, as he followed our party to our reserved places: "Again this awful Cook's party!" The weather was usually bad; only occasionally, traveling on some lake, did we see bits of lovely country through the mist. During a rainy trip to some islands an old gentleman rushed up to us and began to shake our hands, expressing his regret that such misfortune should have befallen our country. When we asked what he meant, he replied solemnly that he had just read in the newspaper that our president had been killed. We assured him that we had no president. He seemed rather disappointed; he had mistaken us for Frenchmen, President [Sadi] Carnot having been assassinated.[3] At last the Scottish nightmare came to an end. It was my first and, I hope, last experience of a communal undertaking under strict supervision.

On our way back we stopped in Paris, where we met the aunt who was studying medicine there. She advised us what to see in Paris and insisted that we avoid the gay places which, according to her, were frequented only by empty-headed foreigners and not by a single decent Frenchman. My aunt, who adored Paris, always blamed the city's immoral reputation on the foreigners, claiming that the French were the most virtuous people in the world. When I got to know Paris better, I found reason to doubt the latter, but there was much truth to her criticism of the foreigners. During our first visit to Paris we followed the advice of my aunt and went to such places as the Louvre, the Luxembourg, and Versailles; only once did we find ourselves in Montmartre and entering some café were horrified to see skeletons standing in the corners and people sitting on coffins. But, as my aunt said, such a strange and horrid idea probably appealed to some foreign tourists. After London we did not like Paris. It was the end of the summer, the streets were empty and hot, with dust and dirt everywhere. Furthermore, our money was running out. We walked aimlessly through the big shops, asked about the prices, and bought nothing.

Back at The Oaks, we were welcomed like heroes and proudly walked about in our English clothes. But soon we were absorbed in our old life and the whole journey seemed like a dream. The autumn was beautiful. The park was full of yellow trees and leaves, the red ash berries adding to the symphony of colors. With all my newly acquired love for England, I had to confess that no country was more

[3] The assassination, and thus the trip, took place in 1894.

[35]

beautiful than my own, no place more gorgeous than The Oaks. Everything seemed to smile at me. I was young and strong, my university years, by tradition the best years of one's life, before me.

But soon the disillusionment began. With the start of Moscow University, in the middle of September, I discovered that in trying to please my father I was going counter to my nature. I had neither talent nor interest for purely scientific work. With great attention I followed different lectures, for hours I sat in the laboratories, but I was terribly bored. Nor did my relations with fellow students go smoothly. Natural science majors were usually serious persons, their chief outside interest being politics, politics meaning to them extreme opposition to the government and secret work toward its overthrow.

Every student, young as he was, considered himself capable of reforming the state. Yet actually he and his comrades were putty in the hands of real agitators, who even then worked for the destruction of academic discipline. You never saw the agitators at lectures, but at the first sign of any disorder they were there, took leadership, and were followed by the mass of students, who did not even know whence the agitators had come and what their aims were. I did my best to be on good terms with my fellow students. I visited them in their rooms and, as most of them were poor, purposely wore an old uniform and tried to hide that I came from a bourgeois family. But to no avail. Envy and class hatred are prime factors in any revolutionary movement, and it sufficed for my comrades to discover that my family was well-to-do and owned factories, to make me soon the target of all their attacks in political discussions and to accuse me of sucking the blood of the people. I tried to explain that factories were necessary and that in those factories nobody sucked anybody's blood, but the term "bloodsucker" was a vital cliché in political discussion and so in the eyes of my comrades a bloodsucker I was and a bloodsucker I remained. The only thing for me to do was to stay away from political meetings, but even this did not spare me from political agitation.

That year the students, probably under the influence of agitators, introduced strikes, following the example of factories. These strikes were usually triggered by hysterical speeches to the effect that in some section some students, unknown to most of us, had been arrested by the police, and that we must show our sympathy for them by striking, i.e. ceasing to attend lectures. Strange agitators, usually long-haired students in dirty uniforms, rushed from room to room demanding that students stop listening to the professors. As students got up and walked out of the lecture halls, there was little the professors could do but gather up their notes and stop talking. In the large auditorium, to which all students flocked, speeches were made attacking everybody and everything. In vain the old dean of the faculty implored the students to return to their lectures, because otherwise the police would come and make new arrests. Nobody listened, the shouting increased, the police appeared, and all of us were driven to the big manege opposite the university, there kept for the night, and then released, the chief agitators usually having disappeared in time. The whole thing was absurd: here we came to the university to study, but instead were caught up in senseless agitation, endangering our entire careers by becoming involved in a revolutionary movement imposed on us by unknown agitators. As I never wanted to be a tool of anybody, I began to avoid all this agitation, attending lectures when possible but leaving the moment we were to protest against something without knowing whether there was really cause for complaint. The fact that all of us wore the same uniform did not suffice to bind us thousands of students in a camaraderie strong enough to justify our self-sacrifice for unknown persons.

In those days father made one of his attempts to teach us to be independent. He rented separate lodgings for the four oldest of us[4] and let us live as we pleased. But the experiment was not very successful. The four of us were different in character and had our own friends and tastes, so that the perfect order which had reigned in our family house, gave way to general chaos in our bachelors' quarters. My older brothers were fond of hunting. They would go on hunting expeditions far away in the country, and come back with innumerable hares, foxes, wolves, and once even a bear; all this was dirty and smelled bad. Soon I noticed that the hunting expeditions served as a pretext for gay adventures with wine, cards, and women. Strange people whom my brothers met on their hunting expeditions appeared in our lodgings and beer, wine, and cards did not leave our table. Once a small insignificant man, who was always drunk and asserted that in his provincial town he was considered a Don Juan whom not a single lady could resist, stayed with us for nearly two weeks and we got

[4] The author, his elder brother Aleksei, and cousins Nikolai and Sergei.

rid of him with difficulty. I had to do the housekeeping and had endless discussions with a fat cook who could not think up what to serve us the next day. When the cook left, I thought I was through with the petty things of this life, but our old servant, who looked like a ghost, glided noiselessly from a dark corner and began to whisper to me that his heart was bleeding, for while we had been studying hard, our cook had been stealing our money by adding five kopeks to the price of a chicken. Enraged, I threw my physics book at the old man, and the whispering shadow disappeared. All this was a far cry from the brilliant and luxurious life about which I had dreamed.

I tried to persuade my father that such independence did not suit me at all and that I would like to return home, but he insisted that it was important for me to see all sides of life. There were some sides of life to which I could never get accustomed, however, and when my brothers arranged some of their gay parties they always suggested that I go to the theater or visit our parents, because, as they explained, to invite me to their parties would be like putting a coffin on the table. What with my disinterest in the subjects I studied, the political strikes and agitation, and the chaos in our new home, my first year at the university was not a success, and when I failed one of the examinations at the end of the year, I took it as a decision of fate and transferred from the Faculty of Natural Sciences to the Faculty of Law, which had the largest enrollment of students and therefore offered greater freedom in the choice of friends without the tyranny of a revolutionary majority. After arranging everything, I felt I deserved a rest and accompanied two of my brothers abroad.

This time we traveled through Austria, Switzerland, North Italy, and back. Russians usually accuse each other of touring other countries in preference to their own, so that those who can afford to travel know foreign places well, but scarcely know anything outside their native town in Russia itself. This is quite true, but after all, when one wants a change and a rest, one is much more likely to find it abroad. Traveling in Russia is not a rest: the distances are enormous, the trains irregular, hotels dirty and uncomfortable, servants are rude, and everywhere there are angry faces and no escape from political discussion. Abroad the air is different. In Vienna we were at once caught up in the general gaiety; the crowds were nice; so were the cafés with their beautiful music; even the political life in Parliament, where the President was vainly ringing the bell to silence a crowd of young Czechs who were rushing about protesting against something, did not look so tragic as our Russian strikes. We enjoyed picturesque Innsbruck, with its narrow streets and medieval buildings surrounded by mountains, as well as Switzerland, where everything was done for the comfort of tourists and even the mountains and beautiful lakes seemed to have been put there for foreigners to admire. When we arrived at our hotel in Interlaken, we found a crowd watching a balcony on which, to our surprise, one of our innumerable aunts, of whose presence in Switzerland we had no idea, was in a state of acute hysteria because her small boy had squeezed his head between two bars and could not get it out again. The boy was howling and my aunt imploring the crowd of onlookers to save her child. At last a workman appeared and liberated the howling boy by cutting one of the bars.

At Vevey, where we stopped for several weeks, we met some other relatives as well as a charming old Russian princess who stayed there because she could not find a cheaper place to live. She used to invite us to tea and tell us stories about her brilliant youth. Suddenly three beautiful American girls with a majestic-looking aunt moved into our boardinghouse. The girls created a sensation. All the young men immediately fell in love with them, and our boardinghouse became the gayest place in Vevey. There was endless dancing, picnics on the lake, serenading with guitars in the moonlight, squeezing of hands and kissing, the majestic aunt not seeing anything and telling the old princess how good and unspoiled her nieces were.

After Vevey we stayed in the wilderness of the mountains in a small place kept by our sweet teacher from Moscow. The absolute quiet among the green valleys, except for the sound of cowbells, and the magnificent sunset which tinted Mont Blanc red, were restful. Moving on, we crossed the Alps at Simplon. In those days there was no tunnel and we went by carriage, spending the night in some monastery. We visited Devil's Bridge, where the famous Russian General [Aleksandr Vasilevich] Suvorov had crossed the Alps and, unexpectedly appearing in North Italy, had destroyed the armies of Napoleon's generals [1799]. There were some Russians in our coach. As we continued our journey, splendid views came into sight, but these people did not pay any attention to the scenery. They talked and

[39]

talked about the superiority of the Russian cuisine over foreign cooking, enumerating caviar, lox, borsht, and Russian pies, and smacking their lips as if they were eating all those dishes, completely ignoring the precipitous mountains and wild torrents in their gastronomic reflections.

At Simplon everything had been covered with snow. As we descended into Italy, it looked like paradise. We stopped at Lake Maggiore and in the morning found ourselves on Isola Bella,[5] all covered with roses and oleander. Walking through the gardens of the villa Borromee, we met a group of Catholic priests led by a cardinal garbed in red. He was the proprietor of the villa. He stopped us, asked from what country we came, handed us some roses and gave us his blessing. In the brilliant sunshine this figure in red, surrounded by flowers, made a wonderful picture. Bellagio passed like a dream as we sat on the terrace of the hotel admiring the calm surface of the lake, bathed in moonlight. In Milan we saw the *Last Supper* of Leonardo da Vinci and climbed onto the roof of the Cathedral. In Venice, the fairyland city where one is taken back into medieval times, we spent a week, absorbing the beauty of the town and its churches and museums like sponges. Back to gay Vienna and a last glimpse of Europe in the form of Berlin with its marching soldiers and heavy marble arches, preparing itself for the role of the most powerful city of Europe—the dream which all Germans have, but the fulfillment of which always escapes them.

At last the long voyage home and gloomy Russia with its endless fields, forests, miserable villages, and people with sad faces. At the frontier station, as you see the first Russian porter and the gendarmes standing at attention, you have a feeling of joy that you are back in your fatherland mixed with sadness that it lacks the gaiety and brilliance of other countries. Suspicion is in the air; as you present your passport you tremble that something will be found wrong; as the customs officer looks through the luggage, you fear that he will find a lot of contraband. But when all these formalities are over and you find yourself in the restaurant before a glass of weak tea with artificial palms on the table, you are glad to be back and repeat the Russian proverb: "It is good to visit, better to be home." Two or three days after returning to The Oaks, all golden in its autumn foliage,

[5] One of the Borromean Islands.

impressions brought back from abroad retreat into the past. Only the present seems real.

❖❖❖

After a few days I resumed my university life in new surroundings. The enrollment in the Faculty of Law was so large that there was no sense of obligation to lead a common life with one's fellow students or to comply with anybody's instructions. You attended your lectures and saw your friends and that was all. In other parts of the university, however, the political troubles continued. Sometimes a group of strange-looking students would rush into our lecture halls and demand that we stop attending lectures and arrange meetings of protest against different injustices toward some unknown persons, but we remained indifferent toward such manifestations of artificial indignation. Most of us in law were of the bourgeoisie, and the agitators looked upon us as hopeless elements in their plans to overthrow the government. In truth, we did not share the hate and envy so necessary in every revolutionary movement. I must confess that this political indifference corresponded much more to my inner feelings than self-sacrifice for some vague purpose.

I was accustomed to the idea that Russia was a monarchy. It was the monarchy that had created contemporary Russia and ruled, as far as I could see, without any display of inhuman cruelty. To be sure, people were arrested and sent to Siberia, but these were people who had conspired against the government and a government which had not defended itself against its enemies would not have been worthy of its name. No one could deny that Russia was making enormous progress in its cultural and economic position; the population was increasing and getting richer. To destroy all that and to start some political adventures seemed absurd to me. Before destroying the past one must be sure of a better future and, at any rate, the students, who have to study for years before they can understand what it means to rule the country, are not called to take part in the political life of the state.

In my new faculty I could adhere to my principles without being accused of sucking the blood of the working class. We had some fine professors whose lectures I followed with great interest. I never missed the lectures of our famous historian [Vasilii Osipovich]

[41]

Kliuchevskii. He was popular with the students, especially the radical ones, because he sometimes allowed himself extremely sarcastic remarks about certain pages of Russian history. But I was present at a scene, which proves of what little value such popularity is. Alexander III had just died, and prior to starting his lecture in the overcrowded auditorium, Kliuchevskii began to speak about the merits of the late Emperor and proposed that everyone rise for a minute in honor of the Tsar who several times had saved Europe from the horrors of war. The suggestion evoked pandemonium. Those students who would not admit that anything good could be said of the monarch began to shout and hiss and to call Kliuchevskii names; others began to applaud. Kliuchevskii watched the scene with a sarcastic smile, probably thinking that there were many fools in Russia, but that he had bested them all. After that his popularity among the radicals was gone and they started a movement to boycott his lectures. The incident gave me real pleasure because so many professors tried to be popular with students by flattering them that they were ripe for political activity.

Outside the university I resumed my role of housekeeper in our bachelors' quarters, holding consultations with the fat cook about the next day's menu, while my brothers continued their hunting expeditions and gay life. I kept aloof, too self-centered or self-conscious to let myself go. This side of my character may have deprived me of many joys of youth; on the other hand it spared me many senseless acts, complications, and regrets. Untouched by hangovers, sudden infatuations, and early marriage, I contemplated life calmly and detachedly. Every time I found myself on the verge of an infatuation, I thought of the possible consequences and retired in time. Love does not like such a man, and did not waste its time on me. There was a friend of my sister, a charming girl, whom I met at that time. Her blue eyes were appealing and my desire to see her became stronger and stronger, but it never went further than holding hands while listening to the Chaikovskii overture to *Romeo and Juliet*. I did think for a while that she was the only girl who could make me happy, but her life took such an extraordinary turn, as I shall relate later, that I did not deem myself good enough to change the course of her life, and consoled myself that all was for the best in what then seemed to me the best of all possible worlds.

Anna and Vera, Abrikossow's sister and cousin

Young man about town. The author, in St. Petersburg, about 1904

Life in Moscow was full and interesting and truly wonderful. The political disorders among the students did not touch other parts of Russian society and the merchant class, which predominated in Moscow, did not participate in politics or finance the radicals to undermine the foundations on which their welfare rested. It devoted its interest to art, the theater, and music, Moscow's magnificent state-supported theaters having a rich repertoire of operas, dramas, and ballets. Every new play was discussed by an enthusiastic audience. I particularly enjoyed the concerts in the beautiful Hall of the Moscow Nobility. All this the Moscow of my youth spread before us with both hands. But even apart from these joys of life, Moscow with its cozy appearance, its countless churches, crooked streets, and friendly crowds was the nicest city I have ever seen, its character not yet spoiled by class hatred.

The Kremlin was open to everybody, the churches were full, and on every holiday the air resounded with the ringing of church bells. Only in Moscow could you feel the impressive contrast between carnival week, when the whole population gorged itself on food and drink and the streets were filled with merrymakers, and the beginning of Lent, when suddenly, as if by magic, everyone became still, and the church bells majestically called people to repent and to prepare themselves for the Resurrection. After seven weeks of Lent came Easter, which we usually celebrated in the Kremlin where crowds of people would wait for the first peal of the great bell of St. John's Church. Processions of priests and singers moved around each of the four cathedrals before the palace, and suddenly at midnight the great bell began to boom over the whole of Moscow, joined after five minutes by innumerable bells throughout the city. You really felt that something great had happened. Only those completely devoid of any idealism and love of fellow man could be so narrow in thought and feeling as to regard all this merely as opium for the people.

In spring I passed my examinations and in the company of my two brothers and their Greek teacher left for our usual journey abroad. This time we decided to go by way of the Black Sea to Constantinople, then Greece, and back through Italy. Our ship reached the Straits during the night, and we had to wait until sunrise for permission to enter the Bosporus. No other town in Europe has so effective an approach as Constantinople, especially as seen from the Black Sea. At sunrise we were all on deck and watched the gorgeous panorama. On both sides we could see small villages with their minarets and cypress trees. The closer we got to Constantinople the livelier became the scene. We passed beautiful palaces and the magnificent summer residence of the Russian Embassy. The Bosporus was crowded with small crafts which glided in all directions, and the noise of the crowd on shore could be heard. Suddenly the vessel turned into the Golden Horn and the entire city loomed before us in the morning mist. From the ship one did not see the dirt or smell the odors. Situated on three hills, Constantinople with its mosques and minarets looked like a picture from a fairy tale. Once we set foot on shore, the magic spell was broken; still, Constantinople remains one of the most fascinating cities that I have seen in my numerous travels. In those days the red fez was not yet prohibited; everybody wore it, and it gave to the crowd a special distinction. We admired the bright red hats so much that we bought some for ourselves and wore them, proud to have become part of the Turkish milieu. But once we met a secretary of the Russian Embassy, who inquired where we were from. When he learned that we were prominent inhabitants of Moscow, he became very angry and abused us, demanding how we could so humiliate ourselves and our origin by wearing this sign of Islam. He was especially angry with our teacher and told him that he was not fit to guide our steps. After that the fezzes disappeared from our heads, and we were restored to grace in the eyes of the Russian diplomat.

We visited the famous Santa Sophia Church, which the Turks had changed into a Moslem mosque. All their efforts notwithstanding, I felt as if I were inside a magnificent Christian temple and could imagine the gorgeous services held here in Byzantine times. It was an old tradition among Russians that Santa Sophia waited for Russia to liberate it from the Turks and to restore the cross on its roof. We were close to doing so after the Russo-Turkish War, but England prevented us; we had hopes again during the First World War when the Revolution shattered our plans. With the indifference of the Soviet government to old Russian traditions, particularly those connected with religion, the dream seems farther from realization than ever.

We spent two weeks in Constantinople sightseeing. We were present when the Sultan, an old Turk with a wicked face, was driven by a pair of magnificent Arab horses to the service in the mosque. His numerous wives remained outside, their faces covered except for the eyes, with which they curiously inspected the foreign ladies who were there. We went to Brussa, the old capital, of which I remember the strong smell of roses and the signature of Pierre Loti in the hotel register with some inscription about the charms of Brussa, the capital of roses. I tried to write something equally poetic, but did not succeed and only spoiled the page in the register.

Proceeding to Greece, we were greatly disappointed. The heat was awful, the dust worse. Modern Greece has nothing in common with the Greece of our schoolbooks. Even the Acropolis does not make any impression unless seen in the moonlight when modern life is asleep. Only the statue of Hermes, lost in a small museum near the ruins of the temples of Olympia where the old games were held, looks really beautiful even in the daytime.

From Patras we crossed to Italy, and Baedeker guidebook in hand, visited Rome, Naples, and Sicily. In Rome I was impressed by all that the Catholic Church and its artists had created. In Naples we climbed Vesuvius, visited the ruins of Pompeii, drove through Sorrento and Amalfi, went to Capri and the Blue Grotto. Everything was beautiful, but the terrible heat diminished our enjoyment. By the time we reached Sicily, we were tired of the perpetual change in scenery. I quarreled with our Greek teacher and persuaded my brothers, who had to return earlier for their school, to go back with him alone, leaving me behind. On my own in Florence, I found that I was much happier being alone than tied to other persons, especially if there was among them someone like our Greek teacher, who imagined himself so clever that he tried to teach everybody and was completely devoid of a sense of humor—in my eyes a sign of stupidity notwithstanding all his knowledge. It was of Florence that I kept the best memories of my journey. Being alone, I did what I liked, went for long walks, sat for hours on top of a hill admiring the view of the town below, and ate delicious ice cream while listening to music. The tune of a march which was very fashionable at the time has remained in my head to this day, and whenever I hear it I see before me the open square in Florence with the figure of Michelangelo's David and the gay crowd which surrounded me.

I visited the Catholic churches and tried to find out whether those

[45]

dark buildings with groups of old women whispering their prayers, clergymen officiating before the altar, and the smell of incense permeating the air brought me nearer to the Great Truth than our churches with their gilded images, their loud singing, and their common prayer. They did not. I was merely confirmed in my conviction that the Great Truth is felt, not reasoned, and that all temples are the result of man's effort to squeeze the Great Truth into human forms, forms too narrow and inadequate for something divine. Consequently we have magnificent temples, crowds of worshipers and processions of priests, yet God seems absent at times, and I feel His presence far more when I am alone. The star-studded sky forms a much more suitable cover for a temple than the most beautifully painted ceiling.

From Florence I went to Genoa and thence, before returning to Russia, to Saint-Jean-de-Luz to visit my French aunt and her two charming daughters. After all her misfortunes she had found a peaceful existence, was absorbed in her children, and led an interesting life in Paris. I felt that conversations with her made me a better person; they helped me to resist a tendency to become overly absorbed in little things and in myself.

Recrossing the frontier, the sight of the Russian station and its porters and solitary figure of a gendarme, the restaurant with its artificial palms and swarms of flies, marked the end of my summer holidays and the beginning of winter with its studies at the university, as well as its theaters and many other Moscow amusements. I particularly loved Moscow in winter when it was all white with snow, sleighs speeding in every direction and the moonbeams playing on the many golden cupolas of the Kremlin cathedrals. The whole of Russian history with its endless struggle against the Mongols and the Tartars passed before your eyes. Peter the Great had discarded Moscow for the European St. Petersburg, but the heart of Russia remained in the old city; and I shall never cease to wonder how the Bolsheviks, after transferring the capital back to Moscow, continue to stick to their Marxism and other theories so alien to Russia instead of returning to the Russian way of thinking, characteristic of old Moscow. We too had spoken of revolution and of changes, but always of a Russian revolution and Russian changes. Europe was an ideal for us and we

[46]

never presumed to leadership in a world revolution. Such cruel and inhuman conceit was alien to the Russia I knew and loved.

Though we continued to live away from home, I spent most of my free time in the Big House, as we called the building where the whole family had lived together until father had got the idea of giving the oldest sons absolute freedom to shape their own lives. To tell the truth, I did not like this freedom. I missed the conversations with Father and the benevolent attitude of Mother. Thus in the evenings I usually left the company of my brothers and their friends, and joined the rest of the family for tea. Easy friendships and senseless flirtations led to early marriage, a good thing in theory, but full of complications in practice. I passed through a short period of romancing, only to suffer a dreadful blow to my dignity when the girl preferred someone else. I must confess I have never forgotten Natalie with her sad eyes.[6] The great fault of my character was that I could never give myself entirely to strong feelings. Without such occasional madnesses, one's personality cannot achieve its full development. I have always preferred the path of reason to the follies necessary to the full enjoyment of life. But it is useless to complain that God has not made one different from the way one is.

In those days I read many books from my father's library and had endless discussions with him about the origin of life, during which it seemed to me that the portrait of Darwin, which hung in my father's study, looked down with sympathy on our efforts to delve into the mysteries of life. One sentence I read at the time made a particularly strong impression on me. It pointed out that the tragedy of man lay in the fact that he had the soul of an angel, the intellect of a human being, and the body of a beast, the true sage having to keep a balance between these irreconcilable sides of human nature. I decided at once to work toward such a balance in my own life, not giving free rein to impractical dreams, curbing excessive reasoning, and subduing animal instincts. Alas, this only led me farther away from the free enjoyment of all the pleasures of life.

[6] Natalie was to become the wife of Grand Duke Michael, brother of Emperor Nicholas II, and, as we shall see later, was to introduce her childhood friend into the world of royalty.

Thus passed my third year at the university, and with the arrival of spring I began to make plans for a new summer excursion.

✠✠✠

This time I went with one of my brothers to Spain, where we toured different Spanish towns, guidebook in hand, studying cathedrals and picture galleries as well as Spanish dances, all the while suffering from the great heat. There were far more ties with the Middle Ages left in Spain than in Italy. Toledo with its Alcazar, the Alhambra with its Moorish palaces, and the wonderful cathedral of Seville with its bell music spoke of the distant past; only Madrid with its gay crowds and innumerable cafés proved that Spain was not satisfied to have merely a past, but desired also a present and a future. In the small provincial town of Málaga my brother ate too many fresh grapes and nearly died from a severe gastric attack. I felt lost in the small hotel where only Spanish was spoken, but everyone showed the greatest sympathy and our room was filled with strangers, everyone of whom tried to give advice. Soon a doctor appeared, who looked like Don Quixote. His long arms went round and round like a windmill as he was telling me something in Spanish. I could make out only one word: cholera. To my horror my brother was losing consciousness. The doctor ordered hot-water bottles and poured brandy into the mouth of my brother. Everybody was trying to help. I have never seen such a noisy sickroom. The doctor who apparently knew everybody seemed to enjoy his own energy; a girl with red cheeks, serving as the nurse, giggled all the time. But the next morning my brother gave signs of life and the doctor began to feed him fresh tomatoes.

I did not know how to occupy my time during the two weeks that it took my brother to recuperate, until a company of first-class bull-fighters came to Málaga and the doctor insisted on taking me to a performance. I was rather horrified at first, but the doctor and the whole crowd seemed to enjoy themselves so much that I could not disappoint them and screwing up my courage, followed the fight. The doctor was so excited that his arms went round and round, and I was afraid he would jump into the arena. The spectators passed around wine bags which they squeezed so cleverly that the spray shot directly into their mouths. When my turn came I tried to do the same,

[48]

but squirted half the wine over myself. After several visits to the arena, always in the company of the doctor who in his excitement forgot that I did not understand Spanish and tried to explain to me the bullfights in detail, I began to enjoy them. Analyzing the chief attraction of this struggle between man and bull, I concluded that the change of feeling from fear for the man, as the wild animal rushes toward him to impale him on its horns, to relief, when he escapes by nimbly jumping over the fence, creates a special sensation of great exultation. At the end of the spectacle, when the crowd disperses with songs and dances, you have the desire to join them. Thus nearly every day the doctor came to see my brother and after his visit we went to the bullfight. His practice must not have been very large, or maybe when a famous bullfighter visited the provincial town nobody had the right to be ill. At last my brother was quite well and the dreadful moment came when we had to call on the doctor to pay the bill. We had no idea what his fees were; when I had tried to discuss the matter with him, reading sentences from a phrase book which had a section on conversation with a doctor, he had only laughed. Thus we had calculated what the fees of a good doctor in Moscow would have been and went to him with our pockets full of money. When we presented him with a bulky envelope and tried to make a hasty retreat, he opened it and roared with laughter. We were sure that he had found the amount insufficient, when to our great astonishment he took only part of the contents of our envelope and shoved the rest of the money back into our pockets. We tried to struggle and to escape, to no avail. He held us firmly until he had returned to us most of our money, gave us a strong hug, and shoved us outside.

With more money to our names than we had expected, we decided to go to Tangier. It was a wonderful excursion. First we visited England's important Rock of Gibraltar, which like a sleeping lion guards her entrance into the Mediterranean. Here I was arrested for taking photographs, but fortunately the major before whom we were brought decided that we did not look like spies and satisfied himself with exposing my negatives to the sun and giving us a short lecture of fatherly advice.

A few hours from Gibraltar we found ourselves in a new world of deep blue sky, palm trees, and whitewashed houses, graceful figures of Arabs and weird-looking people from the interior selling

[49]

their products in the marketplace. We were in Africa. Tangier, though extremely dirty, was picturesque, and all the foreigners who lived there under an international regime were full of praise for the climate and the freedom and inexpensiveness of life. It was really a happy corner of the world. But we had little time to enter into the pleasures of the place. We spent one whole day on muleback traveling along the coast to see a few stones buried in sand—the last remnants of mighty Carthage, which at one time had nearly destroyed the Roman Empire. After a last magic night in Africa, with the palm trees casting dark shadows and Tangier asleep in the moonlight, we returned to Spain, and then by way of France and Germany to Russia, stopping for a week with our aunt and two small French cousins at Saint-Jean-de-Luz.

Russia with its frontier station, bearded porters, and fierce-looking gendarmes appeared as gloomy as ever after the brilliant scenery of other countries. The midsummer dream was over. Yet the Russian reality, however different from life abroad, was dear to my heart and reminded me that here was my home. Our bachelors' quarters now were in another part of town, nearer to the clinic where my eldest brother went daily for his medical studies. It was farther from the Big House, but I could go by way of the Kremlin. I shall never forget the cold nights, the sound of crisp snow under my feet, and the sight of the main palace, surrounded by the cathedrals, the dull golden cupolas of which shimmered in the moonlight. It reminded me always of the old Russian legend in which a town full of churches came out of a lake where it had been submerged for years.

During my fourth year at the university we had no examination, but wrote an essay on a theme announced by the department for those who wished to vie for prizes. At the time the topic was the teaching of Spinoza about the state and laws, and as Spinoza happened to be the favorite philosopher of my father, he persuaded me to enter the competition. I surrounded myself with books from his library and soon became absorbed in the interesting subject. Thus my winter passed under the influence of Spinoza, and his philosophy, which taught not to be satisfied with transitory and changeable events, but to seek behind them the great eternal truth, whose manifestation we must endeavor to see in everything that surrounds us, became to a certain degree the guiding principle in my attitude toward the mysteries of life. How often have I overcome the irritation of endless little annoyances by looking on everything *sub specie aeternitatis*! Spinoza never spoke of a personal God, but his eternal great truth was not very far from our religious conception.

My study of Spinoza indirectly affected my choice of career. I often passed the Archives of the Ministry of Foreign Affairs in Moscow, a building surrounded by a garden but rather dead in appearance. I had only a vague idea about the function of the Archives, and when somebody told me that the building housed a good library where I might find books dealing with Spinoza, I gathered my courage and entered the solemn place. After passing the silent hall where a uniformed old servant was sleeping in a corner, I came to a big room filled with books, where several men sat at their desks steeped in old documents. They hardly noticed my presence. I approached the man nearest me and explained that I was told that I could find among their books material on Spinoza. The man was astonished at my request, but took me to the library, where after a long search we found what I needed. The man explained to me that the Archives contained primarily the diplomatic documents of past centuries and putting them in order and doing research on different questions pertaining to the diplomatic relations of Old Russia were the chief work of the personnel. With great pride he showed me their most treasured document: the original manifesto of the election of the Romanov dynasty to the Russian throne. No wonder the whole building seemed dead. These people were so interested in the past that the present hardly existed for them. According to regulations I could not take the book with me and had to study it on the spot. Consequently for a while I joined this group of people who, once I got to know them better, proved more alive than had appeared at first glance.

With one of them I became great friends. He was kind and took an interest in my future plans. I told him that I was quite miserable because I could not decide what to do after finishing the university. I had no desire to pursue a juridical career, because I lacked the self-assurance to judge others and the interest in my fellow creature to defend them. I could always participate in the different industrial and commercial enterprises in which my family was engaged, but I was ambitious and wanted to build my own career rather than to follow in a path well trodden by others. My new friend then asked why I did not choose the diplomatic service. When I replied that I had thought a diplomatic career in Russia to be the privilege of the nobility and that I did not know anybody in St. Petersburg who could help me enter the Foreign Office, the old man made a sly face and said that there was a shorter and easier way—through the Archives. I could do some research in the Archives of the Ministry of Foreign Affairs, then present myself to the Foreign Office for the diplomatic examination. This was tempting. Recalling the brilliance of diplomatic life that I had glimpsed passing through Constantinople, my ambition and vanity took a new turn. I thanked the old man for his advice and decided on the spot to apply for entrance to the Archives upon graduation from the university. Thus Spinoza affected my career and was responsible for the interesting and brilliant life in store for me. It was not the first or last time that life taught me that chance is far more important than careful planning, for in chance there is a touch of a superior force not confined to our limited human reasoning. In those days there was little contact between commercial Moscow and bureaucratic St. Petersburg, especially the aristocratic Foreign Office. Consequently, had I not been writing an essay on Spinoza, had I not heard about the possibility of finding a book in the library of the Archives, and had I not met the old man who took an interest in me, my whole future would have been quite different; I would not have become a diplomat and would never have been able to escape the narrow life of commercial Moscow.

The whole winter I worked on my theme, and Spinoza became an obsession with me. I began to look at everything *sub specie aeternitatis*, and was losing touch with reality. Toward March I presented my finished work in a sealed envelope to the department and found myself free from all obligations. This gave me the idea to plan my yearly trip on a larger scale, and after studying maps and guidebooks, I decided to go to Jerusalem for Russian Easter. This time I went by myself, because the experience of past summers had shown that traveling alone suited my character much better than having to compromise with others on where to go and what to see. I took a steamer from Odessa to Constantinople, thence planned to continue on a Russian pilgrim ship carrying pilgrims from all corners of Russia to Jerusalem. Most of them were plain peasants who had saved for years to satisfy their lifelong religious craving to see the place where Christ was born.

Many were old people who wished to pray on Christ's tomb before leaving this world. Not a few hoped to die in Jerusalem, thinking that this was the straightest way to paradise. In old times pilgrims made this journey on their own and upon arrival in Palestine found themselves in the hands of unscrupulous Greek priests who robbed the ignorant pilgrims of their last kopek, and our consuls did not know what to do with the numerous Russians, stranded in a strange land far away from home. The plight of the pilgrims attracted the attention of the Russian Imperial family. A Palestine Society was created, a huge piece of land was purchased by the Russian government outside the wall of Jerusalem, and special houses constructed there for pilgrims during their stay in the Holy Land. Well looked after by members of the Palestine Society, the pilgrims found upon arrival a Russian church, a Russian bath, and all that they were accustomed to in Russia. Montenegrin guards met them at the station and accompanied them everywhere, so that they could not fall into the hands of Greek priests. A special ship was rented by the Russian government, and the whole journey was very cheap and comfortable. Eager to introduce into my journey to Jerusalem as much religious fervor as possible, I wanted to go on a pilgrim boat, certain I would find on such a vessel among plain peasants a faith unspoiled by all the doubts sown by too much learning.

The Black Sea greeted me with a furious spring equinox storm, and I suffered terribly from seasickness. But the marvelous sight of the Bosporus with Constantinople suddenly appearing in the morning mist restored my high spirits. I revisited the places of interest and everywhere met groups of Russian peasants, who looked with anxiety and fear, especially the women, on the crowds of Turks who stared at them. In Santa Sophia, where it was explained to them that the mosque had been an Orthodox church until transformed by the Turks following the fall of Constantinople, they showed great indignation and expressed the hope that sooner or later God would repair the indignity and restore the cross on Holy Sophia. After three days in Constantinople I boarded the pilgrim ship. It was a big old vessel, filled to overflowing with pilgrims, most of whom traveled as steerage passengers. With but few first-class voyagers, the ship was packed with peasants from different parts of my country. It was like a bit of Russia, torn from the rest of the territory and sent across the waves to faraway Palestine.

The ship sailed slowly through the Dardanelles, the Aegean Sea, and down the shores of Asia Minor to Jaffa. It was becoming hotter and hotter, but the sea was calm and every one seemed to enjoy himself. The voyage past the innumerable islands of the Aegean Sea was especially wonderful. We had our meals on deck, and the jolly Captain tried to amuse everybody. Only once did we have a small tragedy at our table. Among the passengers was a very old lady who told us that she had buried all her relatives and decided to go to Jerusalem before joining them. As the only lady, she sat on the right of the Captain. At one of the meals another passenger, an old man from Siberia, started a conversation about the discovery of the North Pole by [Fridtjof] Nansen[7] and said that the success of Nansen's expedition was due to the fact that he had left his wife behind. Hearing that, the old lady stood up like an outraged queen and declaring that his slur of Mrs. Nansen had been an offense to all womanhood and that she, as the only representative of the weaker sex, must protest and henceforth would not sit at the same table with this Siberian bear, proudly stalked to her cabin. We stared at each other, barely able to control our laughter at this clap of thunder out of the clear sky, the more comical as Nansen was never married and there was no Mrs. Nansen whose honor had to be defended. Though the Captain rushed to the old lady's cabin with the apologies of the old man from Siberia, the old lady could not be mollified, and only after two days, probably finding it too hot to remain in the cabin, she consented to join us on condition that a separate table would be arranged for her. As the deck was very small, her table was only a few inches from ours. But peace was restored and the honor of the nonexistent Mrs. Nansen saved.

A full moon hung over the islands, famous in ancient history, and as the pilgrims joined in a sad Russian song, all the small things of this life disappeared, and I felt part of the calm sea, the dark silhouettes of the islands, the silvery moon, and the plaintive song which gave voice to the soul of Russia. Our first stop after Constantinople was Tripoli on the Asiatic shore. Coming on deck early in the morning, I saw our ship surrounded by small boats with natives who came to sell fruits, nuts, and various trifles. The dark blue sea and the crowd in brilliant rags were a sight not to be forgotten. Our Russian pilgrims

---

[7] Nansen did not actually discover the North Pole, though he penetrated to the highest latitude then reached by anyone.

looked with fright at the crowd that soon rushed aboard; the old women crossed themselves, thinking that all those shouting people must be in league with the devil. The scene was repeated at Beirut, where the beauty of nature was enhanced by the snowcapped Lebanon Mountains, which looked like a mirage in the blue sky. As our ship stopped in Beirut for quite a while, I was able to make an excursion to the ruins of Baalbek and to Damascus. Crossing the Lebanon Mountains, we stayed at a small hotel near the imposing ruins of Baalbek; the next day we descended into the rose-filled valley of Damascus. The city itself was big, noisy, and very dirty. The broad, covered streets in which the local bazaars were situated, the half-dark passages with small shops whose keepers were shouting to attract the attention of buyers, who streamed through the bazaar in their picturesque attires, made a fascinating sight. The bazaar led into the huge open place of the main mosque, so that one passed from the darkness directly into blinding sunlight and a milling crowd whose attitude toward a lonely foreigner was not very friendly.

I visited the Russian Consul who, as I learned, also came from Moscow, his parents living on the same street as my family. His wife, children, charming old mother, and old Russian nurse were all with him, so that I felt back in Moscow. Pointing out that it was dangerous to walk alone through the streets of Damascus, he assigned to me one of the consulate guards. This gave me an air of importance and I experienced again the beauty of a diplomatic career. Say what you like —it is agreeable to feel superior to the masses. But I had to get back to Beirut, where I found our pilgrims much less frightened of the unusual surroundings, walking about in the streets addressing everybody in Russian, not admitting that there could be anyone who did not understand the language.

The next and last stop on our sea voyage was Jaffa. The dirty train, crowded with noisy Arabs, and the miserable-looking station that greeted us in Jerusalem outraged my religious feelings; it was my first disillusion in the Holy Land. We were met by representatives of the Russian consulate and of the Palestine Society, and the whole crowd of pilgrims was led to the Russian compound, which at once acquired the look of a Russian monastery during a big holiday. There was a nice hotel in the compound, where we found good accommodations. As we arrived on the eve of Palm Sunday, we began our devotions without delay. The first service was in the crowded Russian church in the compound; except for the palm branches, which we did not have in Russia, there was nothing to indicate that we were in Jerusalem. The following day I went with several companions to the Holy Sepulcher. Here I had my second disillusionment. The temple stood on a small place inside the city. The building looked very insignificant, hardly like a church. As I entered, my eyes fell on a guard of Turkish soldiers in red fezzes, smoking and talking in loud voices. Gazing at the shabby inside of the small church, I asked myself what had happened to all the sums collected throughout the Christian world for the decoration of the Holy Sepulcher. What I saw looked cheap and in bad taste.

The chief altar was in the hands of the Greek clergy. To the left was the Catholic section and all around the chapel the small altars of other Christian sects. People used to say that it was impressive when services were held before each altar at the same time: thirty-three languages praising Christ. Personally, I found it a dreadful cacophony. To get to the chapel where the Holy Sepulcher itself was located, I had to pass through a small door, and found myself in a small dark room. When my eyes became accustomed to the darkness, I was shown the place where the angel had stood and announced to Mary and Martha that Christ had risen. Passing through a smaller door to another tiny room, I saw under a mass of candles and lamps the white marble tomb, where according to tradition Christ lay buried. This room, this holy of holies, was filled to suffocation with pilgrims, among them a huge red-bearded monk, such as one often saw in Russia going from one monastery to another, who had assumed the role of policeman. With a huge cotton umbrella he tried to arrange a line among the people approaching Christ's tomb. He was singing about his joy at the sight of the Holy Sepulcher and shouting to the frightened old women not to push and to keep in line. How could one keep one's religious fervor in such a surrounding? With the rest of the pilgrims I kissed the marble cover of the tomb, and was glad to get out of the chapel. In the same church, somewhat higher, there was another chapel with a big crucifix, supposedly Golgotha, the place where Christ was crucified. With heavy heart I left the temple of the Holy Sepulcher, having found nothing that could have provoked in me a semblance of the devotion which I had expected to find in Jerusalem.

I saw how human beings with their vulgarity and cupidity desecrated what could have been a source of inspiration and devotion. It was difficult not to be shocked at the way the alleged events and parables of the Gospel had been reconstructed in minute detail, with wax figures illustrating the events connected with the last days of Christ, only to collect money. As if to confirm my doubt, a young archaeologist, who was studying the antiquities of Jerusalem and was staying in our hotel, told me that after Christ's death Jerusalem had been destroyed to its foundations several times and that when Helena, the wife of Emperor Constantine, had come to Jerusalem nothing definitely pertaining to the life of Christ could be found. He insisted that not a single place or relic shown to the pilgrims and tourists as connected with the life of Christ could be accepted by an intelligent person without doubt, except perhaps a certain Roman arch which, archaeologists agreed, had existed at the time of Christ, though not in town where it now stood. All this made me quite miserable because I did not like to have my faith destroyed, however much I realized that it was a remnant of my childhood and was already fading with maturity. But no doubts assailed our simple pilgrims. They accepted whatever they were told and I could imagine the wonderful stories they would tell their relatives and friends upon returning to their villages.

My doubts did not keep me from observing with the rest of the pilgrims all the prescribed formalities of Holy Week. On Good Friday I followed the path along which Christ had carried His cross. This path, by now an ordinary street in Jerusalem, was in the hands of the Catholics. They divided it into so-called stations in memory of different episodes mentioned in the Gospel. At each station was a small chapel with crude figures illustrating the episodes. I remember a figure of a lady in a red velvet dress applying a lace handkerchief to the brow of Christ; it was St. Veronica wiping the sweat from the Savior's forehead. On the road I met a fellow traveler, the old lady who had defended the honor of Mrs. Nansen, being dragged along by two Montenegrin guards. She told me that though she could hardly walk, she had decided to follow in the footsteps of our Master till the end and that she was sorry she could not be crucified. Then, switching to French, she asked how much of a tip she must give the guards for helping her fulfill her sacred duty.

The strangest sight I saw was the miracle of the descent of the holy

[57]

fire. I had read about it in an old book written by a simpleminded Russian pilgrim on whom it had made a great impression centuries ago, but had not thought that it continued to be performed in our modern times. To my astonishment it was still going strong, and I joined our Consul's party to see it. The miracle took place on the afternoon of Good Friday in the temple of the Holy Sepulcher. The sight was quite wonderful. We watched from a balcony opposite the chapel where Christ's tomb was located. The temple was packed with Arabs and Russian pilgrims. Some Arabs, unable to find a place, were clinging to the pillars of the church. Everyone was holding a package of thirty-three candles in memory of the years Christ passed on earth. The door of the chapel was sealed, and a Turkish general sat before it. There was not a single light in the church. When the hour of the miracle approached, the Greek patriarch in a white surplice, accompanied by a Greek priest, approached the Turkish general who unsealed the door, allowing the patriarch and the priest to enter, then closed the door again. For some time nothing happened. The impatience of the Arabs was strained to the last limit. Everybody was shouting and calling on God to perform the miracle. Then suddenly bells rang, and a lighted candle was passed through a small window to the man who the previous day had purchased at auction the right to be the first to receive a light from the patriarch's candle on which the holy fire was said to have descended from Heaven. There was a general rush for the candle and soon the whole church seemed ablaze. From our balcony we saw a sea of flames illuminating the faces of ecstatic persons who tried to touch their breasts and arms with their candles. It was a fire worshipers' rite, not a Christian ceremony. Meanwhile a fight broke out among the representatives of different sects, and Turkish soldiers tried to restore order. And this in church near the tomb of Christ! The whole scene was disgraceful. When I later asked some Greek priests how they could allow such paganism, they replied that they had to appeal to the imagination of the Arab converts; the Arabs were accustomed to the miracle for which they came from far away, that they would riot if the miracle were not performed. Our Russian pilgrims returned from the ceremony greatly impressed, carrying the candles in special lanterns, hoping to take the holy fire home, but as the voyage back to Russia was long and difficult I doubt very much that any of the pilgrims succeeded in taking the authentic candles back to their villages.

The Easter midnight service was very impressive. We formed a long procession with our Consul at the head and with the Montenegrin guards in their picturesque uniforms carrying torches. As Russian pilgrims were known for their generosity in distributing alms, beggars from all over Palestine came to Jerusalem for this occasion. They formed two lines between which our procession passed. Most of the beggars were lepers and in the light of the passing torches you could see their awful wounds. Plaintively they pleaded for money, but there were so many that it was impossible to give to all, and every coin thrown into the darkness provoked a fight; it was a ghastly sight. The Holy Sepulcher was so crowded that we could hardly get through to our special places. Services were held before each altar and the different languages, the singing of the Greek chorus, and the suffocating heat so enervated me that I could not concentrate on any prayer; at the first opportunity I escaped and returned to the Russian compound, where I attended the last part of the service in the Russian church. The Russian clergy, Russian singing, and the predominantly Russian peasant congregation brought me much nearer to the Easter feeling of my childhood.

After the service the members of the Palestine Society asked us to help them distribute Easter eggs and cake to the Russian pilgrims, a task that took nearly two hours as everyone insisted on proclaiming that Christ had risen and on exchanging the traditional three kisses. My face was drowned in endless beards and I felt that I was kissing the whole of Russia. By the time this ceremony was over, the sun was rising. It was useless to go to bed, and I went for a walk. I passed through the garden of Gethsemane and climbed the Mount of Olives. Before me lay Jerusalem surrounded by its walls and beyond the endless desert. As I looked on this scene, which could not have changed much since the time of Christ, I experienced a real religious feeling— the first since my arrival in the Holy Land.

❖❖❖

With the coming of Easter I had nothing more to do in Palestine, and after an excursion to the Jordan and the Dead Sea left for Egypt.

On the excursion to the Jordan I had Mr. Doroshevich, a well-known Russian journalist, as a companion. He told me that his newspaper had sent him to Jerusalem to cover Holy Week, but that after what he had seen in town, he had telegraphed his newspaper that he could not write a story without shocking the religious sensibilities of the readers, and as this was not the aim of the paper or himself, he did not write a single line from Jerusalem. I congratulated him on his honesty.

Egypt struck me as far more interesting than Palestine. Here the antiquities were real. You could not counterfeit the pyramids or the Egyptian temples, and I was astonished how much had remained from ancient days. At the same time modern Egypt was very much alive. You could sit for hours on the terrace of the Shepherd Hotel admiring the ever-changing colorful street scenes. The pyramids, however spoiled by crowds of tourists who insisted on looking ridiculous perched on top of camels, lived up to their reputation once you found yourself alone in their company as the sun was setting and a purple mist was coming from the desert. Though it was late in the year, I went south to the temples of Luxor and Karnak. The tourist season was over and I could wander freely among the ruins—if ruins is a proper word—for only the roofs were missing, the buildings standing otherwise as solid as they had been at the time of the pharaohs. Thanks to the dry climate all the designs and hieroglyphics on the walls had been perfectly preserved. As I stood in the moonlight and examined the portrayal of a triumphal procession of the pharaoh, I felt engulfed by the mysterious past. I could imagine the old temple come to life with crowds of people acclaiming the pharaoh, but suddenly the moon hid behind the clouds, it became chilly, and there was nothing before me but a stone wall. I went on an interesting excursion in the desert to see two colossuses sitting alone in the endless sand, and visited some other temples, among them one of a later period, belonging to some mystic cult. We had to go through long corridors, whose ceilings were alive with bats awakened by the light of our torches. I remember the beautiful sunsets on the Nile, the dark palm trees silhouetted against the red sky, the miserable villages near the water, the plaintive cry of some bird, and the beautiful outlines of the Egyptian barges. Darkness came suddenly, but soon the enormous disk of a red moon arose from the desert sand. I was so impressed with Egypt that I promised myself to return someday, but this never materialized. My last stop in Egypt was Alexandria, an elegant European city, whence I sailed to Marseilles.

As usual I stopped for a while with my French aunt and her two charming daughters. The youngest, Lucette, was very excited when she learned that I had been in Egypt, for though only five years old, she had read a story of a beautiful Egyptian princess with rose-colored cheeks and insisted that I tell her how she lived in Egypt. I had to invent some fantastic tale of how this princess was imprisoned by a wicked prince in a pyramid and how the Sphinx saved her. Not having to go back yet, I decided to visit my brother [cousin Khrisanf], who lived among the exiled Tolstoyans in a colony somewhere in England.

My brother met me in London and at once took me to the colony, where he lived in the house of the chief member, Mr. Chertkov. He gave me his room and said that it was the rule of the house that everybody do everything himself. He introduced me to Mr. Chertkov, and we all ate our vegetarian meal together in a big kitchen. Mr. Chertkov was a remarkable man. He came of a very good family, had been wealthy and had served in one of the most brilliant guard regiments. Somehow he had started to read Tolstoi's books and had become so influenced by them that he had discarded his riches, divided his estate among the peasants, and generally tried to follow the teachings of Tolstoi. Hearing of the latter's interest in the Dukhobors, who were being persecuted by the authorities for refusing military service, he devoted all his energy to their defense, as a result of which he was asked by the Russian government to leave the country. With his wife and ten-year-old son he went to England, where his mother, who did not share the ideas of Tolstoi, bought for them a farm with a big house near Croydon. Soon other devotees of Tolstoi, similarly exiled from Russia for work with the Dukhobors, established themselves in the neighborhood, and a small Russian colony of the followers of Tolstoi came into being. Most of them were curious people.

I remember one by the name of Biriukov, who had been a naval officer and had accompanied Nicholas II, when still a crown prince, on his world tour. Later he had become a Tolstoyan and, like the others, after involvement with the Dukhobors, had been forced to leave Russia. What was curious about him was that he did not live alone but with three peasant children, whose life had been rendered miserable by a cruel stepmother, and a woman doctor, whom he had invited into

[61]

his artificial family without thought of intimate relations. They lived in a small house near Chertkov. Biriukov was a middle-aged man with a long beard and childish blue eyes. He always wore a long Russian shirt and walked in rubber shoes, because leather goods were made by killing animals. Another curious member of the colony was a nice quiet woman with a charming three-year-old daughter. She was the wife of Prince Khilkov, though as a follower of Tolstoi she had not been married to him in church. After her first two children were born, the old princess, the mother of her husband, obtained from Emperor Alexander III an ukase permitting her to take the two children from the mother in order to give them the proper education. When the mother refused to surrender the children, the old princess chased her across the whole of Russia and succeeded at last in taking them from her. After moving abroad the mother gave birth to a third child, but she could never reconcile herself to the loss of the two others. Meanwhile, her husband was in Canada trying to obtain permission from the Canadian government for the Dukhobors to settle there. Tired of all the difficulties with them, the Russian government eventually let them migrate to Canada, where they flourished, though not without causing considerable trouble for the Canadian authorities.

The Chertkovs were very hospitable and their house was always full of guests who were interested in Tolstoi's teachings and came to discuss them. When I was there, a young Slovak also lived in the house. When he had refused to do military service the Austrian government had put him in prison, where he developed tuberculosis. Upon his release he went abroad and made his way to England, where the Chertkovs had invited him. Too ill to move he remained with them. When I was there people feared he would die. My brother grew very attached to him and looked after him like a nurse. When he felt better, we all would sit in his room after the daily work was finished. The young Slovak with his pale face looked as if he were about to move into the other world. My brother usually sat on his bed. The room was half dark, but nobody thought of bringing some light, lest he spoil the general feeling that something grand was taking place. Mrs. Chertkov, who had a magnificent voice, sometimes started a plaintive Russian song. The whole scene was very impressive and everybody had tears in his eyes. But I am glad to say that the young Slovak did not die. When the doctor said that he could be saved only by being moved to Italy, my brother wrote to father, who allowed him to take the young man there. In Italy he got better, grew fat, and married an Italian girl, becoming a normal human being. But all that happened much later.

My other contacts were less pathetic. I remember a middle-aged lady with short hair, a sign of very advanced ideas in those days, who came to stay with the Chertkovs. She was the widow of a famous terrorist who had been executed for his part in the assassination of Emperor Alexander II. At the time I was interested in photography, and spent much of my time in the darkroom. The lady insisted on joining me there and tried to persuade me that the only revolutionary activity which could be of any use in Russia was terrorism. She criticized the mildness of the Tolstoyans, for one of whom she probably took me, and shouted that I must join the terrorists and start throwing bombs. The reflection from the red lamp and her screaming voice, urging me to throw bombs at every person of authority, gave a hellish touch to the darkroom. The lady was very disappointed when I told her that I was not a Tolstoyan, that indeed I was quite content with the state of affairs in Russia and had no intention of assassinating anybody. She made a speech about the selfishness of the bourgeoisie, and never again offered to accompany me into the darkroom.

Near the Russian colony was an English colony of some cranks who called themselves the Followers of the Philosopher-Carpenter [Jesus]. We had endless discussions with them. Among them there was a young man who felt that we must all return to the simple life of Adam and Eve in paradise, and insisted on working in his vegetable garden naked, but the police, who did not annoy us, protested against this. Fortunately there appeared on the scene a girl who pretended to share the views of the young man and agreed to be his Eve if he consented to marry her. The marriage took place and the wife insisted that the husband return home and be reconciled with his father, who proved to be a rich banker. Thus the whole story had a normal ending. Instead of playing the role of Adam, the young man under the influence of his newly found Eve joined his father's bank.

The chief occupation of our colony was growing vegetables, but this we did with little success. We also tried to propagandize our beliefs. On market day we went to the nearest town and made speeches extolling the teachings of Tolstoi. After three weeks of such a life, I had enough. It all seemed senseless play; I could not understand how such a forcible character as Chertkov could be satisfied with it. In fact he probably was not, for he was always in a bad temper and one could see what effort it cost him to control his passionate nature. Later, as I heard from my brother, the colony moved to Christchurch, its existence ending after the Dukhobor question was settled by their migration to Canada. Then the Russian government allowed the members of the colony to return to Russia. Chertkov became the right hand of Tolstoi and tried to save him from the influence of his family. At one time all of Moscow spoke about the quarrel between Chertkov and the Countess Tolstoi. Eventually Chertkov was the indirect cause of Tolstoi's secret departure from his family, a flight which ended in his death from pneumonia at some obscure station.

When I left my brother I took with me letters for Tolstoi. The Russian police through their secret agent abroad must have learned about my stay among the Russian exiles, for when I crossed the frontier I was interrogated by the gendarmes about my dealings with the Tolstoyans and my luggage was thoroughly searched, but fortunately the letters to Tolstoi were not found. After some time on our estate, I made the pilgrimage to Tolstoi, who spent his summers on his estate in Tula Province. It took me twenty-four hours to reach my destination. I remember I arrived early in the morning and was asked to join the Countess at her morning coffee; the Count was ill and could not join us. I was struck by the Countess' practical outlook. She made no effort to hide that she did not share her husband's principles. Indeed, she did not take her husband seriously. "It is only talk. I would like to see where he and our whole family would be without me," she told me frankly, explaining that while Tolstoi was creating the literary masterpieces which made him famous all over the world, it was she who copied all his novels by hand and saw to their publication. Now that the family fortune had been restored and each of the sons owned a separate estate, her husband could live and philosophize without thinking about the daily bread. All this was certainly in direct contradiction to the teachings of Tolstoi, yet it contained a large dose of common sense. The Countess complained that her husband was like a child; only three days ago in celebrating his birthday he had eaten too much ice cream and now was suffering acute indigestion.

All this was a bad introduction to my meeting with what may

[64]

have been the greatest moral teacher of our time, so that when I was summoned by Tolstoi and saw him on his narrow couch, untidy with his long beard and complaining of pain, I could feel only pity. Tolstoi at once asked me about his friends in England, spoke with great tenderness of my brother, then started to ask me about myself and about my faith. When I told him frankly that I had lost my childhood faith and had not yet found anything to take its place—though I was sure that I would sooner or later, since I was convinced that no man could live without some faith in God—he grew angry at the calmness with which I related my loss of faith. He said that when he felt that he was losing faith, it made him so miserable that he thought of committing suicide. I retorted that suicide was the end of everything and thus would only rob one of the last opportunity to find God. He seemed too tired to continue the discussion, and I left him and joined the rest of the family, drinking tea in the open under the trees. The family did not strike me as particularly remarkable and my attention was again drawn to the old Countess. She was relating that she had called on the new chief of police. Though Alexander III did not allow the police to touch Tolstoi, saying that he did not wish to make a martyr out of him, the Countess tried to be on good terms with the police, and hearing that a new chief had arrived had gone to see him. She said that they had parted as good friends; she had flattered him by finding a likeness between him and the Emperor, he in turn had assured her that he was a great admirer of her husband and had promised not to annoy him.

One of Tolstoi's sons invited me for a ride. During the ride he talked all the time about his father, bemoaning the fact that he had abandoned his purely literary work and had devoted himself to religious and philosophical essays which, he felt, were read only because of the former masterpieces. He said that he was sure the time would come when Tolstoi would discard his philosophy and return to his literary work. This only showed how little the members of the family understood their father. When Tolstoi found his faith in the teachings of Christ, he lost all interest in his former books, indeed he treated them with contempt. Much as Russian literature lost by this change of attitude, Tolstoi himself won a great deal by becoming one of the great teachers of humanity. Toward evening I went to say good-bye to Tolstoi. He felt better, took my hand in his, and said that if I would

[65]

continue to search for a new faith I was bound to find it. With his piercing eyes, he looked most impressive as he lay there on a modest couch in the light of the evening sun.

✛✛✛

After an uncomfortable night on the train I returned to The Oaks, where I spent the rest of the summer. Toward autumn, when our park was so beautiful in its golden attire that you felt a special joy at being alive among dying nature, I started my fifth and last year at the university. This last year was one of the most trying. The political agitation among the students was increasing, and even in the Faculty of Law, where the majority did not take a keen interest in politics, it was impossible to study, because strange-looking students with long hair and untidy uniforms whom you never saw otherwise would enter the auditorium during lectures, interrupt the professors with a protest against the arrest of some students by the police, and shout to the auditors that they must show their solidarity with those who had been arrested, stop attending the lectures, and join a protest meeting. When the professor or other students tried to argue that they saw no logical connection between the arrest of some students for unlawful agitation and the continuation of their studies by other students, the agitators created great pandemonium by throwing smelly chemicals about the auditorium; it was quite impossible to continue the class, and the students were obliged to join the general meeting which usually took place in the university garden. At such meetings one could not understand anything. Several orators, most of them in a state of acute hysteria, tried to talk at the same time. The meeting usually ended with the arrival of the police and the arrest of another batch of students, which caused new protests and new agitation, more arrests and again more protests. The authorities tried hard to calm the students but without success. Milder measures only increased agitation, while stricter ones boosted the number of students who wanted to become martyrs, and all that was clearly directed from the outside.

I counted the days until the end of the school year, the final examination before a special commission, and the receipt of the diploma. But it was easier to dream about the end of my university life, which had brought me nothing but misery, than to reach it. Just before the ex-

[66]

aminations the agitators decided to prevent their taking place by dissuading students from appearing before the commission. The same long-haired students visited those due to appear before the commission to persuade them not to present themselves for the examinations. Most students could reply that if those before them would not turn up before the commission, they too would stay away. But there was no one behind whom I could hide, for my name, beginning with "Ab," was first on the list. Thus I suddenly became the key figure in the eyes of the agitators and they concentrated all their efforts on me; it was a nightmare. While I was trying to study for the examination, every half hour the bell rang, and a strange student of fierce appearance stood before me. He would start in a honeyed voice, expressing his conviction that I would not go counter to the will of the student body and would show my solidarity with those who could not attend the examinations because they were in prison; he would dwell on the nobility of the act, and so forth. When I obstinately refused to sacrifice my five years of university study for the sake of some unknown students who had neglected their studies in favor of politics and had been jailed for violating university regulations, the visitor would begin to shout and call me names. I replied in kind; it was a disgraceful scene. But I was as obstinate as a hundred mules. One deputation of agitators, unable to sway me, threatened to resort to more serious steps. I laughed into their faces, and asked whether they meant to kidnap or kill me before the examination. They solemnly replied that they might do just that. But in those days revolutionary tactics were not yet developed and such melodrama seemed ridiculous.

The day before the examination I received a ticket of admittance from the university. When I went to the university the following day, I found all the gates closed and the buildings surrounded by a crowd of students. When I showed my ticket the police opened the gate just enough to let me pass and I found myself in an empty yard. Behind me the crowd was hissing and calling me a traitor. Safe from the crowd, I calmly walked through the yard and entered the examination hall. The commission from the Ministry of Education looked most solemn in its uniforms and decorations. When the members saw a timid student entering the hall, they were greatly relieved and showed their appreciation by making the examination as easy as possible. After me came the other students who had been hiding some-where, waiting to see if someone on the list before them presented himself for examination.

On one of the following days I saw some of the students who had threatened me enter and take the exams themselves. When I asked if they were not ashamed to do so, they replied that since I had spoiled everything there was no more reason to avoid the examinations. It was with a feeling of great relief that I left behind me my university years which had been poisoned by the fact that the students, instead of pre-paring themselves for life, thought of themselves as great statesmen chosen to show the government how to rule Russia. Actually they were only tools in the hands of hidden forces which worked for the downfall of the government by whatever means, caring not if young persons who had not yet started to live ruined their lives in what then seemed a hopeless struggle.

✣✣✣

After finishing the university and receiving my diploma, I went to England. This time I had to accompany my sister [Anna] who had finished her school and had decided to enter Girton College at Cam-bridge. In those days Russian girls did not think of amusement but of study, going on to the university, studying medicine, and mixing in politics. My sister was not an exception to the general rule, but under the influence of our English governess chose an English college; the whole family approved wholeheartedly, for thereby she would be free from politics and the pressure to bow to the tyranny of solidarity in holding extreme views expected of serious women.

On our way to England we stopped at Heidelberg, where my youngest brother [Ivan], disgusted with conditions at Moscow Uni-versity, was continuing his studies in mathematics. It was a very beau-tiful university town, full of old German traditions. The students did not seem to study much. They were constantly gathering for different celebrations, wearing medieval costumes, singing patriotic songs, and drinking a lot of beer. Dueling was a popular sport. Their faces were full of scars and they were proud of the patches with which their faces were covered. In the evenings they would assemble in cellars to have a good time, which to them meant drinking as much beer as possible and pinching the fat girls who flew among them with big jugs of beer on each finger. After attending the lectures of the famous Professor Kuno Fischer and after some sightseeing in the beautiful surroundings of Heidelberg, we continued to England, leaving my brother to his studies. Meanwhile I kept asking myself what was better, the Russian students with their politics or the German students with their duels and beer.

In England we went straight to Cambridge. It was love at first sight. The beautiful old colleges among green lawns on the shore of a small drowsy river, on which young people, immaculately clad in white flannels, reclining on colorful cushions, slowly paddled, bespoke the highest culture. What a difference between the vulgarity of German university life and the distinction of the surroundings in which the happy English undergraduates passed the best time of their lives. I was sorry for the sadness and shabbiness in which we Russians had to study.

We called on the principal of Girton College, which was situated in the country close to town. Recently founded, the college occupied a spacious new building in which each student had her room. The house was surrounded by open land for sports. The principal, a stern-looking lady, explained to us the rules, which to our astonishment were very strict; if a girl broke one of them twice, she was asked to leave the college. The students could not receive guests in their rooms except in the presence of a teacher. When the principal told us that at nine P.M. all students must be in the college and I asked how this could be checked, she answered that every student signed her name in the book in the hall. Remembering all the tricks common in our schools to deceive the teachers, I commented that one student could easily sign for another. The principal measured me from head to toe with a cold gaze, and retorted: "But this would be a lie." I felt duly squelched, and reflected what our girl students would have said about such a regime, how many meetings they would have called to protest against this tyranny; and all the while at rallies in Russia England was held up as the country of greatest liberty.

I left my sister, and returned to Moscow to make arrangements for my military service.

3

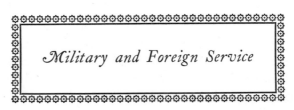

Military and Foreign Service

IN RUSSIA THERE WAS UNIVERSAL MILITARY SERVICE—FOUR YEARS FOR the common people, one for persons with a higher education. University graduates had the privilege of choosing their regiment, Moscovites usually serving in the artillery brigade stationed in Moscow. Surrounded by friends and able to go home every day, they found their military tour of duty, dreaded by most civilians, less demanding than in other regiments. But by the time I returned to Moscow all vacancies had been filled. Fortunately somebody advised me to sign up for another artillery brigade and ask to be attached to the Moscow brigade. This I did, and learning that the brigade was situated not very far from Moscow, I journeyed there. It proved to be a dreadful hole, without good communications, the barracks situated in an old porcelain factory built during the time of Catherine the Great.

The small village near the barracks was inhabited by people whose main occupation was to collect night soil[1] from Moscow, the workmen they employed being of the lowest class of people—mostly drunkards, thieves, and murderers. In the middle of the village stood a church, in a square covered with crows which circled over every carriage that passed and vied with each other to sit on the golden cross atop the building. It was raining and the dirt came to my knees. Luckily a regimental clerk in the chancellery understood what was required of him,

---

[1] The manuscript states "garbage," but it was human waste, or "night soil," that was carted out of town.

and with the help of a few rubles I soon obtained the necessary papers and the transfer to Moscow. I left the dismal place with relief, hoping never to see it again.

The service in Moscow, among friends, was quite agreeable. At first, after our university studies, the perpetual marching, gun drill, and total lack of independence seemed strange and childish. But soon I began to like the change of pace. For fourteen years I had studied without letup, cramming my head with Latin, Greek, history, mathematics, and foreign languages. I had had no physical exercise and was in poor shape. A year of purely physical existence was good for me, and soon I felt stronger and began to enjoy the new feeling of physical fitness. As for the discipline, which most of my freethinking friends found irksome, personally I liked submitting my own will to the will of an iron organization. For a change, it was really agreeable to stop thinking for myself and find everything decided for me. To be sure, many of our new activities seemed extremely idiotic, but if looked at with a sense of humor they could be a source of great amusement. For instance, the first thing we had to learn was how to saluate our superiors. For this we were put into the hands of a sergeant who was very pleased to command people who in civilian life were above him. He took his task quite seriously. He would stand in the middle of the room and oblige every one of us to pass endlessly before him and salute him. Dissatisfied, he would shout that we must not salute a superior as if he were a friend, that we must always remember that a superior was a superior and could put us under arrest, and the saluting would start all over again. First he pretended to be a junior officer, then a colonel, and finally a general. Saluting a general was most difficult, for when you met a general you had to freeze like a stone, devouring the general with your eyes till he passed. But even that was not enough; we had to carry first one, then two dirty pillows, representing parcels, and practice what we would have to do if we suddenly met a general. The pillows had to pass from one hand to the other; if both hands were occupied, utter submission had to be shown with the eyes alone. I found this extremely comical; not so one of my comrades who was big and fat and in later years became a well-known lawyer. He could not get accustomed to what he considered the greatest humiliation in his life and kept repeating to himself: "And to think that I finished the university, studied Schopenhauer and Kant, in order to carry dirty pillows and be shouted at by an ignorant sergeant!" I told him to follow Spinoza and look upon everything *sub specie aeternitatis*. But viewing the matter with a sense of humor or *sub specie aeternitatis* resulted in my never learning to salute properly, and I sat countless times under arrest for not greeting my superiors, especially generals, correctly. Thus the pillow system invented by our sergeant was not very good.

Military service had its compensations, however. We had to attend special classes in artillery. These classes included the most clever soldiers from the whole brigade, especially selected to study the rudiments of gunnery. Aside from the fact that the subject was interesting, it was in these classes that I met the other soldiers on an equal footing. It was a revelation to me how clever some of these soldiers were. Coming to the regiment practically illiterate, they were able after a few months of study to grasp the most complicated problems concerning modern artillery and often put us, with our university educations, to shame. I thought what a brilliant future Russia might have, if all those half-baked geniuses had a better education. I was proud to discover the cleverness of the soldiers who came to the regiment straight from the village, and had many real friends among them. But I must confess that this friendship did not survive my military service. Once out of the regiment, the class difference reasserted itself, and when I invited those friends to our big house in Moscow to celebrate the end of our service and they found themselves in the spacious rooms and had to eat with silver knives and spoons, all the spontaneity disappeared, envy and class hostility came to the fore, and I was glad when the celebration was finished and I parted with my newly acquired friends never to see them again.

In the midst of my new happiness as a carefree soldier, there occurred a change in command of the brigade to which I belonged. When the new commander discovered that all his one-year soldiers were detached to Moscow, he ordered that they return to their outfit, and I had to go back to the dreadful hole, which I had hoped I had left forever, finding it as godforsaken, dirty, and desolate as before, with the same crows circling the church cross. The general met us with contempt and sarcasm, saying that we had been spoiled in Moscow and promising to teach us what real military service was like. He began by ordering us to sleep in the barracks with the rest of the soldiers. This really was a terrible experience. The barracks were dirty and damp. The air was so spoiled by hundreds of soldiers sleeping together that one could hardly breathe. Several of us fell ill. The regiment's doctor became frightened and persuaded the general to let us sleep off the post, lest complications arise with parents who might have influence with high authorities in Moscow. We were again summoned by the general, who said that it was no use to expect to make real soldiers out of us, and that we might look for quarters outside the barracks, but that anytime we arrived even a second late for service, we would be put under arrest. We saluted and left the disappointed general to look for new quarters.

The inhabitants of the village were only too glad to rent us rooms. From an assistant clergyman I obtained a rather nice house. The owner, an old man who lived with his sister, moved to the kitchen and left me the use of the house. As it was bigger than the others could find, I invited them to have meals in my house. The owner and his sister were kind people. They looked after me as if this had always been their job, and many an evening, when I was tired of the company of my comrades—who, as usually happens when one dons a uniform, considered drink and noise part of military service—I spent with them in their half-dark kitchen listening to their stories about the life of the village. They were mostly sad stories and I was ashamed to tell about my own life, so full of variety and happiness, when there were two old persons who had not seen anything and whose life from the cradle to the grave was a succession of monotonous gray days without a single bright spot.

From this couple I learned that the life in Pavlovskaia Sloboda, the village where the barracks were located, had its passions and jealousies. The night-soil collectors were divided into classes, according to the number of barrels they owned and the number of workmen they employed. The rich ones formed the aristocracy and did not mix with the more modest ones. Their sons went to Moscow and were ashamed of the occupation of their parents. Their daughters were considered rich brides, had their dresses brought from Moscow, and when the weather was fine, promenaded down the street arm-in-arm in all their fineries; their only dream was to find someone who would take them out of this night-soil town. The appearance of the superior soldiers from Moscow, therefore, was a great event for those daughters of the local aristocracy. As romancing is also part of a soldier's life, we too started to walk down the street after work; acquaintances were made and meetings were arranged. With the advent of spring even the place of our exile acquired a touch of romance. The lilacs were in full bloom, the nightingales were singing, and not far from my house the silhouette of one of our Don Juans, known in Moscow for his conquests and his poetry which helped him in these conquests, embraced the most fascinating night-soil girl.

I could see more than romance from my window. One evening, as I was gazing at the moonlit square with the crows sleeping on the cross, I saw a strange figure approaching my window: a barefoot man with disheveled black hair and beard, clad in rags, his white face and wild eyes expressing such horror that I wanted to close the window and seek refuge with my host. But my curiosity got the better of me and I stayed at the window. In a trembling voice the man asked me for some wine to help him escape from his enemies. When I inquired who his enemies were, he asked to my shock if I did not see them, and explaining that they were small green devils who persecuted him everywhere, began to tear the imaginary devils from himself and crush them with his feet. I managed to calm him with a bottle of vodka and called my host, who betrayed no surprise at the apparition, took the man to the kitchen and gave him some food. The man soon fell asleep, and my host explained to me that he was a former well-to-do inhabitant of the place. When his wife had died after giving birth to a dead child, he had taken to drink, and when he had used up all his means had disappeared. After years of wandering he had returned, a shadow of his former self. Out of pity he had been given the position of keeper of the local bathhouse. Periodically he suffered attacks of delirium tremens, when he could not remain alone. One could see that he was in terrible agony, but my host assured me that he was harmless and expressed the hope that I would not mind if he spent the night in the kitchen. Such kindness disarmed me and I could not object, though later, when I heard his groans in the garret near the kitchen, I felt uncomfortable at the thought of having a drunkard with his devils near me. In his lucid moments the man was interesting. He liked to come to my window and relate his wanderings. He told me that after his wife's death he had sought consolation in drink, and when this had not helped, had visited different churches and monasteries, also to no avail. After some time he had been drawn back to his native place and had taken up drinking again; he felt that his case was hopeless, that sooner or later the small green devils would get him. Listening to him, I thought how strange and cruel life was. In the midst of happiness would suddenly appear a bottomless pit of misery and despair. To end the story of my friend the drunkard: One night there was a fire in the public bath. By morning the whole place had burned down, and inside the charred body of the keeper was found. The little green devils had got him at last.

Our daily military service was full of hardship. We were allowed no leave. Fortunately my family regularly sent me a large amount of provisions so that we had ample food and drink in our mess. This did not please our superiors. Once we were sitting in my house and were being rather gay, when we saw somebody's shadow on the window curtain. Thinking that it was the drunkard, I opened the curtain and to my surprise found our commanding officer standing before the window. We all jumped to attention. Furious at being discovered and seeing the bottles on the table, the general began to shout that we were having another orgy and put us under the usual arrest, to which we were becoming quite accustomed. But I felt sorry for those officers. Their life was really sad, especially in such holes as Pavlovskaia Sloboda. As one officer pointed out, we had to put up with this place for only a few months, then could return to our normal life, but for him things would remain the same—miserable pay and slow promotion. Those serving in guard regiments in the capital at least had their diversions, but in a place like this there were only drink and cards. He longed for war with its adventure, quick promotions, and higher pay, oblivious of wounds and death. All this was beginning to depress me, when my whole position changed unexpectedly.

One evening I was summoned to the battery commander. I entered his room with the usual "I have the honor to make my appearance!" certain that some new punishment awaited me. Instead, the General greeted me with an amiable smile and told me a long story about having a set of artificial teeth made and needing money to pay for it. He concluded by asking me to be so kind and lend him the necessary funds, naming an amount far greater than any artificial teeth could have cost. I was staggered at this breach of military regulations—a commander asking a loan from a common soldier—but realized that thereby he put himself in my hands, and decided to use this unexpected situation to my advantage. I replied that I could not answer him without consulting my father and for that must go to Moscow. He agreed at once and when I asked for permission to bring my own horse, a request that heretofore had provoked his wrath, he cheerfully consented. And so, to the great astonishment of my comrades, to whom I never confided the true cause of my chief's benevolence, I left for Moscow.

When my father learned the reason for my unexpected visit, he was furious and told me to inform the General that my father would not allow me to lend him the money. When I explained that it would be quite impossible to refuse, and pointed out the humor of the whole situation—the artificial teeth, the sudden change in attitude of the ferocious commander and the advantages that I could gain from the change—my father agreed, but was firm that I must offer only half the amount requested.

Money in pocket and supplied with new provisions I made a triumphal return to Pavlovskaia Sloboda on my beautiful horse. The General was so pleased to get even half the money, that he embraced me and gave me a resounding kiss—another violation of the rules and regulations concerning the relations between commanding officer and common soldier. From this time on I was the spoiled child of my battery, suffered no more arrests, received permission to go home, and had endless pleasure in riding my beautiful horse, which soon became the object of admiration and envy of the whole brigade. To my surprise the commander proved to have been more honest than I had realized. At one of the reviews I heard him sending his orderly to fetch the artificial teeth which he had forgotten in his bedroom. The orderly could not understand what the General meant by "artificial teeth," and the latter explained that they were like pincers. The orderly galloped away and returned with a pair of sugar tongs. But the story of the artificial teeth had not been a fabrication.

Soon we moved to our summer camp. I liked the march through the peaceful countryside, where peasants were doing their spring sowing, our entry into villages with the band at the head, the whole population running to see us, sleeping on fresh hay, and the general friendliness of the officers and soldiers. The summer passed very quickly with the strenuous exercises and maneuvers and my lonely rides through the surrounding country. Our camp was on the spot where a century earlier Russian troops had made their last stand against the invading forces of Napoleon before quitting Moscow.

With the advent of autumn the end of our military service approached. The last exercise we, the one-year soldiers, had to perform, was a practical demonstration before the artillery chief of the Moscow district. Each of us had to command his own battery, destroy a faraway target, then a moving target. By this time I had acquired a certain amount of military psychology in which the desire to show off plays an important part, and persuaded my men to perform the exercise at full speed. It was very effective: everybody galloping in a cloud of dust, the noise of the guns, I myself in front on my beautiful horse like a great conqueror leading his army to victory. When I had to order the guns to stop by signaling with my sword, my sword got stuck and I had to do it with my stick. But among the smoke and noise I had successfully destroyed the targets, and felt that there was great beauty in war. After the end of the exercises, we were summoned to the hill where the commander was surrounded by officers and ladies. Seeing me, he made a stern face and said that I had had no right to do my exercise at full speed, because if one horse had fallen, there would have been many casualties; as for giving the cease-fire order with the stick, only one general had allowed himself to do that, and he had been a favorite of Catherine the Great; but as the whole thing had been extremely effective, he forgave me. Thus the commander was human and did not wish to spoil the beautiful day and the gay gathering of smiling ladies by falling into the military habit of finding fault with subordinates. After that we obtained our commissions as reserve officers and returned to civilian life. I confess I did so with some regret, for I realized that now I must stand on my own feet and that nobody would regulate my life and tell me what to do. I was a bit frightened of the uncertainty which lay before me.

❖❖❖

I at once applied to the Archives of the Ministry of Foreign Affairs, reminding officials of their promise to help me enter the Foreign Service by this door. Everybody was very kind. The usual application was sent to St. Petersburg. Meanwhile I was given some work to do and started my daily visit to the Archives. My work consisted in put-

ting in order twelve boxes with documents, found in the chancery of
Prince [Grigorii Aleksandrovich] Potemkin on his death in the south
of Russia, when he was commanding the troops against the Turks. It
all sounds interesting—Prince Potemkin, the colorful favorite of
Catherine the Great, and documents found on his death—but actually
the documents were dull, consisting mostly of the formal ukases of
the Empress. No wonder that nobody had had the patience to put
these papers in order and that the boxes were usually given to beginners. I saw that many people had set out with great energy to classify
the documents, but, losing interest, had never gotten to the last boxes.
I succeeded in staying with the material all the way through and during my year in the Archives completed the task, but the result was so
uninteresting that my catalogue was added to the documents and
probably lies there forgotten to this day. The only document of interest that I found in the whole collection was a private letter from Paris
written at the beginning of the French Revolution. It showed that
contemporaries are usually the worst prophets of things to come.

The Archives were headed by the old Prince [Pavel Alekseevich]
Golitsyn, who had a nice house in the compound of the Archives and
there lived with his old wife. He never came to the Archives and had
little interest in the old documents. The only reasons for his appointment as head of the Archives were that he was an old diplomat and
that the Grand Duchess Elizabeth, the wife of Grand Duke Serge,[2]
governor general of Moscow, was greatly attached to the old Princess
Golitsyn and wanted to have her nearby. These Golitsyns were a
charming couple. Most of their time they lived abroad; for years he
had been attached to our legation in Brussels. He did not take his
diplomatic career seriously and viewed it as a means of having a good
time in foreign lands. He inherited a large fortune, mostly in land,
from his father and spent it freely.

The old couple lived in the past. They were bored in their comfortable house in the Archives compound, filled with beautiful things
from their brilliant past, and insisted that somebody from among their
subordinates keep them company at lunch. It was mostly I, since the
others could not tear themselves away from their documents. For the
Prince it was a source of wonder that I should aspire to become a diplomat. He thought that members of commercial families never left

[2] Sergei Aleksandrovich.

their factories and their shops, and would never dream to compete with members of the nobility in what he considered to be their special sphere. I tried to explain to him that times had changed and that what was good for the nineteenth century was not good for the twentieth. In the end he sympathized with me, and we became great friends. He even decided to teach me what was expected from a diplomat. His tutoring did not go beyond the answering of dinner invitations. He handed me such invitations from imaginary princesses and ambassadresses and I had to answer them. These lessons later proved of great help, social correspondence playing an important part in diplomatic life.

One day, when entering the room before lunch, I found the couple reading a book which they tried to hide from me. When I asked them about it, they confessed that they had gotten hold of a work, banned because of its revolutionary tendencies. They wished to find out what it was that agitated the public and what the revolutionaries wanted. When I asked their opinion about this book, the Princess, who was much smarter than her husband, replied that there was nothing new in it. The lower classes had always wanted to take the place of the upper classes in order to enjoy all the things they did not possess; it was the duty of the ruling classes to see through these maneuvers in order not to be duped by grand phrases. I thought this a good—albeit cynical—definition of the perennial struggle between those who have succeeded in rising to the top and those who wanted to take their place.

Moscow meanwhile enjoyed itself with theaters, concerts, parties, and sleigh rides through the cold night to outdoor restaurants with their gypsy songs, so dear to the ever-tormented Russian soul. In vain the new governor general, the uncle of the Tsar, tried to create a semblance of court life. The independent Moscow bourgeoisie preferred its own ways and refused to play the part of courtiers. With the arrival of the Grand Duke the struggle against all liberal movements increased, and attempts on his life followed. But in those days the terrorists were more gentlemanly than today. As the wife of the Grand Duke was very popular among all classes of Moscow, the terrorists sent her an anonymous letter asking her not to accompany her husband when he went out, because they did not want to harm her. The letter had the opposite effect, the Grand Duchess making it a point to accompany her husband everywhere. But one time, when she was away, he went out alone and was blown to pieces by a bomb. The assassination of the Grand Duke made a great impression on Moscow. It showed that the revolutionists meant business, though years were to pass before they were to overthrow the government, and our happy life continued.

❖❖❖

At last it was time for me to present myself before the Foreign Office in St. Petersburg for my diplomatic service examination. In the past I had taken hundreds of examinations without being nervous. But now I was afraid. I did not know what to expect. Failure would mean the collapse of all my plans and a dreadful blow to my dignity, success a complete change in living—departure from Moscow which I loved so much and a new life in St. Petersburg which had always struck me as inhospitable and cold and where I knew scarcely any one. Accompanied by the blessings of the old Prince Golitsyn I headed into the unknown. The first days were terrible. The long soulless corridors of the Foreign Office, the presentation to the high bureaucrats, who seemed never to have time to receive me and made me wait for hours, and the feeling of hostility I encountered—as if everybody I met was asking himself what this merchant from Moscow was looking for in the Foreign Office—were disheartening.

The diplomatic examinations were less concerned with testing specific knowledge than with evaluating general behavior, appearance, and quick thinking. I had to wait in a half-lit room. When my name was called I passed into a brilliantly illuminated room, where everything seemed gilded. I sat down on a gilded chair, alone in the middle of the room, before a long table with a green cloth, facing a row of uniformed high officials covered with decorations. In the center was the Vice Minister, who stared at me through dark glasses. The first few minutes passed in absolute silence. Then the questioning began. The queries were phrased in such a way that they seemed designed to catch one in some nonsense. For instance, the eminent professor of international law asked me with the air of a cat playing with a mouse: "Please tell me what the Red Cross is." When I began to recite the history of the founding of the Red Cross, he looked annoyed and said that he was not interested in historical research, he simply wanted to know what the Red Cross was. Angered, I replied that the Red Cross was a flag with a red cross on it. He beamed with pleasure, said that that was just the answer he wanted, and gave me a high mark. The others tried to imitate him and I realized how much easier it is to be in the place of the examiner than of the examinee. You invent the question and at the same time the answer you expect to get, and then simply wait to see how close the answer given is to the one you have invented. Thus the whole examination was reduced to a mixture of repartee and mind reading. All the while the Vice Minister said nothing, only stared at me through his dark glasses. The comedy lasted for an hour. It was slightly amusing but very tiring, and I was glad to find myself back in the dark room.

For a week I did not know the outcome of this strange examination. I did not have much hope; the dark glasses of the Vice Minister made it impossible to be optimistic. But when the results were posted, though half of the persons examined had failed, my name was among those who had passed. To my astonishment I did not feel triumphant. The examination had been conducted in such a way that I had no sense of particular achievement. Later on, when I was presented to the Vice Minister with dark glasses, the first question he asked me was did I belong to the rich Abrikossow family; when he had been in the Crimea he had several times passed a magnificent estate belonging to a Mrs. Abrikossow and wanted to know if I were related to her. I remembered that one of my innumerable aunts had an estate in the Crimea and answered in the affirmative, though the fortune of this aunt had absolutely nothing to do with me or the Abrikossow money. It impressed the Vice Minister greatly and was of a certain importance in my future career. He was a rich man himself and, as I was told later, adored everything that had a touch of money. Thus the fact that the Vice Minister had been in the Crimea and had been impressed with the appearance of my aunt's estate may have played a part in my being accepted into the Foreign Office. Little and seemingly insignificant facts, therefore, may be of great consequence in one's life. The moral of the story is never to treat little things with contempt, but to try to turn them to your advantage. After all, luck consists to a large extent of not ignoring little things which may be of use to you.

To become better acquainted with my future colleagues I stayed a few more days in St. Petersburg and joined in the celebrations of our successes. Those who had failed joined us to console themselves. The celebrations consisted of dinners and suppers in the most expensive restaurants. I remember the endless succession of champagne, music, and women. The restaurants had stages where dancers and singers of different nationalities performed in the evening. This was not considered enough, however, and the artists and choruses were invited to give special entertainment in separate rooms until early morning. I remember an Italian woman who started to cry when she saw me very sad, a huge German woman in a hussar uniform sitting on my lap, and crowds of feline gypsy women singing those plaintive songs which made the half-drunk public either sad or wild. I disliked orgies and always ran away at the beginning, but this time I persevered. As I was starting a new life among new people, I had to see them not only at work but at play. The wine rendered them more human and less artificial. Yet all that meant the senseless waste of money and hangovers in the morning. In the end I came to the conclusion that I could suffer through such a round of parties once but not constantly; there was a limit to my adaptability.

I had to decide how I would live in St. Petersburg. All my relatives, friends, and acquaintances were in Moscow. I did not know anybody in the capital except two cousins of my mother. Married into a typical St. Petersburg set, with families of their own, they had drifted away from their former Moscow life, and though I meant to renew my acquaintance with them, I could not burden them with my company. To have my own quarters in St. Petersburg did not particularly appeal to me. Even in Moscow, where everything was arranged for me, I was tired of housekeeping, with its endless discussions with the cook about food, quarrels of the servants, and the like. To live in a hotel sounded better, but I was too accustomed to family life to be satisfied with the loneliness of a hotel. At the same time I wanted to avoid the sort of "gay" life that I had just observed and would be likely to encounter in a hotel. Seeing that all this was more complicated than I had foreseen, I longed to be back in Moscow, where everything was so simple and where I could always rely on someone else. But it was useless to regret what had already been decided. As the French say, once the wine has been poured, you must drink it.

One morning, walking along the gorgeous Neva River, of which St. Petersburg was justly proud, I was passing the English church on the English quay when I suddenly got the idea to try to find an English family which would take me as a lodger. This would improve my English and remove me from the Russian atmosphere which, I felt sure, would be quite different in St. Petersburg from what I was accustomed to in Moscow. I rang the bell of the chaplain's house, and was received by a typical red-haired English clergyman. When I put the matter to him, his first reaction was that this would hardly be possible since most of the English families living in St. Petersburg were wealthy, and, as was usual with Englishmen, kept aloof from the Russians and would never dream of taking in a Russian to live in their home. As I insisted that every rule has its exception, he agreed to make inquiries, and I left him, promising to come back for an answer in three months. Considering the question settled—the young are full of optimism—I returned to Moscow and after a family celebration, set out on my annual trip abroad.

❖❖❖

This time I decided to visit North Africa. From snow-covered Moscow I went to Algiers by way of Genoa and Tunis with its deep blue sea, white Arab houses, palm trees, and brilliant sun. I enjoyed myself immensely and thought how beautiful the world was. After traveling for hours through desolate sands I was particularly struck by the oasis of Biskra with its comfortable hotel, elegant society, and native dancers. It was astonishing how much France had done in North Africa, especially in the cities, whither the French had successfully transplanted a part of Paris.

But my holidays passed quickly and I soon headed back to Paris on my way to Russia and a new life. As always I stopped with my aunt. Deciding that I had grown up, she gave me a key to her place so that I could stay out in the evening to see what she called the places of perdition. I went to the Folies Bergères and to different Montmartre cabarets and to the great delight of my aunt found them extremely dull.

❖❖❖

At the beginning of the year I was back in St. Petersburg. My first visit was to the English chaplain to find out if he had found an English family with which I could stay. He informed me that, as he had thought, no English family was willing to accept me, but a young curate, recently come from England to help him, was interested in Russia and the Russians and would be quite willing to share his apartment in the church with me. When I said that that would be splendid, the curate was called. He proved to be a young fellow, just out of Cambridge University, with all the nice attributes of an English undergraduate: good manners, a lively nature, and not much pedantry. We agreed to live together for a month, sharing our expenses. If we found that we did not suit each other, we could separate then without giving any reason or offense. I found the agreement very sensible and we actually stayed together for the whole two years I remained in St. Petersburg. I acquired in the Rev. Capel Young a true lifelong friend. He was a very nice fellow. He liked music, and we went to operas and concerts together. He took singing lessons from a Russian teacher and I remember how for two years he constantly tried to sing with his dreadful accent the same Russian song about the winter that had reigned in his heart until she had come and the winter had turned into spring. His ecclesiastical duties he performed very conscientiously, not because a special sacred fire burned in him, but because such was his duty. I think he preferred the pomp and luxury of our Orthodox service to the simplicity of the Protestant church, and we often went together, especially to the magnificent Easter service, in the Cathedral of St. Isaac. His chief work was among the innumerable English governesses who lived in St. Petersburg and liked him very much.

The fact that I came to live with him created a great stir in the English colony. Many of the more prominent members, who were connected with the administration of the church, were not at all pleased—as if they did not pay their curate enough so that he had to take in boarders! The chaplain advised me to call on the chief families and try to make a favorable impression. This I did and met with their approval. As the curate told me, I even got the highest compliment that an Englishman could pay a Russian, namely that I was so nice it was a pity I was not English.

The English families in St. Petersburg were quite peculiar. Though some of them had lived here for generations, they rarely mixed with Russians, sent their children to England for their education, and kept all the characteristics of early Victorian times. Some of them looked, thought, and acted as if they came straight out of one of Dickens' novels.

All this was very amusing and gave me the chance to lead a double life. In the Foreign Office I was a serious and ambitious young man, trying to find my footing in new surroundings, where nobody knew me and looked on me if not with hostility at least with surprise. Outside the Foreign Office, in the company of the young English curate, I felt like an English undergraduate full of life and ready to enjoy myself in a way unknown to Russians with their disinterest in sport and their premature seriousness. Through my curate I was admitted to the tennis, skating, skiing, and sailing clubs of the English colony and thereby could avoid those restaurant dinners which were part of the life of the countless officials and clerks of the different ministries and their numerous branches, which formed the machinery by which Russia was ruled. Thanks to my double life I kept in perfect health and avoided becoming a typical Russian bureaucrat, intent only on getting a promotion and gaining the protection of his chiefs. I am certain that but for my English life, I could not have endured St. Petersburg and work at the Foreign Office.

Not only did I no longer feel that I was my own master, as I had in Moscow, but all my illusions about diplomatic life were quickly dispelled. The work of those in high position, who behind closed doors participated in shaping Russian foreign policy, may have been interesting, though even they, as I discovered later, spent most of their time intriguing against each other and gossiping about court news and possible promotions. But the position of the beginners was absolutely desperate. There were too many of them, and there was not enough work. Nobody took any notice of them; they were shoved into some insignificant department where they performed minor clerical tasks. Those who belonged to rich families and had protection in higher circles did not do any work. They came elegantly dressed, spent half an hour, gossiped about their friends, and left to have lunch at some fashionable restaurant. Their ambition was to be moved to the chancellery of the minister, the holy of holies of the Foreign Office, through which all appointments abroad had to go, and where they would be near the Minister himself. The officials of this chancellery stuck together tyrannically and did not admit any outsiders.

Realizing that I had no chance of being admitted to this sanctuary, I had to rest satisfied with a position in the section dealing with money left by Russians in foreign countries. It was a far cry from the brilliant

[85]

life abroad and the diplomatic secrets that I had imagined. I felt so humiliated that I did not have the courage to tell anyone in Moscow the truth about my life in the capital, and I parried all questions with vague answers. Fortunately Moscow was so content with itself that its interest in St. Petersburg was limited.

I feel that I showed a great deal of character in not chucking the whole thing and going into business. Unlike my brilliant colleagues who did nothing, I modestly sat at my desk and tried to put order in the general chaos which prevails in all bureaucratic institutions. Most of the persons who did the real work were modest people, dependent on their salaries and having few illusions about their future. As all officials in Russia were divided into ranks and from time to time received decorations, their only ambition was to be promoted to a higher rank or to receive a decoration. I must say that they were amiable, but uninteresting. Many of them, because of the selfsame work year in and year out became regular bureaucratic types, such as described by the great Russian writer [Nikolai Vasilevich] Gogol in his satires. I remember an old man who sat in our room, copying different papers. He was small and dirty, and had a red nose which he powdered when he thought nobody was looking. He would tell the same old story of how Nicholas I once visited a government office early in the morning and finding it empty except for a small clerk, who on seeing the Emperor was so frightened that he fell on his knees, said to him, "Get up, Your Excellency!" rewarding his punctuality by promoting him on the spot to the highest bureaucratic rank. Impressed by his own story, the clerk with the red nose always tried to reach the office before anyone else, no doubt hoping that the same thing might happen to him. Alas, the time when emperors could freely walk about the capital was over, and Nicholas II not only never left the palace without a strong guard, but for safety's sake even lived in Tsarskoe Selo, some twenty miles from the capital. Thus the old man's dream could never come true. His end was sad. Every Saturday he used to go to the public steam bath; there he was found dead one day. Let us hope that in his last vision he saw the Emperor telling him: "Get up, Your Excellency!"

In Russia much fun was made of the bureaucrats and their red tape. With the outbreak of the Revolution they became the main object of the people's wrath. I do not think that such an attitude was justified.

The bureaucrats in Russia were no better and no worse than the rest of the population. The Russian government, like any other enterprise, could not exist without officials and clerks. The task of administering so huge a territory, inhabited by people of different races and mentalities, was a problem of such magnitude that the astonishing thing is that it could have been done at all, and done not so very badly. For centuries Russia had existed and made enormous progress, progress in which, as every impartial historian must admit, the bureaucracy played an important role.

When I first came from Moscow, where the bureaucrats of St. Petersburg were regarded as quite unnecessary even though private concerns were full of clerks who were bureaucrats in all but name, I too asked myself what all those countless clerks who at five o'clock came streaming out of different government offices carrying portfolios were doing. But my daily work in the section dealing with Russians who had died abroad enlightened me. I remember the case of a Russian sailor who upon arrival in Australia on a merchant ship died in Sidney, leaving some thirty dollars and a silver watch. The local authorities informed the Russian Consul, the Consul wrote to the Foreign Office, the Foreign Office communicated with the governor of the province, where according to the passport the sailor had been born. In some little village the old mother of the sailor was located, the governor wrote thereof to the Foreign Office, the Foreign Office got in touch with the Consul and the thirty dollars and the silver watch were brought to Russia and—after the appropriate judicial authorities determined that the old mother was the only relative of the dead sailor—were transmitted to her. All this certainly took a long time, but I was greatly impressed by the insignificant case. I realized that it was one of millions of similar cases. Somebody had to do it. My admiration for the work of the Russian bureaucracy rose and everytime I heard it abused, I related the story of the sailor who died in Sidney and his old mother in a small village in the Baltic provinces, rejoicing at the receipt of the thirty dollars and the silver watch of her son.

All this did not increase my love for my new occupation, however, and when I got to know my colleagues better, I used to pretend that I was suffocating from the stale bureaucratic atmosphere and, rushing to the open window, pretended that I was about to throw myself from it. A kindhearted but humorless baron who sat near the window would catch me by the arm and try to console me. What depressed me most at the Foreign Office were its endless corridors, where the clerks walked up and down, enviously gossiping about promotions and complaining about the injustice of their chiefs, and where those who returned from abroad met their friends who had remained in the Foreign Office. They would tell about their successes in foreign posts and about the promises made to them of new posts and promotions. But gradually their hopes dwindled and after some time they had to return to their old posts. This picture of shattered hopes and humiliation was so sad that I promised myself, if I were lucky enough to obtain a post abroad, never to come back without first obtaining a definite transfer. In view of the number of candidates for foreign posts, chances of my starting a real diplomatic career were becoming dimmer and dimmer, however, and had I not been so happy in my private life, I would have sunk into a state of acute depression.

✠✠✠

Meanwhile, Russia was entering that period in her history which spelled the beginning of those misfortunes that ultimately led to her collapse. There are such periods in history when destiny seems to be stockpiling causes for a future disaster—really clever statesmen disappear or are no longer heeded, power passes into incompetent hands, decisions become foolish or belated, and all forces work against you till you gradually slide into the abyss. This was the situation in which Russia found herself in 1904, when I was starting my career in the Foreign Office. The Boxer Rebellion in China [1900] had brought Russian occupation of Manchuria. Earlier [in 1896] we had obtained from China the right to construct the last link of the Siberian railway across [north] Manchuria. This had caused a display of great energy on the part of Russia, the dream of an ice-free port nearing fulfillment. The best engineers were sent to Manchuria and the railway with a branch line to Port Arthur rushed to completion. Russian settlers were moved into Manchuria, towns were built, and life and civilization were brought to this wild and sparsely populated part of China.

All this attracted world attention; other powers began to protest. At that time, however, Japan was the only power vitally interested in this question. Forced out of her seclusion, she was beginning to show imperialistic tendencies. Having re-entered the world arena too late to participate in the distribution of colonies in the Pacific, all islands being already occupied by others, her attention was directed toward Korea and Manchuria, whose weak governments seemed to make them easy prey, when Russia, who once before [in 1895] had thwarted Japanese attempts to gain a foothold in Manchuria following the Sino-Japanese War, crossed her path. No wonder Russian occupation of Manchuria sounded to Japan like the death knell to her ambitions and she took steps to counteract it!

Not yet spoiled by success, Japan moved slowly and cleverly. First she obtained the support of England and the United States, who also looked with suspicion upon the bold policy of Russia. It was quite logical for Japan to do so, but I must say I could never understand how England and the United States so readily gave their support to Japan, oblivious to the fact that beyond the question of Manchuria was a conflict between West and East; and that for them, the two biggest nations of the West, to take the side of the East was an unpardonable crime for which they would ultimately pay dearly. But in politics statesmen do not look beyond their noses. At the time both England and the United States thought that the occupation of Manchuria went against their interests, and when they saw that Japan was ready to fight Russia, they were only too glad to support the Japanese, forgetting that thereby they were contributing to the "Yellow Peril," that they were creating a new force which in the end would turn against them, for East is East and West is West and to invite an Eastern country into one's family quarrels is very poor policy. When President [Theodore] Roosevelt finally understood that and, disturbed by Japan's formidable strength, helped bring the War to a close, it was too late. The poison of power lust was in Japan's veins, and she was dreaming of new conquests.

All this does not justify Russia's Japan policy, which was based on absolute ignorance. St. Petersburg had no idea of the real strength of Japan, and thought that tiny Japan would never dare to make war against mighty Russia. The reports of our military agents in Tokyo, like most reports, presented things not as they were, but as the central authorities wanted them to be, confirming the belief that the Japanese army was no match for a European army. The Foreign Office had a better understanding of the real situation, but at its head was a weak person, without the courage to go counter to general opinion. The main cause of the absence of any fixed policy toward Japan, however, was the personality of the Emperor himself. Kindhearted and patriotic though he was, Nicholas II lacked the two most important traits necessary to rule a big country—a strong character and the knowledge of human nature—and, as is often the case with weak personalities, he did not tolerate strong individuals and surrounded himself with unscrupulous persons instead. Destiny had sent him two really great statesmen: Count [Sergei Iulevich] Witte and [Petr Arkadevich] Stolypin. But he did not trust either of them and thus deprived Russia of the full benefit of the talent of these men, who might conceivably have forestalled the disaster of the Russo-Japanese War and the catastrophe of the Revolution.

Not listening to his ministers, Nicholas in the days before the Russo-Japanese War put his trust in two adventurers[3] who had some knowledge of the Far East. Interested in some commercial enterprises on the border of Korea, they rhapsodized about the glorious future that awaited Russia on the Pacific shores and for a time became the most influential persons in our Far Eastern policy. In vain the Minister of Foreign Affairs [Count Vladimir Nikolaevich Lamsdorf] pointed to the danger of such a policy, and the Vice Minister complained that he could not sleep, for as soon as he closed his eyes, he would see Japanese creeping from every corner to attack. Russia played into Japanese hands. While continuing to negotiate with Russia and pretending to seek a compromise, the Japanese put the finishing touches on their preparations for war. When they were ready, they recalled their Minister from St. Petersburg. Taking leave from our Foreign Secretary, the Minister expressed the hope that his absence would be temporary and that he would return to continue the negotiations, but while St. Petersburg was waiting for the resumption of negotiations, news was received that the Japanese had attacked Port Arthur and disabled our three best cruisers.

I remember the horror and indignation with which this news was received. All the ministers and high dignitaries were immediately summoned to the palace. We looked through the windows as carriage after carriage, bearing the military and the civilians in full uniform, rolled through the snow to the palace. The Emperor made a patriotic

[3] Aleksandr Mikhailovich Bezobrazov and A. M. Abaza.

speech assailing the perfidy of Japan. A crowd gathered before the palace, the Emperor appeared on the balcony, and there was a patriotic demonstration as the snowfall increased in intensity, but there was a complete lack of enthusiasm, half of the population not even knowing where Manchuria was located. The only people who rejoiced were the revolutionists who had always seen their only chance for success in the demoralization of an unsuccessful war. The conflict found us unprepared, with an insufficient number of troops in the Far East; it took a long time to select a commander and when General [Aleksei Nikolaevich] Kuropatkin was appointed at last, he did not hasten to the Far East at once, but traveled from town to town, appearing at dinners and accepting holy images that were to insure victory. The public, which was critical of what the government was doing, quipped that when the Japanese would hit us with ammunition, we would hit them with holy images.

Meanwhile the Japanese, with English and American moral and financial support, pushed through Manchuria, beating us at every turn. Meeting the General who, as Military Attaché in Tokyo before the War, had reported that the Japanese army was no good, a high-ranking civilian asked him at one of the receptions in the palace how he could have sent such reports. The General got angry and replied that he still felt the Japanese army was no good. When the civilian asked how this could be in view of the fact that the Japanese were beating us at every step, the General shouted that what he had not known at the time of his reports was that our army was even worse.

Generally speaking, St. Petersburg did not take seriously the developments in the Far East. The War seemed some distant colonial affair, and there was always the expectation that eventually Japan would exhaust her resources and Russia show her real strength. Thus St. Petersburg continued to dance and hope for the best, many content that the government would learn its lesson and embark on the necessary reforms. There was little display of real patriotism, the extreme radicals openly showing their joy at the constant defeats and preparing to stage the first act of the tragedy of the Russian Revolution.

❖❖❖

My own life, meanwhile, went on as before, punctuated by increas-

[91]

ing dissatisfaction on my part with my work at the Foreign Office and by my attempts to persuade my English acquaintances that a Japanese victory would not be to their advantage. I continued to go with my curate friend to various functions for which he could obtain tickets through his embassy. I shall never forget the anniversary celebration of one of the guard regiments in its manège—the sun brilliantly reflected from the silver cuirasses and eagle-topped helmets of the officers and men, the hurrahs that greeted the Emperor and the stirring strains of "God Save the Tsar." It was such a demonstration of the might of the Russian Empire that even the foreigners were impressed and for a moment the disasters in far-off Manchuria were forgotten. Returning to our quarters and waiting for lunch, I gazed out of the window into the street adjoining our house. There was some commotion near the gate of the house across from us. A crowd of passersby stopped and looked into the yard of the house. Soon I saw two sleighs coming out of the yard, one with a miserable-looking student and a policeman, the other with bundles of paper. Our servant told us that the police had discovered a secret printing press and were taking the student who lived in the cellar and the revolutionary proclamations found there to the police station. Turning to the curate I ventured a prophecy: "You remember the brilliant scene of this morning, the Emperor surrounded by his troops; now watch this miserable sight of a consumptive student with his revolutionary proclamations being taken to the police station. What can be of greater contrast? But I fear that in the end, it will be the student who will win."

We were approaching the second year of the War with no hope for the future and no way out of the difficulties. It is always easy to start a war, but very difficult to end it. Prospects for any change in my personal life seemed equally dim. But I was forgetting the unexpected element in human life. In my case the unexpected came in the shape of a dog. Unconsciously I was following the example of the famous Greek statesman Alcibiades who cut off his dog's tail to attract public attention. I did not cut off the tail of any dog, yet it was to a dog that I owe the beginning of my career.

One day the curate expressed the wish that we had a dog. Shortly afterward I was offered a magnificent borzoi, which in the sunshine looked golden and had the most expressive black eyes. This dog became our companion. As I always returned home for lunch, I would take the dog with me to the Foreign Office and leave it at the foot of the staircase, chained to the railing. No one who passed could fail to notice the dog and ask to whom it belonged. In such a way I succeeded in standing out in the crowd and attracted the attention of those on whom my fate depended. I became known as the man with the magnificent dog. I realize that such a ruse was undignified, but I was desperate and had to do something out of the ordinary.

One morning I was called to the Chief of Personnel, who, after complimenting me on the dog, asked casually what I would say to an offer to go to London. He explained that our ambassador there, Count [Aleksandr Konstantinovich] Benckendorff, had asked for an increase in staff, stipulating that the clerk sent be a good worker with sufficient means to lead a life befitting a member of the Embassy. Apparently the combination of industry and money was hard to find, most candidates lacking either one or the other, and somebody had mentioned my name. Asked about me, my chief had attested that I was quite capable of working even on such dull matters as Russians who died in foreign lands and as for means, a man who owned such a dog could not be poor. I certainly confirmed all that and said that I was ready to start the following day if necessary, but the Chief of Personnel, an elegant man who wore the court uniform with one spur attached to one boot, answered that the conversation was purely exploratory, that nothing had been settled yet and that I must keep everything in secret.

For a long time I did not hear anything further and had a miserable time with my dead people, the old clerk with the red nose and corridor gossips, but then I was summoned by the Vice Minister, the same man who had been so impressed with my aunt's estate in the Crimea. He repeated the offer, but dwelt for a long time on the high cost of living in London and said that I would have to spend at least five pounds a day. As I had always considered the question of expenses a purely personal matter, every man spending according to his character, I was quite willing to promise to spend a million a day, not because I could do so, but because I wanted so much to leave the stale atmosphere of the Foreign Office and see for myself if my ambition for an interesting life would be satisfied by service in the most important and brilliant Embassy.

The question was settled, my nomination appeared in the Foreign

[93]

Office bulletin and at once became the subject of gossip in the Ministry corridors. Nobody could understand how I could have been transferred from an insignificant section dealing with people who have died in foreign lands directly to London. They did not know, of course, about my aunt's estate and about the part a dog can play in diplomatic nominations. I was sorry to leave the curate, who had become a true friend during the two years we had lived together, but he said that he would soon return to England and we would see each other there.

Before leaving for my new post I went to Moscow to say good-bye. Everybody rejoiced at my good fortune and did not believe the story of the dog, but then my relatives were always too kind and had a higher opinion of my capacities than I had myself; nor could they conceive of the atmosphere in the government offices, where talent was not of primary consideration. In Moscow I found much more interest in the War and in its results, but equally little patriotism. The War was looked upon as a lesson for the government, and in vain I argued that during a war there cannot be any distinction between government and people, because a lost war would be a misfortune for both. I thought this increase in opposition a most dangerous thing, since it greatly strengthened the power of the revolutionists, the only people who really knew what they wanted. The political atmosphere in Moscow dampened my enthusiasm for my work in London. Not foreseeing a change in the military situation, I anticipated difficult times for Russia, and life among a people whose sympathies were on the other side was not likely to be very agreeable. But the die had been cast, and I could only hope for the best.

4

London

I ARRIVED IN LONDON JUST AFTER CHRISTMAS. THE SHOPS WERE closed and the streets were empty. In the past I had always come to London in the summer, when the sun and the season dispelled the city's gloom and brightened it with brilliant life and endless pleasures; the parks had been full of riders on magnificent horses, the restaurants and theaters had been crowded and London had looked like the world capital, to which the millionaires of all countries flocked to join, however briefly, in its cavalcade of brilliant court, high-sounding titles, beautiful women, and immense riches. Now the town appeared gloomy, dirty, and dull. After three years in London I was to grow attached to it and find a special charm in its dark winter days, when the whole of town was enveloped in a yellowish fog through which the sun vainly tried to penetrate, but to appreciate the special beauty of London one must really see it in the summer, especially in spring, when the grass in the parks is particularly green and the flowers particularly bright.

True to tradition, I stopped in the same hotel Father had recommended to my brother and me when we first visited London, because it was mentioned in one of Dickens' novels. In the summer, with the windows open onto Trafalgar Square, our boyish interest captivated by the new sights, the hotel had looked young and bright. Now, with its dark corridors and cold rooms, it heightened my feeling of sadness and loneliness. In the hall stood a Christmas tree, but except for three old gentlemen buried in their newspapers, there was nobody to give the room a touch of Christmas. I did feel somewhat less lonely, however, when an old waiter recognized me and asked about my brother. After eating an unsatisfactory Christmas dinner in a cold room, I went out.

Decidedly London looked much more English in winter: dark, solid houses, narrow crooked streets, little shops with all their goods piled up in the windows, two-wheeled cabs with the coachmen sitting behind—there were as yet no motorcars which make the streets of different towns so much alike—men in silk hats, bars where you sat on high chairs and flirted with barmaids in very elaborate hairdresses, small theaters to which hansoms brought elegant ladies and gentlemen in evening dress, the shouting of newspaper boys, and in the dark streets the figures of prostitutes, who according to police regulations had to disappear from the main streets at curtain time so as not to shock the virtuous ladies and girls coming to the theater. The self-contentment of virtue must not be spoiled by the indiscreet appearance of vice. Such was London when I arrived in the winter of 1905 to begin my diplomatic career.

The first evening everything was half-hidden by the fog, and looked unreal. I entered a brilliantly lit bar, which turned out to be a German delicatessen, and suddenly found myself transposed to Germany, confronted by fat German faces, huge beer mugs, and enormous ham sandwiches. I ordered an excellent sandwich and a glass of hot milk. The good-natured proprietor struck up a conversation, telling me how easy it was to make money in London and how foolish the English were, leaving all those opportunities to foreigners. He opined that the English were either too proud or too lazy to work, preferring to lie on the grass in the parks or to walk through the streets carrying advertisements, leaving the positions of waiters in restaurants and hotels or of owners of small eating establishments to the foreigners, who made their piles of money and returned home to live it up. So much the better, he concluded, and all the fat Germans roared with laughter. Returning to my hotel, I could not help thinking what the Vice Minister would have said had he seen me spending a few pennies on my first supper in London in a delicatessen instead of paying pounds at a place like the Savoy or the Carlton.

The following day, dressed in all my finery, a silk hat balanced on my head, I was ready for my first visit to the Embassy. In London a proper address is a thing of very great importance. If you wish to be taken for someone of prominence, you must live in what is regarded as the aristocratic part of town, which in my day was the Mayfair section, not far from Hyde Park. When our Attaché lived a few blocks away from Mayfair, an English lady commented: "Such nice people. What a pity they have an impossible address!" The remark so depressed the wife of the Attaché that they moved from their comfortable house overlooking the park to a tiny place situated in Mayfair. In like fashion the Russian Embassy had to be in Mayfair. As it was difficult to buy a big-enough house, our government bought two houses and connected them into one, but the owner of the corner house, situated between the two buildings that formed the Embassy, refused to sell his property. This caused him much trouble, because most people mistook his entrance for the Embassy entrance and his bell was constantly rung by the wrong people. He posted signs in four languages, telling people to go around the corner, but the notices contained more mistakes than words and did not help at all, and he wrote us rude letters complaining that he had no rest because of our visitors. Things went from bad to worse during the Dogger Bank incident, when the Russian fleet, en route to the Far East and warned of a possible torpedo attack by the Japanese near the English shores, in the mist mistook some British fishing trawlers for Japanese torpedo boats and opened fire, sinking several trawlers and killing a number of fishermen. The ensuing uproar in London was so great that war with England seemed inevitable. A furious London crowd set out to attack the Russian Embassy, but by mistake bombarded the corner house with empty beer bottles and stones. The old gentleman had some of his windows broken before the arrival of the police. He claimed money from us, but our answer was that no court could hold us responsible for the disorderly conduct of an English mob. I am afraid all this shortened the old man's life.

On my way to the Embassy I had to pass through Piccadilly Circus, where old women sat near the fountain with the statue of Eros on the top, selling flowers. In Russia it would have been considered effeminate to wear flowers, but in London most men, even serious statesmen, did not leave their rooms without a boutonnière. The famous [Joseph] Chamberlain always appeared with an orchid in his buttonhole, and when he made his speaking tour in South Africa to promote his system of protection, he took with him pots of orchids so as not to disappoint his listeners by appearing without the traditional orchid. In Parliament I saw a member wearing such an enormous bunch of violets in his buttonhole that he looked ridiculous, but as I followed the debates in the House I missed the bunch of violets whenever this member was not present. Our own ambassador, Count Benckendorff, the most elegant man in London society, always wore a gardenia boutonnière to dinner parties. Statesmen must have had much more leisure in those days to be able to combine their important work with such childishness, yet undoubtedly there was more beauty and dignity in life then.

After Piccadilly Circus I had to follow Piccadilly Street, the most elegant street in London. When I asked whence it had gotten its Italian name, nobody knew, but in a book on the meaning of London street names I read that "Piccadilly" was derived from the name of the fashionable Italian short coat (called "piccadilly" or "small sin" because of its shortness)[1] worn by elegant young men on that street in years past. As the English do not imitate the modern tendency of renaming streets or towns in honor of writers or statesmen, Piccadilly retained its name, though the short coats disappeared long ago. I like this conservatism of the English people. After all, I do not think that anything is added to the stature of a writer or statesman by calling some dirty street after him; it strips the street of a name that rightfully forms a part of history and causes considerable confusion. When St. Petersburg was renamed Petrograd part of its dignity was lost; when it became Leningrad its fame as the proud creation of Peter the Great was besmirched, as if a queen had been degraded to the position of a charwoman. In my day Piccadilly Street was lined with dignified mansions: the old Albany, the house of the Duke of Devonshire, and the magnificent buildings of different clubs, among them St. James's Club.

To go from St. James's Club to the Embassy I had to continue along Piccadilly to Hyde Park Corner. How beautiful and typically English these London parks were, especially in the spring, when the first flowers came out and everybody tried to look young and elegant. In my day morning gallops, afternoon drives, and Sunday church

---

[1] The English word "peccadillo" is derived from the Spanish "pecadillo," a diminutive of "pecado," a sin.

parades were fashionable. As I admired the beautiful horses and magnificent carriages, I felt how English snobbism was seeping into my simple Moscow nature. The English upper classes looked so magnificent, so proud of their position, that it was not astonishing that one felt a touch of envy and a desire to imitate them. The days were not yet near when animosity and bitterness would prevent one from admiring any display of luxury and social superiority without an immediate desire to pull them down to one's own level. The London of Edward VII was the most gorgeous city in the world, with the riches and pride of the English aristocracy apotheosized. Perhaps there was a touch of vulgarity in all that, but to me, who had always been attracted by the brilliant side of life, it looked beautiful and I prepared if not to participate in the pageant, at least to contemplate it with pleasure. We have a Russian proverb: "When one lives with wolves one must howl like a wolf." Thus as most Englishmen were snobs, as long as I lived with them, I became one myself. I did not consider snobbism a vice. It cemented the English together. They loved their royal family, their aristocracy, even their rich people. They were interested in their activities and spoke as if they were something near to them. They tried to imitate them, and so snobbism became a kind of progressive force which pushed them forward. Everybody criticized his inferiors and did everything to be taken for more superior than he really was. Pride in English culture and achievements produced the gentleman type, a combination of nobility, selfishness, lack of meanness, great calm, good manners, and a certain smartness in dress. The English are so proud of these qualities that if you wish to degrade somebody, it is sufficient to say that he is not a gentleman. The English outlook is not without its negative side, of course. All foreigners are regarded as inferior beings. In my day there still were Englishmen who considered everyone beyond Calais as Negro, but notwithstanding all that I got on very well with the English people and always used to say that England was my first love.

❖❖❖

But I am still on my way to the Russian Embassy. Turning left at Hyde Park Corner you enter Mayfair. The streets are quiet with rows of comfortable houses. There are nice squares with trees; everything is clean and dignified. Luxurious carriages wait for their masters, their resplendent interiors revealed whenever a liveried servant holds open the door. The whole atmosphere exudes comfort and decency. In the summer, window boxes with bright geraniums add color to these streets. Here we are far removed from poverty and squalor. All this may be unfair, but social justice will rob our lives of a great deal of beauty.

One of these comfortable buildings was the Russian Embassy. It was not very different from other houses, except for a magnificent marble staircase for which the architect had sacrificed much space in combining two houses into one. The reception rooms and the living quarters occupied a secondary position. The chancery, where all work was done, occupied two small rooms on the fourth floor, accessible by narrow back stairs which the elderly members of the Embassy found very hard to climb several times a day. One Counsellor, who later became our Minister to China, suffered from heart disease; every morning after climbing these stairs he would collapse and have to rest for half an hour. Thus in terms of comfort we were not exactly spoiled in the Embassy; on the other hand, the marble staircase gave grandeur to the receptions.

Thanks to their own beautiful things, brought from Russia, the Benckendorffs managed to furnish their own living rooms very comfortably, much more so than the reception rooms, which generally looked bare and cold. When I arrived, the Ambassador and his family were still on leave in Russia, and I had time to accustom myself to my new position gradually without being overwhelmed by the hustle of diplomatic life.

The Embassy was under the direction of Chargé d'Affaires [Sergei Dmitrievich] Sazonov, who had considerable experience in our Vatican Legation and was to be Minister of Foreign Affairs at the time of World War One.[2] He was a nice and decent man, with little of the bureaucrat in him. He was a cultured and idealistic Russian gentleman, with whom it was easy to get along, but he did not strike me as a great statesman and his appointment as head of our Ministry of Foreign Affairs at such a critical juncture of history was a mistake. He lacked calm impartiality and allowed himself to be swayed by personal sympathies. But as a man and a colleague he was second to no

[2] Minister of Foreign Affairs from 1910 to 1916; Counsellor and Chargé d'Affaires in London.

one. In Russia he lived mostly in Moscow and, therefore, we had much in common. The Sazonovs did not remain in London long, however, as he was soon transferred back to Rome as our representative at the Vatican.

❖❖❖

The most interesting personality in the Embassy was Poklevskii [Stanislav Al'fonsovich Poklevskii-Kozell] who was First Secretary at the time of my arrival and became Counsellor after the departure of Sazonov. His grandfather, a Pole, had been mixed up in an insurrection against Russian rule and had been exiled to Siberia. During his stay in Siberia he had been impressed by all the possibilities of this rich country and after the end of his exile, instead of returning to Poland had remained in Siberia, soon becoming one of the biggest industrialists in this region. He owned mines in the Ural mountains, big steel works and the like, and became a multimillionaire. His son lived in St. Petersburg and continued the activity of his father. The grandson finished the school for sons of the nobility and entered the Foreign Office. I think his first post was in Japan,[3] where thanks to his money he soon became an outstanding figure in diplomatic society. Years passed and Tokyo was still talking about the feasts he had used to give. As he was very generous he never refused to lend money and did it in such a way that people felt they were giving him pleasure in taking it. Even some Japanese could not resist the temptation to oblige him by taking money from him, and when some twenty years afterward I came to Japan I found an old Japanese at the court who still received a pension from Poklevskii.

It was not astonishing that with such means Poklevskii always wanted to have a post at some big capital in Europe. When he arrived in London no one knew him, and he was snubbed by English society. Our ambassador, Count Benckendorff, who had an enormous position in London, did not wish to share the limelight with an unknown figure, and even had he wanted to do so, it would have mattered little, for English society did not attach any importance to the mere fact that a person was a member of some embassy. To have success in London, a foreigner must create his own position by rendering himself agreeable and interesting to the inhabitants of this peculiar island.

[3] As First Secretary in 1897-1901.

If you do not take a successful first step, you may remain ignored during your whole stay in London. All that did not stop Poklevskii. He decided to conquer London society, relying on his money and brains. Money alone would not have attracted the attention of the English aristocracy, because at that time wars and taxes had not yet ruined their own fortunes, but the combination of money and brains could be of great advantage. Poklevskii was clever enough to render himself extremely useful to the Ambassador and soon understood the mysteries of English politics; he could flatter the proud duchesses and prominent members of society and at the same time he knew how to satisfy the greed of persons who found it difficult to make ends meet. The English ladies adored presents, accepting them even from persons they did not know well. Hence every Christmas Poklevskii sent out presents by the hundreds, usually in the form of Russian enamels; everybody knew where these presents came from and the popularity of the generous Secretary of the Russian Embassy grew from one Christmas to another. At the same time Poklevskii rented a beautiful house, found an excellent cook, and kept the best-looking lady from the London demimonde. No wonder that after two years in London he became a prominent member of the most exclusive society. He was seen everywhere and an old duchess, who was a personal friend of the King and whom Poklevskii helped very discreetly by paying her expenses for the entertainment of His Majesty at the regattas at Cowes, introduced Poklevskii into the intimate circle which surrounded the King. Once Poklevskii came to the Embassy very excited and told me as a great secret that the King had teasingly told him that he had heard that Poklevskii had a very good cook and that he was astonished that until now he had not been invited to dinner; the necessary arrangements had at once been made and a guest list drawn up. When Poklevskii confided this to me, I said that he had attained the summit of success and could not climb any higher and that, therefore, the only thing for him to do was to give the dinner and after that to die in order to avoid the humiliation of sliding down.

The high position occupied by our Ambassador and Poklevskii's success benefitted the remaining members of the Embassy. We were invited everywhere, our Embassy was the best informed, and the work of the Ambassador was greatly facilitated by his personal contact with the King and the prominent statesmen of England. I soon realized how fortunate I was to begin my diplomatic career in London. No-where else could I have found such a display of the most important and interesting diplomatic work. In those days the Embassy staff was small. Besides the Ambassador, the Counsellor, and the First Secretary, there were two Second Secretaries, [Matvei Markovich] Sevastopulo, a man of Greek extraction, Old Russia receiving with open arms representatives of different nationalities, and Prince [Mikhail Nikolaevich] Sviatopolk-Mirskii, a clever but extremely cynical and immoral type.[4] The Prince took special pleasure in ridiculing my enthusiasm and his characterizations of everybody whom I tried to put on a pedestal were so clever and devastating that the pedestals became lower and lower until I realized that pedestal-building was a silly occupation which brought only disillusion and disappointment. He liked to take me to unmentionable places and play the part of Mephistopheles trying to demoralize a young Faust, but my Moscow education saved me from the downfall which Sviatopolk-Mirskii would have enjoyed. Eventually it was he who fell. One night, in a fashionable club, he lost about ten thousand pounds, while he had only eighty pounds in the bank. According to club rules he had to pay his debt in a week. He asked to be released from any chancery work in order to find a moneylender who would agree to let him have the necessary amount until he sold part of his estate. As failure to pay the debt would reflect on the whole Embassy, he cynically announced that his work now was of the greatest importance, for he was trying to save the honor of the Russian Embassy. The week passed without his being able to raise the money. In the end Poklevskii paid for him, and Sviatopolk-Mirskii was transferred to our Legation in Serbia. Our Foreign Office could be very indulgent.

✤✤✤

In addition to the above, we had an old sexton of the Embassy church who helped us at the chancery. He had the face of St. Nicholas, had served in the Embassy for years and years, and in the old times had made a fortune carrying dispatches from London to St. Petersburg. Once on his way back to London, in Cologne, he married a German woman, took a dowry of a hundred thousand marks, bought

[4] Abrikossow does not specify his own position in London; his cousin in a letter to the editor, dated April 20, 1962, gives it as Attaché.

a house in London, and entertained different destitute old English ladies from good families. All that did not prevent him from continuing his work at the Embassy, registering incoming and outgoing letters and copying various insignificant papers. He was extremely obliging and whenever he circulated in our small chancery, feeling that he was in our way, tried to make himself invisible by lunging toward the floor. It was strange to see the old man with the face of St. Nicholas trying to avoid one and bumping into someone else. But in his own house he was a different man, a tyrant before whom everybody trembled. His German wife hardly opened her mouth, perhaps for the better, because he did not understand German and she did not speak Russian.

I liked to hear him tell about the Embassy in bygone days and about former ambassadors, many of whom appeared to have been very eccentric. He told me, for instance, how Ambassador Baron [Phillip] Brunnow, who, I think, was there even before his time,[5] entertained Tsar Alexander II when he came to London for the marriage of his daughter to the Duke of Edinburgh, the son of Queen Victoria. During the stay of the Emperor in London, the Ambassador's wife fell ill and died. The Ambassador was horrified, because the next day he was giving a ball in honor of the Emperor. He called together his staff and declared that an Ambassador's wife cannot die when the Ambassador is entertaining his sovereign; nobody must know, therefore, that the Ambassadress is dead and her body must be put in the cellar on ice. The ball took place, and when the Emperor during the royal quadrille asked the Ambassador how his wife was feeling, the latter replied with a smile that she was much better, and all the while her body was lying on ice. Only when the Emperor left London did the Ambassador gather his staff again to thank them for keeping the secret, and invited them to do the last duty to the deceased. I found something grand in this story. Such loyalty toward the Emperor did not exist in our time. Another Ambassador was very fond of shooting and set up a regular shooting gallery in the ballroom, inviting his staff to join him in this ambassadorial recreation.

It is usually said that diplomats do not do much work, but in our case this was far from true. Three of us were obliged to cipher and

[5] Baron (later Count) Phillip Brunnow was Ambassador in London in 1840-54, and again in 1858-74.

decipher all telegrams, which at a time of crisis were very numerous, and to copy the dispatches written by the Ambassador in French in such a handwriting that often one could not make head or tail out of what he had written. Today there would be a crowd of typists and clerks to relieve the work of the secretaries. We had no such assistance; the one Embassy typewriter was a prehistoric machine on which only the old man with the face of St. Nicholas could write. Once or twice I tried to use it, but something always happened and after a few words some springs fell out and the whole thing stopped, much to the joy of the old man who was extremely jealous about his work and did not want anyone else to usurp part of it. At the same time my colleagues were always busy with their social obligations. The telephones rang constantly and women's voices asked for one or the other of the secretaries, and usually after a playful conversation such a secretary would rush out, asking to be excused. I came to the conclusion that to be in love or to have some sort of affair was normal for a young diplomat, and could understand why the Ambassador, when he had written to the Ministry, had insisted upon a young man willing to work. I was quite ready not to disappoint the Ambassador, for my indifference to this sort of excitement made me immune to the temptations which distracted the other young diplomats.

I spent most of my time alone in the chancery. I really liked it. I felt a special gratification in being the first to divine the meaning of a ciphered telegram and to rush to the Chief with the news. I found the archives of the Embassy in a dreadful state. The necessary documents could be found only after hours of search, while the telephone from the Ambassador's study would be ringing frantically and everybody would be shouting. Hence I sacrificed my first months to putting order in our chancery, spending many evenings alone among heaps of documents, nearly frozen with cold, the fire in the open fireplace dead. Somewhere downstairs I would hear the carriage bringing the ambassadorial couple back from a dinner party. Very late, in absolute darkness, I would descend our narrow staircase and walk home through the deserted streets, often through a dense fog. But I was soon rewarded for my labors in that I became the only member of the Embassy who knew where to find a particular document, and thus rose in importance. Let the others have their intrigues with the charming ladies; as for myself, I was satisfied with the realization of my usefulness and regarded love affairs as a great strain on one's emotions. Thus I was always first in the chancery, fresh as a daisy, and when the others arrived with tired faces after a sleepless night and in bad temper from indigestion after heavy suppers, I reflected that one has to pay for all those successes in the gay world.

Diplomatic life can be demoralizing for a young diplomat in a foreign land. By virtue of being a member of an embassy or a legation, without any merit of his own or without doing a stroke of work, he finds himself a member of high society, with its brilliant, pleasure-filled life. If such a young diplomat has good manners, is not ugly and not quite an idiot, he is received everywhere; ladies flirt with him and he passes from one conquest to another. If the diplomat is clever and knows what he wants, he accepts these pleasures without allowing them to destroy his personality, marries brilliantly, and in his later years becomes an ambassador or minister; but the majority lose their heads, begin to think that their successes are due to their own merits, develop great conceit, speak with contempt about those who do not belong to their class, and become perhaps amusing but absolutely useless members of society.

Such people feel like strangers when they return to their own country. This was particularly true in the case of Russian diplomats, because in prerevolutionary Russia the upper classes lived in the twentieth century, while the majority of the people remained in the fifteenth or sixteenth, so that a diplomat who abroad might be considered clever and charming would be taken seriously by hardly anyone upon his return to Russia. It was for this reason that so many Russian diplomats upon retirement preferred to live abroad. I remember reading in the newspapers that our former Ambassador in Paris, Baron [Artur Pavlovich] Morengeim, who had played a considerable role in preparing and signing the Russo-French Alliance, died somewhere in France, the only friend who followed his coffin being his barber. I found this extremely sad and pathetic—brilliant banquets to celebrate the Russo-French Alliance[6] and the highest decorations during his lifetime, a modest coffin followed only by the barber at the end of his career—and had some misgivings about my chosen profession. But not for long. I was young, interested in life, and spoiled by every-

[6] The manuscript states "Russo-Japanese Alliance," but it is obvious that Russo-French Alliance is meant.

body. But I was also ambitious, and firmly resolved not to let the temptations of life abroad overwhelm me. I already suffered from too much admiration for everything English and felt I must see more of the Russians living in London.

The Russians who could have been interesting were mostly political exiles with whom a member of the Embassy could not have any contact. Those I could visit in London were representatives of Russian tea firms. When the wife of our Naval Attaché, who until my arrival considered herself the only true Russian in the entire Embassy, invited me to join the Russian New Year celebration of the commercial colony, I agreed with pleasure, the more so because I felt lonely and rather depressed after reading about new reverses in Manchuria.

The celebration took place in a big boardinghouse, where most of the young Russians, sent by their firms to study English business methods, were staying. I met some fifty or sixty Russians in very high spirits. When they learned my name and my Moscow origin, I became popular at once and an old man, who called himself the Dean of the Russian Colony, exclaimed that at last there was a true Russian in the Embassy. As always at Russian parties food and drink were most important. The man who regarded himself as the Dean put me next to him and produced a bottle of wine from under his chair, saying that this wine was only for the two of us, because the rest did not understand the difference between Mouton Rothschild and ordinary red wine. In order not to disappoint him, I pretended to be a great connoisseur and made the appropriate noises while drinking this truly excellent wine. The ordinary wine was apparently quite sufficient for the rest of the party, for soon everybody became very gay and noisy. It was really a bit of Russia transplanted to London.

In the middle of the dinner the old man stood up to make a speech. For a minute he stood still, then roared: "Ivan has awakened!" At first nobody knew what he meant, but it soon became clear that he was speaking of the coming Revolution in Russia, the first rumors of which had begun to appear in the English press. The more he spoke the fiercer he became, attacking especially the Russian bureaucracy. He said that all bureaucrats must be hanged and, not satisfied with this, added that before they were hanged, their faces must serve as spittoons for the rest of the population. He finished his speech with a toast in my honor. I was horrified, because I was the only so-called bureaucrat at the party and the idea of becoming a spittoon did not appeal to me. I thanked the speaker for his toast, but said that it seemed to me a contradiction first to invite everybody to spit in my face, then to drink to my health. I spoke in defense of the Russian bureaucracy, pointing out that just as their firms could not exist without clerks so a state could not exist without bureaucrats. I expressed the fear that by preaching the annihilation of the bureaucracy, they preached the destruction of order, and in so doing worked against their own interests, for without order they would not be able to continue their businesses. As I was the last speaker everybody agreed with me, and the old man kissed me. Russian dances and singing followed, somebody played the violin very badly, and the old man produced a second bottle of Mouton Rothschild.

I could leave the party only after midnight, and walked all the way to my place. It was cold and began to snow. A policeman looked at me suspiciously, but seeing my silk hat and white scarf decided that I was a harmless fellow returning from a gay party, asked me good-humoredly if I had had a good time, and wished me good night. I thought how strange my compatriots were. Our country was in the midst of a dangerous crisis and was suffering defeat after defeat, yet instead of being depressed, they showed such joy at the first sign of possible disorders that their sympathies seemed to lie more with the Japanese than with their own people. I could have understood such an attitude on the part of revolutionists whose hatred of the Russian government was stronger than love of country, but these were Russian merchants, who should have been the most conservative element in Russia, for their ability to make money, indeed their whole existence, depended on stable government. How right are those who say that in every Russian there lurks a potential anarchist! It is for this reason that the revolutionists had such an easy task in Russia.

❖❖❖

Rumors of the outbreak of disorders in Russia in the wake of military defeats began to appear more frequently in the newspapers. The Ambassador, who returned from St. Petersburg after Christmas, was very pessimistic. He did not believe in a turn of fortune on the front, and thought that internal disorders were on the increase. It seemed that the revolutionists—at that time people did not know about the

Bolsheviks and did not differentiate between diverse radical elements, grouping them all together as revolutionists—thought the time ripe for an open struggle with the government, weakened as it must be by the unsuccessful war. But no one realized how serious the situation really was. The War was far away, censorship withheld news about the true situation, airplanes which in later years were to bring war close to everybody did not exist, and the feverish activity of the revolutionists was as yet underground, so that the inhabitants of St. Petersburg could close their eyes to the mounting dangers and continue their gay life.

In London we were better informed by the local newspapers, who in their sympathy for the Japanese tended to exaggerate our misfortunes, but the surrounding life with all its pleasures, from which the Embassy could not keep aloof, to a certain extent made us too forget the seriousness of the situation.

The London of Edward VII was the most brilliant capital in Europe. So long did Edward have to wait for the throne that it was not astonishing, especially after the last years of Queen Victoria's reign, to see a general change in the social life of England, as Edward surrounded himself with people who could help him make life interesting and brilliant. King Edward had not played any political part during the reign of Queen Victoria, who was very jealous of her power, but he proved to be a very astute diplomat and a great help to his ministers; he gave a personal touch to the policy of England. He had the great gift of attracting people and of saying the right thing in the right place. Because of the personal touch, the personalities of the foreign representatives were of great importance. An ambassador who could not adapt himself to this personal diplomacy and clung to more formal official relations with the English sovereign was at an obvious disadvantage in his work. From this standpoint Russia was fortunate to have Count Benckendorff.

It is difficult to give an objective appraisal of Count Benckendorff because of the many defects he had in the eyes of an average Russian. First of all, he could scarcely speak Russian. This sounds rather absurd—a Russian ambassador who could not speak Russian—but he came from one of the Baltic provinces and was a descendant from the mayor of Riga at the time the town was taken by Peter the Great and a continuous line of faithful servants of the Imperial Russian Court.

His great-uncle [Aleksandr Khristoforovich],[7] Chief of Police during
the reign of Nicholas I, had received the title of count for his loyal
service; his marriage to an Austrian lady of high birth had placed the
Benckendorffs in the first rank among the European aristocracy. The
Ambassador had received his education abroad and as the Russian
language was not necessary for Russian diplomacy at that time, all
correspondence being conducted in French, they had forgotten to
teach him Russian.

The fact that Benckendorff did not speak any Russian did not prevent him from having a clear grasp of the needs of Russia and being
a first-rate diplomat. But undoubtedly he felt much more at home in
foreign countries than in Russia. As our great wit Sviatopolk-Mirskii
used to say, abroad Count Benckendorff was considered a perfect gentleman and in every restaurant he would be trusted to the limit of five
pounds, but once he crossed the frontier into Russia, no one would
take him seriously with his foreign looks and monocle, and he would
not be able to get credit in any restaurant. Russians did not like well-
dressed people and especially resented monocles. I remember when
my brother became a professor, his colleagues used to say, "what a
pity that he is always so well dressed, nobody will think him a serious
man." Every country has its peculiarities. For all these faults, which
were not of his own making, our Ambassador was one of the greatest
gentlemen I have ever met. He was a real grand seigneur, a type
which has quite disappeared from this rough world. He never low-
ered himself to intrigue, so dear to the Russian bureaucrat. His relations with his staff were always excellent and I soon grew greatly
attached to him. He was highly respected among the English ruling
classes and many diplomats tried to imitate him. Seeing his elegant
figure with his gardenia boutonnière at the great gatherings, speaking
and laughing with the King or the Prime Minister, I felt proud that
the representative of my country occupied such a position in England,
then without doubt the greatest and most enlightened country in the
world. His prestige rubbed off on us and my dream of a brilliant and
interesting life became a reality during my four years in London.

Count Benckendorff was married to a very intelligent lady. Born
the Countess Shuvalov, she belonged to one of the best families in
Russia, one of her ancestors being the founder of the first university

[7] The manuscript mistakenly states "father."

in Moscow. Considered one of the most clever women in London society, she attracted to the Russian Embassy many interesting and bright persons outside the usual diplomatic circle. Sviatopolk-Mirskii used to say that Countess Benckendorff was like an aunt of Wagner who never admitted the talent of her nephew and was quite depressed when the world hailed him as a genius; in order not to make a similar mistake she started to see genius in every clever man. Whenever the Countess Benckendorff heard people speak about the cleverness of some young statesman or writer, she wanted to meet him. Thanks to that we met quite a few intelligent personalities at our Embassy; some shone only for a short time and soon disappeared not to return, but others, such as Winston Churchill or the writer Maurice Baring, became quite prominent and were regular visitors in the salons of Countess Benckendorff. We of the Embassy had a standing invitation to lunch at the Embassy; we only had to inform the butler in the morning and join the family. The same rule applied to the English friends of the Countess and thus our luncheons were often extremely interesting and informative.

During the first few weeks I felt shy in my new surroundings and probably shocked my colleagues by not thinking or acting like a typical diplomat, but gradually I adapted. Realizing that it would be fatal for me to imitate the other members of the Embassy in their gay flirtations and social life, their gambling and other pleasures that constituted the usual life of young diplomats in a brilliant capital—I felt that in such a life I would always be left behind, and I did not like being left behind—I chose a life in which I would not meet any competition from my colleagues. I decided to be a working diplomat, a rare bird at the time. I was always first in the chancery, tried to do most of the work, and soon became the most essential member of the Embassy. This could have earned me enemies had my colleagues not been so busy outside or had I become arrogant. As things stood, I think everybody was only too glad to know that I was always at the chancery and their presence was not required. Tired of restaurant meals, I lunched at the Embassy regularly; thus I saw a lot of the Benckendorffs, indeed became part of their daily existence. Life has taught me that if you do not hide your sympathies for people and at the same time do not annoy them with demonstrations thereof, they will treat you in the same simple and natural way. Such were my relations with the Benckendorffs, and my life in London, of which I had been so afraid at the beginning, became very agreeable.

As I saw much of the Ambassador, I soon had an idea of his policy. Little things did not interest him, and I remember how annoyed he was by the endless telegrams about the international control over Crete, one of the most important diplomatic questions of the day. Greece dreamed of annexing the island. The great powers were quite willing to help Greece, but did not want to irritate the Ottoman Empire to which the island belonged and therefore invented a very artificial solution: the island was to be administered by Greece, its sovereignty remaining in Turkish hands. As is always the case with such artificial solutions, it did not satisfy anybody. Greece continued to support popular uprisings against the Turks, the famous Greek statesman [Eleutherios] Venizelos playing a very active role, but the powers insisted on the maintenance of Turkish sovereignty. As a result both Greece and the Ottoman Empire were against the powers, and the amount of money spent on telegrams would have sufficed to buy the whole island. Disgusted, Benckendorff used to say: "Let them settle the question among themselves. They will do it much better than all those international commissions." And really, when Europe lost interest in the once famous Cretan question, the matter was settled quite easily, the Ottoman Empire ceding the island to Greece.

The chief consideration of the Embassy at the time of my arrival in London was, of course, the Russo-Japanese War, which had entered in its second year without any hope of settlement. Our defeats continued, due to our utter unpreparedness, bad luck, and miscalculations. The War became increasingly unpopular and the hand of the revolutionists was seen everywhere. We were very depressed at the Embassy. Benckendorff considered this War to have been the greatest stupidity that Russia could have done; he was sure that a long war would precipitate an internal upheaval, but did not see any way of stopping it. To our Ambassador the whole thing seemed especially tragic, because in spite of his German origin, he was fully convinced that Russia's real danger lay not from Japan but from Germany. He dreamed of bringing about an understanding between Russia and England. From this point of view, the Russo-Japanese War not only weakened Russia for the future struggle with Germany, but rendered it difficult for her to reach an understanding with England, because of her alliance with Japan; the whole situation was desperate. The attitude of the English Foreign Office toward Benckendorff was not only correct but cordial throughout the War. This made it possible to avoid English intervention on behalf of Japan at the time of the Dogger Bank incident. The King too was friendly to Benckendorff and as his anxiety about the activity of the German Emperor increased, he hinted that it would be desirable after the War to take steps toward a Russo-English understanding. In St. Petersburg, where there was always the tendency to attribute all Russian misfortunes to English intrigue, such a proposition was not acceptable; and in answer to Benckendorff's telegram concerning his conversation with the King, the government stated that no such understanding was necessary.

Here I must tell about a mistake I made in addressing a telegram that could have cost Count Benckendorff his position, might have retarded the realization of his dream of a Russo-English understanding, and could have put a stop to my whole career. We received a telegram from St. Petersburg, asking us to take steps against the conversion of a Japanese loan in England. Benckendorff, who discovered that this conversion was only a formality and would not give the Japanese any additional money, sought the opinion of our ambassador in Paris before approaching the Foreign Office, telegraphing his own feeling that any step in this matter would not be tactful. The ciphering of telegrams was usually done by two people. In this case I did the whole thing myself. As most of the telegrams went to St. Petersburg, I mechanically addressed the telegram to the Foreign Office instead of to Paris and the Minister discovered that the two ambassadors were plotting against his instructions. He began by sending Benckendorff a very sarcastic telegram in which he said that he did not understand his wire, which had probably been intended for somebody else. Subsequent telegrams became increasingly disagreeable and one telegram even implied that the Ambassador might be recalled. I was in a terrible state, would not join the Benckendorffs for lunch and was telling everybody that if the Ambassador were dismissed there would be nothing left for me to do but to commit suicide. Prince Sviatopolk-Mirskii tried to console me, saying that Benckendorff was too important a personage to be dismissed, and that at worst he would be transferred to Madrid. When I exclaimed that then I would ask to be transferred to Spain too, Sviatopolk-Mirskii retorted that this would be rather stupid, for the Ambassador would hardly want to see before him always the cause of his downfall. I spent some truly harrowing days, but Benckendorff himself did not seem to mind the whole thing very much. Once when I brought him a disagreeable telegram from St. Petersburg, rejecting his proposal to start negotiating with England, he made one of his characteristic hand gestures and said that it was only a cloud that would pass. After some time, to my great relief, the cloud did pass, but I was too ashamed to reappear at the luncheons until the Countess called me a fool and said that I surely did not expect her to come to the chancery to invite me. Thus the incident ended, and my position in the Embassy was restored.

The news from St. Petersburg was getting worse and worse. We read about the march of the workers to the Winter Palace with a petition to the Emperor and how the police fired into the peaceful crowd. Poor Nicholas, he was the worst man to be at the helm of the state during a serious crisis. One day he listened to one advice, another day to an opposite one. Reforms were promised, then retracted, and everything that was done only added to the chaos and benefitted the revolutionists.

At our luncheons in the Embassy we had endless discussions about the situation in Russia. Counsellor Sazonov favored strong measures and wanted all agitators hung; Poklevskii was more liberal; Sviatopolk-Mirskii with his usual cynicism maintained that everything would turn out for the worse. I was for a middle course: elimination of the agitators and reforms for the people. I think the most liberal of us was the Ambassador, but he was careful in expressing his opinions and several times, when we went too far in our discussion, told us to stop, lest he express an opinion which he as a representative of the Emperor had no right to voice. This usually terminated our discussions, which like most discussions among Russians were quite useless and could not in any way change the course of events.

There were too many distractions to allow us to concentrate on events in Russia. The London season was approaching and the court and the English aristocracy were preparing to astound the world with their display of luxury. I shall never forget the first reception at the court at which all the diplomats had to be present. It was gorgeous. The fat King, looking like Henry VIII, was seated on the throne with Queen Alexandra, who was covered with diamonds. Thanks to her enameled face she seemed as young and beautiful as when she had come from Denmark as a young girl to marry the Prince of Wales. The orchestra was playing old English airs. Men in resplendent uniforms and ladies in magnificent dresses passed and curtsied before the throne. From the standpoint of beauty there is much to say in favor of monarchy.

For us the feast proved to be a sad one, the first rumors of the destruction of our fleet in Tsushima Strait reaching our ears. There was nothing in the newspapers as yet. In the palace, waiting to be received by the King, we stood in one corner, the Japanese in another; we did not greet each other; the atmosphere was heavy. It was evident that something had happened, the neutral diplomats moving from our group to the Japanese to find out the news. We did not know anything, but the Japanese Ambassador, as we learned later, had already received a telegram with full details about the destruction of the Russian fleet. Nonetheless, apparently not wishing to spoil the general rejoicing, in answer to the query if rumors of a new Japanese victory were true and congratulations in order, he replied that he had heard something but that the rumor was probably exaggerated. In those days the Japanese were most gentlemanly foes. As the rumors became more persistent, however, we left the palace.

Reception followed reception, one more splendid than the other. I remember a reception at the Lansdowne House—magnificent rooms with rows of statues, palm trees, crowds of guests, ladies in tiaras—Prince Sviatopolk-Mirskii pointing out to me the most prominent figures, among them the Duchess of Marlborough, née Vanderbilt, with strings and strings of pearls. But, to my secret pride, the chief guest was our Countess Benckendorff, wearing the famous Shuvalov pearls, accompanied by the host, the Marquis of Lansdowne [Henry Charles Keith Petty-Fitzmaurice], at that time the Foreign Secretary. All this splendor is now gone; most of the people are dead, and the house has passed into the hands of a department store owner. *Sic transit gloria mundi.* Another reception, repeated every season, was given at the Stafford House, the resplendent Duchess of Sutherland, an American by birth, standing on the steps of a marble staircase with a few lilies in her hand, an insignificant-looking husband at her side, welcoming her guests as they passed upstairs. When I asked Sviatopolk-Mirskii from where the money for the music, the beautiful pictures, diamonds, pearls, and other precious stones came, he replied that for centuries England had robbed the whole world, spending the proceeds in London. Cruel as this may have sounded, there was some truth in it.

During the reign of Queen Victoria the English had displayed their greatest enterprising energy, making material progress and personal fortunes, acquiring new colonies and sending the young generation there to toil and return with considerable wealth to be spent in England. Edward VII, who ascended the throne upon Victoria's death, was already an old man [sixty years of age] and, being by nature a lover of life and its pleasures, made a much greater display of the position England had acquired during the reign of his mother. English society followed its sovereign. London became the world's capital and England openly dictated its policy to Europe. This was resented in several countries, notably in Germany, whose young and foolish monarch William II envied England's position and thought that his uncle, the King of England, wanted to patronize him. A certain strain developed between England and Germany. I am sure that England did everything to diminish it, but there was too much of the personal touch of its capricious monarch in the policy of Germany to respond to the advances of England, and English diplomacy, mindful of the possible consequences, abandoned the country's splendid isolation and sought friends in France and Russia.

France had never ceased to fear Germany and met England half way, but Russia, unable to forget the role of England in the Russo-Japanese War, which was still in progress, turned its back on English overtures, and only our Ambassador in London maintained the hope that once the War in the Far East was over Russia would turn toward England. All these behind-the-scenes developments continued over a long period of time. The Kaiser was undecided, France openly sought an alliance, while Russia was sulking. I remember the visits to England of the French President [Clément Armand] Fallières and the Emperor of Germany. What a difference between the old Fallières, tired by all the court festivities, nearly asleep at the ball in Buckingham Palace, with [Theophile] Delcassé, his Minister of Foreign Affairs actively trying to tie England closer to France than the English wanted, and William II, who sought to charm everybody except Count Benckendorff, whom he ignored, and riding to the city for the traditional luncheon with the Lord Mayor assumed the equestrian pose of the future conqueror of England. All this was extremely interesting, especially for me, at the first stage of my diplomatic career.

I listened with great attention to the opinions expressed at our Embassy luncheons by Count Benckendorff, and had to modify several principles which underlay Russian diplomacy. While it was generally stipulated that Germany was our traditional friend and England our traditional enemy, Count Benckendorff, who had a profound knowledge of European history, pointed out that in diplomacy there cannot be any traditional friends or enemies. It is a fundamental rule that every country thinks only of its own interests; there is no altruism in diplomacy. Whenever a country tries to be unselfish, as was often the case with Russia, it was duped. It was for this reason that England was called in Russia the perfidious Albion, although its "perfidy" consisted merely in pursuing a policy which would serve its interests at the time: when Russia was advancing in Central Asia toward India, England deemed it in its interest to stop the Russian advance, and when it saw in Japan's hostility toward Russia a means of doing that, it supported Japan in its war with Russia, but when danger threatened from Germany, the same England worked toward friendship with Russia. Once England had made up its mind and an agreement was signed, however, England remained true to the agreement; and when the agreement had outlived its usefulness tried to find an honorable way out. There may have been a certain unscrupulousness on the part of England in thus pursuing its interests, but to call it "perfidy" was not correct. Often, as was the case with the Russo-Japanese War, English policy turned out to have been shortsighted, because it helped to make Japan a great power which ultimately turned against England herself, but the diplomat who can truly look into the future has yet to be born. All that is very cynical and sad, but human relations are full of cynicism and sadness. The struggle of life goes on, and he who wishes to succeed must adapt himself to it.

❖❖❖

If such depressing thoughts came to my head, they were greatly mollified by my pleasant surroundings. How could I dwell on the sad side of life, when all my time was occupied by work in which I could see the shaping of human destiny and by evenings of wonderful concerts and brilliant crowds? In my day the London opera was magnificent. Such singers as [Enrico] Caruso, [Nellie] Melba, and [Luisa] Tetrazzini were at their best; and the Wagnerian cycle was given as I have never heard it since.

Soon the English friend with whom I had lived in St. Petersburg returned to England and obtained a good position as a curate in the country near Henley on Thames. Whenever I wanted a peaceful weekend I went to see him. He lived with his old mother and a sister. His charming house and flower-filled garden were a picture of English country life—comfortable, decent, and cozy. In the morning, when he was busy in his small church, I wandered through the beautiful woods, where deer roamed in perfect freedom. What a happy country! In Russia you could not see anything like that. The dimensions were too large, the landscape was never cozy, and the people were gloomy. There was none of the appearance of general contentment and happiness. In the evenings we sat before the fireplace and reminisced about our life in St. Petersburg.

I also liked to visit Oxford, where I knew a liberal professor from Moscow University [Sir Paul Vinogradoff] who, unable to stand all the restrictions that had been introduced as a result of the perpetual student agitations, had accepted an invitation by Oxford University to lecture on the history of the British Constitution. He was perfectly happy in the cultural atmosphere of Oxford, and took me to dine at his college. The sight of the healthy undergraduates, the general discipline, and the beauty of traditional ceremonies made me envious, and I wondered whether the day would ever come when our young people would have the same good time instead of the agitation, strikes, and hysteria that poisoned the best years of our lives.

Mail from Russia revealed that internal conditions were becoming more and more dangerous. Everybody was tired of the War, the purpose of which no one could understand. After the destruction of the Russian fleet, which had been dispatched as a last resort, nobody expected a turn in fortune. Even in conservative circles there was talk that a defeat could be a blessing in disguise, because experience had taught that there were less chances for reform after a successful war than after a defeat, and cited the times of Alexander II who had ascended the throne after the disastrous Crimean campaign as an example. Such a point of view seemed to me extremely narrow, since I felt that for a revolution to be beneficial in Russia it must come from above; every revolution from below would only bring disaster. But it was Russia's great misfortune that at the most critical moment of her history there stood at the helm of the state a man incapable of starting any big movement beneficial to Russia, a man who constantly changed his mind and did not trust anybody except his wife. She, though stronger than her husband, was not quite normal and looked on Russia's future from a strange, mystical point of view.

Thus problems piled up and as early as 1905, Russia found herself with a war that nobody desired, mounting revolutionary activity on one hand and not a single statesman at the head of the government on the other. Most thinking people understood that no energetic measures against the approaching Revolution could be taken as long as the War continued, but nobody could suggest how to end the conflict, for after all those victories Japanese demands were likely to be far greater than anything the Russians could accept, and the War would have to go on. A new commander-in-chief was appointed and gave assurances that after the winter respite he would be able to stage an advance. There were signs that Japan was nearing exhaustion and these assurances, as well as the confidence of the Emperor that everything would turn out all right, might have been justified had the Russian people been more patriotic and had the specter of revolution not been knocking louder and louder. The situation was saved by the American President [Theodore] Roosevelt, who offered his good offices as a mediator. Japan, which at that time looked to the United States for help in the development of the fruits of its victories, could not refuse, neither could Russia in view of its internal problems, though Nicholas, who never truly comprehended the real state of affairs, did so with great reluctance.

Once the War was over, Russia could concentrate its efforts against the revolutionists. Most troops remained as yet faithful and the revolutionary movement was crushed. The events of 1905 may be regarded as a rehearsal for the Revolution of 1917. The rehearsal was unsuccessful and the revolutionists retired to their lairs in foreign countries. The sentences imposed by the tribunal on those who did not succeed in fleeing abroad show how lenient the old authorities were toward their enemies. No one was executed, most of the accused were exiled to Siberia, whence many were able to escape. Among them there were persons who were to figure prominently in the Revolution of

1917. How much horror could have been avoided had these people been liquidated in 1905, when their danger to the state was obvious. In this respect the Bolsheviks were far more clever: they promptly eliminated their enemies. If, as it appears, success in revolution demands the abandonment of all scruples, the same rule must apply to the defense of the existing order against such a revolution.

The selection of a representative to negotiate peace terms with the Japanese was not an easy matter. Witte, the former Minister of Finance, would have been the most logical choice, but Nicholas did not like him, for Witte was clever and independent and the Emperor feared such people. Only after two other functionaries declined the position did the Emperor nominate Witte, stipulating that Russia would cede no part of territory and pay no reparations. Impossible as it seemed to end the War under the circumstances, Witte displayed such ingenuity in the negotiations that gradually all initiative as well as sympathy passed from the Japanese to the Russian side, and the Imperial stipulations were modified only to the extent of ceding half of Sakhalin.[8] Otherwise Russia came out of the War as if she had not been seriously defeated. On his way back from Japan Witte stopped in Paris and arranged for a loan to cover the losses incurred during the War. Thus he returned to Russia with peace and money. But it is difficult to please the Russians. Though the Emperor granted Witte the title of count, he never forgave him the cession of part of Sakhalin, and Witte did not get the triumphal welcome he so amply deserved.

The struggle with the revolutionaries continued. Though the danger passed, it was clear that something must be done to satisfy the population in order to prevent the more moderate elements from turning toward the left. Some sort of representation had been clearly held out, but as always happens, once the danger had passed, the reactionaries began to lift their heads. They tried to persuade the Emperor that absolutism was the cornerstone of Russia and that he must hand down to his son untouched the same absolutism he had inherited from his father. These arguments were dear to the Emperor and especially to the Empress, who began to take more and more interest in politics. But she knew little about Russia, did not like the Russian society out-

[8] The southern half, which had been acquired from Japan in 1875 in exchange for the northern Kuril Islands.

side her narrow circle, and lived under the delusion that somewhere there existed an unspoiled Russian people which adored the Emperor and did not want any diminution of his power. This misconception, which was to prove fatal when the real Revolution came, led her to persuade the Emperor that his ministers wanted to deceive him when they insisted a constitution was necessary. Instead of assuming leadership in instituting the necessary reforms, Nicholas only looked for loopholes in the proposed changes to preserve his rights.

The whole reform question was in a muddle. In addition to Count Witte, who as Prime Minister did the major work in outlining the reforms, several other high bureaucrats presented plans to the Emperor. Not wishing to offend these persons Nicholas encouraged them, and in the end Witte himself did not know how far the Emperor was prepared to go. When he consulted with leaders of the liberal movement, he found no less confusion and no more practical statesmanship. As a result the October Manifesto was full of grand phrases and high-sounding promises which meant different things to different people. The liberals saw in it the granting of a constitution, the conservatives the preservation of the absolute rights of the throne. But the longing for reforms was so great that the Manifesto was received with popular jubilation. Everything seemed to be forgiven to the Emperor. Had Nicholas sincerely followed the new path, he could have become one of the most popular monarchs. Alas, human character cannot be changed.

When the text of the Manifesto was received in London and we were ready to join the chorus of believers that at last Russia had a real constitution, Count Benckendorff became furious and exclaimed that the Manifesto was the most stupid thing the State could have done, for unlike a constitution with articles clearly defining the rights of the people and of the monarch, it consisted of vague promises which would be easy to modify or ignore. History was to prove the Ambassador's pessimistic view of the October Manifesto well founded. But enough of that; I was abroad during most of this struggle between the Crown and the people and cannot add anything new to what competent eye-witnesses have already written.

The concluding of peace was welcomed by everybody in London. Many prominent people came to congratulate the Embassy. The press was interested in the future of Russo-Japanese relations. One correspondent wanted to know who would first call on whom after the conclusion of peace, the Russian Ambassador on the Japanese Minister or vice versa. When I answered that the question was nonsensical because a Minister always called first on an Ambassador, he tried to argue that the Japanese had won the War, but I stopped him by pointing out that when a war is ended by mediation there is no question of conquerors or vanquished. All this conversation found its way into the newspapers. I do not know if the Japanese were pleased, but Baron Hayashi [Tadasu] called first.

When we received a cheque for seven million pounds for transmittal to the Japanese Legation in payment for the maintenance of our prisoners of war a crowd of photographers came to the Embassy asking permission to photograph the cheque for such a large sum. As it was not pleasant to advertise that such a large number of Russians had been captured, I refused, saying that as it was made out to the Japanese Minister it already belonged to him and he alone could decide whether a photograph thereof should appear in the press. The photographers hastened to the Japanese Legation, whither the cheque was taken shortly, and it was duly reproduced in all the illustrated papers. With the exchange of visits between the representatives of Russia and Japan, the conflict became a thing of the past.

❖❖❖

The War over, our Embassy plunged into the gaieties of the London season. I remember an Embassy ball which the King and half a dozen other royal personages attended. A modest Russian doctor who came to London as a member of the Red Cross conference was invited to the ball and when I showed him during supper the table at which the King of England, the King of Spain, and other royal persons sat, he did not want to believe me. "Is it possible," he wondered, "that this fat old man who eats and drinks with such pleasure is the King of the mighty British Empire?" He seriously believed that kings never left their thrones, always wore a crown, and ate from golden plates. He was visibly disappointed. I recall also a small dinner party for the King, who had declared that in his royal functions he met enough strangers and preferred to be entertained at small parties, surrounded by his friends. One of the main guests at such parties was Mrs. George Keppel, a beautiful and clever intimate of the King, treated by everyone, even a crowd when she appeared in public with the King, with certain tenderness. Other guests included the Portuguese Minister Soveral, whose witty remarks amused the King, the Austrian Ambassador Count Mensdorff [Count Albert von Mensdorff-Pouilly-Dietrichstein], the greatest snob one could imagine, who gave excellent dinners and had volumes and volumes of books showing how to select and place guests, books that we constantly borrowed, the Duchess of Manchester, a fat old lady from Cuba who liked to help deserving young men enter society, our own Ambassador and Poklevskii, plus several others whose names I have forgotten.

At the end of the season society moved for a week of yacht racing to the Isle of Wight, where Poklevskii usually rented a house and invited all the King's friends. Ostensibly the affair was given by the Duchess of Manchester, but actually Poklevskii bore the expenses. The King lived on his yacht, but would come to the house to visit his friends. Poklevskii grumbled about the cost, but being a snob was flattered and paid.

Once I was ordered to take some dispatches, which had arrived at the Embassy, to Benckendorff in Cowes. I found the whole crowd at dinner, the ladies covered with diamonds, the men in formal wear, eating the most refined food and drinking champagne, and trying to be witty. I was put up for the night in a small garret under the staircase. Poklevskii impressed upon me that the room of Mrs. Keppel, who slept very badly, was next door and that I must be quiet and not snore, lest she be in a bad mood the next day. This would affect the whole party, and the King was coming in the afternoon to play croquet. I tried to be as quiet as a mouse.

The following morning the whole party was invited aboard the recently constructed *Dreadnought*, the pride of the British fleet, to watch its gunnery practice. The King was present and the *Dreadnought* passed rows and rows of warships, their crews lined up in review to greet the King. Then we went far out to sea. The weather was beautiful, the noise of the booming guns deafening. It was all very impressive; you could feel the might of the British fleet. A great experience.

In the afternoon we sat in the garden. The King insisted on a game of croquet. Cowed by the array of grandees, I asked the Countess Benckendorff to take me under her protection. During the game there suddenly appeared on the lawn a group of people all dressed in black.

Everybody stood up and the King with great deference saluted the old lady who headed the solemn procession. "The Empress Eugénie, widow of Napoleon III," Countess Benckendorff whispered, and I stared with wide-open eyes on this bit of history. But I was glad to return to London. All these grandees were very tiring.

It is difficult not to say the wrong thing in the presence of royalty. Nearly every spring our Empress Dowager Maria Feodorovna, the widow of Alexander III, came to London to visit her sister, the Queen of England. We had to be at the station to meet her. The King, the Queen, and several ministers were also present. The whole group was elegant in frock coats and silk hats. The Russian guests who arrived on the train looked as if they had come from the North Pole. The Empress Dowager in an old-fashioned fur coat, the lady-in-waiting in a prehistoric coat, rushing about and looking for the Empress Dowager's dog, which had disappeared at the last moment—it was so typically Russian that it reminded me of my dear Moscow. And to say that royalty was not human!

The day after the arrival of the Empress Dowager the King usually left for Biarritz, the two sisters remaining in London enjoying themselves immensely. Once they came to lunch at the Embassy. After lunch we stood in a circle and the Empress Dowager and the Queen passed from one of us to another with a few gracious words for everybody. When the Empress Dowager approached me, she said that she remembered seeing me in Copenhagen. As this was quite impossible, since I had never been to Copenhagen, I politely pointed out that she was mistaken. She insisted, and when I said that I had never been in Copenhagen, she became angry and moved on to the next person. When the two sisters had left, I was told that it had been tactless on my part to contradict the Empress Dowager, that I must be terribly conceited to imagine that she was really interested in whether or not she had met me in Copenhagen, that when she had approached me it had simply been the turn for the question about Copenhagen. I should have felt flattered, ought to have agreed at once that our last meeting took place in Copenhagen. In such an artificial atmosphere did royalty live. But enough of this light side of my London life; it was interesting and amusing but not very important.

I was much more interested in the mysteries of English politics. In my desire to monopolize the greater part of chancery work, I succeeded in being assigned even the writing of reports on current non-political affairs. It meant reading a number of newspapers and frequently visiting Parliament. Those were very interesting times. After a long period of administration by the Conservative party, the Liberal party was voted into power by an enormous majority and commenced a series of great reforms, which at the time were considered so radical that the government was accused of Socialist tendencies. Lively parliamentary debates ensued, and I spent many hours in the visitors' gallery listening to the speeches. All the orators of the day passed before my eyes. My boundless admiration for the parliamentary regime in England was reflected in my reports, which the Ambassador usually signed without reading. When Poklevskii saw my report on the new education bill, he was horrified and told me that I was giving the Ambassador the reputation of a radical, hardly designed to please the Ministry. Henceforth he strictly censored all my reports.

✤✤✤

My activity brought me in touch with a relic of history: Mrs. Olga Novikov, who had played an important political role at the time of [William Ewart] Gladstone. She had come to London some forty years ago at the time of the Russo-Turkish War and had begun strong propaganda in favor of Russian liberation of the Slavic peoples from the Turkish yoke. Announcing that she would be at home every evening after dinner, she attracted to her place many people. It became fashionable to meet at Mrs. Novikov's and an excuse to escape from a dull party soon after dinner. It was said that Gladstone, when he wanted to meet somebody without attracting attention, would make the appointment at Mrs. Novikov's tea. She was brilliant and patriotic and like most Russians talked well. At that time the struggle between the Liberals and the Conservatives was concentrated on the fight between Gladstone and [the Earl of] Beaconsfield [Benjamin Disraeli]. The former favored the liberation of the Slavs, the latter supported the Turks. Gladstone got his arguments from Mrs. Novikov and once in Parliament, answering Gladstone, Beaconsfield even remarked ironically that it was known that the arguments of his honorable opponent came from the drawing room of a certain lady who could be called "a member for Russia." This remark made Mrs. Novikov quite famous.

[125]

When I knew her she was very old and lived in the past. She tried to continue her tea parties, but hardly anyone would come. She was full of recollections of her friendship with Gladstone. I remember her story of how she had once passed with Gladstone near the monument honoring the soldiers who had fallen in the Crimea. Pointing to the word "Crimea" which was inscribed on the monument, Gladstone had told her that the "a" ought to be scratched off. When the Liberals came back to power with a huge majority, Mrs. Novikov announced that she would give a dinner party with only two guests, the Prime Minister [Sir Henry] Campbell-Bannerman and the Russian Ambassador. To everybody's astonishment the Prime Minister accepted the invitation and Mrs. Novikov was quite excited that the question of Russo-English[9] friendship would be settled at her dinner. But as Benckendorff told me afterwards, it was a ghastly affair. Mr. Campbell-Bannerman had a cold and hardly could speak. Mrs. Novikov talked only about Gladstone. The food and the room were cold. Campbell-Bannerman left soon after dinner, his health became worse, and he died shortly. Such was the last appearance in the political arena of poor Mrs. Novikov. It is dreadful to outlive one's fame. When Viscount [John] Morley was writing his biography of Gladstone, Olga Novikov insisted that he peruse Gladstone's letters to her, for without them Gladstone's biography could not be complete. Benckendorff took these letters to Morley, but the latter said that most of the correspondence consisted of replies to her invitations and that the great friendship between Mrs. Novikov and Gladstone was a myth.

The Liberal party program included an understanding with Russia, and Mr. Asquith, who succeeded the late Campbell-Bannerman as head of the Liberal party and Prime Minister, had several conversations with our Ambassador on this matter, but while he reported these conversations to St. Petersburg, he always received the same answer—the matter could wait. Strong influences worked against such an understanding. Once the Foreign Office sent us copies of secret documents dispatched by our Ambassador in Constantinople—copies of telegrams from the Turkish Ambassador in London regarding his conversations with Sir Edward Grey, the British Foreign Secretary—showing that England was trying to persuade the Turkish government

[9] The manuscript states Russo-Japanese friendship, but Russo-English friendship is probably meant. See mention of Liberal party program in next paragraph.

to invite an English military commission to aid the Turks in the forti-
fication of the Dardanelles against Russia, our Minister adding sarcastically that it was strange that the British government offered us its
friendship at the same time that it tried to help the Turks fortify the
Straits against us. Benckendorff considered the whole thing incredible,
and suspected that the documents were forgeries. He decided to take
the bull by the horns, went with the documents to the Foreign Secretary, and asked for an explanation. Grey, a soul of honor, was horrified and denied categorically that he had had any such conversations
with the Turkish Ambassador. Indeed, he proved quite clearly that he
could not have had such conversations, because on the dates indicated
in the documents he had been out of town. He even sent us extracts
from the central post office books showing that there had been no
telegrams from the Turkish Embassy on those dates. It was found
later that our Ambassador in Constantinople had received these documents from his secret agent, a Turk who made a regular business out
of selling "secret documents" to different embassies. As the Russian
Ambassador in Constantinople belonged to the old school of Russian
diplomats who saw in everything that transpired English intrigue, he
had been only too glad to spoil the efforts of Count Benckendorff and
had paid a high price for those spurious documents. He was furious
when he learned that the documents with which he had tried to impress his own Foreign Office had been shown to that of England and
been proven false.

Meanwhile the German Emperor did not lose time. He came almost yearly for a visit to England and annoyed his uncle, King Edward, with fantastic propositions, above all to obtain equality of naval
power with England. At the same time he tried to warn our Emperor
of the duplicity of English diplomacy and to undermine the foundations of the Russo-French alliance. In one of his meetings with Nicholas II, when the latter was cruising on his yacht with his family, thinking only of having a rest from all politics, William persuaded him to
sign a document which sounded harmless but in fact discarded the
Russo-French alliance. It cost our Minister of Foreign Affairs and
Count Witte great effort to explain to Nicholas the real significance
of the document which he had signed and to have it nullified. Only
after Count Lamsdorff relinquished his post of Minister of Foreign
Affairs and after a brief interlude by Count Lobanov-Rostovskii, who

died on the train during his first journey to Vienna to remove the tension in the Balkans, was replaced by our Minister in Copenhagen, [Aleksandr Petrovich] Izvolskii, did Count Benckendorff's policy triumph.

Izvolskii was generally considered one of our most clever diplomats, but it was only after service in Copenhagen, where he constantly met members of the Russian Imperial family, that he demonstrated to our court his suitability for the post of Minister of Foreign Affairs. Before going to St. Petersburg, he came to London for an exchange of opinions with Count Benckendorff on future Russian policy. Our Embassy wit, Prince Sviatopolk-Mirskii, assured us that the chief reason for Izvolskii's visit was to learn from Benckendorff how a real diplomat and perfect gentleman must behave. Exaggerated as this may have been, it was amusing to see these two high personages trying to impress each other. At the Embassy lunches to which Izvolskii came, they would perpetually compete in saying the most clever things and showing the greatest amount of knowledge. Both wore monocles, which I have always regarded as very useful in impressing your interlocutor. When you have no ready answer, you swing the monocle in place and critically look at the talker; he at once begins to wonder if he has not said some nonsense, and you gain time to think of a suitable reply. Our Ambassador was much more clever in these tricks and usually had the last word until Izvolskii would switch to some question of higher mathematics and leave poor Benckendorff quite bewildered.

These little vanities aside, the two diplomats agreed that with the appearance of the Russian Duma with its liberal tendencies, the foreign policy of Russia must be radically changed; and the Minister-to-be declared that he would base his policy on two principles: an understanding with England and a bid for friendship with Japan. This had the full approval of Count Benckendorff, whose whole work had consisted in trying to remove all obstacles with England, as he was fully persuaded that the real enemy of Russia was Germany. Convinced that Germany under its impetuous monarch was preparing for war, Benckendorff deemed it highly dangerous to leave Russia, greatly weakened as she was after the War with Japan, allied only to France and hostile toward England. Izvolskii with his energy and position of influence apparently succeeded in persuading Nicholas of the necessity of an understanding with England, and it was a great moment when we received a telegram instructing the Ambassador to announce to Sir Edward Grey that Russia was ready to enter into negotiations with a view to removing whatever misunderstandings existed between the two countries. At the beginning the scope of the agreement was rather limited, touching only on our relations with Persia, Tibet, and Afghanistan; but as Count Benckendorff pointed out, the most important thing was to begin. Izvolskii, who wished to concentrate the execution of his new policy in his own hands, insisted that negotiations be conducted in St. Petersburg. This was a good thing for our Embassy, because with his reputation as an ardent Anglophile, Count Beckendorff would have run the risk of being accused of sacrificing Russian interests for the benefit of England. As it was, the most important Russian newspaper *Novoe Vremia* printed articles to the effect that the Russian Embassy in London was filled with foreigners: Benckendorff was a German, Poklevskii a Pole, Sevastopulo a Greek, Sviatopolk-Mirskii a Lithuanian, and though there was one Russian—Abrikossow—he was too young to help the situation. The paper was forgetting that this was bound to happen in a country which consisted of many nationalities, the more so since Russians as a rule did not like to exile themselves abroad—they liked to visit foreign countries for amusement not work—and since the Russian character was much more difficult to deal with than that of the disciplined Germans, the main reason perhaps why our diplomatic service was full of barons from the Baltic provinces.

With the change in relations between Russia and England the popularity of the Embassy increased, and we had time to see more of England. I took a trip to Scotland with my friend the curate. His small car kept breaking down and we were obliged to stop in different provincial towns. Once in Scotland, we stayed in a spot known for its fishing. The curate spent his time standing in the middle of the stream, trying to catch trout. This did not appeal to me, and I went for long walks, often losing my way among the moors. In the evenings the visitors of the inn drank whiskey and spoke about fishing, falling asleep one after another. After London with its excitements, this peaceful existence was a real pleasure. The English country is truly beautiful and I fully understand why Englishmen, scattered all over the world, dream of the day when they will have enough money to return home to the English landscape with its green, green fields, magnificent old trees, and misty contours, compared with which the luxuriant tropics seem restless and vulgar.

Often I crossed over to France to stay with my aunt. She had built a modest villa in Brittany amidst pine trees through which you saw the ocean. In the intellectual atmosphere which always surrounded her, I forgot the vanity and snobbishness of my London life; and in the company of my two clever cousins felt transported to my childhood. Once we went to see the French castles on the Loire. The whole trip was a plunge into French history, which my cousins knew so well that I felt ashamed.

When we returned to the hotel, we found a bit of London—the whole group of the King's friends, including Mrs. George Keppel and several other beauties, having dinner. It was a scene of the usual English luxury, the costly dresses, diamonds, and pearls. At the end of the season an American millionaire had invited this whole group on a motor trip to France and Italy. The proud English ladies and their friends had not been able to resist the temptation, but though he bore all expenses, in their snobbishness they had their own conversations and laughs and took scarcely any notice of him. My virtuous aunt was deeply shocked and felt that the sooner I left London the better; the temptations were too great.

❖❖❖

Back in England, I resumed the life which was so dear to me because it was my own creation. I found the Embassy perturbed by a telegram from St. Petersburg, ordering the Ambassador to insist that the English government take steps against the projected conference of Russian revolutionists in England. Sir Edward Grey explained that English tradition did not allow measures to be taken against political refugees, and that prohibition of the conference would evoke inquiries in Parliament which would put the Foreign Office in an impossible position. St. Petersburg could not understand this point of view and insisted that England must block the conference as proof of its new friendship toward Russia. Benckendorff did not know what to do, then the head of the Russian secret police abroad appeared on the scene. He was furious when he discovered that we had received instructions to do everything to prevent the projected conference. He said that at least one-third of the members of it were in his pay and that he had come especially to find out what would be decided at the conference, and now the Embassy tried to stop it. He at once telegraphed to the home office in St. Petersburg and to Benckendorff's great relief his instructions were cancelled. In speaking with the chief of the secret police, I realized the complexity of the struggle against the revolutionists, how difficult it was to trust even those in your pay. At this time I first heard the name of Lenin. Though the secret police chief called him the most clever and most dangerous revolutionist, nobody really worried about him or the other extremists. With the restoration of peace, all anxiety disappeared and at first nearly everyone seemed satisfied with the reforms. Gradually, however, disillusion set in, and the new institutions became arenas for the renewed struggle between people and government, a struggle that was directed by the revolutionaries, hiding abroad.

✠✠✠

In those days I often saw my friend Professor Vinogradov at Oxford. He was skeptical about the reforms in Russia and was so accustomed to the freedom and luxury of a professional position at an English university that he did not express any desire to return to his country. At that time my sister finished Girton College and went back to Moscow. She had been my closest friend during my stay in England. I was proud of her. She was a brilliant girl, and I always hoped that she would meet an intelligent man and have a brilliant life. But fate decided otherwise. In Moscow she fell in love with a cousin of ours [Vladimir Abrikossow], in my eyes a complete nonentity. In some ways he was like me, and I used to say that he had all my defects, without any of my virtues. When she wrote me about her feelings, I was horrified and promptly warned her that it was madness. I even wrote to my father asking him to stop this nonsense, but with his usual philosophy he replied that it was a law of nature for strong characters to be attracted to weaklings, because in their love there was always a touch of motherly feeling. Unimpressed, I continued my attempts to change my sister's mind, not sparing in my letters the object of her affections, with the result that one day I received a short note in which she pointed out that I had forgotten one thing, namely that she loved him. It was the end of our friendship.

After her marriage, my sister and her husband went to Rome. For a long time we did not hear anything about them except that he was studying early Christian art. Years later we suddenly learned that both of them had been converted to Roman Catholicism.[10] It was a great blow to our family, especially to the old generation, which considered itself a pillar of the Orthodox faith. In vain my relatives hoped that they would at least continue residing in Rome. Once they became Catholics, they were sent by the Vatican authorities back to Moscow to propagate Catholicism. During one of my leaves I saw them. They had changed greatly. My sister, who had been broadminded, now impressed on everybody that hers was the supreme truth. She was extremely kind to everyone, but with a touch of pity for all those who had not attained the happy state of knowing the real truth. Eager to enlighten anybody who wanted to be enlightened, she gathered in a year's time a considerable following, especially among hysterical ladies who did not know how to occupy themselves. Contaminated by her faith, her husband had been transformed from a young fop, constantly admiring himself in the mirror, into a Savonarola, ready to fulminate against everybody who did not share his faith. I tried to renew my friendship with my sister, but soon felt that we had nothing in common. I still loved this life, but for her it had meaning only insofar as she could help her fellow creatures find the truth. At our family gatherings she patiently listened to our conversation, but it was clear that her mind was far away and that what interested us seemed insignificant to her in comparison to the truth she had found.

Years later, in Peking, I fell ill and was put in a Catholic hospital, where Catholic nuns looked after me. When one of them died from typhoid, the other nuns to my astonishment rejoiced for her that she had joined Christ. I was so struck by this faith that once, when one of the nuns tried to convert me, I said that as long as I lived I had no intention of changing my religion, not because I considered it to be the only true one, but because my whole life, my entire childhood, was connected with it, but that if I died in this hospital I was ready to become a Catholic just to give them pleasure. She replied that what I had said obliged them to pray for my death. I commented that I thought it a strange hospital where the nurses prayed for the death

[10] According to Mr. Paul Abrikossof, Anna had originally been drawn to Roman Catholicism because the Orthodox Church opposed marriage between cousins.

of their patients, and wrote about it to my sister. She answered that the nuns were perfectly right, and that she was joining her prayers to theirs.

She and my brother-in-law went further than ordinary converts and preachers in their service to the new religion. The Catholic Church allowed in Russia that married couples without children could separate in order to don the cloth. This my sister and her husband decided to do; he was ordained a priest, she a Carmelite nun, both continuing their work in Russia. When the Revolution was approaching they rejoiced, saying that the Russian people were too self-indulgent, preoccupied with material things, and that the sufferings which accompany revolution would turn their minds toward higher things. When the Bolsheviks came to power they remained in Moscow and my sister, who at that time headed a group of Carmelite nuns, arranged that she could work in the prisons, where many Catholics were kept in most miserable conditions. When the Soviets started their war against Poland, she and other nuns were arrested on accusation of spying for the Poles. Not allowed to defend herself against this absurd charge, she was sentenced to ten years' solitary confinement in northern Siberia. The other nuns were scattered to different parts of Siberia. Her husband was more fortunate; he was ordered to leave the country. He went to Rome, and from there to Paris as clergyman of a special Catholic church for Russians. Freed from the influence of my sister, he gradually discarded Catholicism, was even seen in the bars of Paris. As for my sister, nothing was heard about her for nine years and even my eldest brother, who worked with the Soviets and became a prominent scientist, could do nothing to help her. Then suddenly she reappeared in Moscow. Relatives who saw her wrote to my aunt in Paris that she gave the impression of a saint. She did not utter any complaint, though from what she said one could judge that living conditions in a small village, buried in the snow, were terrible; she nearly died from cancer and was operated on by a local man who did not have the proper instruments. Her faith had sustained her. The Soviets allowed her to remain in Russia on condition that she desist from any sort of religious propaganda. Nothing could stop her, however. She was rearrested and put into prison, where she died.[11] Till her last moment she never thought of herself, and tried to help and support by

[11] Probably of cancer, according to Mr. Paul Abrikossoff.

her faith other unfortunate prisoners. Such was the fate of this remarkable woman.

When I was in Japan, some Catholic told me that he had read in a Catholic magazine that the Church was collecting all data on her life with a view to possibly consecrating her as a saint of the Catholic Church. How destiny plays with human life! A family of rich merchants, considered in its native town a pillar of the Orthodox Church; an ambitious girl who wants to create her own life; an English university; an unambitious marriage; a visit to Rome; the overwhelming influence of the Catholic Church; a complete mental transformation; return to Russia; taking the veil; Revolution; imprisonment; nine years of solitary confinement in Siberia; return to Russia; prison again; death and apotheosis, possibly sainthood in the Catholic Church —who could have believed all this possible, had anyone prophesied it? My sister herself would have called it the dream of a madman. But I have strayed from my story.

✦✦✦

After nearly three years in London I decided to spend my leave in Russia. It was summer, and I went straight to our estate near Moscow. I was welcomed like a man from the moon, but after a few days felt as if I had never left home. My father was busy in his laboratory trying to discover the origin of life. I tried to help him, but the mysterious question escaped me.

I found the political situation much calmer. Our intelligentsia tried to make something of the newly established Duma, but creative work did not interest them. They wanted to continue their struggle with the government, and uttered grand phrases and speeches full of pathos, but empty of substance. The experienced and sly old bureaucrats played with them like cats with mice, delighted that the Duma showed no practical sense and only compromised the idea of popular representation. Meanwhile the revolutionaries waited for another opportunity, pleased that the representatives in the Duma by their perpetual opposition to the government did some of their work for them. The new Prime Minister, Stolypin, a clever and strong man, understood the situation and tried to guide the Duma along practical lines, but this only set the Duma and the government against him. "Give me twenty years without war, and I shall save Russia from revolution," he used to say. Gradually Russia began to make progress in all areas, and the people began to trust Stolypin, when at the celebration of the three hundredth anniversary of the Romanov dynasty he was killed at the Kiev Opera House in the presence of the Emperor. His last movement was a sign of the cross in the direction of the Emperor. Yet mysteriously his assassin had been an agent of the secret police.

Returning to London, I found a new colleague, a Mr. B. [Petr Sergeevich Botkin?] at the Embassy. He too came from Moscow, and we became great friends. He was a big, healthy person with a loud voice and even louder laugh, which shocked the English. He had started his career in Washington and was full of stories about his experiences in America.

Alone at the Embassy in Washington, he had asked the Foreign Office in St. Petersburg for an assistant. He was informed that a young attaché from Brazil was being sent, and after some time a strange-looking, very tall and very thin man with the face of a corpse appeared, dressed in black, and announced that he was the man from the Legation in Brazil. Mr. B. was rather upset, because he had not expected anyone so gloomy, but the newcomer was a good worker and a good listener and B. got accustomed to him. He rented an apartment somewhere near the Embassy and would visit B. nearly every evening and silently listen to his conversation. In those days life in Washington was simple and instead of ringing the bell, the man would always shout from the street to announce his arrival. One morning B. was notified by telephone that his colleague had been found dead, shot through the head. Mr. B. rushed to his house, summoned the police, and as nothing was known about him, thought to look through his papers. As he opened his desk he received a dreadful shock, for his eyes fell on a large photograph of the deceased, lying in a coffin with three candles around it. In the evening he heard the same voice from the street, calling to be let in, but when he opened the door, there was nobody there. As this recurred night after night, B. decided, work or no work, to close the Embassy and go to Newport, a merry place where he soon forgot the whole incident.

Mr. B. came to London as the First Secretary of the Embassy. Though he could have gotten a higher post elsewhere, his wife, an American of great ambition, wanted to be presented at the English court and shine in London society. B. himself was a typical good-natured Russian who did not care very much for the merry-go-round of the London season, but for the sake of his wife, whom he adored, he willingly used all his energy to force open the doors of the most exclusive drawing rooms, and constantly annoyed Count and Countess Benckendorff with his requests for introduction to prominent members of English society. B. always complained to me that the Benckendorffs did not do enough for his wife, warning grandiloquently that a slight of himself he could easily forgive, but a slight of his wife he would remember until death. As a result his relations with the Ambassador became strained. B. openly criticized the policy of his chief and began to express Germanophile tendencies. Whenever we were preparing the diplomatic pouch with ambassadorial dispatches, he shoved in his own letter, addressed to his friend the chief of the personal chancery of the Emperor, and proudly announced that his dispatch would be in the hands of the Emperor before that of the Ambassador. When I told him that such things were not done, he repeated his favorite phrase that a slight of himself he could forgive, but a slight of his wife never. He was so possessed by the idea that the stay of his wife and himself was not a social success that once when after a dinner at the Embassy the King amiably told him that he had not seen him since the races at Ascot, he became red in the face and stuttered something incomprehensible. When I asked him afterwards why he had seemed so confused in answering the monarch, he replied that he had understood the King to say: "Your stay in London, what a fiasco!" The snobbishness which permeated the whole of English society thus could make a clever man quite foolish and ridiculous.

Soon B. was transferred to Lisbon, where he rented an old historical palace and I hope was happy among the shadows of its former grandeur. I met B. again in St. Petersburg on the eve of the First World War. With his usual good nature he assured everybody that there would be no war, that the diplomats would find some "formula" to settle the matter. When the formula was not found and war was declared, he announced that he was going back to Lisbon to bury himself in his "sarcophagus."

During my last summer in England Father came to see me while attending a sociological congress. He insisted on putting my name on the list of participants, though I had nothing to do with sociology. To please my father I listened to very dull lectures and attended different functions in honor of the members of the congress. I remember a big garden party, given by Sir John Lubbock at his country place. It was quite formal and very dull, much to the despair of the secretary of the congress, a small Frenchman, who considered himself responsible for everything connected with the congress and always tried to think of something to add more life to all the gatherings. This time, when the orchestra began to play a Strauss waltz, he rushed to the hostess, a stately elderly lady, and whirled her round and round. Everybody thought that he had gone mad, but his gaiety was so contagious that one guest after another joined him, and soon a most solemn gathering was turned into a party of old goats hopping about on the lawn.

Several times I took my father to sessions of Parliament. He was greatly impressed by the dignity and restraint, but thought that we were not cold-blooded enough to achieve such political self-discipline in Russia. He thought so particularly when I explained to him that the Liberal party, having obtained a huge majority at the last elections, had decided to deprive the privileged classes of the last remnant of power, namely the House of Lords of its right of final veto. When my father was wondering what would happen if the House of Lords refused to accept the appropriate bill, I explained that the Prime Minister could then ask the King to create enough new peers to give the Liberal party a majority in the Upper House and that most lords were such snobs that they would sooner accept the bill than see the House of Lords filled with a crowd of newly created peers. My father repeated that we were decidedly not ripe for a constitution in Russia. "And never shall be," I added, "because our people will never obey anybody who does not have a stick in his hands." To cheer up after such sad prognosis, we went to a music hall where a man in a frock coat and silk hat was dancing on the stage and making silly jokes. My father was delighted. He said that when he had visited this music hall as a young man some forty years before, the same man in the frock coat had been dancing on the stage and making the same silly jokes. "What conservatism and what solidity in taste!" he exclaimed. "Why can't we Russians follow this example, instead of always desiring changes and new things? Life would be so much simpler."

A delegation from our Duma came to London at that time and many grand phrases were exchanged on the theme that the youngest parliament came to greet the oldest one. During the stay of the delegation in England the first Duma was dissolved and at a big gathering in honor of our delegates, the Prime Minister had to change his speech, exclaiming: "The Duma is dead; long live the Duma!" Our government, which had had much trouble with the first Duma, took offense at this phrase and Benckendorff received instructions to tell the Prime Minister that Russia considered his speech very tactless. Benckendorff, who treated the new friendship between Russia and England as his favorite child, was greatly upset by this turn of affairs, the more so since he did not see anything offensive in the words of the Prime Minister; he considered it as a matter of course that the first Duma would be followed by a second one. Thus he chose a middle course, and instead of writing an official note, took the Prime Minister aside at some public reception and in a fatherly way explained to him the point of view of our government. The Prime Minister was touched by such a friendly appeal and said that he never would have uttered these words had he thought they would make a bad impression in Russia. This was telegraphed to St. Petersburg as an apology of the Prime Minister, and the whole matter was settled.

The diplomats of the old school had such tact that they could always find a way out of a difficulty without ruffling anybody's feelings. It is easy to write a stiff note, but it is likely to evoke an even stiffer one, to which you then reply in kind, one note leading to another, until the guns start booming. Benckendorff taught me that there was no situation out of which two gentlemen could not find a way without fighting. The great misfortune today is that there are so few gentlemen left in this world.

Not to forget in my admiration for English ways that I was still Russian, I frequented the Russian colony, where I was always received with open arms. Inevitably, discussions ensued about the superiority of the Russian character over the English one, my predilection for the English always leaving me in the minority. The talks usually ended in a huge supper with the famous French wine, which the old man who called himself Dean of the Russian Colony kept for special guests.

At that time a certain Mr. Hughes came to London with his Russian wife and three daughters. He was the grandson of the founder of the famous Hughes Works in south Russia. His grandfather had been a plain miner who had come to Russia because his wife had served as a nurse in the Imperial family. An enterprising and clever man, he obtained through his wife's influence the right to look for coal in south Russia. Successful, he founded the Hughes Works, which grew so large that a whole town was named after it.[12] The entire family migrated to Russia to direct work on the mines. The Hughes whom I knew in London had retired because of ill health. He had spent all his life in Russia, surrounded by Russians, was married to a Russian, and presented the very rare sight of a Russified Englishman. The Hugheses had a big house and many Russians had a standing invitation to dinner on Sundays. I spent many happy evenings with them.

Once we started to discuss the possibilities of a successful Russian revolution. The young people voiced the usual rot about Russians obtaining freedom and then creating a paradise on earth. The old Mr. Hughes, who, suffering from consumption, never left his armchair by the fireplace and usually did not join the general conversation, suddenly lost his temper and shouted that they did not know anything about the Russian people and their ability to introduce freedom and paradise in their country. He had spent all his life in the interior of Russia and in his work had had to deal with thousands of Russian workers and common people and had a clear idea what revolution would bring to Russia. To illustrate, he related an incident which had occurred at their mines. For years relations with the workers had been good, then under outside influence the workers became restless and started to strike. At first the strikes were settled amicably without the help of the police. But one day an agitator arrived and began to spread the rumor that a revolution was imminent. The idea of a revolution pleased the workmen and they decided to do their share. To them revolution meant the destruction of everything: the mines, the houses, the owners, and so forth. The fact that thereby they would deprive themselves of their livelihood did not seem to concern them. They thought only of destruction and murder. The situation became dangerous and the management had to send for troops from the neighboring town. But the town was at some distance and the huge crowd of miners, quite out of control, began to attack the houses of the directors and their families with sticks and stones. Fortunately some of the miners felt thirsty and turned to the destruction of the local inn to obtain wine and soon the whole crowd followed suit and a general

[12] Hughes town (Iuzovka, later Stalino, today Donetsk).

orgy began. When all the wine was drunk, somebody suggested that there must be more wine in the cellar, and part of the crowd descended below. Then one of those who had remained outside decided it would be great fun if they set fire to the inn to see what those who were in the cellar would do. The drunken crowd approved of the idea and soon the building was aflame. When those who were inside tried to escape, the crowd threw stones at them, roaring with delight. Meanwhile the soldiers arrived and quickly quelled the disorder, the miners later asking the management for forgiveness and re-employment. Mr. Hughes concluded that it was this sort of thing that one could expect from revolution in Russia; and he expressed the hope that he would not be alive when such a revolution occurred. This story impressed me deeply and I was to remember it a decade later, when the first signs of the coming Revolution appeared on the Russian sky.

Meanwhile I was still in London, which also had no inkling of the future. The great difference was that England had an intelligent king and a fair number of clever statesmen, who looked ahead and tried to cope with the danger posed by the personality and ambition of the Kaiser, while Russia had a weak Emperor and practically no outstanding statesmen, except perhaps for Stolypin (who was shortly assassinated), and Witte, who in his ambition was more concerned with his own career than the welfare of Russia. As a result England survived the calamity of the First World War, while Russia collapsed. But all this was in the future, and I fully enjoyed my stay in London.

❖❖❖

After more than three years in England common sense told me that I must start thinking about advancement in my career. The worst part of the Russian diplomatic service was the irregularity in appointments. Just as I had been sent to London because of the Vice Minister's fantastic notion about my family wealth, so future advancement would depend on outside influence. Since I had nobody in St. Petersburg influential enough to ask for my promotion to a higher post, it would have been normal for me to go to St. Petersburg myself and annoy different chiefs with requests for a better position. However, as I have noted, I so disliked the whole bureaucratic atmosphere of the Foreign Office and had such a horror of walking up and down the corridors waiting for an appointment which might never materialize, that I decided to go to the Foreign Office only with a new assignment already in my pocket. Thus I asked the Ambassador to write the Minister on my behalf, and requested Poklevskii, who was going to St. Petersburg en route to his new post as Minister of Teheran, to talk about me to Izvolskii, whom he knew well from the time they had served together in Tokyo.

Feeling that I had done all that could be done, I sat back and waited without impatience, indeed almost hoping that no change would occur soon, for I feared that nowhere else could I be so happy as I had been in London. But when change is imperative, yet the man is so attached to the past that he has not the strength to close his eyes to the past and look ahead to the future, life has a way of introducing a new factor which will make the change not only easier but sometimes even desirable. The factor may be something grand that awaits you in your new life; it may be something that threatens to poison your old life. In my case it was the arrival of a replacement for Prince Sviatopolk-Mirskii, who had to leave the Embassy. The new Secretary was an awful person, envious and wicked. He resented the position which I had created for myself in the Embassy and did everything, as he used to say, to put me in my place. The atmosphere in the chancery, where I spent most of my time, became unbearable, and I began to long for a change. Judging from what I heard about this man years later, my dislike of him had been absolutely justified. I learned that on the eve of World War I he astonished everbody with his grand way of living in spite of his limited personal means, but as it was considered bad form in Russia to ask people about their money, nobody raised any questions. It was noticed also that he spent most of his time in the German Embassy, but this was dismissed on the grounds that he was of German origin and thus felt at home with Germans. When reports of the Ambassador began to disappear from their usual place, he was asked about the matter, but his explanation that he took them home to make copies for the archives was accepted. He continued to be seen with members of the German Embassy even after war was declared. Only after he failed to return from a leave was it realized that he had been in the pay of the German Embassy all the time. No wonder my constant presence in the chancery had bothered him so much. At the time I had not known about all that, and had thought that he disliked me simply out of envy.

When the Ambassador saw how miserable I felt, he consoled me that it was good for me to work with such a man and learn how to get along not only with people who liked me but also with those who disliked me. Perhaps he was right, but fortunately the new experience did not last long. One morning the Ambassador called me and showed me a telegram from the Foreign Office offering me the post of Second Secretary in Peking. I was delighted and accepted it at once. I was particularly glad that the position was not in Europe, where I would always make comparisons with London and feel miserable. Now I could start a new chapter in my life, so different from the old one that no comparisons would be possible. As I discovered later, I owed my appointment to Poklevskii. When he arrived in St. Petersburg, there were already eight candidates for Peking, but thanks to his eloquence the Minister penciled my name at the top of the list. Thus I could proceed to St. Petersburg with my head up, not obliged to face those sad walks up and down the corridor, and took leave of the Benckendorffs. I had been very fortunate in starting my career under such a chief as Count Benckendorff. He was a true diplomat as well as a man of most noble character. His only shortcoming was that he belonged to the twentieth century, while the majority of his countrymen still lived in the sixteenth.

On my last evening in London, on my way home from some dinner party, when the public was returning from the theaters, I stopped in the middle of Piccadilly Circus. I watched the hansoms with beautiful ladies and elegant men, the electrical advertisements and Eros aiming his arrow from the fountain, and felt a great sadness at having to part with this place which I had passed so often. I took off my hat and to the great astonishment of a policeman bowed to the four corners. Thinking that here was another gentleman who had imbibed too freely, the policeman drew near, but I assured him that I was only taking leave of London and maybe of my happiness.

❖❖❖

On my way to Russia I visited my aunt and my cousins, because I could not leave Europe without their blessing.

In Moscow little had changed. With the restoration of order, all thought about the Revolution had disappeared. Everybody was making money and spending it lavishly. There were rumors from St. Petersburg that the government was trying to go back on the concessions it had made when everybody was expecting a revolution, but no one in Moscow seemed to care much one way or the other. My youngest brother, the gayest and most popular of us all, insisted on taking me to different places of amusement. Champagne was flowing, the gypsies singing—the usual carefree Russian life from which I had fled some six or seven years before to create my own career. Assignment in pocket, I could limit my stay in St. Petersburg to a few days, during which I made my bows to my superiors. I was duly impressed by Foreign Minister Izvolskii, who said that he had heard me praised so much by Count Benckendorff and Poklevskii that he expected great things from me. I replied that I should do my best to fulfill his expectations, but that I did not know what great things a junior secretary could accomplish. He did not appear pleased with my answer, for his utterance had been merely a pompous phrase not to be enlarged. I visited the rooms where I had begun my career and had nearly suffocated from the bureacratic atmosphere. Everything had remained the same, including the chief and the old clerk with the red nose. The only novelty was the employment of women typists. They filled the offices, walked arm in arm in the corridors, and flirted with everybody. The whole solemnity of the place was gone. I was glad that my days of service in the Foreign Office were over. With my curate back in England, life in St. Petersburg would have been sad indeed.

In spite of my four years of independent life in London, my family still regarded me as not quite grown up and unable to provide for myself. For a short time this reversion to childhood was quite agreeable and I willingly submitted to it. At last the day of my departure arrived. I took the Siberian express from Moscow. My family had only a vague idea about living conditions in Peking, and mother loaded me down as if I were going on an expedition to the North Pole. I had to take along a huge fur coat, the sort that people wear when they go bear hunting in the middle of winter. I later found it quite useless, because it was never too cold in Peking and during the journey across Siberia, if it was cold outside, the compartments were so overheated that one would feel hot even in summer clothes. The whole family saw me off. There were endless farewells, and my enthusiastic sister-in-law, who was interested in astrology, saw the first evening star and assured everybody that it must be my star, watching over me. I was greatly flattered that celestial bodies should take an interest in my life. The train began to move, and after the usual shouts about writing, Moscow disappeared from my sight.

5

Peking

ON MY WAY TO PEKING I HAD TO CROSS THE WHOLE OF SIBERIA, Manchuria, and North China. No one can fail to be impressed by the journey through Siberia, especially the first time. The dimensions of Russia are staggering. You travel a day, you travel a week, you travel ten days, and you are still in Russia. Except for the Ural Mountains and a stretch near Lake Baikal, the country is absolutely flat. After you leave European Russia the population becomes scarce; you pass hours and hours without seeing any village or habitation. Near the stations are a few houses. Usually, when the express train arrives at the station, the entire local population comes to stare at the travelers. Especially in the evenings, when the train is brilliantly illuminated by electricity and the elegant figures of some inhabitants of Shanghai or other Far Eastern ports are visible inside, the travelers must appear to the local residents like men from another planet. What envy and dissatisfaction the exotic creatures in furs must provoke in the hearts of those doomed to spend their entire life in some miserable station!

I imagine a young girl, who has not yet lost the capacity to dream, waiting on the station platform. She hears the express approaching and sees it all illuminated. The train stops for five minutes. The passengers, looking like people from a fairyland, jump on the platform; they laugh and joke. There is a whistle, the train with its passengers disappears, and darkness, emptiness, and dullness reign again.

It is unjust that some should move from place to place in luxury, while others must remain in some forsaken place in misery. Small wonder that this should cause irritation and discontent. I am convinced that the Siberian express played an important part in the awakening of the population of Siberia and thereby hastened the coming of the Revolution.

The sight of unlimited space and the absence of life begins to affect you, and the passengers prefer to pass their time in the diner, drinking endless glasses of tea and playing cards.

The ease with which Russians, when they travel, make each other's acquaintance is remarkable. At one of the stations a tall man in the uniform of an engineer enters the restaurant, takes a seat at a table where a fat lady is sitting, and orders tea. After a few insignificant phrases, they are deep in conversation. The lady begins to relate her whole life; she tells that she is on her way to Hankow, where her husband has a tea business, that she has four children, that life in Hankow is very gay and that she is fond of amateur theatricals. In the evening the engineer and the lady dine together and discuss the question of suicide. He maintains that suicide is always ugly; she, that one can die beautifully, for instance by drinking poison from a lovely goblet, and with a glass of beer demonstrates how it must be done. The train stops and the engineer takes leave of the lady. Such is the conversation between two Russian passengers who meet in the Siberian express for but a few hours.

It is quite different with foreigners. We had passed half of Siberia before the Englishmen started to talk with each other and then mostly about the weather. I do not know which is better. Personally, during long voyages I like to find out everything about the other passengers. My knowledge of languages helps me a great deal in this detective work.

I discovered that one passenger was a Belgian who had a contract to build tramways in Tientsin; another was a young English engineer, going to work on some coal mine in China; a nice-looking woman was a French governess on her way to join the family of the manager of the Chinese post office; another lady was a dressmaker en route to Vladivostok. The dressmaker, incidentally, believed that she had invented a flying machine. She insisted on showing her invention to us and nearly pierced the eyes of the constructor of tramways when she threw a strange apparatus about her compartment. With conversation time passed quickly.

Soon we found ourselves entering Manchuria. To my great disappointment, except for the ever increasing crowds of Chinese, who made an awful noise, as if they were perpetually quarreling with each other, everything remained more or less identical—the same Russian train, the same Russian station with the Russian station master in the red cap, the same three bells at the departure of the train, and, as we entered Harbin, the same Russian provincial town.

My first acquaintance with the Chinese Eastern Railway filled me with great pride. To come to the wild, robber-infested country and create in such short time the enormous enterprise that brought the vast region to life was proof of Russian genius. Once only a small Chinese village, Harbin was now a flourishing Russian town. It attracted many thousand Chinese who grew rich as a result of the Russian activity.

But we Russians had forgotten, when we created all this, that success provokes envy and that to maintain one's success one must be able to defend it. Furthermore, success breeds pride and greed. Unwilling to share our fortune with others, we did not realize that if the Chinese, the real owners of Manchuria, were too weak to do anything alone, they could intrigue and collaborate with envious neighbors. As a result the Russo-Japanese War ensued, and we lost half of our great work in Manchuria. But now, three years after the conclusion of peace, following an agreement with Japan[1] we had resumed our work, limiting our activity to Northern Manchuria. Thus even after the lost War, as a Russian entered this part of Manchuria where the influence of Russia could be seen at every step, he could not but take pride in the tremendous effort that his country had made in bringing this part of the world to life. I realize that the Chinese cannot share this feeling, but if they are incapable of doing the job, surely they can allow others to do it for them, especially since they themselves will be the first beneficiaries. Alas, the word "independence" has such an attraction for human beings that they prefer to live like pigs but feel independent.

[1] July 30, 1907.

At Changchun,[2] where the Japanese-dominated part of Manchuria began, the Russian railway met the Japanese one. The difference between the two was remarkable. The Japanese had changed the wide Russian gauge to their narrow one. The big and heavy Russian express approached the station from one side; on the other waited a small and light Japanese express with elegant pullman cars. It was already dark. The Russian train was half-lighted with candles, the Japanese one was brilliantly lit with electricity. There were flowers on the tables in the diner and numerous servants in white coats were waiting to serve dinner. The whole train in the midst of Manchuria looked like something out of a fairy tale. Apparently the Japanese wanted to impress the travelers with the contrast and underline that here one had to do with a higher civilization. It was my first impression, if not of a higher Japanese civilization, then of the Japanese ability to impress foreigners. At that time the Japanese still enjoyed the friendship of England and America and were on their best behavior.

With a certain amount of regret I parted with the comfortable Russian train and moved to the Japanese side. At once I was surrounded by wonderful politeness. Everybody smiled and bowed. After a good but diminutive dinner I found my berth, also diminutive, and went to sleep amid the snores of other passengers.

On the next day we arrived at Mukden and changed to a Chinese train. Here nobody wanted to impress one with a high standard of civilization. The train was dirty and crowds of Chinese filled every corner. Though the railway was under the supervision of the English, there was little order. At every station, crowds of Chinese rushed in and out, shouting at each other, buying food and eating it in a most disgusting way.

The foreigners sought refuge in the dining car. The train moved very slowly. The whole landscape looked very Asiatic—flat, predominantly yellow, especially in late autumn, when everything seemed to have dried up and clouds of dust covered everything.

Before coming to Tientsin I was shown the remnants of the Great Wall which had been built many centuries ago to defend China proper from the invasion of different Mongolian tribes in the north.

[2] Also known as Hsinking.

Here the wall, after climbing from hill to hill like a huge snake, descended into the sea. Though half in ruin, it was still magnificent. One of those mysteries that puzzles later generations is from where all the millions of workmen who built the Great Wall were taken.

There were many villages, but they did not enliven the dull landscape, because they too were colorless. The houses were built of mud, and everything had the same yellow appearance. There were small, half-ruined temples and a great number of tombs, deeply venerated as they contained the local ancestors. Though there was much talk of the awakening of China, the Chinese at that time still lived with their faces toward the past, especially in the countryside, where the people continued to live as they had a thousand years ago. It gave the whole landscape a sleepy, half-dead appearance. Only the pale blue sky and the brilliant sun looked alive and beautiful. Peking was to have a remarkable climate—perpetual sunshine from August to June, with the same transparent pale blue sky and the same brilliant sun every day. Of all this I learned on the train as I approached the Chinese capital with great impatience. The past seemed to recede, and I was ready to begin my new life.

The approach to Peking was disappointing. Passing through the opening in the city wall, the train stopped at a miserable-looking platform on which a Chinese policeman in rags stood near a white post bearing the inscription "Peking." I was met by my colleagues, who grinned when they saw me descending from the train in my fur coat, but the Chinese were greatly impressed.

The first thing I learned from my colleagues was that the day of my arrival was not an ordinary one. The old Chinese Empress Dowager [T'zu Hsi][3] had died during the night in the Forbidden City.[4] Not wishing to show my great ignorance in things Chinese, I pretended that I was greatly struck by this event. Only later did I understand why the death of the old lady was of such importance. It was the breaking point between Old China, with its centuries-old

[3] The Ch'ing Dynasty, which ruled China from 1644 to 1912, was Manchu, not Chinese. Abrikossow, like many authors, uses "Manchu" and "Chinese" interchangeably.

[4] The walled section of Peking, encompassing the Imperial palaces and "forbidden" or closed to the public.

[149]

tradition and a certain amount of order, and New China, with its high-sounding phrases about progress and general chaos, which after near forty years still persists.

❖❖❖

The old Empress Dowager had started her life as a concubine of the debauched Emperor [Hsien Fêng]. Clever and beautiful, she knew how to subject the old Emperor to her will. When he died she governed as regent during the minority of the new Emperor [T'ung Chih]. She ruled with a firm hand and knew how to remove all rivals and enemies from her path. It is difficult to estimate the number of crimes committed by this woman during her lifetime. The Forbidden City knows how to keep its secrets. When the Emperor attained his majority, the Empress Dowager pretended to surrender her power and retired to the magnificent summer palace near Peking, but she continued her old relationship with the servants at the Court and through them kept informed of everything that went on in the Forbidden City. The Emperor Kuang Hsü [who succeeded T'ung Chih] surrounded himself with young progressive Chinese who spoke about reforms and a constitution. Frightened, the old bureaucrats urged the Empress Dowager to intervene, but she bided her time, doing everything to increase discontent with the projected reforms. Soon the young Emperor realized that as long as the Empress Dowager was alive nothing would come out of his new policy and he was persuaded to take steps against her.

The Emperor ordered General Yüan Shih-k'ai to proceed to the summer palace and arrest the Empress Dowager. But Yüan himself belonged to the old school and knew very well that his career would be finished if power passed into the hands of the reformers. Hence he announced to the Empress Dowager that he had come to arrest her, but that if she would order him to arrest the Emperor, he would prefer to do that. She gave the order and the poor Emperor was arrested; some of his advisers were executed, others escaped. The Empress Dowager once again took up the reins of power. She kept the Emperor near herself, but did everything to render him harmless by debauchery. She allowed him to be present at her audiences, but she sat on the main throne, he at a small table in the corner of the room. From that time she ruled China with a firm hand. She supported the Boxer

Rebellion and had to escape with the Emperor from Peking as the foreign powers took the city. When peace was signed and China was saddled with a huge indemnity, the Empress Dowager returned to the capital. In order to reconcile the foreign powers with her rule she started to speak about reforms, gave audiences to the foreign ladies, and tried to charm them. Soon she actually became popular with the foreign legations.

Now this woman was dead and so was the Emperor, whom she had poisoned, it was said, when she had felt death approaching. As to her succession, she seemed to have done everything to prevent a strong man from appearing as her successor and had named as Emperor the late Emperor's nephew, an infant three years old, with his father, Prince Ch'un Tsai-feng, a weak and foolish man, as regent during his minority. It is not surprising that the Manchu Dynasty outlived the Empress Dowager by only one year[5] and was succeeded by a republic and general chaos. Thus I arrived in Peking at the moment when China entered the most critical period of its history, and I witnessed a most fascinating historical drama.

✤✤✤

From the station we walked to the Russian compound, where the Legation and all the houses of the staff were situated. Occupying an enormous house, which a former Russian Minister had built in the style of Villa Juglia in Rome, the Legation was pretentious but ill-suited to the climate of Peking. The houses of the secretaries were much more modest. I was delighted with my bungalow but horrified at the appearance of the servant who had been engaged for me: he looked like a huge gorilla with smallpox. My colleagues explained that the servant was a descendant of the Cossacks whom the Chinese had taken prisoner in the seventeenth century after destroying a small fortress near the Manchurian border. Taken to Peking, his ancestors had intermarried with the Chinese. Though they had a Russian church and some remained Orthodox, the Cossacks and their descendants became completely assimilated. Now when Russians arrived in China servants were hired from among their ranks, but as there were no worse thieves they were not retained for long. This was my experience

[5] Actually by three years. T'zu Hsi died in November, 1908; the Revolution broke out in October, 1911.

too, and after a few weeks I parted with this gorilla-like descendant of the Russian Cossacks and took a Chinese servant, who, like all Chinese servants, was also a thief, but his stealing never went beyond the established limits. Anybody who has lived in China knows how hopeless it is to teach a Chinese honesty from a moral point of view. The lessons must be purely practical: Do not steal more than a certain amount or you will lose your job.

My first days passed in arranging my house. In this I had the help of Sergeant Baturin, a Cossack who spoke Chinese and Mongolian fluently and thus was a most important and useful man at the Legation. Indeed, one could not take a step without him. The Chinese knew what an important personage he was and were afraid of him. Whatever discipline there was among the Chinese staff was to his credit. Baturin was a kind of Figaro: Baturin here, Baturin there.

The Diplomatic Quarter, where all the Legations were situated, had been created after the Boxer Rebellion. It occupied several blocks near the wall which divided the Chinese and Tartar parts of Peking. Constructed primarily to prevent the repetition of a siege such as the foreign legations had experienced during the Boxer Rebellion, it contained special military barracks and big open places where an approaching mob could readily have been dispersed by gunfire. Chinese carts were not allowed in the Diplomatic Quarter, which was under exclusive foreign administration. Consequently the foreigners could live in Peking according to their own customs, unabsorbed by the Chinese crowds, Chinese noise, and Chinese dirt. The Diplomatic Quarter with its clean streets and magnificent Legations, built with the money taken from the Chinese after the Boxer Rebellion, contrasted sharply with the rest of Peking with its narrow, crooked and dirty streets, its noisy crowds, its beggars and its peddlers, who sold the most nauseous food.

After the conquest of China the Manchus had tried not to mix with the Chinese, the Manchu garrisons and officials living in separate parts in every town; but gradually the Chinese had absorbed the Manchus, and the Manchu and Chinese parts of the towns had come to differ in name more than in substance. The so-called Forbidden City, where the Emperor and the numerous Court officials lived, occupied nearly a third of the Tartar City and was situated near the entrance of the Diplomatic Quarter. It was surrounded by a high wall, dirty pink in color. Nobody was allowed to enter the Forbidden City and in spite of its proximity to the Diplomatic Quarter, its life and events remained little known.

At this time nobody thought of discarding extraterritoriality, and we lived subject neither to Chinese jurisdiction nor Chinese customs. It may have been unfair toward the natives to put ourselves in the position of superior beings, but I must confess that the feeling of superiority was agreeable and was, I think, the chief reason most foreigners adored life in China and felt miserable when they retired and had to return to their own countries. Extraterritoriality allowed every little clerk to feel like a small lord. It was much later, when the Chinese were taught the principles of democracy, that they started the agitation against extraterritoriality and succeeded in getting rid of it under the false pretext of having ameliorated their laws and thus having rendered unnecessary the special status of foreigners in China.

But in many cases the termination of extraterritorial privileges has rendered life in China quite impossible. Perhaps centuries ago the Chinese may have been a highly civilized people, compared with the savages among whom they were living, but they froze in their development. In the course of time Europeans outstripped the Chinese and the roles have changed. Now the Chinese must learn the lesson of civilization from the foreigners, but ignorance breeds conceit and the Chinese will never admit this. Exploiting the foreigners' rivalry and the mistakes they make in their Far Eastern policy at every step, they will gradually attain full equality with the foreigners. The foreigners will have to pack and leave China. Without the civilizing influence of the Westerners the Chinese will quickly revert to savagery. Thus the presence of the foreign settlement in the midst of Peking was the best way in which the Chinese could learn, if they wished (which I doubt very much), how to change their cesspool of a town into a place fit for civilized people.

My first days in Peking were exciting. Everything was new. The excursions to buy all the necessary things for my household were adventures. Everything seemed cheap, though the Chinese merchants, who at once recognized in me a newcomer, inflated their prices tenfold. Fortunately the Cossack Baturin was with me, and all their tricks were useless. But the noise was terrific. I was nearly torn to pieces as various merchants tried to drag me into their shops. I bought mostly Chinese things, including Chinese furniture, the foreign imitations which the Chinese made from imagination being quite awful. Nonetheless my house soon began to reflect my own personality, and feeling at home, I turned my attention to the chancery.

The chancery was a big room full of sunshine. It was my rule to render myself indispensable, and finding the archives in an awful state, I started to put them in order. Often I sat until midnight absorbed in the most interesting documents, to the great astonishment of my colleagues, who did not understand such diligence.

Gradually I became accustomed to Peking's social life. It was peculiar. As all diplomats lived on the same two or three streets, it sufficed to take a few steps in order to meet a number of "dear colleagues," all of whom reported the latest news. If there was none, it was invented on the spot. Soon I remarked that any news that one conveyed made the round of the city in twenty-four hours and came back to one enlarged beyond recognition. Most of the Legations had little to do and the chief occupation of their members was gossip. As there was nothing to prate about the Chinese, all gossip concentrated on the foreigners themselves. Reputations were ruined with great ease, but this was done in such a good-natured way that no one took offense. Horseback riding and dinner parties filled much of the Western life.

The Chinese had no desire to mix with the foreigners and did not yet seek to imitate them. Many still wore pigtails and were never seen in foreign clothes. It gave them a more dignified appearance, but at the same time made it more difficult for them to mix with the foreigners. Few Chinese could speak any foreign language and all communication with the Foreign Office was done in Chinese. This increased the importance of the interpreters, the only persons who could speak Chinese.

The first time I was present at negotiations with Chinese officials, I realized that the Minister was absolutely helpless; everything was in the hands of the interpreter. The interpreter in a Legation generally was a person who had devoted his entire life to the study of Chinese, and unlike the ministers and other members of the Legation who usually came for only three to four years, he tended to have a permanent appointment. The interpreter frequently had more understanding and sympathy for the Chinese than for his own Minister. Every new Minister found himself in the hands of his interpreter who could easily, especially if he disliked his chief, place him in a very awkward position. The Minister thus had to be very careful in his dealings with the interpreter.

The interpreter in our Legation was a difficult man. His knowledge of the Chinese language, as the Chinese themselves said, was perfect, but after nearly thirty years in China he had become somewhat Chinese in mentality, and he liked to drag out the negotiations, thinking that speed only rendered the attainment of favorable results more difficult. Often, especially if the Minister was energetic and wanted quick results, the interpreter found himself much more in sympathy with the Chinese than with his own Minister.

I was astonished how well the Chinese knew the weaknesses of the foreigners and how skillfully they exploited them. Their whole diplomacy was based on playing one Legation against another, and they did this so cleverly that the Legations never suspected it. At one time, for example, two groups of bankers wanted to arrange a loan for the Chinese government. One group was favored by Russia, the other by England and France. The Chinese foreign office started negotiations with both. Accused of a double game, it assured the English and French representatives that it dealt in earnest only with them, negotiating with Russia merely because it must throw "some kind of bone to that dog" too, while telling a similar story to the Russians, underlining to them Chinese contempt for the English and French "dogs." In the end the Chinese obtained money from both parties.

The first lesson a diplomat learns in China is that what the Chinese say may mean one thing one day, another the next. In this they are helped a great deal by their language, in which one character can have several different meanings. All our old agreements with China, by which we obtained different advantages, were gradually undermined by this juggling of Chinese characters. Often the Chinese themselves did not have a clear idea of what they meant, and it was quite a task to read and understand a Chinese note. At a glance our interpreter could vaguely indicate its general content. He would then retire to his chancery and with the help of his three Chinese assistants translate each single character separately. Often there were long discussions, because the meaning of a character varied with context.

Thus it took hours of crossword-puzzlelike efforts to render the Chinese text into Russian.

No less complicated were the oral negotiations. At the Foreign Office the Minister, his interpreter, and secretary would be received by a smiling Chinese secretary and ushered into a room with a long, green tablecloth-covered table. After some time the Foreign Minister with a crowd of secretaries would enter and sit down at the table, opposite the Russians. There would follow an exchange of greetings, tea, and small talk before the chief subject was introduced. Each word had to be translated from Russian to Chinese, then from Chinese to Russian. As the Chinese did not trust anything the foreigners said, there ensued endless discussions among themselves, understood only by the interpreter. The answer that followed would usually be very vague, necessitating endless explanations and translations. If the Minister was not accustomed to Chinese ways, he was apt to lose his temper, but the interpreter alone would feel this. The Chinese would continue to smile and be as vague as ever. After hours of discussion it would be decided to postpone the negotiations. At the next meeting, when one reminded the Chinese of what had been more or less settled during these negotiations, they were likely to make astonished faces and say that one had not understood them, and everything had to be begun all over again.

I remember that the Foreign Minister at the time of my arrival was an opium addict. Sometimes he was in such a state that he looked half asleep and could not understand anything. Our interpreter, who knew how opium affects the human brain, could see at once in what state the Foreign Minister was, and if he saw that the opium was affecting him adversely, he simply told our Minister in Russian that it was hopeless for the moment to expect anything sensible from the Foreign Minister and we retired after some amiable phrases. At other times, the Foreign Minister was in the state where opium made him especially brilliant and on such occasions the negotiations were fruitful.

In their negotiations with foreigners the Chinese were born humorists. I remember how once our relations with them had become strained when, with their trick of giving different interpretations to their characters, they had suddenly started to deny various concessions to which they had agreed in their commercial treaty with us. As it

[156]

would have placed us in a difficult position, if before the conclusion of a new treaty they changed the nature of the old one, we
decided that we must insist on the original interpretation of the old
treaty. When the Chinese persisted in their interpretation and the
negotiations reached an impasse, St. Petersburg decided to present
to the Chinese government an ultimatum demanding a satisfactory
answer within forty-eight hours. A Cossack regiment was assembled
near the Russo-Chinese frontier in Sinkiang with orders to cross the
border if no satisfactory Chinese answer was received in the stipulated
time period. It so happened that a big fancy dress ball to which the
Foreign Minister had been invited had been scheduled at the Legation
for the critical day. Lest the Chinese realize that we were anxious
about the result of the ultimatum the affair took place as planned. The
Chinese remained noncommittal until the last minute. We were greatly
excited at the chancery, and in order not to lose any time the Minister
prepared two telegrams: one to the effect that the Chinese had
accepted our claims, one that they had not. A few moments before
the expiration of the time limit, we received a telephone call from
the Foreign Office asking if our Minister could receive the Foreign
Minister. Our Minister agreed, certain that the Foreign Minister was
bringing the final answer, on which the question of war and peace
depended. Instead, the Chinese Minister announced with a smile
that he had come to ask if masks were to be worn at our fancy dress
ball. Only just before leaving did he hand over the expected answer,
which was considered satisfactory and thus eliminated complications.
Our Minister, who could appreciate a joke, was enchanted with the
behavior of the Chinese Foreign Minister. As he put it: "Here we
were all excited about the Chinese attitude on which the question of
war and peace depended, and the smiling Chinese came and asked if
he must wear a mask at the fancy dress ball, making fools of us with
our deep diplomacy." And so instead of the Cossacks crossing into
Chinese territory miles and miles away, we danced in silly fancy
dresses, the Chinese Foreign Minister drinking brandy and smiling.
When talks about the treaties were resumed, the Chinese proved as
evasive as ever but we could not use the same threat a second time.

In all their dealings the Chinese acted fully persuaded that notwithstanding all the concessions they had to make, ultimately every-

thing would turn out in their favor. The astonishing thing is that they proved right. Whole provinces were given away to the foreigners, but in time they reverted to China. I remember once when a secretary of the Chinese Foreign Office had been summoned by our First Secretary in connection with negotiations concerning navigation on the Sungari, during which the Chinese were procrastinating as usual. Our Secretary, who had a very loud voice and a patronizing attitude when dealing with Chinese, told him that he was astonished at Chinese behavior and that if it continued Russia would lose its patience and China would suffer. At this moment he was called by our Minister and passing through the chancery asked me to keep the Chinese diplomat company. I found the latter seated in an armchair with a benevolent smile on his face. To say something, I commented that our Secretary seemed very strict with him. Laughing he answered that he did not mind at all, and added that if our roles had been reversed, Russia being in the bad position in which China found herself at the time, he would have spoken with the Russian Secretary likewise, and he barked like a dog. Here was a brief but true definition of diplomacy, for it was frequently reduced to the barking of a strong dog at a weak one. I am sorry to say that the time came when the Chinese felt stronger than we Russians and then their barking was cruel, but this was as yet far away. With the approach of the Chinese Revolution we had the upper hand, and our diplomacy then was really brilliant.

What I found so fascinating in Asian diplomacy was that the personality and policy of the representative played a much more important role than in Europe and that the results of his policy were apparent more quickly. In Europe countless conferences, the intervention of other powers, and instructions from above constantly modified individual policy. Years passed before any results could be discerned, and then one could not always recognize them as the fruit of one's own ideas. Not so in Peking. There you were the creator of policy. No conferences interfered with you and after a short time you could see the influence of your policy on the relations between your country and China. This was especially true in the case of [Ivan Iakovlevich Korostovets], the Minister with whom I had to work in China.

The Minister was a peculiar man, a great cynic but brilliant. He considered the majority of human beings to be either fools or rascals and took great pleasure in proving it by provoking them into losing their tempers. Most of his career passed in China, where he had started as a young secretary. Suspected of having poisoned the dog of his chief's wife, the perpetual barking of which robbed everyone of sleep, he had been exiled to Chefoo as Vice Consul. Later he had served on the staff of the Viceroy in Manchuria and had stayed at Port Arthur before the War, returning full of cynical stories about the Russian generals and predicting the inevitable Russo-Japanese War. He had accompanied Count Sergei Witte to the Portsmouth Peace Conference and had come back full of admiration for the way in which Witte had succeeded in turning the sympathies of the Americans from the Japanese toward the Russians. With his usual cynicism he asserted that Witte had done this by shaking hands with every Jew he met. After several years in the Far Eastern Section of the Foreign Office he was appointed Russian Minister in Peking, where he found full scope for his cleverness and eccentricity. He started by quarreling with the Military Attaché, Colonel [Lavr Georgievich] Kornilov, who, years later, during the Russian Revolution, was to become so famous as the last hope of the White Russians and was killed during the Civil War. But in those peaceful days the Minister and the Military Attaché still could afford to quarrel, and, as no secrets could be kept in Peking, the quarrel became one of the usual topics of conversation. Our Minister had a tender spot in his heart toward the Chinese. He loved to make people lose their tempers, but much as he tried to provoke the Chinese, he could not ruffle their placidity. He admired them for it and thought them much more clever than all our bureaucrats. Yet he never lost an opportunity to outwit them; it was a perpetual game of chess.

Perceiving the character of my chief, I decided to follow the example of the Chinese and imitated their placidity. After several vain attempts on the Minister's part to make me lose my temper and thereby put me in a silly position, we became great friends, and his witty conversation added to my enjoyment of life in Peking. He had a clever wife, who knew him thoroughly and used to say that no trick of his could astonish her. His household included also a charming daughter and a nice-looking French governess, who became the rage of the young diplomats. The Russian Legation soon became the center of Peking social life. Small wonder that my London experience began to fade among the joys of my new life, which was so different that any comparison was difficult.

❖❖❖

In Peking I found the free life of the country, with horseback riding the chief recreation. The horses were small Mongolian ponies, wild and bad tempered, but full of energy. The foreigners went in for racing and as ponies were very cheap and it was great fun to train them, nearly everybody kept a racing stable. I too was persuaded to start one, even though I had no instinct for gambling and cared little which horse came in first. The Cossack sergeant, who loved horses, knew everything about Mongolian ponies and had connections with the horse dealers, was especially keen. Assured that with his help the best Mongolian ponies would find their way into my stable, I left everything in his hands, agreeing to bear all expenses, the profit, if any, to be shared equally between us. Thus, for the first and last time, I became the owner of a racing stable and had to pretend that I knew everything about horses.

What I really liked about this new occupation were our early rides to the racetrack to watch the training. We usually started about five A.M., when the streets of Peking were beginning to wake up from the night's sleep. As we rode out into the countryside, we usually found the city gates jammed with camel caravans, which were not allowed to enter the capital during the night. With a Chinese servant racing ahead and shouting to his countrymen to clear the way for the white lords of creation, we galloped among the frightened camels, staring Mongols, and Chinese. Beyond the gates we rode along the city wall, the morning sun adding a special beauty to the whole landscape, then galloped through small villages with half-ruined temples. Out of pure joy of life I saluted the Chinese who sat placidly before their houses or worked in the fields. They grinned back, foreigners in their eyes always being half mad.

At the race course we found hot coffee and other sportsmen. The Chinese grooms were exercising the ponies and each owner tried to find the faults of his competitors' horses. Our Cossack, who mixed with the Chinese grooms, was the only one who really knew anything about the chances of each stable. When it was time for trial runs, everyone sought to hide the results from the others, and the Cossack insisted sometimes that we be on the spot about three A.M. to try the horses in the dark. On such occasions the reflection of the moon on the medieval wall, the sleeping camels waiting to be admitted into town at sunrise, the dozing villages whose quiet was broken only by the barking of dogs, the deserted race course and the ghostly ride around it, added a touch of mystery to our outings.

At nine o'clock I had to be back at work. Sometimes the Minister, who was greatly interested in racing, joined us in the excursions and our return took longer, for he was always ready to discuss his policy plans. When the racing season was over, our morning rides usually took us to the Temple of Heaven, which stood on an open place in the corner of the Chinese city. You passed through a small gate and found yourself in a huge garden with alleys of old trees. In the middle stood the Temple of Heaven with a marble altar from which in old times the Chinese Emperor made yearly offerings to Heaven. Next to the altar stood a round pavilion with a roof of tiles of such magnificent peacock blue that you could not decide, as you went past, which was more beautiful, the pale blue of the sky or the deep blue of the roof. In this pavilion the Emperor gave audiences after the sacrifice. At that time the Temple was in a state of great dilapidation. Grass grew through the crevices of the marble altar and the pavilion was empty. But you could imagine the gorgeous scene the offering of a sacrifice presented, with the Emperor clad in magnificent robes and surrounded by a crowd of officials, and the smoke rising slowly unto Heaven. The whole idea was very beautiful, but now, like so many beautiful ideas, it belonged to the past. The Chinese no longer came near the Temple; only the foreigners who galloped there on their morning rides.

No wonder that we foreigners shock the Chinese and that their only dream is to get rid of us. But it is too late. They have overslept the arrival of an alien civilization, far more vigorous than their old Chinese civilization. When they saw the harm this new civilization was doing to their old way of thinking, they could do nothing to stop it. They tried once, during the Boxer Rebellion, but with tragic results. Now the only question which confronts them is whether they are capable of digesting this new civilization in order to oppose effectively the foreigners whom they hate and will always hate. I am afraid that the foreigners with their senseless fratricidal wars are doing their best to help the Chinese in their dream to get rid of all foreigners, but it is a great illusion to think that the world will fare better under the domination of the yellow race, even in a small part of the globe. I am glad that I was in China when the foreigners still could play a leading role in the introduction of European civilization. Even though in many cases such leadership went to the foreigners' heads, and they allowed themselves many things which reflected adversely on their civilization, they were far superior to the Chinese as leaders.

Speaking about the recreation of the foreigners in Peking, I must mention the picnics in the western hills. All you had to do was to tell your principal boy the number of guests you expected and you found when, after a ride of several hours through the sand and dust of the Chinese countryside, you arrived at the western hills with their trees and running water and temple ruins, a magnificently set table with your silver and such a choice of food in the courtyard of one of the temples that it no longer resembled a picnic. For several hours the solemnity of the forsaken temple would be desecrated by the noisy foreign devils, who walked about the place and casually inspected the huge Buddhas which sat silently among the dusty ruins of their past glory. When the heat of summer made life in Peking very trying, some of the foreign representatives would rent those temples and pass the season in the company of the silent idols.

Another place frequented by the foreigners was the section of the city wall near the Diplomatic Quarter. Since the time of the siege of the Foreign Missions [in 1900] Chinese had been barred from this area to protect the Missions from a possible mob attack from the wall. Americans stood guard at one end of this section of the wall, Germans at the other. We could walk between these two posts and since life in the Far East as a rule was regulated by the Anglo-Saxons this part of the wall was used by "dear colleagues" for their constitutionals, and you met different members of the Diplomatic Corps, marching seriously to and fro between the American and German posts. Many grave diplomatic problems were probably settled on this wall.

I enjoyed my walks. On one side you could see the Chinese city with the Temple of Heaven far away, on the other the Tartar city with the Forbidden City close by. You could see the top of the law buildings of the palace, the Coal Hill where the last of the Ming had committed suicide when Peking had fallen to the Manchus, a high wall hiding whatever went on there now. As I walked on the wall, the crowd with its noise and dirt was somewhere below. The town lay hidden among the trees and above there was always the same pale blue sky in which flocks of pigeons turned round and round. The Chinese had attached small whistles to the pigeons, and as the birds flew they emitted a silvery sound. My memories of Peking have remained associated always with the transparent blue sky and the silvery music of the flying pigeons.

I soon realized that my original ideas about life in Peking had been wrong. I had thought that after London my stay in China would be semibarbarous. Instead, I found the charming society of foreign diplomats who, in the middle of the Chinese capital, had arranged a purely European mode of living. Exiled from everything to which they were accustomed, and having little to do, the diplomats turned their lives in China into a perpetual merry-go-round of parties. Every Legation tried to eclipse the others: a ballet in the Russian Legation, where the charming daughter of the Minister was a comet surrounded by stars; a musical at the French Legation, where the beautiful wife of the French Minister danced the bolero to the music of Ravel; a fancy dress ball in the French bank, with everyone under the influence of champagne, exotic costumes, Chinese lanterns in the garden, and romance in the air. I always wondered what the solemn Chinese servants who moved about with refreshment trays must have thought of the representatives of a higher civilization. Probably nothing that would have been to our credit. These parties were purely foreign affairs and unless it was an official dinner party in honor of the Chinese Foreign Minister one hardly saw any Chinese guests among the crowd.

One got the impression that the foreign diplomats had been sent to China for the sole purpose of amusing themselves. Actually they were quite busy at their chanceries, enciphering and deciphering endless telegrams, as was the case in our Legation, or reading the Ministers' reports proposing ways of obtaining some new concessions from the Chinese or describing conditions in the country.

✠✠✠

The situation in China was becoming more and more complicated. With the death of the old Empress Dowager, the strong hand which had kept China together was gone. From the south came rumors of a revolutionary movement. In the Forbidden City there was no fixed policy. The three-year-old Emperor [Hsüan T'ung][6] was fit only to be a puppet, but there was no one strong to manipulate him. The one strong man, who had been the right hand of the dead Empress Dowager and who commanded the only reliable troops, General Yüan Shih-k'ai, was in exile. As will be recalled, he had betrayed the Emperor [Kuang Hsü] and had delivered him into the hands of the Empress Dowager. When the brother of the Emperor had become Regent following the Empress Dowager's death, he had to avenge his brother, but lacking the courage to execute Yüan Shih-k'ai, simply banished him to his native province where, according to the Chinese newspapers, he passed his time fishing. Prince Ch'un, the Regent, was a complete nonentity; the Emperor's widow, who according to the testament of the Empress Dowager was to share in the government, was stupid and in the hands of eunuchs. Thus there was no one in the palace who could act decisively, and as it happens so often at the moment of greatest crisis, there was general chaos at the helm of the Chinese government.

The effect of such a state of affairs soon became evident. First of all, the old discipline vanished, the young princes being seen about town. One of the Regent's brothers was made head of the Army, the other head of a nonexistent Navy. One of the Legations, the German one, as I recall, invited one of the princes to a dinner party. To everyone's astonishment he came. Diplomats tend to be somewhat snobbish, even if in Timbuktu, and it became the rage to have a Chinese prince at your party. They were nice-looking young men, beautifully attired in sable coats. They tried to behave in a dignified fashion and soon learned to lead the hostess to the dining room. The great difficulty was in the language, but in our Legation lived our former interpreter's daughter, who had spoken Chinese since childhood. She was put next to the prince and astounded him by trying to flirt with him in Chinese. Apparently the princes had not been taught how to flirt with a decent person and their language, especially after some glasses of champagne, became rather unsuitable for a dinner party, but luckily no one other than the young lady could understand the high personage, and she seemed to enjoy it.

The ladies began to invite Chinese court ladies and their presence greatly added to the gaiety of our parties. Once the wife of the Bel-

[6] He is better known by his later name of Henry Pu-yi.

gian Minister asked several princesses with their ladies-in-waiting to
an afternoon concert. During the performance one of the princesses
expressed the desire to retire and was taken by the hostess to the restroom. Soon she returned greatly excited and whispered something to
her companions. The whole row of distinguished guests got up and
rushed with the princess to the restroom. The astonished hostess followed and saw the princess flushing the toilet. The ladies were fascinated; the sound of the rushing water amused them much more than
the music of Beethoven and Chopin.

Our Minister, who liked everything out of the ordinary, arranged
a big ball to which all the ladies of the court were invited. They arrived accompanied by their servants and eunuchs. Everybody wanted
to enter the Legation and measures had to be taken to prevent the
servants and palanquin bearers from coming in. Kept outside, they
pressed their faces against the windows and watched. The Chinese
ladies with their painted faces and huge, flower-adorned Manchu
hairdos, wore heavy, embroidered clothes. When they saw the foreign
ladies in their décolleté dresses, with hardly anything on their backs,
in the arms of men who turned them round and round, their excitement had no limit. They sat in corners, showed each other the couples
that passed by, and laughed, having probably seen nothing so amusing
in their theaters. An old Mongol princess who had brought a young
and pretty granddaughter and never left her side even though several
enterprising young foreigners tried to invite her to dance, was especially shocked. The party was considered a great success, although for
days and days thereafter the Legation stank of garlic, cheap perfume,
and special Chinese smells.

❖❖❖

Meanwhile the revolutionary movement was increasing in strength
and the entire Yangtze valley seemed to be in the hands of the rebels.
The government did not know what to do. Every day new promises
of reforms were given, but nobody believed in them. Peking was full
of rumors. Then came word that the Court had decided to recall Yüan
Shih-k'ai. This was a terrible loss of face for the government, especially
as Yüan Shih-k'ai received as condition for his return absolute power
to deal with the revolutionaries.

I well remember the return of Yüan. Most of the foreigners had assembled on the wall, from where the entire railroad station was open to their view. First came a train which disgorged the personal bodyguard of the general, fierce-looking soldiers, who cleared the whole station and took up position in two lines, bayonets ready for action. Then came another train from which Yüan Shih-k'ai stepped, surrounded by friends. Without taking cognizance of anyone, he slowly moved toward the entrance. In the Peking sunshine, the whole scene was very impressive.

With the arrival of Yüan the government began to show signs of activity. Troops were dispatched against the revolutionary forces and pushed them back toward the Yangtze, but just as success seemed to favor the government, Yüan halted the advance and entered into negotiations with the revolutionary leaders. To the astonishment of everybody he accepted their conditions of peace, and persuaded the Manchu Dynasty to abdicate in favor of a republic. In return the court was to be treated most liberally after abdication. The whole thing was done quickly; it was a peculiar arrangement, the sort possible probably only in China. The Dynasty abdicated and China became a republic, but the Emperor kept his title and his court, received an annual income from the Republic, kept all his treasures, and continued living in the Forbidden City. If you want to find something absolutely illogical, you must go to China.

Sun Yat-sen, who is known as the Father of the Revolution, had been provisional President of the republic.[7] His role was less in the practical field than in the theoretical foundation of the new regime. His are the famous Sun Yat-sen principles, which became the gospel of the Chinese republic. As is the case with many principles, they are so vague that anyone can interpret them in accordance with his own interests. Even Japan, when it tried to subjugate China, sought to persuade the Chinese that the unification of China's and Japan's policies had been a principle of Sun Yat-sen. At any rate, Sun was an honest man who realized that his talent lay in framing the theoretical structure of the republic, not in its practical realization. Once the abdication of the Dynasty had been attained, he stepped aside in favor

[7] Abrikossow states that Sun was "the first President of the new Republic." Actually, he was provisional president of the revolutionary government prior to the abdication of the Manchu monarchy. Yüan Shih-k'ai was the first president (also still "provisional") of the republic of China.

of Yüan Shih-k'ai, on condition that the latter come to Nanking, the capital of the new republic. If becoming president suited Yüan's plans, the transfer of the capital did not. His base of strength was in Peking and North China, where he had faithful troops and many friends, while in Nanking he would be alone, surrounded by hotheaded revolutionaries, who would not allow him to rule according to his own ideas. Thus, when accepting the presidency he said that he would be quite willing to come to Nanking, but that he feared that this would precipitate a revolt in North China, Mongolia, for instance, feeling that its connection with China hinged on its relations with the Ch'ing Dynasty and that the abdication of the latter had freed Mongolia of all its ties with China. This point of view was so logical that it may have been suggested to Mongolia by its northern neighbor [Russia]. But the revolutionaries were not impressed, and sent a formal deputation to bring the new president to Nanking. Yüan thereupon staged an uprising, and one evening, when the diplomats as usual were entertaining each other, the rattle of machine-gun fire erupted, and the rumor spread that Peking was in the hands of soldiers in revolt.

The dinner parties were interrupted, and we all rushed to the wall to see what was happening. The night was calm and we could clearly hear the shots in different parts of the city. Fires had started in two or three places; the clamor of many voices drifted toward us. There was a certain excitement among the ladies in evening dresses and their escorts, but no one was afraid. I must say that in this respect the diplomats were generally courageous, filled more with curiosity than with anxiety for their own safety even at times of real danger. Thus they viewed the disorders as a new entertainment.

When it became obvious that the fires and disorders were increasing, it was decided to mobilize the Legation guards. The gates were closed and the sound of galloping horses could be heard as officers carried orders to the various Legations from the British general, the senior officer of the foreign detachment, whose duty it was to defend the Diplomatic Quarter.

I returned to the chancery. The Minister was away on leave, and I found the Chargé d'Affaires [Mikhail Sergeevich Shchekin] giving orders left and right, using, as was his habit, foul language. This Chargé liked to create an emergency situation and pose as the only person who could deal with it. He was seated with a fierce expression on his face and was bellowing at the officer who commanded our Legation guard and who had just reported that half of the soldiers were away in the other part of Peking at Lenten services. The Chargé was shouting that we had increased our forces because of the danger of an uprising among the Chinese, and now that the uprising had come, most of the soldiers were away. The officer tried to explain that this was not his fault, for he commanded only the Cossacks. The common soldiers received orders from his commander who was also away at the Russian Orthodox Mission. The voices were rising, the Chargé d'Affaires shouting that he would send a telegram to St. Petersburg asking the recall of the officer. Luckily, the other Secretary, who had been dining at another Legation, entered just then and the Chargé turned on him, yelling that here we were in danger of losing our lives and the Secretary was away flirting. The Secretary, who was extremely patriotic, saw that the Chargé was sitting with his hat on and began to shout how he dared to sit before the portrait of the Emperor with his head covered. With all this shouting the Chancery was like a madhouse.

At that moment we heard the voices of a Cossack guard and a crowd of women who were trying to get past him, demanding to talk to someone from the Legation. I went out to investigate and found that the prostitutes, mostly Russian Jewesses who lived outside the Diplomatic Quarter, had come to seek asylum in the Russian Legation. This calmed our Chargé down and he peacefully began to discuss with the officer where to put these women. I noticed that the Chargé took off his hat, and the Secretary smiled triumphantly. Peace had been restored. Some old barracks were found, and after a fatherly speech by the Chargé that as long as they were in the Russian Legation they must forget their profession, the prostitutes were led away by a grinning Cossack. There was nothing more to be done, and I returned home. Before falling asleep I could hear the shooting continuing, but it sounded far away.

The morning brought little change in the situation. Peking was still in the hands of soldiers in revolt, who spent most of their time robbing shops and hauling the loot to their barracks. They attacked the deputation which had come to take Yüan Shih-k'ai to Nanking, the revolutionaries saving their lives by jumping through the windows of their hotel. Frightened, they reported to Nanking that it was too dangerous for Yüan to leave Peking.

With the gates shut, the Diplomatic Quarter seemed safe. The Chinese still remembered the lesson they had been taught after the Boxer attack on the Foreign Legations, and there seemed no desire to complicate matters by doing anything against the foreigners. Our interpreter, who knew the Chinese and had his sources of information, assured us that the whole revolt had been arranged artificially as a pretext for preventing the departure of Yüan Shih-k'ai from Peking. We even ventured to ride outside the Diplomatic Quarter and saw how the soldiers were carrying goods from the shops into their carts. There was no sign of hostility toward us.

The next day the situation worsened somewhat, the town rabble joining the soldiers in the pillaging. Meanwhile, news was received that Nanking no longer insisted on Yüan's move south. This was the signal for the suppression of the revolt. The soldiers returned to their barracks unmolested, but the beggars and the hooligans who were seen robbing the shops were seized and executed on the spot. Their chopped-off heads were left in the streets with suitable inscriptions as warnings to would-be imitators. The scenes were ghastly, but nothing could deprive the diplomats of new excitement, and conversation turned to the calm and indifference with which the Chinese met their execution. I must confess that I renewed my morning rides to the Temple of Heaven even though I had to pass under trees from the branches of which the heads of some poor devils were hanging. At first I was horrified, but after some time, when with the approach of hot weather the heads dried up, I became quite indifferent to the sight. Venerable old Chinese would sit under these very trees in the morning with their birdcages and listen to the singing of their fine-feathered friends. In such a peaceful atmosphere it was difficult to think about the horrors of Chinese life.

❖❖❖

Once Yüan Shih-k'ai had succeeded in remaining in Peking, he began to scheme for the restoration of the monarchy with himself as Emperor. In this he followed Chinese tradition, the whole of Chinese history being a chain of dynastic successions. Who knows, if Yüan had succeeded in his aim, China might have been spared those years of civil war that followed his downfall. A nation cannot with impunity break with its old tradition and embark on experiences absolutely alien to its history and character. The road Yüan had to follow was extremely difficult, but he knew the Chinese character thoroughly and would have succeeded had external factors not interfered.

At first, when the republicans had come to Peking flushed with victory, Yüan had conducted himself modestly, pretending that he was willing to obey them. Parliament was open and Yüan made a speech in which he promised to follow the will of the people. It became the fashion for heroes of the revolution to come to Peking and to play the part of the new masters. Yüan usually arranged a grand reception for the heroes and, as there was a touch of humor in everything the Chinese did, these receptions were very comical.

Somewhere in the Palace stables an old carriage was found which had been built for the German Crown Prince whose reception had been expected a year before the revolution. I remember how the German Minister, Count Rex, had been opposed to this visit, as the visits of members of the German royal family to foreign countries were usually followed by international complications and Count Rex, a peaceful man, had wanted to avoid such complications, but the royal command must be obeyed and he had informed the Chinese of the Crown Prince's coming. The Chinese built a huge special carriage and, since the monarchy still existed, covered it with yellow silk on which the imperial dragons were painted. Meanwhile a plague epidemic had broken out in Manchuria, killing people by the hundreds, and was slowly moving toward Peking. When the first dead were discovered in the streets of Peking, the German Minister raised a great fuss. A meeting of the Diplomatic Corps was summoned at which he insisted that the Chinese government take energetic measures to halt the spread of the epidemic. A list of such measures was presented to the Chinese, but though they promised to take the necessary steps, they did nothing, and a member of the Foreign Office, talking with our interpreter, expressed astonishment that the foreigners should make such ado about a little thing. He added that if the foreign diplomats knew Chinese history better, they would realize that the happiest times for China were always after wars or epidemics when thousands had died and for those who remained life became easier; without wars

and epidemics the Chinese would starve from overpopulation. So energetic was Count Rex, though only one case of plague had been discovered in a Chinese beggar, that he insisted that the gates of the Diplomatic Quarter be closed and no communication be allowed with the
Chinese city. A well-known foreign wit suggested that Count Rex had
forgotten that he was in Peking and not in Countrexville, but Count
Rex's determination ended as soon as the Crown Prince's visit was
cancelled as a result of all this fuss. He was not so silly as his colleagues had thought. The carriage with the golden dragons remained
forgotten in the imperial stables until it became necessary to meet the
heroes of the revolution at the station. Then the carriage built for the
German Crown Prince was remembered, and the fierce revolutionists
entered the capital sitting among yellow pillows with imperial crests.

The program for such receptions included visits to the foreign legations, where the heroes through an interpreter told of their deeds and
future plans. After the dignified Chinese bureaucrats in their Chinese
robes, these youths in some kind of military uniforms, with their short
hair and grand phrases, made a strange and rather comical impression.
I especially remember a fat general whose chief exploit during the
revolution had been the losing of the fingers on his right hand when
a bomb had been thrown at him. He sat with his wounded hand exposed for public inspection, a proud grin on his face.

Sun Yat-sen, the father of the revolution, made a better impression.
Most of the heroes went from the reception to different restaurants
and brothels, received money from Yüan Shih-k'ai, and returned to
Nanking. But Sun tried to arouse the indifferent Peking population
and talked so much that people began to lose interest in what he was
saying. At that time his chief idea was that China in order to prosper
must be covered with railways. Yüan encouraged him in his talking
and offered him the presidency of a board, with a big salary and a
residence in Shanghai, to study the question of railway construction.
Sun Yat-sen accepted the position and also disappeared from the
Peking horizon.

Thus gradually Yüan Shih-k'ai got rid of his enemies and started
to agitate for the restoration of the monarchy, with himself as founder
of a new dynasty. All the conservative elements supported him. Most
of the foreigners, sick of the perpetual disorder that had followed
the establishment of the republic, were also in sympathy with this

return to the old traditions. As Yüan Shih-k'ai showed special attention to our Legation and was very helpful in settling different difficulties between China and Russia, and as the latter was extremely skeptical about the efficacy of a republican regime in the Chinese atmosphere, the return of the monarchy was most welcome.

As we discovered from confidential sources, the cause of the special friendship shown by Yüan Shih-k'ai toward the Russian Legation dated back to the Sino-Japanese War of 1894-95. At that time Yüan had been the Chinese representative in Korea. The War had started unexpectedly and Yüan had not been able to escape from Seoul when the Japanese occupied the city. He secretly asked the help of our Military Attaché, Colonel Vogak, who was in Seoul and was leaving for Peking. In applying for permission to leave town, Vogak included him among his Chinese servants under a false name. As Japan at that time was doing everything not to provoke Russia, there could be no question of verifying the list presented by the Russian Military Attaché, and Yüan returned safely to Peking. He never spoke of this incident, but showed his gratitude in trying to meet halfway different claims presented by the Russian Legation.

Most of these claims concerned Mongolia, which until the Chinese revolution was considered part of China. As this huge but sparsely populated land was situated along the Siberian frontier, far from any other country, the temptation to subject it to Russian influence was great. After all, the forward movement of Russia into Asia, which had started in 1581[8] when some 840 Cossacks under the command of Ermak had conquered nearly the whole of Siberia, had never stopped. In subsequent years Russian expeditions had brought order to the newly acquired lands. Different Tartar and Mongol chiefs voluntarily submitted to the White Tsar, as the Asian tribes called the Russian Emperor, and by the twentieth century all Siberia from the Ural Mountains to the Pacific Ocean had become an inalienable part of Russia.

Today this would be labelled "aggressive imperialism," but I think it would be more correct to call it the healthy growth of a big state,

[8] The manuscript states 1587. This may be one of many typing errors. Probably Abrikossow had in mind 1581, the year in which Ermak Timofeevich embarked on his conquests. The date 1587 cannot be correct, for Ermak was killed in 1584.

which cannot tolerate at its frontiers undefined, vast empty lands with nomadic tribes in a primitive state of civilization wandering about. The Chinese realized this and in the years before the revolution began to colonize these lands and submit them to Chinese administration. The Mongols did not like it and with their horses and sheep moved to the north, where they fell under Russian influence and easily became tools in anti-Chinese intrigues. This created a great deal of misunderstanding between Russia and China and gave the clever and ambitious Russian representatives in Peking opportunities to display brilliant diplomatic fireworks.

I remember one morning, when I was trying to put the archives into order, the Minister entered after his morning ride, and said that he was greatly annoyed by the tendency of our Foreign Office to let slip past all opportunities for the adjustment of our relations with the Mongols, and asked whether I had not found in the archives something exciting with which we could arouse St. Petersburg from its slumber. I replied that only the day before I had found some correspondence about the part of Outer Mongolia known as Uriankhai.[9] According to this correspondence some fifty years ago an officer attached to the Governor General of Irkutsk had discovered in the archives that during the reign of Catherine the Great the Khan of Uriankhai had submitted to the Empress, agreeing to pay an annual tribute of several skins of sable. With time the Khan had disappeared, no skins were sent, and the land, with the rest of Mongolia, became Chinese territory. The Governor General had sent the officer to Uriankhai, where he had discovered some stone markers, which could be taken as proof that according to the old frontier this land was Russian. The Governor General had sent a report to St. Petersburg and the Emperor had written on it that it was inadmissible that part of Russian territory should be included in the Chinese Empire. The report was sent to the Foreign Office, which, fearing complications, had given the Emperor some explanation and the whole matter had been forgotten. The Minister asked me to send him the whole correspondence.

The next morning I found him beaming. He said that the correspondence was ideal for his purpose and at once sent a report to the

[9] Proclaimed independent in 1921, Uriankhai became known as Tannu Tuva, or the Tuvinian People's Republic; in 1945 it was incorporated in the U.S.S.R. as the Tuva Autonomous Region—or, simply, Tuva.

Foreign Office and the Governor General of Irkutsk, expressing astonishment that nothing had been done to implement the decision of the Emperor. In vain the Foreign Office tried to stop the Minister, the matter came to a head, a representative of the Governor General of Irkutsk coming to Peking to aid the Minister. At the same time the Governor General of the Priamur Region sent a Colonel to claim some territory along the Amur, insisting that the river which served as a frontier between Russia and China had changed its course, and that the land from which the Cossacks had used to get hay for their cattle found itself on the Chinese side. Each colonel tried to persuade the Minister that his claim was more important than the other's. Each took his affair so much to heart that they quarrelled and stopped speaking to each other. In the end the Chinese, whose troubles were increasing daily, agreed to satisfy both claims. Russia got a piece of land bigger than the whole territory of France, and the Cossacks got the fodder for their cattle. Peace was restored between the two colonels, and at the farewell dinner in their honor they got slightly drunk and sang an endless duet about some prisoners in Siberia.

Soon the career of our clever and humorous Minister came to an end. He had made so much fun of others that he was punished by becoming the laughing stock of Peking. He fell in love with a sixteen-year-old French girl and tried to elope with her. The girl's infuriated father, who occupied a high position in the Chinese service, stopped the train and the whole thing came to light. The girl was restored to her parents; the Minister continued to St. Petersburg alone. For weeks there was no other topic of conversation in Peking, and the correspondent of some liberal Russian newspaper quipped that the difference between an Austrian and a Russian diplomat was that while the Austrian diplomat annexed a province (Austria had annexed Bosnia and Hercegovina), the Russian diplomat annexed a French girl young enough to be his daughter. This was not really fair: our Minister had annexed both a province and a girl. But I was sorry for the Minister's wife, who had remained in Peking, not knowing anything. She was a charming lady, and showed how a clever woman can find a way out of a most difficult situation. She wrote to her husband that nothing he did could astonish her and that she was ready to do anything he found necessary in order to protect their children from scandal. The husband replied that she must join him in St. Petersburg and that they must appear everywhere together in order to silence all gossip. This they did, and when people lost interest in the incident, she divorced him, and he married the French girl. Even the Foreign Office changed its attitude and allowed him to continue his career. He was sent to Urga, the capital of Mongolia, to conclude a very important agreement, and after that was Minister in Persia. Later, when I was in St. Petersburg, I visited his former wife and found with her a charming boy who called her grandmother. It was the son of her former husband and his new wife. As the climate of Teheran was bad for the child, she had offered to take him and keep him as long as the parents were in Persia.

✤✤✤

As stated, Mongolia had proclaimed its independence following the abdication of the Chinese Emperor. Russia, not wanting a change that might provoke international complications, made an agreement with the Chinese in which Russia promised to persuade the Mongolian government to recognize the suzerainty of China in return for Chinese recognition of the autonomy of Mongolia, no Chinese soldiers or officials to be sent there. The Mongols proved more difficult to persuade than the Chinese, but our former Minister in Peking who was sent to Urga succeeded and a Russo-Chinese-Mongolian tripartite agreement was concluded. Thus without hostilities, annexation of territory, or international complications the vast Mongolian region was opened to Russian political and commercial activity. By the time the foreign powers began to take interest in the matter, everything had been finished in such a way that there was no cause for any legal argument against the arrangement. Our Legation had a right to be proud of this diplomatic triumph.

The difficulty after the conclusion of the above-mentioned agreement was to create in Mongolia a government capable of ruling the autonomous country. There were two authorities in Mongolia: the princes who ruled the separate parts of the territory and the body of lamas, clergy of a branch of Buddhism in which the chief role was played by the innumerable monks who filled the monasteries. Because of the general superstition of the people they wielded great influence. The head of those lamas, the so-called Khutukhtu in Urga, was considered a reincarnation of Buddha. These Living Buddhas usually came from Tibet, where they were chosen by the local monasteries, after complicated ceremonies, from among the newborn babies; after strict religious training, at the age of eight or ten, they were sent to Mongolian monasteries, where they were ruled by the lamas, and became objects of great veneration. In order to avoid a civil war that would inevitably have ensued if one of the princes had been placed at the head of the government, the Russian advisers decided to follow the example of Tibet, and put at the helm of the state the Khutukhtu of Urga and a Council of Ministers chosen from among the princes, the Russian Consul General at Urga playing the role of chief adviser to the new government to train the princes in the art of ruling.

Such a setup now would be called a "puppet" government, but if a people is absolutely incapable of ruling itself, such a puppet government is the only alternative to complete subjugation of the country to alien rule. The Mongols had not progressed since the time of Genghis Khan who had led them to world conquest; indeed they had so degenerated that they were incapable of ruling themselves and could not keep their independence, and Russia had all the trouble of creating a semblance of self-government. A Russian officer who served as instructor of the new Mongolian army once related how, when a Russian general arrived to inspect the Mongolian troops, the Mongolian Minister of War had been invited to be present at the review, but could not be awakened after a heavy dinner. When he did come at last, he showed no interest in the proceedings until he espied the general's spurs. Then he came to life, squatted down behind the general, and started to turn the little wheels. With such material it is difficult to build anything other than a puppet government. As to the Living Buddha, he was perpetually drunk and created a scandal by taking a wife who ruled in his place.[10]

Meanwhile Yüan Shih-k'ai continued to further his ambition to become emperor. At his order the provincial authorities began petitioning for a return to the monarchy. Steps were taken to put the Temple of Heaven in order. There he intended, after proclaiming himself Emperor of China, to resume the offerings to Heaven. We were preparing ourselves for the great ceremonies which were to captivate the

---

[10] According to Prof. Robert Rupen, the Living Buddha who took a dancing girl for his wife was Bogdo Gegen, Gebtsun Damba Khutukhtu. The terms "Gegen" or "Khutukhtu" are roughly equivalent to "Cardinal" in the Roman Catholic Church.

imagination of the Chinese people and put an end to the chaos created by the republic. But for all his cleverness Yüan had made one vital miscalculation. Concentrating on gaining the sympathy of Russia and other Western countries, he had left Japan in the cold in the expectation that Japan could not go counter to the decision of the other powers. One morning the Japanese Minister called on Yüan and after asking about his plans for the restoration of a monarchy announced that Japan would never allow it. With one blow the whole clever building Yüan had constructed collapsed. Realizing belatedly that nothing would stop Japan from sending troops to back up her threat, all blame being put on his shoulders, the old man became so depressed he fell ill and soon passed away. With him died China's last chance of reviving its strength and unity. In my eyes Yüan was the last Chinese statesman who could have saved China from its sad present fate.

As for Japan, its policy was clear. The Japanese government realized that there was not room for both a strong China and a strong Japan. As history had proven that they could not go hand in hand, which would have been disastrous for Europe, the only thing for Japan to do was to prevent the appearance of a strong and united China. Since the policy of Yüan Shih-k'ai could have led to such a strong and united China, the only thing for Japan to do was to prevent the fulfillment of his policy. But I was sorry for old Yüan, who, notwithstanding his cruelty and unscrupulousness, had a great deal of charm.

Foreigners who live in China usually sympathize with the Chinese and dislike the Japanese. With all their lies, dirt, and antiforeign feelings the Chinese seem more human than the Japanese, who outside their country always seem to wear a mask and, keeping to themselves, not mixing with foreigners, give the impression of plotting against everybody and everything. As long as I was in China I shared the opinion held by most foreigners that Japan was the cause of all the complications in China; only when fate brought me to Japan did I realize that the common Japanese, not contaminated by the ambition of their politicians, were very lovable. Only while abroad did they behave as if everyone of them had some secret task to perform. The Chinese knew how to turn the general dislike of the Japanese to their own advantage, and were always ready to shift onto the Japanese the responsibility for all the complications they themselves created. The

Chinese had the capacity to exasperate even the angels and then blame them for it.

We all felt that the situation in Manchuria had become more complicated after the Russo-Japanese War. Instead of two powers—Russia and China—struggling for domination, there now were three, Japan having obtained half of the railway which passed through the whole of Manchuria and, holding the railway, control over the whole territory through which it passed. It was one of the surprises of the War that not only did Russia keep half of Manchuria, but Japan kept the other half and China did not get anything. As a result China sought to undermine the position of Russia in North Manchuria, especially in Harbin, a town created by Russian money and Russian energy in the railway zone, which in accordance with the Russo-Chinese agreement allowing the construction of the Chinese Eastern railway, was under its administration.

The intrigues of the Chinese, supported by other foreigners, rendered the administration so difficult that after the War Russia had to choose between allowing an increase in Chinese influence in the administration of the railway and the reinforcement of her own position in North Manchuria by agreement with Japan, Japan's position now being so strong that neither China nor any other foreign power could oppose her. As the Chinese Eastern Railway was part of the Siberian Railway, Russia could not afford to lose control over it, at least not until the construction of the Amur Railway had been completed. Russia decided in favor of an agreement with Japan; Manchuria was divided into two spheres of influence, the northern part being reserved for Russian activity, the southern one for Japanese enterprise. The Chinese, whose territory Manchuria supposedly remained, were free to display their industrial and commercial activity in both parts, but except for making money out of the foreign enterprises and intriguing endlessly to draw attention to the abnormal situation in Manchuria, the Chinese activity did nothing to further real cultural and economical progress.

The enormous advances that Manchuria made after the Russo-Japanese War were due to Russian and especially Japanese activity. Russia had too much to do in other parts of her vast empire to display great energy in Manchuria, but Japan with her small territory could concentrate tremendous effort on southern Manchuria. Japanese construction of the South Manchurian Railway, together with the indus-trial and cultural work that this involved, was something of which any nation could have been justly proud.

The United States tried to modify the situation in Manchuria, pro-posing the so-called Knox plan,[11] which called for the purchase and administration of all Manchurian railways, including the Russian and Japanese lines, by an international syndicate. Both Russia and Japan understood, however, that the internationalization of the railways in Manchuria would mean the end of Russian and Japanese influence, as neither country could ever compete with American capital and Ameri-can enterprises, and they refused to accept the proposed plan. For Russia the acceptance of this plan would have meant the internationali-zation of part of the Siberian Railway and the penetration of American influence into Siberia; for Japan it would have meant the loss of the fruits of her successful war, including the great power status she had attained. Hence the proposal fell through, and with it the chance to change the whole course of events in the Far East.

The American project caused a violent quarrel between our Minis-ter and the First Secretary. The Minister was of the opinion that the American proposal would undermine our whole position in the Far East, put us, not only in Manchuria but also in Siberia, at the service of the American dollar, and would spoil our relations with Japan. The First Secretary, on the other hand, maintained that the appearance of the United States in Manchuria and in Siberia would forever free us from danger from Japan, would help us to develop Siberia, and would allow us to concentrate on our interests in the Near East, which he considered much more important than our interests in the Far East. It was impossible to reconcile these points of view and in the end the Minister and the First Secretary were not on speaking terms, though the Minister agreed to send the Secretary's report to St. Petersburg. There nobody took any note of it and the situation in Manchuria re-mained unchanged.

The new understanding between Russia and Japan was strong. No plans which went against the interests of both Russia and Japan could succeed. Japan thought of strengthening her ties with Russia even further and when she heard that our Minister of Finance was coming

[11] After its propounder, Secretary of State Philander Chase Knox, champion of "dollar diplomacy."

to Harbin, she sent her foremost statesman, Prince Ito Hirobumi, to greet the Russian Minister and discuss with him the possibility of closer relations between the former enemies. But the meeting finished tragically. As Prince Ito walked with our Minister of Finance, Vladimir Kokovtsov, at Harbin station before the guard of honor, a Korean assassin rushed out of the crowd and shot Prince Ito to death. The latter had not yet broached his plan to Kokovtsov, and as he had acted wholly on his own initiative and Japan did not follow up the matter, it remained a mystery what sort of an offer Prince Ito had intended to make. At any rate, our relations with Japan were becoming closer and closer, and our position in the Far East, which had been undermined by the unsuccessful war with Japan, was becoming strong again. At last, after years of strenuous work at the Legation from morning until night, we could think of rest.

✤✤✤

I decided to see Mongolia. Wishing to travel simply, without a lot of baggage, and under the pretext of seeking to buy horses for my stable, I applied for permission to use the ordinary post horses which the Mongols were obliged to furnish to people traveling on official business. In the middle of summer, when the dirt and smell of Peking were becoming unbearable, I supplied myself with two bags of dried bread and left the city, accompanied by my Cossack sergeant friend and another Cossack.

From Peking to Kalgan we proceeded by railway. Kalgan proved hot and dirty, our Chinese inn noisy and full of insects. From Kalgan to the Mongolian plateau, where we hoped to obtain the horses for our excursion across the endless steppe, we crossed the mountains in a sort of palanquin carried by two mules. You were quite helpless in the palanquin; if one of the mules were to slip and tumble down the precipice, it would drag you with it. I was glad, therefore, when late that evening we reached a solitary inn. I was so tired that I fell asleep at once in spite of billions of insects which poured from all corners to test the foreign blood; they must not have liked it, however, for I awoke in the morning without having been eaten alive. The inn, which in the moonlight had appeared like a small castle lost in the surrounding emptiness, in the daylight looked dirty and dilapidated; it was surrounded by swamp in which huge black pigs were lying in supreme bliss. After endless conversation and the inspection of our papers, everyone in the inn participating, we were brought three miserable horses and negotiated the remainder of the climb on horseback.

When we reached the plateau I felt like a new man. Before us lay the endless steppe, covered with wild flowers. The air was marvelous; all the heat and dirt had been left behind. The Cossacks soon obtained fresh horses, and we started to gallop across the steppe.

Reared on fresh grass, the Mongolian horses develop such energy that it is difficult to make them go slowly. Soon all houses disappeared and I imagined that this whole vastness belonged to me. From time to time we reached the stations where horses had to be changed, but it was a dreadful job to find new animals, because the Mongols, obliged though they were to supply horses to official travelers, made every effort to avoid doing so. Usually they insisted that they had no horses and it required all the eloquence of my Cossack friend to obtain them. Two or three times, when the Mongols persisted in their obstinacy, Baturin located the horses himself, lassoed and saddled them, and we simply rode off. Only later, when the Mongols discovered what had happened would they send somebody to accompany us to the next station in order to bring back the horses.

At night we would stop at a Mongolian camp, which consisted of several yurts (Mongol tents) in which the nomads lived as they moved from place to place, staying as long as their horses and sheep had enough grass to eat. Coming to such a camp, Baturin usually announced that I was a very important personage. Believing this, the Mongols emptied the best yurt, killed a sheep, and under Baturin's supervision prepared it in an edible way. Inside the yurt I sat opposite the entrance in the place of honor, and as custom required of important personages did not utter a single word. All the talking was done by Baturin, who spoke Mongolian like a Mongol. Soon the yurt was crowded with the population of the entire camp, listening with admiration to Baturin's tales. Excellent mutton was served which we ate with our hands. An alcoholic beverage prepared from milk was offered also, but it was too nasty to drink. Before long the whole sheep disappeared and the Mongols, intoxicated, became noisy and gay.

The women did not join the feast: they stood near the wall, in the darkness, and looked on with curiosity. Mongol women as a rule were far superior to Mongol men. They were healthy and strong, resembling somewhat Russian peasant women. All work was done by them. The men spent most of their time drinking, eating, and sleeping. Looking at them, it was difficult to realize that there had been a time when Mongol hordes had conquered half of Europe and kept Russia under their yoke for more than two centuries.

At the time of my journey Mongolia was still under Chinese rule, and in the south I met Chinese officials and Chinese merchants who infiltrated everywhere like ants. The arrival of a member of the Russian Legation with two Cossacks aroused the suspicion of the officials. In one place we were ordered not to proceed farther until instructions could be obtained from Peking. In vain I fumed and threatened. Only when the Cossack Baturin calmly explained to the official that if he detained us he must supply us suitably—that we would kill one sheep a day out of his own flock—did he become pensive, and after three days, during which we claimed more and more food, he announced that a favorable answer had been received from Peking, supplied us with horses and gladly got rid of us. The story of a message from the capital was, of course, a lie. There was no telegraph in this locality and it would have taken a messenger weeks to reach Peking. The official simply wanted to put me in a position where I had no choice except to turn back, but he had not realized that this would cost him so much.

We continued our journey, stopping now in Mongolian tents, now in small monasteries. These monasteries were crowded with lamas of every age. Except for the daily services, which seemed to be very short and without attendance, the lamas had absolutely nothing to do. It was pathetic to see this multitude of strong and healthy men who did not know how to occupy their time. Only once did I experience something akin to religious feeling in one of the monasteries. The sun was setting as several monks, seated on the roof of the main building, blew into enormous trumpets. A peculiar plaintive sound filled the endless steppe, as if a lost soul were calling in despair for something it did not have on this earth. The red sun disappeared behind the horizon; dusk set in, then the darkness. Millions of stars appeared. But the lament continued and became more tragic in the black of night. You had the feeling that this complaint would be heard and that something would happen. It was a moment when you lost all touch with reality. Your soul seemed to leave the body and float toward something unknown. Hours later the plaintive sounds stopped, and I heard the voices of the monks who carried their instruments downstairs. I remained alone in the stillness of the night; only the stars seemed to be coming nearer and nearer.

Soon we reached our main destination, the famous Mongolian monastery of Dalai Nor. We had calculated our time so as to arrive for the annual holiday of the monastery, when pilgrims from all over Mongolia flocked hither and Chinese merchants brought their wares and squeezed the last farthing from them. The place looked animated. Near the monastery buildings one could see the camps of Mongolian princes. The small town surrounding the monastery was filled with Chinese merchants, who came with their families, the Chinese women with their painted faces looking like some frightened, exotic creatures compared with the healthy Mongol women in their fineries, who walked about as if the place belonged to them. Thanks to Baturin's friendship with the Mongols I was invited to stay in one of the buildings of the monastery. I accepted the invitation without realizing that I would thereby place myself in the midst of political intrigues which divided different sections of the monastery.

Like all religious centers in Mongolia, the monastery of Dalai Nor had its own Living Buddha, who in his childhood had come from Tibet. Now a man of sixty, he had fallen under Russian influence. Several times he had visited Irkutsk, returning full of admiration for Russia and all things Russian. Inside the monastery he had built a small Russian house for himself, filled it with gifts from Russia, and even drove about in a Russian carriage. The Chinese had not liked this at all and had begun to intrigue against him, but in spite of the great risk he had shown great independence. At last Peking had succeeded in inducing Lhasa to send another Living Buddha to Dalai Nor. Upon his arrival most temples and the majority of the monks had passed to him, but the old Living Buddha could not be deprived of his sanctity and had remained in one section of the monastery, surrounded by monks still faithful to him. Undoubtedly there were some among the latter who served as Chinese spies, but the old man did not seem to mind. He was considered very rich, owned a big place not far from Dalai Nor on the supposed site of the former capital of Kublai Khan; there he kept horses and whiled away most of his time without hiding his contempt for the new Living Buddha.

I can imagine what consternation the arrival of a member of the

Russian Legation as guest of the old Living Buddha must have aroused among the Chinese and the supporters of his successor. At once my journey acquired political significance and the Chinese began to be very curious about my mission, refusing to believe that I had come merely to buy horses. The old Living Buddha made me very comfortable. As I did not speak Mongolian, Baturin interpreted. He told me that the old man always turned to politics and was asking when the White Tsar would take Mongolia under his protection. I could only reply with a mysterious air that the White Tsar had not confided his plans to me.

The holiday celebrations in the monastery lasted nearly a week, presided over by the young Living Buddha, surrounded by hundreds of monks. I went to the services, at which rows and rows of monks were reading their prayers in unison. From time to time they rang small bells. Mongols swelled the temple. The front row was occupied by the princes and their families; the women in their gorgeous dresses, with their silver head ornaments, looked magnificent. At the end of the service the congregation knelt before the Living Buddha, who was seated on a high silk cushion and distributed his blessings in the form of small silk towels. One afternoon there was a kind of sacred dance before the temple. The monks were dressed like devils, dragons, and other animals, and were going round and round, trying to frighten the spectators. In the brilliant sun these monsters and the picturesque crowd were a queer sight indeed.

Another day was devoted to racing. My host, the old Living Buddha, was a great lover of horses and invited me to his box. And a box it was literally, standing on high poles and reached by a ladder. When I climbed up, I found the old man attired in brilliant yellow, and there we sat in full view of the huge crowd, the incarnation of Buddha and the foreigner. There was great dignity in his manner and had he worn a frock coat and silk hat he could have been taken for an English lord at the races in Ascot. He tried to explain the races to me, but they were so disorderly that I understood little. As a comical part of the program there was racing on camels. The crowd seemed to enjoy itself immensely. At the end of the performance the Living Buddha descended the ladder and surrounded by monks, also dressed in yellow, left the place without noticing the kneeling public.

The next morning I was invited to accompany the old man to his

country place and look at his horses. The excursion proved very interesting. The Living Buddha drove in a light two-wheeled carriage, also
brought by him from Russia; he held the reins. I followed with the
two Cossacks on horseback, close behind the carriage; a dozen monks
rode in the rear. In the bright sun our procession, with the Living
Buddha and the monks in their usual yellow robes, was a wonderful
sight. The people we met, recognizing the incarnation of Buddha,
stopped and knelt till the procession had passed. Baturin explained to
me that the old man was doing all this to annoy the Chinese.

It took us the whole day to reach his place. It was dark when we
arrived, and we were met by barking dogs and a man with a lantern.
I noticed that we had to pass between huge stones, apparently the remnant of an old wall and all that remained from the old capital of
Kublai Khan. In the middle of the enclosure stood a small Russian-
style house, in which we found food and comfortable beds. Tired, I
went to sleep early. As I dozed off, the flickering candle transformed
Baturin and the Living Buddha into enormous shadows whispering to
each other about the future of Mongolia or perhaps about the prices
of horses.

The following morning we rode to the place where the horses were
grazing, a vast stretch of land with hundreds of horses running about
freely. Recognizing their master, several of them galloped toward us.
The Living Buddha was like a changed man. He dismounted and was
soon surrounded by his horses. Baturin whispered to me that we would
not find any better horses elsewhere and recommended that we make
our purchases at once. I gave him a free hand, and soon he and the old
man were absorbed in picking the horses and bargaining about their
prices. Among the ponies I saw a big European horse and chose it for
myself. At first the Living Buddha did not wish to part with it, but
eventually consented, thinking perhaps that it might help him obtain
Russian protection over Mongolia. In three days the horses were
chosen and purchased. I sent them straight back to Peking with the
second Cossack and a Mongol. Baturin and I returned by a longer
route, across the province of Jehol. I had heard so much about the
magnificent summer palace in which the Chinese Emperor Ch'ien
Lung had received Lord Macartney, the first English representative,
that I thought it a sin not to visit Jehol even though it meant another
week on horseback, traveling across a strange country without a guide

and with little food. My trust in the resourcefulness of Baturin was so great, however, that with him at my side I would have calmly faced even the wilderness of the Sahara.

We took leave of the Living Buddha. I was to see him once more when he came to Peking to return my visit. His fate was sad. When civil war broke out in China bands of Chinese soldiers wandered through the whole country, killing and robbing. Reputed to be wealthy and living in relative isolation with only a few monks, the Living Buddha was set upon by one such band. Though tortured, he would not reveal where he kept his fortune. In the end he was killed and his house was burned down, but nothing was found. Thus he died without seeing his dream of a Mongolia under Russian protection fulfilled.

❖❖❖

After days of wandering, asking directions to Jehol of everyone we met, we left Mongolia and re-entered China proper. The endless steppe with its cool air gave way to a hilly country with nice shady valleys. It became increasingly difficult to find horses and we had to content ourselves with Chinese carts, which were real instruments of torture. But at last we arrived in Jehol, a typical Chinese town, full of soldiers and unspeakable dirt; there was no outward sign that the city had once been the seat of the luxurious court of Ch'ien Lung. We spent the night in a noisy inn. In the morning, armed with instructions how to find the famous palace, we walked along the streets, filled with Chinese shops and smelly restaurants, to the outskirts of the city. Here we found a big gate, where a guard checked our permit.

As we passed through the gate, we entered a veritable fairy land. Beneath us lay a lake covered with small islands, on each of which there stood quaint Chinese pavilions, every one a real object of art. The different designs that covered them had once been vivid; they were faded now but still beautiful. Small arched bridges, originally covered with red lacquer, connected the islands. A porcelain-tile-covered pagoda stood on shore. It was a picture of the past, of China's ancient culture and art. One could imagine how beautiful it must have been when the pavilions had been bright in color and were surrounded by flowery shrubs, the pagoda reflected in the water, as boats, filled with beautifully dressed court ladies, glided from island to island. In the office near the entrance I was met by a fat Chinese official, the guardian of the palace, whose duty it was to show the place to distinguished visitors. He took us on a boat cruise of the lake. Everywhere we found signs of decay: the pavilions stood empty, their colors faded. The Chinese did not know what it means to be proud of the relics of one's glorious past. They did nothing to preserve or restore them. What was past was past and they saw no use in spending money on its preservation. All the priceless treasures which had once adorned the palace were kept in local warehouses with broken windows, exposed to rain and snow. Many had been pilfered by the guards and sold to curio dealers in Peking. Yüan Shih-k'ai tried to save the remainder by moving items to a small museum in the Forbidden City of Peking. But during the civil war which followed Yüan's death, Peking passed from one general to another, and I doubt that much is left of this museum.

A luncheon had been prepared for me on the main island. The fat Chinese, who spoke a little English, was very proud of belonging to what he called "progressive China," and tried to prove this by drinking a lot of whiskey and pointing to the soup, which he called "chicken broth."

During the next two days I visited different temples which Emperor Ch'ien Lung had built around Jehol in the hope of making the seat of his summer residence into a spiritual center. He planned to transfer the residence of the Dalai Lama from Lhasa to Jehol and in order to receive him properly built near his palace an exact replica of the Potala monastery in which the Dalai Lama usually resided. The Dalai Lama came to Jehol but died before long. His successor, elected in Lhasa, would not move to Jehol and Ch'ien Lung's ambitious plan came to naught, but the monastery still stands and, as it was built almost like a fortress, it is in better shape than the other temples.

I remember another temple whose roof was said to have been covered with gold. Four enormous dragons had once graced the four corners of the roof. Now only two remained standing; the other two had fallen down and you could hardly find them in the tall grass which had overgrown the whole place. It is sad to see how little has remained from a whole century of glory, but perhaps the Chinese are right not to preserve the old palaces and temples. The comparison with the present would be too pitiful.

The rest of my journey was uneventful. We took a boat down the slow current of a broad river to the spot where the Chinese wall entered the sea. Foreign soldiers stationed in Peking spent the summers in barracks nearby, and I stopped for a few days with some friendly Italian naval officers. Several diplomats and their families lived here also in order to escape the heat of Peking. When I listened to the gossip of these foreigners I realized with slight regret that my journey was over.

❖❖❖

In Peking I found a grumbling Chargé d'Affaires, who complained that I had been away too long. But as he was the grumbling type, I took no heed of his remarks and soon was absorbed in my old work.

In those days Yüan Shih-k'ai was still making plans for the establishment of a new dynasty, and our Chargé had the idea of publishing a French newspaper to promote Russian interests. He found an unemployed French journalist, an energetic but also unscrupulous person. Every day the Frenchman would come to our Chargé and together they wrote the whole newspaper. I had to supply extracts from the reports of our different consuls, and these were printed as correspondence from the special correspondents of the paper. At the beginning there was always a political article dictated by our Chargé. As the latter was a man who could not tolerate any contradictions, our newspaper soon became involved in a polemic with the English newspaper published by the Chinese Foreign Office. In the heat of the polemic the aim of the newspaper was forgotten. As the English paper promoted the interests of Yüan Shih-k'ai, our newspaper began to attack him. Amused, the other diplomats asserted that their breakfasts had become more entertaining since the publication of our newspaper. I told our Chargé that we were becoming the laughing stock of the diplomatic corps with our newspaper. The Chargé got very angry and said that neither I nor the rest of the diplomats understood anything, and for a week we were not on speaking terms. As we both came from Moscow and I felt that the grumbling Chargé had a tender spot in his heart for me, we soon made up, but the newspaper attacks continued.

One day the English paper stated that the attacks of our newspaper did not deserve any attention, because it was a well-known fact that they were written by a man who received money from a certain Legation. True as this was, our Frenchman became furious and went forth, in the best French tradition, to challenge the Chinese editor to a duel. When he appeared at the office of the Chinese paper with a second, the panic-stricken editor tried to hide under the bed. The Frenchman found him and calling the whole staff together showed them the editor under the bed and expressed his regret that they had to work for a man so contemptible he did not even deserve to be challenged to a duel. The next day he published the whole story in our newspaper. When our Minister came back from leave, he was greatly amused by the episode and allowed the fight between the two newspapers to continue. But after his unsuccessful elopement with the French girl, the Minister was replaced by a serious man who did not have the same sense of humor, and put a stop to the whole business. As for myself, the incident undermined my confidence in newspapers. I had seen how easy it was to distort facts and camouflage public opinion.

❖❖❖

With the arrival of the new Minister [Vasilii Nikolaevich Krupenskii], the whole atmosphere at the Legation changed. At first I missed the brilliant fireworks of his predecessor, but soon I began to appreciate the steady work of the new man. He too had a certain amount of experience in Chinese affairs, having been First Secretary in Peking during the Boxer Rebellion.[12] He owned a collection of magnificent Chinese objects, among them the red lacquer throne from the Summer Palace and the silk embroidered ceiling from the tent of Emperor Ch'ien Lung. While he was Minister our Legation looked magnificent and his receptions had a touch of the European capitals. He was extremely conscientious. He may not have displayed the same brilliant yet often misplaced initiative as his predecessor, but when he received his instructions from the Foreign Office, he responded with such fervor that he usually attained the desired results regardless of difficulties.

With the disappearance of the newspaper and its attacks on Chinese

[12] Krupenskii had served in China as First Secretary from 1899 to 1902. He returned as Minister in 1913.

[189]

policy, our good relations with President Yüan Shih-k'ai were restored. It was then that we started our Mongolia policy which brought such brilliant results. The initiative in this policy belonged to the Chief of the Far Eastern Section of the Foreign Office [Kazakov], in whose capable hands the new Foreign Minister Sergei Dmitrievich Sazonov, who knew little about the Far East, left our whole Far Eastern policy. To the collaboration of Kazakov and Krupenskii Russia owes the successes that marked our policy in the Far East after the Russo-Japanese War.

As my time to leave China was approaching, the idea of a change, as always, made me quite miserable. When quitting London, I had not expected to find anywhere such happiness as I had enjoyed in Peking. Now I wondered what other place could offer such an exciting life, with something new happening every day, with a multitude of friends yet with none of the bureaucratic officialism that made one old before his time. But a career is a career, and nice as it might be, one cannot stay put. Without an influential aunt or anyone else who could solicit a new post for me, I was not willing to return to St. Petersburg empty handed and beg for a new assignment. Thus I had to delay my departure until I chanced upon an opening.

Before leaving the Far East, which I did not expect to see again, I wanted to visit Japan. The Minister was kind enough to allow a short trip without first requesting Foreign Office authorization as required under the general regulations. After consultation with people who knew Japan, I drew a plan for a lightning visit.

My first stop en route to Japan was Mukden, where I visited our Consul, whose eccentric wife insisted on taking me to the tombs of the Manchu emperors. Before I had time to consent, she summoned a carriage in which she installed her two children and a dog, leaving scarcely room for me. Then, at the last moment, she shouted through the window to the wife of the British Consul next door and invited her to join us. She moved the children to the right and left of the coachman, ordering him to hold onto them well, and took the dog on her lap, letting me squeeze in between the English lady and herself. Fortunately the horse was so old it could hardly move and trotted along without guidance, so that the coachman could concentrate on holding the children. In such an undignified way, through clouds of dust, with the two Consuls' wives talking incessantly, we arrived at the Manchu tombs. Situated in a wood and surrounded by a wall, the tombs were impressive, but, as all the old monuments, in a state of utter dilapidation. From a box attached to the carriage the Consul's wife produced a homemade pie and bottles of beer. She never stopped talking, shouted to her children to beware of snakes, and chased the dog who refused to keep quiet. It was a typical Russian picnic, with the only difference that it was consummated on the tombs of the Manchu emperors, buried centuries ago, never suspecting that they would be subjected to such profanity. We returned at dusk, with the same clouds of dust and the same torrent of conversation.

The following day I left for Dairen, curious to see this Russian creation [Dalny] on which we had spent millions only to cede it to Japan after the Russo-Japanese War. I was astonished to find how much had remained from the time of the Russian occupation. A Russian cathedral stood opposite the station, and a number of Russian droshkies, driven by Chinese coachmen, rumbled down the streets. The Japanese were planning to make Dairen into the biggest port of Manchuria and the center of administration of the South Manchurian Railway. Already the place hummed with Japanese activity.

The following day I visited Port Arthur. It too was filled with reminiscences of its former masters. Indeed, the Japanese had changed scarcely anything. The houses stood empty, the walls covered with remnants of Russian advertisements. In the middle of the town was a typical Russian park with a rustic bandstand. I sat on a bench and imagined smart Russian naval officers promenading with their Port Arthur ladies to the strains of music of a Russian naval band. But alas, it was only an illusion; not a soul was in the park and except for a small Japanese garrison the whole place seemed empty. I visited a little military museum in which the Japanese had collected everything relating to the siege of Port Arthur, including some old Russian uniforms. With the aid of a Japanese guide, who spoke a little Russian, I retraced the course of the siege, walking from the smaller hills to the celebrated two-hundred-meter hill, the key to the fortress. Standing on this hill one realized that once the Japanese had taken it, no further defense was possible. From the hill I could see how small the bay of Port Arthur was and how shallow it was at low tide. Half the fleet had to remain outside. No wonder that the Japanese surprise attack, preceding a declaration of war, had succeeded in disabling the three best Russian warships. As I looked down on Port Arthur bay, it struck me as a most unsuitable place for a big fleet. I failed to understand why our military authorities had been so proud of its occupation by the Russian fleet, and recalled how the Minister of the Navy was rumored to have told the Empress that he offered to her Port Arthur as a most valuable diamond for her crown. No wonder the Japanese decided not to restore Port Arthur as a fortress. My excursion to Port Arthur took nearly the whole day, and I returned to Dairen tired and sad; although less than a decade had passed since those tragic events, the spirit of Russia still lingered over the place.

The next day I was back in Mukden and gladly pushed on. Aside from the imperial tombs the most remarkable thing about the city was the awful dust, which penetrated everywhere and covered everything. From Mukden to Antung I had to take a toylike railway which the Japanese had constructed during the War for the transfer of their troops. It was a slow and uncomfortable journey; in the two carriages there was barely room for a dozen passengers. The train did not operate at night and I slept in small, primitive Japanese inns.

The only foreigner whom I met on this train was a Frenchman, an assistant surgeon, attached to a French detachment in Hankow. The first thing he told me was that he was going to Japan with the sole aim of sleeping with Japanese women. Hankow, he said, was an awful place in this respect, and he had been saving money to go to Japan to reward himself for his abstentious life in China. At the first inn where we stopped for the night, a fat and ugly Japanese girl served our dinner. The moment the Frenchman saw her, he rushed to her and began to touch her breasts shouting in French: "What beautiful apples!" The girl dropped the soup and ran away. After that we were served by a man. I told the Frenchman that if he behaved like that I would not sit with him; he should restrain his feelings until we arrived in Japan. We parted company at Seoul and I did not see him again until I ran into him in Yokohama. He looked depressed and told me that during his first romance he had been robbed by the woman and had had to borrow money for a return ticket to Hankow from his Consul; he was leaving with the first boat, his dreams of romance in Japan shattered.

Our train was moving slowly and we reached Antung on the second day. The Japanese were building a magnificent bridge across the Yalu, but it was not yet completed and we crossed the river on a ferry. On the other side we found a regular and very comfortable train which took us to Seoul. The character of the country was changed. We passed picturesque hills covered with grass of such intense green that the whole landscape appeared artificially painted. In the fields were figures in the unique white dress of the country. I was told that in antiquity the people had been ordered to wear white, the color of mourning, following the death of one of their emperors. When the term of mourning passed, the authorities forgot to countermand the order and the population has remained dressed in white. From afar the white robes looked picturesque against the green background, but at close range they appeared so dirty and so cumbersome that one could only wonder at the conservatism of the population which did not discard them.

Seoul is a charming town. The Japanese spend a lot of money and work to keep the country and its capital in perfect order, and though the Koreans grumble, it is the first time in their history that so much is done for the progress of their country. But it is an old truth that people prefer to live like pigs yet keep their independence, and so the Koreans grumble and listen to different agitators who speak about the country under the Japanese yoke, forgetting that they had been far more miserable under their own emperors and that the whole history of Korea teaches that they will never be able to stand on their own feet.

The whole country seemed asleep. The tomb of the old Empress [Queen Min] who had been assassinated by the Japanese at the time when Russia and Japan had been struggling for domination of the country, though a relic of turbulent times, did not disturb the impression of absolute calm. As I walked and gazed at the beautiful green valleys and peaceful small villages, where even the dogs were too lazy to bark, I could not help recalling that Korea was called "Land of the Morning Calm." Perhaps "Land of the Evening Calm" would have been more appropriate, for the morning calm can give way to an energetic day, while only profound sleep can follow the evening calm.

With difficulty I found my way to the hotel. The proprietress, a

German woman who had spent her entire life in Seoul, bemoaned the passing of Old Korea. She did not deny that the Japanese did a lot for the country, but complained that it was difficult to work with them. They wanted everything for themselves and were suspicious of foreigners.

I called on the Russian Consulate, which occupied the house of the old Legation. Before the Russo-Japanese War the Legation had competed with the Japanese in trying to win influence over Korea. I was shown the pavilion to which the Korean Emperor had stolen one night to implore the Russian Minister to save his country from the Japanese. But Russia had not been able to do anything. Defeated by Japan, she had been forced to renounce her interest in Korea and eventually to allow its annexation by Japan. The Legation was changed into a consulate, the old Emperor soon died, and his heir was taken to Japan by the Japanese, married to a Japanese princess and absorbed into their own Imperial Family. The Russian Consulate had little to do. With its beautiful garden it looked like a villa somewhere on the Riviera and was a place to which the old consuls were sent for a rest before their retirement.

From Seoul I went to Fusan [Pusan], where I embarked for Japan. The crossing took a night. In the darkness I passed Tsushima Island, where the Russian fleet under the command of Admiral Zinovii Rozhestvenskii had been destroyed by Admiral Togo.

At Shimonoseki I first set foot on Japanese soil. After the yellow Chinese landscape and the noise and dirt of Peking, Japan was strikingly charming. In spring, when the sun did not blind and the cherry blossoms were in full bloom everywhere, the whole country looked like one big garden. The toy houses, the graceful women in bright kimonos, the charming children dressed like dolls, and everybody smiling—it all seemed completely unreal. Thoroughly charmed by Japan on my first visit, I pursued no serious task; I had no intention of writing a treatise on Japan or of studying Japanese politics. All I wanted to do was to enjoy life and wander from place to place with a guide book in my hand. Had anyone told me that I would spend nearly a third of my life in that country, I would never have believed him.

My first stop in Japan was at Miyajima, a small island with a temple so near the sea that during high tide its gate stood in the water. At sunset, when the sea was red and golden, the gate seemed to float on the water. No horses and no cars were allowed on the island; deer fed from your hands, there were crowds of pilgrims. . . . It was Japan as the American author Lafcadio Hearn had described.

Hearn had come to Japan some fifty years earlier, tired of the noise of American cities. In Japan he found the paradise for which his soul had been longing, married a Japanese woman, and became a Japanese subject. He left volumes and volumes of writings in which he idealized what he saw. His portrayal may not have been quite true, but anyone who has lived in Japan knows that there are moments when the beauty of the Japanese landscape—the quiet temples among the huge cryptomerias, the groups of pilgrims, the clear streams among the moss-covered stones—grips your soul, reality disappears, and you share the feeling of Lafcadio Hearn that you are in a sort of paradise. After a few days in Japan I realized how right were the people who had insisted that to know the Japanese one must see them in their own country. Gone was their arrogance, their air of mystery, their suspicion of every foreigner; instead there were people as human as those of other races, admiring the cherry blossoms, playing with their children, laughing and getting drunk. It was the foreigners with their big statures, rough manners, and loud voices who looked incongruous in Japan.

From Miyajima I moved to Kyoto, the former capital of Japan, where until 1868 the emperors had lived among dilapidated palaces and temples, shorn of all power by Tokugawa shoguns, who kept the country closed for nearly three hundred years, until reopened by Commodore Matthew C. Perry and the American fleet. Kyoto was full of remnants of Old Japan, but contemporary life was steadily encroaching on the past. From the point of view of beauty, this was a great pity, since Old Japan was the creation of the genius of its own people; New Japan was the result of imitation and, as all imitation, especially if done by a people whose art is very different, extremely ugly.

In Tokyo I called on our Embassy, where a pompous Ambassador [Nikolai Nikolaevich Malevskii-Malevich] gave me two fingers and expressed his displeasure with our policy in China. When I tried to tell him about the successes of our Legation in Mongolia, he grew quite angry and accused us of spoiling his policy in Japan with our policy in Mongolia, where, as he put it, our whole interest consisted of selling one match box a year. When I told him that we followed instructions from the Foreign Office in our policy and that he must address his complaints to St. Petersburg and not to a modest secretary, he changed the subject.

The Ambassador had served all his life in the Ministry, where he had been chief of some department. After the War Russia had to conclude a fishery agreement with Japan and the Vice Minister, who was to have presided over the negotiations, backed out at the last moment on the grounds that his knowledge of fishing was limited to eating fish in a restaurant. The department chief was appointed in his stead and impressed the Japanese with the grandness of his manners. Upon the conclusion of the negotiations, in order to forestall the military from nominating a general, the department chief was named first Russian Ambassador in Tokyo. Thus it was through fish that he became Ambassador, and, remaining in Tokyo for nearly a decade, he had ample opportunity to display his grand manners. But grand manners alone do not make a great ambassador. When at the beginning of World War I he was asked by our Foreign Office on which side Japan would be, he joined the French Ambassador in drafting a long proposal for keeping Japan neutral, at a time when it was known in St. Petersburg that Japan would side with us. It was not proof of sagacity, when, after ten years in the country, the diplomat could not tell whether in case of war the country would be our friend or our enemy. During the War we desperately needed Japanese ammunitions; the Ambassador in Tokyo was so slow in his efforts that the annoyed military had him replaced with our energetic Minister in Peking [Krupenskii]. This came as a great blow to the Ambassador [Malevskii-Malevich], because he was sure that there could not be a better representative than he. The diplomatic career is full of sad surprises.

I visited Nikko, where the first shoguns lay buried among gorgeous temples and dark cryptomerias. I rode to Lake Chuzenji, never suspecting in crossing it that I would spend many a happy summer there. I visited Karuizawa, a summer resort created by foreign missionaries, climbed the active volcano Asama-yama and stood at the edge of the crater, surrounded by smoke, and listened to the frightening noise inside. When the mountain began belching stones, I dashed away from the hellish surroundings. I returned to Yokohama and from there departed for Shanghai on a German steamer.

In those days everything German was considered very comfortable. Germany was making enormous progress everywhere, German activity and German trade in the Far East outstripping even that of England. The boat was really very comfortable and every half hour we were invited to eat. Sometimes it was a regular meal, another time merely a cup of soup or tea, but eating was our chief occupation aboard ship.

Shanghai was very impressive. It was a monument to Anglo-Saxon activity. Not so long ago it had been an empty shore, inhabited by a few Chinese fishermen; now it was a tremendous city with millions of inhabitants, broad streets, magnificent houses, and, as the height of luxury, a race course in the middle of town. The pride of achievement was written on the face of every Englishman. The display of wealth was simply sickening, and to the great annoyance of the Chinese there was a notice in the local park excluding Chinese and dogs. In later years agitators were to exploit this inscription and it was to cost the English dearly, but when I was there the first time no one gave it a second thought, the chief reason for the notice being that it was impossible to keep the park clean with the Chinese crowd inside.

As a member of the Embassy I was feted everywhere: I visited the famous bar which was supposed to be the longest in the world, dined with the manager of the Russian Bank and saw such a display of silver and well-dressed ladies that I was reminded of London, and played bridge for such high stakes that I was trembling at the possibility of losing everything and remaining stranded in this Babylon of the Far East. I was glad when I found myself on a steamer to Hankow on my way back to Peking.

For three days I traveled slowly upstream against the current of the Yangtze, with its flat shores and yellow water, one of the grandest rivers that I have ever seen. The passengers were mostly missionaries with no sense of humor. During the meal a kind of cloth with frills was moved before our eyes to lessen the heat. When I said that this reminded me of watching a ballet performance from the first row, with the skirts of the dancers directly before one, they were deeply shocked.

[197]

In Hankow I was welcomed by a large colony of Russian tea merchants. They were making a lot of money and were trying to imitate the English in their way of living. Calling on some merchants early in the morning to avoid the great heat of midday, I was asked what I wished to drink. When I replied that a glass of ice water would be fine, the host looked at me with great contempt and said that they never drank water in Hankow and ordered a bottle of champagne. I was duly impressed, but champagne at ten o'clock in the morning made me quite miserable, especially as it was followed by an enormous lunch, tea at the club, and an endless dinner with barrels of the same champagne. Nothing can cure Russians of their hospitality which consists of making you eat so much that you risk getting indigestion for the rest of your life.

After three days in Hankow I had my fill of Russian hospitality and was ready to depart for Peking, when one afternoon in the local club I ran into an English naval officer whom I had known in London, but whose existence I had quite forgotten. Since then he had been transferred to China as commander of a British gunboat on the Yangtze and was leaving the following morning for Changsha, whither he had been summoned by the Consul who expected some trouble among the Chinese. Life is full of surprises: we had last seen each other on a houseboat on the Thames; now, four years later fate brought us together on the shores of the Yangtze. In half an hour we had renewed our friendship and the young and rather irresponsible officer insisted on my accompanying him to Changsha.

I could not resist such an interesting trip and the next morning at five o'clock I found myself aboard a tiny gunboat which was going, perhaps, to quell a disorder in a provincial Chinese town. The river had overflowed its banks and looked like an enormous lake. From time to time the roofs of inundated villages could be seen sticking out from the water. Our small gunboat seemed lost in this enormous space of water. We stopped at Yochow [now Yoyang], where the river was narrower and we could land. It was Sunday and as my companion, an Irish Catholic, was greatly interested in religion, we decided to visit the different foreign missions.

We started with the Protestant missions, but found most of them closed because of the approaching heat, during which all the missionaries forget their religious work and enjoy themselves in the cool of a hill near Hankow. Only in one of the missions was there a missionary; he was furious that he was obliged to stay at Yochow because an old Chinese who ought to have been dead was taking a long time in joining his ancestors.

This was not the first time that I saw how lightly Protestant missionaries took their work, as if the teaching of the Gospel and Christian work among the Chinese depended upon the climate. The only missionaries who were always on the spot and did not allow themselves any holidays were the Catholics, and it was a great relief to find the whole Catholic mission working hard, their hospital full and no one grumbling that the patients kept him from his vacation. Usually when a Catholic missionary left his native land for China, he did so forever. But such devotion did not really affect Chinese attitudes toward the foreign missionaries and the faith they preached. The Chinese are a very practical people. They joined the missions, because the missions, financed from abroad, provided free hospital care and education, but I have always doubted that their hearts were really touched by the teachings of Christ. After all, there was little in Chinese culture to prepare them for the principles of Christianity. The only Chinese I have known who proved to be a sincere Christian was the well-known Chinese diplomat Lu Cheng-hsiang, who was married to a Belgian woman. Several times he served as Minister of Foreign Affairs and was one of the few honest Chinese bureaucrats. After the death of his wife, he joined one of the strictest religious orders in Belgium and was known for his devotion to Catholicism.

In the evening we sat on the deck of the gunboat under the star-studded sky and discussed whether religion could ever kill the beast in man. As if to supply us with a negative answer, Chinese junks with girls to tempt the British sailors rounded our vessel. The commander shouted at them and they slid away, but for a long time the sound of their oars echoed through the darkness. When we arrived at Changsha the following day, we discovered that there had been a false alarm and after spending a day in the quaint town of Changsha, far from any foreign influence, we returned to Hankow.

The train journey from Hankow to Peking took nearly three days. It was very hot and dirty; the country was flat and devoid of beauty; crowds of Chinese were everywhere, shouting, eating, and rushing about. Though there was talk that brigands might attack the train, nothing happened, and I was glad to find myself back in Peking. In the yellow vastness of China, Japan with its green hills, majestic Mt. Fuji, and smiling population seemed a dream.

❖❖❖

Soon I received a letter from my friend, Kazakov, the Chief of the Far Eastern Section, who informed me that I would be nominated as one of his assistants, a new position to be created after a general reform of the Foreign Office, appropriate legislation having been introduced in the Duma. Meanwhile he offered me a post in the Embassy in Tokyo, expressing the opinion that one could not have a proper understanding of the Far Eastern political situation without having lived in Japan. I could not refuse the offer of my future chief, but requested permission before moving to Japan, where I had just been as a tourist, to pay a short visit to Russia, which I had not seen for almost four years. Permission was granted, and after shedding the usual tears and gorging myself at innumerable farewell dinners, I left Peking, where I had been so happy, and headed for Moscow on the Siberian express.

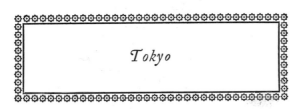

Tokyo

THE GREATEST CHANGE THAT I FOUND IN MOSCOW WAS IN THE tremendous increase of interest in politics. Everywhere I heard discussion as to what one ought to do to promote political liberty. In the house of my gregarious brother, I met crowds of people whom I had never known before. Some were in constant danger of arrest, but they did not seem to mind. When I tried to defend the policy of the government, I usually found myself alone. The policy was really indefensible, because you cannot grant a certain amount of liberty and then devote your energy to taking it back, as Nicholas II was doing under the influence of reactionary circles. The Manifesto of October 17 [30], 1905, had granted Russia a kind of constitution, but it was being interpreted in such a way as to nullify it. The name of the Empress began to crop up in political discussions, for it was her theory that the Emperor, having received autocratic power from his father, must hand it down intact to his son. This unstatesmanlike nonsense irritated the public and turned its political credo more and more to the left. A millionaire Moscow merchant I knew [Savva Marozov] was spending a fortune on the support of the extremist party, from which the Bolsheviks ultimately sprang. Being in the government service I tried to find some justification for the policy of the government, but was beaten on every point. All I could do was to warn prophetically that unrestricted freedom would bring to

[201]

the fore forces which would sweep away everything and leave us with but the memory of our grand phrases.

Only in the company of my father, who in his contemplation of eternity regarded politics as insignificant, and in the family circle of my elder brother, who was completely absorbed in scientific research and whose wife and two boys made me feel quite old by calling me "uncle," could I escape these discussions. Generally speaking, life in Moscow had become broader, and I was proud to find so much culture in my native town, which the inhabitants of St. Petersburg used to call a "big village."

I could not be in Europe without visiting my aunt in Paris. As interesting as always, she had much in common with my father. The conversation of the one seemed the continuation of the conversation of the other, though they both denied it and always criticized each other. She complained that her brother lived too far removed from real life, he that she attached too much importance to little things. My aunt's life seemed complete with her two daughters, who already then showed signs of remarkable intelligence. For a while I was welcome in the midst of their "egoism of three," but after some time I began to feel superfluous, and went to London to see the Benckendorffs. But I learned that it is always a mistake to try to resurrect the past. Glad as the Benckendorffs were to see me, they had aged and I felt outside their interests. Their daughter had married and my friend the *dame de compagnie*, found me too reactionary as I vainly tried to defend the policy of the government. The Chancery had been transferred to another place and was full of strangers. The one Secretary whom I knew and who later was to turn out to have been a German spy met me with such rudeness that I had no desire to return. New people had brought new customs. But as Count Benckendorff said when I was taking leave of him, the Golden Age of the Embassy had been in the past, when Poklevskii, I, and even Sviatopolk-Mirskii had been there. With such consolation I left London, which will always remain my first love, never to see it again.

On my way back I spent three more days with my aunt in her villa in Brittany. An ardent believer in peace, she had named it Villa Pax. Alas, twice war was to turn her out of the villa and her youngest daughter, the charming Lucette, who followed in her footsteps and became a doctor, was to die in Paris during the German occupation, a victim of war. When they accompanied me to the station, the day was gloomy and the ocean roared across the pines, agitated by the wind. I never saw them again.

❖❖❖

It was time to return to the Far East, and I decided to take a boat from the Black Sea. Before doing so, however, I had to pay my respects to my superiors in St. Petersburg. I did not find the capital much changed: the same magnificent Neva River with its granite shores and rows of palaces, the same gloomy Foreign Office with people walking along the corridors and waiting for a promotion. Once again I had my nomination in my pocket, and thus had no reason to stop in the corridor. I called on the high officials and had the usual conversations about nothing, and was honored by a luncheon with the Foreign Minister [Sergei Dmitrievich Sazonov] and his wife, both of whom I knew from my early days in London. Time and position made them appear more important, and when I made some mistake in discussing their Chinese porcelain the Minister reproved me with a contemptuous look. The only important conversation I had was with Kazakov, my future chief in the Far Eastern Division. I complimented him on the success of his policy in China and confessed that I did not look forward to life in Japan, which I had seen only recently, and that I was not enamored with Ambassador Malevskii-Malevich. He consoled me that my tour of duty in Japan would not exceed a year and that I would see how important a knowledge of Japan from the point of view of an official would be for me.

I returned to Moscow and after bidding farewell to my whole family, proceeded to Odessa, where I embarked for the Far East on a ship of the Volunteer Fleet. At one time these ships had been considered very good passenger vessels, but after the construction of the Siberian railway they were used almost exclusively for cargo, accepting as passengers only persons on official business. My ship was a small vessel, destined for the Vladivostok-Sakhalin run. There were only three passengers: a young naval officer going to join the fleet on the Amur, a tea merchant en route to Colombo, and myself. On board were also two pigs for our Easter dinner which would take place somewhere in the Indian Ocean. As for comfort, there was none. When I wanted to take a bath, I was told that this was impossible since the tub had been filled with potatoes for our journey.

It was the period of the spring equinox and thus of frequent storms. On the second day of our journey we were caught in such a storm, and our boat was tossed about like a small piece of wood. I lay in my cabin half dead from seasickness, and thought what a blessing it would be to go to the bottom of the sea and stop suffering. My two companions had fortified themselves with alcohol and above the noise of the wind I could hear their drunken voices through the thin partition: the tea merchant was shouting that it was too early for him to die because he had not yet made his fortune, the officer did not want to die because women still loved him. But no one had to die. The next day the sea calmed down, and we reached Constantinople without mishap.

It was my third visit to this place and again I thought that nothing could surpass the beauty of the approach to Constantinople from the Black Sea. Still feeling the effect of the storm I did not leave the boat, and amused myself by contemplating the lively scene on the Bosporus. We stayed in Constantinople just long enough to coal. The rest of the journey was not particularly interesting. We ate and drank, and the naval officer told about his conquest of the ladies. Somewhere in the Indian Ocean under the dark but star-studded sky we celebrated Easter, feasting with the Captain and the ship's officers on the pigs we had brought from Odessa. As we neared Colombo we ran into a thunderstorm. The sky became black as ink and hundreds of flashes of lightning and deafening claps of thunder enveloped the ship; it was a scene from the last act of the *Götterdämmerung*. Toward evening the clouds passed and the row of electric lamps on the Colombo waterfront appeared as a bright line on the horizon.

❖❖❖

I left the Russian vessel at Colombo. On shore I was struck by the vivid colors—crowds of people all in white, dark green trees covered with bright red flowers, and a sun so brilliant that it hurt to look at it. It was like a modernistic painting. You felt as if new life were entering your veins; even the heat made you feel more vigorous. The same day I left for Kandy, the old capital of Ceylon. The railway ran along the mountain slope, all covered with tea plantations. The view was becoming broader and broader. In the evening I found myself on the shore of a small lake where the ancient Kandy was situated. The only interesting building which had remained from the old capital was a magnificent temple with figures of huge bronze dragons and with a staircase coming down to the water. For a long time in the evening I sat on the steps absorbed in the contemplation of eternity. The air was full of glowworms dancing all around me. It looked as if some of the stars had left the sky and had joined in a mysterious dance near the centuries-old temple.

The following day I went on an excursion to the countryside around Kandy with a number of prosaic Britons. The party was dull. I really think that in a majority of cases human society only spoils the proper appreciation of nature. Most people belong to cities and are lost away from the crowded streets, shops, and offices. The feeling of eternity, which the beauty of nature sometimes evokes, does not come upon you when you are surrounded by fellow men. It is probably for this reason that I have always preferred solitude to crowded gatherings, where everybody insists on your listening to their opinions, as if other peoples' thoughts can replace the feelings and conclusions of the inner self.

A fortnight later I found myself in Singapore. I have always regarded Singapore as the ugliest and dullest place I have ever seen. It is such a thorough creation of the Anglo-Saxon colonial genius that the entire beauty and interest of the place have gone forever. The climate is awful and except for canned food one lacks everything; I would have exchanged all the tropical fruits, of which the local residents were so proud, for one apple. An evening's walk through the native part of town makes one sad about the moral standard of foreigners in the subtropical countries. I think that every decent foreigner thinks only of making his fortune as quickly as possible and of retiring to England, there to forget tropical life; but often by the time the fortune has been made he has become totally depraved and is no longer fit to live in a civilized community. I promised myself never to come near the tropics again. The only event of real interest during my ten-day stay in Singapore was a small excursion into the jungles.

The local agent of the Russian Volunteer Fleet, whom I happened to meet, told me that he was very anxious about a young Russian couple who had come to Singapore on their honeymoon, the husband being sent there by the University of St. Petersburg to study the life of white ants, a rather strange occupation for newlyweds. After some days in Singapore the young couple had left for the interior and for a fortnight nothing had been heard of them. As he knew more or less the locality where they had gone, the agent decided to look for them and invited me to accompany him. As I had absolutely nothing to do in Singapore except to wait for my boat, I accepted with pleasure.

We passed the residence of the Sultan of Johore, an elaborate foreign-style palace, which could be seen from the train. The Sultan, who reigned over millions of Malays under the protection of the British Empire, seemed fond of foreign women. At least, he had married an English woman, proud to bear the title of Sultana, then divorced her and married a Rumanian. Apparently, if you are a Sultan, you can always find a white woman willing to marry you, even though you be a Malay.

After a journey of a few hours we got off the train at some small station and proceeded on foot through the jungle, walking in file, a guide at the front, bearers with our luggage in the rear. I was struck by the orgy of vegetation, standing like a wall on both sides of the footpath. It was full of life: clouds of monkeys jumped from tree to tree and birds of brilliant color flitted about. We did not hear any sinister sounds or encounter any savage beasts, however; we were still too near civilization.

Toward evening, when it became quite dark under the trees, we came to a small open place in the middle of which there stood a small rest house, built by the government for travelers who had to cross the jungle. Such houses usually consisted of three to four rooms with a kitchen and some provisions in the cupboard. Travelers could stop there and with the help of their servants make themselves at home. By a stroke of luck we found the Russian couple in the house, where we had decided to stop for the night. The young wife had a touch of dysentery, but this did not prevent her husband from being absorbed in his white ants.

Supper was prepared and we sat on the terrace surrounded by the mysterious jungle with its strange noises. But soon the world around us was forgotten and the four of us, in the middle of the Malay jungle, started one of those endless discussions which Russians like so much and which has no beginning and no end. As we argued whether modern Russian literature with its pessimistic themes was good or bad for the development of the Russian mentality, the jungle seemed transformed into a peaceful garden somewhere in the suburbs of St. Petersburg and the names of Chekhov and Gorkii drowned out the roars of strange beasts.

The next morning the young professor took us on an expedition in search of white ants. I had not expected that it would be so interesting. I do not know who imitates whom—the human beings ants or the ants human beings—but the organization of life in the anthill has much in common with human society. The ants have their queen and king, their military caste and their workmen. When you start to break an anthill you hear a noise inside; the soldiers are being mobilized to defend the ant kingdom. They look quite fierce as they rush on the spade with which you try to break the anthill. The nearer you approach the dwelling of the queen the more excited the ants become. When you extract the hard piece of earth, where the queen—a horrible-looking insect with the upper part of an ant and a huge white body out of which a perpetual stream of eggs flows—is located, the whole anthill is dispersed and remains in chaos until a new queen is born. To make the similarity greater, when the ant kingdom has to move to a new site, the soldiers stand at attention on both sides while the queen is dragged between two rows of soldiers. Apparently the sympathies of nature are on the side of monarchy and not democracy.

After a short time we all returned to Singapore, carrying jars with queens preserved in alcohol. I spent my last days in town with our Consul, one of those men who always consider everybody else in the wrong. The Russian Foreign Office consisted of fools, because it did not consent to give Russian decorations to his English friends; the whole foreign society in Singapore was made up of idiots, because it made a fuss when he sent his wife home and brought a Japanese woman to live with him. When I ventured the opinion that there might be some justification for the points of view of the Foreign

Office and the foreign society, I felt that I had made an enemy for the rest of my life.

❖❖❖

The following day I left Singapore. From the deck of my ship I looked at the crowd which had come to see someone off. The whole Singapore society seemed to be there. Several hundred Boy Scouts stood at attention. A very elegant lady and a tall, military-looking Englishman were taking leave of their numerous friends. Pointing at the lady, the Volunteer Fleet agent, who was seeing me off, told me that she was a Russian Jewess who had come some twenty years ago to Singapore to join a local brothel. A young British officer, attached to the Governor General, had fallen in love with her and decided to marry her. As this was impossible, even in Singapore, he sent her to England to make a lady out of her. The transformation took about five years. He then left the service and married her.

Since he had large commercial interests in Singapore, he took her there. Her transformation into a lady was so successful that she was received by everybody and was invited to the Governor General's house, the highest honor in English colonies. I have always had a soft spot in my heart for people who succeed in life by clever daring and liked the way this lady had taken hold of her life and made a success of it.

One evening aboard ship she approached me and asked if I were Russian. When I answered in the affirmative, she confessed that she had been born in Odessa and still had a tender feeling for Russia. But when she started to speak Russian, all my illusions were dissipated; before me was the inmate of a brothel. She had learned everything necessary to become an English lady, but there was nobody who could make a Russian lady out of her. I was rather sorry for her and advised her not to speak Russian to a Russian. I think she understood, and for the rest of our journey never spoke Russian with me.

As the ship on which we traveled was French, we stopped at Saigon for three days. Tired of the Anglo-Saxon culture which had been imposed wherever foreigners lived in the Far East, I was delighted to see Saigon, a typical French town, with shady streets and tables under trees, tables at which after five o'clock bearded Frenchmen relaxed, talking and laughing loudly and gesticulating. I went to hear the opera *Louise* in a charming opera house. My Jewish compatriot from Singapore sat in a box, beautifully dressed, and waved to me with her ostrich fan. All this had a touch of Paris about it. During the intermission I heard people ask each other who this "belle anglaise" was.

When I returned to the hotel and went to the bar, the proprietor, half drunk, insisted on speaking Russian to me. These Russians seemed to be everywhere! He related that he was a Pole and had fled his country when falsely accused of murder, since once a person has been accused of murder, even unjustly, something always sticks. He had found his way to Indochina, where he was doing not badly. Indochina[1] is a wonderful place; it collects and feeds all sorts of people. But when I went to bed I locked my door. Who could tell? If he had been accused of murder once, he might wish to repeat the experience.

I continued to Hong Kong on the same vessel. The approach to this fortress, which gave England her predominance in the Far East, was magnificent. The port was filled with ships from all nations. Chinese junks flew about like sea gulls. The town was situated on a hill, rows of houses descending straight to the sea. The sky was blue, the sea bluer yet, and the sun was hot. An approaching ship is greeted by British authorities; English is spoken everywhere. Everything breathes of British might. Thousands of Chinese, though they love to complain of British tyranny, make millions under the protection of this tyranny.

Wanting to visit Canton and Macao, I left the ship and moved to a hotel in Hong Kong. There was little to see in town. I took a cable car to the top of the hill, where the house of the Governor General dominated the whole cliff. There was a well-kept park, a polo ground, on which a group of energetic English officers were playing polo in spite of the heat. Everything was very efficient, very decent, and very dull.

The next day I went to Canton, the most typical Chinese town I have ever seen. The streets were narrow and filled with noisy crowds; smell and dirt prevailed everywhere. The Chinese here differed markedly from the Chinese and especially the Manchus in Peking, who had greater poise and looked more dignified. The general nakedness of the Chinese in Canton made them look like devils; it was not pleasant to be lost in the crowd. When the foreigners had come to Canton as victors, they had chosen to build their houses in the best place, and

[1] The manuscript states "China"; the context suggests "Indochina."

[209]

though they were surrounded by millions of Chinese they succeeded, as they did everywhere in China, in creating an oasis of civilization among the struggling masses of humanity. I do not envy the foreigners who will be obliged to live in China when all the advantages obtained by their thoughtful ancestors will be gone, as is bound to happen in the coming era of democracy and general equity.

The next day was Sunday. The upper part of Hong Kong, with its British population, reposed; virtuous ladies in their Sunday best went to church. But in the Chinese quarter the struggle for existence continued unabated. Everybody seemed to have something to buy or to sell, notably most unappetizing food, and to think that the louder he shrieked the more successfully he could effect the transaction.

In the port I boarded a small steamer for Macao. Though the deck was filled to overflowing, the excursion proved very agreeable. The boat followed the shore, a light breeze diminishing the heat. We arrived in two hours. The difference between Macao and Hong Kong was remarkable. One could see at once that England had nothing to do with the foundation of Macao. It clearly belonged to the time when Spain and Portugal had ruled the distant seas. The whole place had a touch of Spain. The houses were surrounded by high walls; there were many churches and very little order. Even the public seemed more easygoing.

Though it was Sunday and the bells were ringing, the devil too had his share, the gambling houses which lined the streets near the port operating openly. I did not know the game, but apparently anybody who came could join. The players, mostly Chinese, sat at a long table as well as on a balcony, all around the room. As cards were dealt and wagers made, small baskets with money passed back and forth between the balcony and the main floor. Sometimes the people on the balcony quarreled with those downstairs, but most of the time the crowd looked solemn, as if something very important were going on. Not being a gambler and not understanding the game, I preferred to wander about in the streets.

Returning to Hong Kong I met several Englishmen on the boat. They were drunk, and tried to explain to me what an advantage it was to have Macao so close to Hong Kong, so that every time a person wanted to have a good time he could take the boat and go to Macao, where he could enjoy himself without shocking anybody. This was typical English hypocrisy; in London, a respectable family man would go to Paris when he wanted a rest from his virtues. Many used to speak about this with indignation, but I have always felt that hypocrisy is the highest compliment one can pay to virtue.

The following day I left Hong Kong for Shanghai. Here our Consul informed me that the Ambassador in Japan had cabled that I was lost somewhere between Odessa and Tokyo and had asked what could be done to find me. In this sarcastic telegram I recognized my new chief, who was ever eager to remind his subordinates that they must always consider his interests first. Not wishing to increase his displeasure, I did not leave the boat and continued directly to Japan.

✥✥✥

Mt. Fuji greeted me in all its magnificence as I arrived in Yokohama early in the morning. The mountain was really marvelous; it never looked the same. This time the lower part was hidden by mist, and the snow-covered summit floated high in the sky. It looked too beautiful to be real.

At the Embassy I was met by old friends, among them the gloomy Counsellor [Shchekin] who had been transferred from Peking to Tokyo. He was gloomier than ever, and, taking me to his room, started to abuse the Ambassador and the rest of the staff. He bemoaned that everybody was a fool and that as Counsellor he was obliged to listen to all the nonsense of his chief without being able to correct anything. But I had known the Counsellor too long to take all this seriously. When the Ambassador received me, he made a scene, accusing me, instead of having rushed to my new post across Siberia, of having chosen the longest route and getting lost on the way. My modest justification that I had received the Foreign Minister's permission to go by sea and had put all my faith in his well-known indulgence, mollified him, and he began to explain my Embassy duties. He declared that the Second Secretary must help him in his social functions, that is to say he must be thoroughly familiar with protocol—who follows whom and who sits where at dinner—and must listen to all the gossip and report it to him, for he alone could judge what gossip was worthy of attention. To underline this, he related how he had once listened to some gossip while playing bridge and had discovered a most important diplomatic secret. As he talked, I kept asking myself whether he could be serious. At any rate, he had to entertain a low opinion of me if he thought that I, after all these years of diplomatic service during which my former chiefs had deigned to be interested in my opinions, would now stoop to play the role of a butler and gossipmonger. I knew that I would show such ignorance in these fields that the Ambassador would be only too glad to get rid of me.

Malevskii-Malevich then lectured at length how a member of the Embassy must dress and demonstrated with his own wardrobe. He even touched on the delicate question of my relations with women, and demonstrated how to use the telephone by calling the Italian Ambassador and inquiring after his health. When I met the Italian Ambassador later on, he complained that the Russian Ambassador kept calling him constantly to ask about his health and to express his pleasure that it was good, and asked that I tell him that the phone in the Italian Embassy was in a cold corridor and that the perpetual calls would lead to his catching cold. I could not refrain from the sarcastic remark that all that this would change would be that Malevskii-Malevich, after telephoning about his health, would express regret instead of joy. Thus began my work in Tokyo.

Fearful lest we at the chancery forget that he was our chief, the Ambassador never left us alone. The telephone rang every minute, and we had to rush across the garden to his study for the most insignificant things. Even after finishing our work in the chancery, we would find message after message at home requesting some document. In the morning the Ambassador would no longer require the ardently desired document. It was very exasperating. From the beginning I had decided not to satisfy Malevskii-Malevich in what he considered to be my main duty, i.e., the placing of the guests at official dinners in accordance with protocol. I remember how he and I had argued once about the number of guests he wished to entertain at a dinner to which a Japanese prince had been invited—he kept miscounting—and how to seat them properly. Repeatedly we telephoned old Yoshida,[2] the only man in the Japanese Foreign Office who knew the ranks of prominent Japanese. This Yoshida had wanted several times to retire, but every dinner party given without his advice resulted in innumerable complaints from Japanese guests, who felt they had been slighted.

---

[2] Yoshida Masaharu [?].

Yoshida claimed that he had tried to teach several young Foreign Office men the "science" of protocol, but that it was so complicated they had gone insane. Thus he himself retained the most important position until he died from old age. His death came as a great blow to the whole Diplomatic Corps. Not wishing to go insane like the pupils of Yoshida, when a young Baltic baron with a talent for protocol and gossip appeared on our horizon as Attaché, I advised the Ambassador to try him instead of poor me in this line of work. He did so to everybody's satisfaction. I returned to my chancery work and soon was absorbed in my favorite occupation of putting the archives in order.

The Russian Foreign Office was full of Baltic barons and even the newspapers, when they found fault with Russian diplomacy, frequently criticized the Foreign Office for having too many barons in posts abroad. Being quite Russian, I read such articles with a certain amount of joy, but the further I moved in my career the more I understood the preference for barons. As a rule a chief dislikes the contradictions which are in the character of every Russian. A baron makes an ideal bureaucrat since he never dreams of having an opinion different from that of his superior. Should the chief make a mistake in his report and instead of writing that a chicken had hatched an egg, record that an egg had hatched a chicken, a Russian would attempt not only to correct the mistake but add some thoughts of his own, which might change the whole meaning of what the chief was trying to say. A Baltic baron, on the other hand, would copy the mistake as he found it, believing, if he noted the absurdity of the thing, that the very absurdity must have a special meaning. Such an attitude was flattering to the chiefs and consequently they preferred to surround themselves with well-mannered and correct barons, rather than willful and capricious Russians with a tendency to consider themselves more clever than their superiors. Thus, at any rate, it was in our Embassy in Tokyo.

The gloomy Counsellor spent his time referring to the Ambassador as an "idiot"; the First Secretary, a Russian Prince [Lev Vladimirovich Urusov], would stand with his back toward the open fireplace and discourse eloquently on the policy he would follow toward Japan were he Ambassador, while the two barons silently copied the Ambassador's dispatches or ciphered telegrams. At twelve o'clock the Prince would finish his tirade and declare that it was time for lunch. Usually we would eat at a local hotel at a special table for diplomats. As we saw each other constantly our conversation was neither original nor interesting. Everybody tried to be witty and pretended to have some secret information, but in the end conversation usually degenerated to gossip about local events. The drawback of life in Asiatic countries is that the diplomats are reduced to their own society. The Japanese do not admit foreigners into their own life and one's contact with them is limited to official relations. Even at official functions, when they do know a foreign language, it requires superhuman effort to engage them in conversation. One charming and vivacious lady told me that the effort she made to keep a conversation going when she found herself next to a Japanese at a dinner party would be sufficient to till a big field. As you realize that your partner experiences the same agony, you gradually give up, reduce your conversation with the Japanese to a few platitudes about cherry blossoms, and turn toward your foreign neighbor. If you have no foreign neighbor, you merely repeat your comment about cherry blossoms.

Under the circumstances the Japanese seem to do little more than animate their landscape, and your whole life passes in foreign society, though I personally always felt that I had not come to Japan for this. To be sure, you can penetrate into Japanese life by living with a Japanese girl. Japanese women are pretty and quaint, but those who agree to join their fate with a foreigner usually belong to such a class of people that you can learn little from them, and it is they who gradually drag you down to their level. The whole touching romance of Madame Butterfly exists only in Puccini's imagination. I preferred to admire the women as part of the Japanese landscape, where in their charming houses, surrounded by flowers and children, they really looked as beautiful as a print. The Anglo-Japanese Alliance was still in effect and Japan was on its best behavior. There was little talk about the influence of the military and the diplomats were hard pressed to find material for their dispatches. It required great effort on the part of our Military Attaché, who had built himself up as the foreigner best informed about Japanese secret plans, to live up to his reputation. As for the young diplomats, the general calm gave them ample time to gossip, to play bridge and tennis, to dance—in a phrase, to lead a typical diplomatic life.

❖•❖•❖

I missed the energetic and active life in Peking. In Japan, especially during the heat of summer, we were half asleep. When the weather was hot, most foreigners went to the seaside or into the mountains. Our Ambassador stayed at Chuzenji, a place above Nikko, near a beautiful lake. In later years Chuzenji became my favorite place too, but at the time we were not allowed to leave Tokyo, the Ambassador insisting that the Secretaries stay in the Chancery to handle dispatches which he might send from the mountains. Thus we sat in the shade of the trees outside the Chancery, drinking innumerable cups of tea and cursing our Chief, who enjoyed himself in the coolness of Chuzenji. Once in a fortnight we climbed the mountain with a typewriter, and the Ambassador would dictate dispatches about imaginary conversations with the Japanese Foreign Secretary. Sometimes fog drifted into the room and his voice, sounding as if it came from a cloud, was very impressive. As a great honor he invited us for a walk along the lake. We passed through the village, the small children of which had been taught to bow to the Ambassador politely; he beamed at such attention. The foreigners had their regattas on the colorful lake, but all that was not for us; we had to go back to Tokyo with the typewriter and the dispatches which probably no one in the Foreign Office would read.

Having a lot of spare time, I tried to learn the Japanese language in order to find out what was hidden behind those smiling yellow faces. It was easy to learn sufficient Japanese to make myself understood in shops and in everyday life, but I could not learn enough to converse intelligently with an educated Japanese; one lifetime was too short. I found that the written characters simply refused to enter my head. It depressed me, but our Military Attaché, who could speak and understand Japanese, consoled me that were I to understand what was spoken around me, I would only be disillusioned, for conversation was confined to food and prices.

The Military Attaché [Vladimir Konstantinovich Samoilov] was a very original and amusing person. He had come to Japan before the Russo-Japanese War and had promptly fallen under the spell of Japanese women. When war was declared he had departed, leaving behind his Madame Butterfly. When I had met him in London, where he served as Assistant Military Attaché during the War, he was miserable, and constantly spoke of the charms of Japanese women. After the War he was reassigned to Japan, where he was met by his old mistress, who at once began to rule him with an iron hand. She was an awful person, quite unique among Japanese women, who usually are gentle and submissive and whose whole life is devoted to making a man comfortable. This one was a real dragon. She subjected the poor General to endless scenes. Occasionally she even turned him out of his own house and he had to sleep at a hotel. At the same time she wanted to place her female relations in the households of bachelor foreigners and every time a new member of the Embassy was expected in Tokyo, she had such a relative ready, and it was the General's duty to hint to the newcomer that a charming Madame Butterfly was waiting for him. Yet the General adored her, and when he died he left all his money to her. She died soon after him and had no time to enjoy the money, which passed to some coolie relative of hers.

I heard of three Russians who on a world tour stopped at Japan, became involved with Japanese women, and never completed their trips. Before the Russo-Japanese War, when our fleet would come from Vladivostok to winter in Nagasaki, it was a regular profession to supply the officers with Japanese wives, and they say that the population in this port acquired some Russian features as a result of this pre-war friendship between the Russian navy and the Japanese girls. When I was in Nagasaki I was shown a nice-looking young Japanese who was supposed to have been the son of a Russian grand duke. His mother used to show as proof a golden watch with a Russian Imperial eagle.

Other celebrities connected with the Russian Imperial family were two ricksha coolies who had saved the life of Nicholas II when he had visited Japan as Crown Prince [1891] and a fanatic had set upon him with a sword.[3] The Russian government had awarded the two ricksha men with a pension; they had retired to their village

[3] See G. A. Lensen, "The Attempt on the Life of Nicholas II in Japan," *The Russian Review*, Vol. XX, 3 (July, 1961), 232-53.

and, it was rumored, had drunk themselves to death. At my time money was still being sent through the Embassy. Once a member of the staff visited the village to verify if the two saviors were still alive. The village arranged a grand reception and two men were presented as the ricksha men who had knocked down the assailant of the future Emperor of Russia. Whether they were the real persons one could not determine, however, because even the police would have supported a fraud in order not to deprive the village of its glorious reputation. Every time I thought of the incident, I could not but wonder on what little things hung the destiny of a whole nation, if not of the whole world. Had these two Japanese coolies not turned the ricksha in time and saved the Crown Prince from the full force of the sword blow, the entire course of Russian history would have been different. There might not have been a Revolution and consequently no Hitler and no Second World War with its horrors and endless complications.

❖❖❖

As usual I became attached to the place where I felt happy, and the prospect of changing life in Japan for service in the Foreign Office in St. Petersburg did not appeal to me. As Easter and cherry-blossom time approached, I planned a two-week visit to Manila. By now I knew how to obtain the Ambassador's permission for things which before had seemed quite impossible, and with his sanction I left for Nagasaki to catch a steamer for the Philippines.

I was already aboard ship when a telegram arrived from Tokyo informing me that I was being summoned to St. Petersburg. I was lucky that the steamer had not yet departed, for my absence in the Philippines would have provoked great displeasure in the Foreign Office and I might have endangered my chance for a brilliant career. With the consolation that all is for the best in the best of all possible worlds, I turned back to Tokyo and began to make my farewells. I was sure that this time I was leaving Japan forever, but again life was to teach me that human calculations are often wrong, and I was to remember the advice of my father always to accept with thanks what life sends and to try to make the best of it. My last impression of Japan was a brilliant fancy-dress ball given by our Ambassador to inaugurate the new ballroom added to the Embassy. The beautiful

daughter of the Ambassador, dressed as Cleopatra, couples of Colum-
bines, Pierrots, Walküres, boyars, and toreadors were whirling round
and round. Beaming with pride the Ambassador told everyone how
the idea of the beautiful ballroom had been born. Even the Emperor
seemed to approve as he looked down from his picture frame on the
brilliant crowd. A glimpse into the future would have killed the
joy—the Emperor shot, the Ambassador imprisoned and starving
to death, his beautiful daughter forced to work in the fields. It is
a blessing that we cannot look ahead.

On my way back to St. Petersburg I visited Peking, where I had
been so happy, and found once again that it was a mistake to revisit
the place of one's former happiness. Other people had brought other
customs; everything had changed. It was always depressing to see
how easily one could be replaced. I continued to persuade myself
that in my time everything had been much better, but had it? The
only person whom I was glad to see and who was glad to see me
was the Cossack sergeant with whom I had made the journey across
Mongolia. Even the stable, which I had passed on to my successor,
was doing better than in my day. No, it is allowed to look back only
when there is no future left. At the time I still believed in the
future, and without regret left Peking and for the third time journeyed across Siberia.

I saw the same endless woods and open spaces, the same curious
stares of the inhabitants of the dwellings near the small stations;
the Ural Mountains and Russia with its special smell of leather,
mushrooms, and hay, its slow movements and its beautiful Russian
language.

Arriving in Moscow, I stopped for several days with my family.
I found my father happy to have retired from his business with its
concern for money making, which he had always considered the
most undignified occupation for a human being. Books, lectures, and
thinking now occupied his time. As always, after a few days with him
I felt purified from all the little things in this world and had the
feeling that ambition, diplomacy, and my other interests, though all
right, were not the chief things in life. As I left for St. Petersburg
I was pleased that I was not going far away, that I should be able
to see my parents frequently and in the summer relive my childhood
at The Oaks.

7

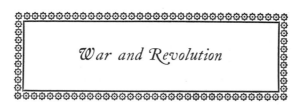

War and Revolution

THIS TIME, IN THE MOMENTOUS YEAR OF 1914, I CAME TO THE capital[1] no longer the youngster who anxiously contemplated what diplomatic life might hold in store for him, but a man who had passed already through the initial steps of his career and had no illusions about the future. I knew that I was becoming part of the bureaucratic machine on which the administration of the huge Empire was based and which, after my free and easy life in Moscow, appeared so soulless that I sought refuge in service abroad. I was not afraid of this machine any more, because I was no longer an insignificant young man who had to resort to such tricks as a fancy dog or a rich aunt to impress his superiors, but a man with a certain standing, chosen by virtue of his merits to occupy a post of some significance and could be a stepping-stone to something really important. I knew that I would still have a long line of superiors whose support I must win and that I was entering a world of intrigue in which some people would want to crush me to remove a dangerous competitor from their own paths, but I was not afraid. Spoiled by service abroad and removed from the realities of Russian life though I was, I had in me the will to fight; and though, because of my background, I was yet a stranger in the

[1] During World War I, the capital's German name—St. Petersburg—was patriotically changed to its Russian equivalent, Petrograd. Abrikossow, who did not approve of the change, continued to refer to the capital city as St. Petersburg; his usage has been retained.

aristocratic spheres with which our Foreign Office was connected and still lacked influential aunts who could sing my praises in those circles, I had enlisted the services of some important friends, not to mention Foreign Minister Sazonov, who knew me from London. Thus I was beginning my new life with courage and optimism.

I was sorry that my friend, the English curate, was no longer in St. Petersburg and I could not renew my half-English life with him, but this may have been for the best, because my new position demanded that I keep nearer to the Foreign Office circles. When I thought about all that, I had to confess to myself that I was becoming contaminated by the general bureaucratic atmosphere of St. Petersburg and was losing the spontaneity of my character, but as the saying goes, if you live among wolves you must howl like one. It depressed me somewhat, but I consoled myself by deciding that everytime I felt I was becoming a dry bureaucrat, I should visit Moscow to restore the human part of my nature in the society of my father.

My first concern was to arrange my personal life. Remembering how useful the association of great riches with my family name had been at the beginning of my career, I took a room in the new and luxurious Hotel Astoria, even though I could afford only a small room on the fourth floor. The Astoria was a fine place to receive superiors returning calls; furthermore, it was near the Foreign Office and its lobby, always crowded with the most diverse specimens of humanity—brilliant officers, businessmen, beautiful women of easy virtue, shady foreigners, and all sorts of adventurers—was an interesting post of observation, useful if one did not want to sink in the dry bureaucratic atmosphere of a typical small functionary.

I was well received in the Foreign Office and in the Far Eastern Section, where all of our Far Eastern policy was concentrated. It was here that my new post was and I felt quite at home. The chief of the section, Kazakov, was one of the nicest men I have met in the service: clever, hardworking, and absorbed in his work. The Minister left our entire Far Eastern policy in his hands. He explained to me that he had insisted on having me as one of his assistants because he was tired of the typical products of the Foreign Office who looked on their work merely from the point of view of advancement and at the first opportunity tried to escape to some other place where they thought they would be more conspicuous. He felt that the fact that I had spent several years in the Far East away from the demoralizing atmosphere of St. Petersburg showed that I had a real interest in Russia's position in the Far East and would make me more useful in the reorganized Far Eastern Section. I was greatly flattered by his good opinion of me, and promised not to disappoint him.

We did work hand in hand, and it was interesting to see how one man, possessed with the idea of restoring Russia's Far Eastern position, could in such a short time make everybody forget the disasters of the War. He did so without thought of his own advancement, for few people knew who the author of our successful Far Eastern policy was, all credit going to the Foreign Minister. When I spoke to him about that he used to answer that he would be amply rewarded if in the future some historian, studying our policy in the Far East, would discover that it had been conceived and executed by a modest member of the Foreign Office by the name of Kazakov. It has been my experience in diplomacy that one clever man interested in his work can do more than a number of commissions, which try to reconcile the divergent opinions of a number of persons, each insisting on his point of view. I attribute the successful modification of our Far Eastern policy to the fact that it was the product of only two men: Izvolskii, who laid its foundations, and Kazakov, who developed it further.

After the Russo-Japanese War it was clear to both sides, that as Russia could not ignore the interests of Japan, so Japan could not ignore the interests of Russia. The latter remained a great power, and the only way to avoid future difficulties was for the two countries to collaborate. Thus we started the policy of mutual spheres of influence in Manchuria and Mongolia. It was astonishing how Russia and Japan during all the years which followed the War and preceded the Russian Revolution remained faithful to their mutual obligations; I do not remember a single case of misunderstanding. I am fully persuaded that if there had been no Revolution and our Foreign Office had been allowed to continue its policy, the whole course of history would have been quite different. Japan would have been kept within its boundaries and would never have been allowed to be driven by insane ambition under the influence of Hitler. Our moderate policy in China, about which I had occasion to speak, also had a restraining influence on

Japan. When I recall how agreeable and interesting my work in St. Petersburg was at this time, I cannot help but repeat how much nicer everything was in Old Russia.

Soon I moved from my luxurious hotel to a charming apartment, where I could house my Oriental collection. I arranged my life as I pleased, an old Russian woman looking after me. As everywhere, I tried to find a friendly family who could replace my own, a place where I would always be welcome. I actually found two such families in St. Petersburg, so I was never lonely. The capital was very gay at the beginning of 1914, the dangerous months of 1905, when the Revolution had seemed so near, were forgotten. Misunderstandings between the government and society, which continued to lean toward the left, persisted; but the government was strong enough to prevent any serious upheaval, and the danger of war was not clearly realized in the first half of 1914.

Yet there was no lack of events which clearly indicated that we were moving toward a situation that could only result in war. The first step was Austria's annexation of the two Turkish provinces of Bosnia and Hercegovina. Russia objected strenuously and tried to take a strong stand vis-à-vis Austria, but had to back down when Germany declared that she would support Austria. Russia could not forgive this humiliation, especially Foreign Minister Izvolskii, who felt that he had been deceived by the Austrian Minister. He resigned and became Ambassador to Paris, where he continued to brood about his humiliation on the part of Austria. There would be fewer wars if personal feelings of dignity and offense could be excluded from international relations.

Sazonov, who succeeded Izvolskii, was a kindhearted man who personally would never have thought of resorting to war to settle international difficulties, but he was a sentimentalist and subscribed to the beliefs of the Slavophiles, who felt that Russia was called upon to protect all Slavs. Beautiful as such policy sounded in theory, it was most dangerous in practice. It concerned the Balkans, the tinder-box of Europe, and the various Slavic peoples were clever enough to exploit Russian protection for their purposes, not hesitating to drag Russia into war if such a war seemed to their advantage. Russia had fought the Ottoman Empire to liberate Serbia and Bulgaria, yet instead of showing their gratitude, Serbia, under King Milan, had turned its back on Russia and flirted with Austria; while Bulgaria under Prince Ferdinand, the old fox of Europe, discarded Russian friendship for an understanding with Austria. After a change in dynasty, Serbia again claimed Russian protection against Austria, sending to St. Petersburg a clever Minister who successfully wooed the Slavophiles. The new Russian Minister in Serbia worked in the same direction, giving a political touch even to the entertainment at the Russian Legation. Living pictures were acted out, the wife of the Minister posing as Russia receiving homage from the kneeling Balkan states. As the German and Austrian Ministers were among the guests, the portrayal could hardly have been conducive to better relations. When war is in the air, everything, even the most insignificant event, increases tension. But if every power in Europe contributed to the outbreak of the First World War, Germany and Austria were unquestionably the chief villains, especially Germany which thought itself strong enough for big conquests and by giving Austria a blank cheque, promising to support its Balkan policy by force, made war certain. Serbia on her part, counting on the help of Russia, did everything to irritate Austria. By provoking the assassination of the Austrian heir to the throne, Serbia gave Austria the needed pretext for war, which had already been decided upon by the cabinets of Germany and Austria. Such was the situation in the summer of 1914.

From what I saw and heard in our Foreign Office, Russia thought little of war and was not prepared for it; German accusations that the war was Russia's doing were emphatically untrue. Nobody in Russia wanted the war. The Emperor did everything to avoid it, though his character prevented any truly firm and final decision. He was not like his father, Alexander III, who, determined to avoid hostilities with Germany, said to his Minister that even if Emperor William spat in his face he would not declare war. Nicholas II could not say such a thing. Personally he was a peaceful man, but he listened to others and wavered. And so events followed their fatal course.

President [Raymond] Poincaré came to St. Petersburg to return the visit of the Russian Emperor, and was feted as a friend of Russia. In private conversations it was probably confirmed that Russia and France would support each other. Summer vacations were in full swing, and all the important people were leaving town for their estates. My chief, the head of the Far Eastern Section, and his other assistant took their holidays and I had to replace them. It gave me the opportunity to be near the heads of the Ministry during those critical days. Foreign Minister Sazonov was a simple man, and treated his nearest coworkers without ceremony. Usually when the heads of different sections had some business with the Minister, they sat in a room next to his office, drinking tea and waiting to see him. At the other side of the office was the reception room for foreign diplomats. Often the Minister came out of his office and joined us at tea. The conversation became general and to use a grand phrase, I felt that I was present at the making of history.

All these days the Foreign Minister looked anxious and depressed. He admitted that things were not going as he wished, but he still hoped that Austria would stop in time. Listening to Sazonov I could not help but think that with all his desire for a peaceful settlement, he played into the hands of Germany and Austria by clinging to the idea that Great Russia must protect little Serbia, even when little Serbia could not stop its subjects from participating in the assassination of the Crown Prince of a friendly country. Russia advised Serbia to be moderate and gossips in our Foreign Office corridors predicted a Russian diplomatic triumph and the preservation of peace. But the fatal day came undeterred.

How well I remember that day! I had to obtain the signature of the Minister for an agreement with the newly formed Mongolian government concerning some postal arrangement, and went to the room where other section chiefs waited to see the Minister. I explained that my business with the Minister would not take more than five minutes, and it was agreed that as soon as the Austrian Ambassador, who was with the Minister, would leave, I should rush into the Minister's study. This I did, but found the Minister absorbed in a paper. It was a copy of the Austrian ultimatum to Serbia; our Minister, who had been hoping that his offer of a conference would be accepted, had been given it when twenty-four of the forty-eight hours' time limit had expired. Looking up, the Minister said that he had no time to see me and hurried out of the room. I returned with my postal arrangement unsigned.

At once a council was summoned at the Palace. The Emperor, who presided, asked his Ministers what should be done. The whole question was reduced to one alternative: to support Serbia or let her be crushed by Austria. As so often happens, most Ministers tried to avoid the responsibility of decision. The War Minister said that if war were decided upon the army was ready, but whether or not there should be war was a political question to be decided by the Foreign Office; the others similarly shifted the burden of responsibility onto the Foreign Minister. Sazonov showed great courage and declared that although there was no definite obligation, Russia could not forsake Serbia. He even went so far as to say that under present circumstances Russian refusal to support Serbia would provoke such indignation inside Russia that the dynasty itself would be endangered. After his firm stand, some other ministers spoke up in his support and the Emperor agreed that Russia had no choice but to fulfil its duty. The old struggle between the Slavonic and Germanic worlds decided the issue, and the mobilization of the Russian army against Austria was determined. The War Minister explained that the Russian mobilization set-up was such that it could not be done piecemeal, nor could it be kept secret like German mobilization, which to the best knowledge of the War Office was going on already.

Even after these decisions Nicholas tried to find a way out. Late in the evening he telephoned the War Minister and asked him if it were possible to postpone general mobilization, but was told that the order had already been issued. Then he telegraphed the German Emperor giving his word of honor that the Russian army, even if mobilized, would not cross the frontier if it were agreed to refer the Austro-Serbian dispute to the Hague Tribunal. This telegram remained without an answer. Instead, the German Ambassador presented an ultimatum: if Russia did not cancel mobilization, Germany would consider herself in a state of war with Russia. They say that the German Ambassador shed tears when he presented this ultimatum to Sazonov, but the same Ambassador lustily sang "Deutschland, Deutschland über alles" with his staff, as they returned to Germany by boat.

✛✛✛

And so the war was with us. I often wondered what Sazonov must have thought when the destruction of the dynasty, which he had predicted in the event that Russia did not go to war, occurred because she did.

[225]

After initial successes on the Austrian front, we entered the period of disasters. Neither the government nor the opposition had enough sense to understand that in such critical times the continuation of the struggle could only have fatal results. Things went too far, and no common language could be found. The opposition believed that the war could not be won without drastic reforms, but the rulers thought that war was not a time for reforms. Dark forces on both sides did everything to increase the rift. Gossip and rumors inundated the capital, and the number of people who began to lose all hope was increasing.

Following the outbreak of the war the chief question in the Foreign Office was whether England would support Russia. Count Benckendorff, our Ambassador in London, was showered with telegrams, insisting that he determine England's attitude. Having worked under Benckendorff when he had struggled and at last succeeded in persuading St. Petersburg that England was our friend, I realized through what anxious moments the old man must be passing. Not only the future of the war, but his whole reputation depending on the question whether England would remain neutral or come to the support of Russia. An honest man, Benckendorff replied at the beginning that as long as the war was fought over Serbia, the British government could not obtain the necessary majority in Parliament to enter the conflict, but that as the scope of the war widened—and he was sure that it would—English participation would be inevitable. He was right. As is known, when Germany invaded Belgium, England declared war on Germany. Thus we were in good company: France, England, Belgium, and Japan were with us. The faith in ultimate victory increased. If only we had not been our own enemy!

❖❖❖

The forces of internal disintegration continued their destructive work, as if Russia had been doomed beyond redemption. The most incredible, sinister rumors spread everywhere. You could not enter a single home without hearing fantastic stories about happenings at court. To accept half of them would be to believe that people were going insane. As officers on leave were in most homes together with their orderlies, the gossip and rumors spread through all classes of society. You had the desire to silence all these conversations by shouting that even if the stories were half true, only greater harm was done by disseminating half truths, and then you found yourself repeating the same stories.

I began to hear more and more about the sinister monk[2] [Grigorii Efimovich] Rasputin. So much has been written about him that I shall not repeat everything that was said. To understand how the appearance of such a man at court was possible, one must take into consideration that Russia had always been full of wandering monks who went from monastery to monastery, attracting the attention of credulous people, by their strange talk. Under ordinary circumstances Rasputin would have died somewhere by the roadside without leaving any imprint on the history of Russia. But fate decided otherwise, and this obscure peasant of low morality, a drunkard and a horse thief, was to play the most important part in the downfall of Old Russia and the destruction of the Romanov dynasty; the young Empress Aleksandra Feodorovna, a person brought up in a strict Protestant court, far away from all the dirt and insanity of this world, making possible the enactment of this incredible tragedy. Her marriage to Nicholas had been a love match, but she had come to Russia at a sad time—Alexander III was dying and the old Empress had no time to help the future Empress with her first steps. In accordance with the laws of the Empire, Aleksandra Feodorovna had to change her religion and join the Greek Orthodox Church. She did not want to discard the religion of her parents, but she had no choice; yet it was more than a formality to her. Accustomed to a strict, virtuous German court, she found everything in Russia strange and distasteful, the more so as nobody tried to help her understand. By nature introverted and shy, she could not take the first step to win the good will of her new relatives and of the people. Left alone, her faults increased, and she had many—she was proud, ambitions, suspicious, and self-centered. She and her husband never realized that as Emperor and Empress they were no longer private individuals with personal sympathies, that duty toward the country rather than absorption in family life should have been their prime consideration. The Russian people once had adored the monarch and his family, but with time they saw less and less of Nicholas, and the Empress ceased to smile in public. She was certainly not happy, egocentric and suspicious

[2] Actually a religious quack.

as she was of everything and everybody. No wonder that when the real tragedy of the Crown Prince's incurable illness was added to all the imaginary misfortunes, the poor woman began to develop such features in her character that people began to suspect that she was not quite sane. Had she been a private person, it would have been possible to isolate her temporarily; unfortunately this was out of the question in the case of the Empress, especially because it was not a matter of outright insanity, but absorption in false ideas. One of these delusions was her conviction that it was her sacred duty, even after the granting of representative government by the Emperor, to maintain the autocracy for her son, who had hemophilia and could not live long. Her inclination toward superstition first became apparent when, after the birth of her fourth daughter, disappointed that she had not given birth to an heir to the throne, she began to believe different cranks, who claimed to be able to influence the sex of the coming child. Thus a certain Dr. Philip, a Frenchman, became an important figure at the court until his theory proved false and he had to leave Russia.

The Empress became ever more absorbed in religion. A person in her position will always find those who will seek to further their own interests by flattery and encouragement. The Montenegrin princesses who were married to grand dukes had contacts with different religious circles and supplied the Empress with information about different "holy" men who appeared in St. Petersburg. Various members of the Orthodox Church also tried to further their careers by promoting such movements. Thus Rasputin had his predecessors in the desire to exploit the increasing mysticism of the Empress, but he was more favored than the others because he appeared at a more opportune time and because he possessed special gifts.

After long years of waiting, the Empress had at last given birth to a boy. Her joy and that of the whole court was enormous. Those in position to know said that the Empress was a changed person. Who knows, if the boy had been normal and healthy, the mother herself might have become normal, and the gloom that enveloped the court and deprived the Imperial couple of a sane appreciation of events might have disappeared. Unfortunately it soon became apparent that the child suffered from hemophilia, and in case of the slightest wound or bruise was liable to bleed to death. As it was known that hemophilia was in the Empress' family, it was a crime to allow her marriage to the Emperor, but one thinks of such things when it is too late. One can imagine the tragedy when the Empress was told that the heir to the throne suffered from this dreadful disease and that it had been she who had transmitted it. Much could be forgiven her after all that she suffered—a mother seeing her lovely and lively child, destined to one of the highest positions in this world, doomed to living death. No wonder that her peculiar traits—her mysticism, her suspicion, her desire to isolate her family and herself from everybody —increased tenfold. It was at this moment that Rasputin appeared on the scene.

One of the Empress' closest friends, [Anna] Vyrubova, told her about Rasputin and arranged a meeting with him at her house. A sly peasant, who during his stay in St. Petersburg had learned how to impress hysterical women of high society, Rasputin with his exaggerated simplicity and illiterate pronouncements, to which those who were ready to see in him a saint attached much deeper meaning than they deserved, made a deep impression on the Empress. She asked him to pray for her son and insisted that he come to see the infant. Thus began Rasputin's visits to the palace. The Emperor, who by this time had come to see things with the eyes of his wife, tired of all the intrigues around him, was also taken by the rough familiarity of the sly peasant. Rasputin, who had an uncanny understanding of human nature, knew exactly what was expected of him. In the palace he exhibited only those sides of his character that would make him appear a saint; at the same time he treated the Imperial couple as if he were their equal, addressing them as "Little Father," "Little Mother," and "thou," not as "Your Majesty." As a result the Emperor and the Empress regarded him not only as a saint but as a real representative of the simple Russian people, uncontaminated, as were the intelligentsia, by revolutionary ideas. Yet this alone would not have gained Rasputin such boundless influence. Unquestionably he possessed a peculiar gift, acknowledged even by the Tsarevich's doctors though they could not explain it; approaching the boy during his attacks, he could stop the bleeding. Rasputin became the most important personage in the whole country to the Empress and his every word was accepted as the gospel truth, nothing that was said against him being believed. Had Rasputin been the man he pretended

[229]

to be before the Imperial couple, he could have done much to reconcile the Empress with the misfortune that had befallen her, appealing to her religious feeling that this was the will of God. But Rasputin was nearer to the Devil than to God. By nature a drunkard and a lecher, once he was out of the presence of the Imperial couple he gave free rein to his filthy inclinations. Soon unscrupulous persons sought to exploit his influence with the Empress by taking advantage of his weaknesses. They gave him money and invited him to different restaurants, where they got him drunk and persuaded him to promise that he would recommend them or their plans to the Emperor. Soon Rasputin was so demoralized by his own importance that he allowed himself anything. When he was drunk, he boasted about his influence with the Empress and said that "Little Mother" could not refuse him anything. As everything that he said at those orgies was repeated from mouth to mouth, the whole thing soon became the greatest national scandal and what little popularity the Emperor still had was dissipated. Many patriots in high government posts tried hard to open the eyes of the Emperor. He would listen politely without saying a word; shortly afterward the person who had dared to speak up against Rasputin would lose his position. For this, well-informed people said, the Empress was responsible. In her eyes anybody who said a word against this "saint," the only person in the whole of Russia whom she could trust, was an enemy of the Emperor and the country.

There was the case of a highly respected general [Gen. Dzhunkovskii] extremely devoted to the Emperor. Appointed Vice Minister of the Interior and Head of the Police, he came into possession of all the information that the police had gathered about the activities of Rasputin. He was so horrified that he went straight to the Emperor and informed him about Rasputin's behavior, pointing out how his drunken boasts compromised the Imperial family. He asked Nicholas whether he should continue investigating, and Nicholas replied in the affirmative. But when the Empress learned of the investigation she was furious, and the loyal General soon was removed from his job. All this undermined the position of the honest and loyal servants of the monarchy, while multiplying tenfold the authority of those unscrupulous enough to use the influence of Rasputin for their own purposes. Thus on the eve of the Revolution Russia was ruled by people who under normal circumstances would never have gotten near the throne, and it would not be an exaggeration to say, that the real master of Russia was a sinister monk with his inarticulate talk about the will of God.

When I was in St. Petersburg, well informed though I was, I did not want to believe all the stories about Rasputin's role in politics and in the appointment of ministers. It was too humiliating for a Russian who wanted to keep his illusions about autocracy, and I had always considered autocracy the best system for Russia. But when the Bolsheviks published the private letters of the Tsar, there could be no more doubt that there was a touch of insanity in the Empress' obstinate belief in Rasputin. His assassination, which occurred when I was no longer in St. Petersburg, was the work of exalted young people who wanted to save Russia. Alas, it came too late, and as Rasputin, when alive, used to say that his end would also be the end of Russia, his death only added to the fatalism with which the Imperial couple accepted the Revolution. I am ashamed to write such harsh words about the last Russian Emperor and Empress, especially in view of their terrible suffering and their inhuman murder by the Bolsheviks, but the events which I witnessed during my years in St. Petersburg were too important to pass over in silence.

✦✦✦

It was my acquaintance with some friends of the Imperial family that helped me to gain a better understanding of what was transpiring in Tsarskoe Selo, the residence of the Imperial family, where the last act of the Russian tragedy was enacted. I have mentioned already my student-day romance with Natasha,[3] a school friend of my sister, a girl with beautiful, sad eyes. I had been so young and shy in those days that I had not found the courage to express my admiration and the romance had come to nothing. While abroad, I had heard that she had married a young officer who took her to St. Petersburg, where his regiment was stationed.

The Grand Duke Michael, brother of the Emperor, was honorary chief of her husband's regiment. He had met Natasha and had fallen in love with her. At first no one took the matter seriously, but Natalia Sergeevna proved ambitious and not easy to forget, and all efforts to

[3] Form of endearment for Natalia or Natalie.

remove the Grand Duke from her influence were to no avail. He insisted on a divorce and the young officer agreed, yielding his place to a more important rival. The affair caused quite a stir in royal circles, for at that time, before the birth of the Tsarevich, the Grand Duke was still considered heir to the throne.

The Grand Duke was separated from his love and gave his word to the Emperor that he would never marry her. He was transferred to some provincial town as commander of a local regiment, while she returned to her family in Moscow, but this did not prevent the Grand Duke from spending every weekend in Moscow, where he stayed in the house of her parents. The situation thus created was very peculiar. Natalia Sergeevna's father, a prominent Moscow lawyer, ignored the origin of the Grand Duke and treated him like a simple mortal. The Grand Duke, who never before had been in the society of common people, enjoyed the lack of ceremony immensely. Those who met him found him very charming and were astounded how little he knew about real life.

But things could not go on that way indefinitely. One day, at a theater in St. Petersburg, Natalia Sergeevna met an officer from her ex-husband's regiment, who plainly showed that the whole regiment resented that she had caused the Grand Duke's removal from the regiment and was compromising him further. Returning to Moscow, Natalia Sergeevna declared to the Grand Duke that she was not accustomed to such treatment, she could not continue such a false life, and insisted that they separate. The Grand Duke replied that he could not live without her and that although he had promised the Emperor not to marry her, he was prepared to go back on his word rather than lose her. Natalia Sergeevna agreed to marry him and as they could not do so in Russia, they sneaked abroad and somewhere in Vienna were married by a Serbian priest. When this became known at court, indignation was general, and a decree was issued forthwith, putting Michael under a guardianship and not allowing them to return to Russia. By this time the Tsarevich had been born and the position of the Grand Duke had lost some of its importance. The newlyweds moved to England, where they rented a house not far from London. They were very happy; indeed, as they said afterward, these years in England, far away from any formalities, were the happiest of their lives.

Upon the outbreak of the First World War the Grand Duke, too patriotic to remain in exile, implored the Emperor to allow him to return to Russia with his family. Permission was granted. The two brothers were reconciled, the guardianship was removed, and the position of Natalia Sergeevna was legalized, the title of Countess Brassova being bestowed on her. Thus the fairytale about an attorney's modest daughter who became the sister-in-law of the Tsar had a happy ending. The couple took a house in Gatchina, some twenty-five miles[4] from St. Petersburg, site of the palace of Alexander III, where the Grand Duke had spent his childhood. Soon he was appointed commander of the Wild Division, named after the wild Caucasian tribes of which it was composed, and went to the front, but every free moment he passed with Natalia Sergeevna.

When I came to St. Petersburg I heard that my childhood friend Natasha was nearby, but she had risen to such high position that I did not dare to renew our acquaintance. One day, walking down the street, however, I met a very elegant lady, who was entering a luxurious car bearing the Imperial crest. Suddenly she rushed toward me and accused me of having forgotten her. I replied that our paths had separated so that I did not want to annoy her, but she called this nonsense. She assured me that she had remained the same to her friends and insisted that I come to Gatchina the first Sunday. As for the Grand Duke, she said, I must look on him as her husband and not as brother of the Emperor.

When I duly arrived at her house, the first person I met was the Grand Duke, and was immediately captivated by his charm. Eventually we became good friends, and I must say I have never met another man so uncorrupted and noble in nature; it was enough to look into his clear blue eyes to be ashamed of any bad thought or insincere feeling. In many ways he was a grown-up child who had been taught only what was good and moral. He did not want to admit that there was wickedness and falsehood in this world and trusted everybody. Had his wife not watched over him constantly, he would have been deceived at every step.

Once, during my presence, a brilliant guard officer persuaded the Grand Duke to go and see some military invention. Natalia Sergeevna was not at home, and Michael went. He returned so enthusiastic about

[4] The manuscript incorrectly gives the distance as forty miles.

the demonstration, that he signed a paper recommending that the inventor be granted some foreign exchange by the Ministry of Finance for the development of the invention. It proved to have been a complete fraud. When Natalia Sergeevna lost her temper and exclaimed, "But you promised me not to sign anything without consulting me," Michael replied that it was impossible to live if one could not trust anybody. And this was a man who had been brought up amidst the corruption of the court, which revolutionaries criticized so much. I used to tease Natalia Sergeevna that I had known her from childhood, at one time had nearly fallen in love with her, and had always been extremely skeptical about her marriage, but that after making the acquaintance of her husband I had found him to be far superior to her. When you were as clever and ambitious as she, you could not remain a thoroughly good woman; such a pure character as that of the Grand Duke, on the other hand, could not be spoiled. But if Michael was a superior being from the standpoint of morality and religion, he was ill-equipped for a man born in the shadow of the throne. If Nicholas by his nature and character was unsuited for tsardom, the reign of Grand Duke Michael would have been a real tragedy. He realized this himself and until a boy was born to the Imperial couple felt quite miserable at the prospect of becoming Emperor.

After my first visit I spent nearly all my Sundays at Gatchina. There I met other members of the Romanov family and listened to their conversation, gaining an insight into the manner of Russian rule and the cause of the perpetual struggle between the Imperial family and the general public. The first impression I had was that the Romanovs had ideas which were centuries-old, that they did not know how the rest of Russia lived and did not want to learn. Fundamentally they felt that Russia existed for the Romanovs, not the Romanovs for Russia. Such an impression ought to have made a revolutionary of me, but as I continued to believe that monarchy, in spite of its many drawbacks, was the sole form of government suitable for Russia, I felt only pity that the current representatives of the Imperial family had such a distorted notion about their duties.

Natalia Sergeevna had acquired a certain amount of regal manners —a vacant look, an artificial smile, elegance—but her mentality remained that of an independent girl who could not hide her feelings. I was present at some awkward scenes. At a luncheon attended by three grand dukes, for instance, she reacted to news of another disaster on the front with the exclamation: "It was you Romanovs who brought Russia to such a state!" There was a general hush in the room and the grand dukes looked down on their plates. As I told Natalia Sergeevna afterwards, it was no wonder she was regarded at court as a revolutionist.

But her old liberalism did not prevent Natalia Sergeevna from enjoying her new position. She was always elegantly dressed and wore magnificent jewelry; she enjoyed attracting the attention of the whole theater as she appeared in her box at the ballet. She always invited me, and sitting somewhere behind her, I could not help taking pride in the gorgeous creature into which the modest schoolgirl I had once adored had been transformed. I was invited to different private parties in the houses of other grand dukes, not for my own sake, I was sure, but probably on Natalia Sergeevna's suggestion. I accepted such invitations partly out of curiosity, partly out of snobbery; but I did not enjoy them. Not a single interesting word was said, most of the conversation consisting of gossip and snide remarks about people I did not know.

I remember a luncheon at the house of Grand Duke Boris at Tsarskoe Selo. Probably because I had just come from Japan a ricksha was brought forth and the Grand Duke pulled Natalia Sergeevna through the garden while asking me questions about geishas that I could not answer, my experience being limited in this respect. In a wine cellar to which we were taken, where wines from all over the world had been collected, the host produced a bottle of Japanese sake and obliged me to drink sake, though I never touched it—even in Japan. A German attack on St. Petersburg was feared at that time and steps were being taken for the evacuation of government offices. Looking with sadness on his collection of wines, Boris bemoaned the possibility of its loss to the Germans, as if there were no greater tragedy that could befall Russia. None of these people seemed to realize the crisis through which Russia was passing; they could not deprive themselves of the pleasures to which they had been accustomed all their lives. I remember how I arrived in Gatchina one time and was at once taken to a small hunting lodge, hidden in the woods, where a magnificent supper was served. Gypsies were singing, and much wine was drunk. I tried to escape from the orgy, but it was dark and cold outside and I did not know my way back. The only man who shared my gloom was Grand Duke Michael, but he bowed to the wishes of his wife, who liked crowds and flattery. Another time, when the same people decided to go for a drive, I declined on the pretext that I should remain with Grand Duke Michael, who was not well.

Whenever I think of this lovable man and his sad fate, I see him as I saw him that Sunday. The house was very quiet, everybody else having gone out; he did not wish any light, though dusk had come early and we faced each other in the twilight. Lying on a couch, shivering from fever, he talked in a sad voice about the difficulty of living among the sorrows, wickedness, selfishness, and deceitfulness of men, and that God was far away. He told me that he often thought how difficult it was for his brother, who sincerely wanted to do only what was good for the people, but who was hindered by his wife. Several times he had tried to convey to Nicholas what people were saying about him and about the dangerous influence of the Empress; Nicholas would listen with great tenderness but would say nothing until Michael felt so upset that it was his brother who consoled him. Nicholas seemed indifferent to his fate, leaving everything in the hands of God, but under the influence of Rasputin God had assumed a strange shape; Michael was afraid of the future. I tried to console him, but could not find words equal to the intensity of his grief. Tears choked his voice. It had become quite dark. When I turned on the light I was shocked by the utter despair on the pale face before me and had the distinct feeling that we all stood on the threshold of great misfortune. At that moment our gay party returned and my only intimate conversation with the Grand Duke was ended.

✠✠✠

My work in the Foreign Office and my personal life went on smoothly now that I had moved out of the hotel, which the war had turned into a meeting place of shady characters—speculators, contract seekers, and profiteers.

I escaped all these excitements to a quiet corner of my own. My Oriental collection had arrived from Japan and I surrounded myself in my small apartment with weird figures, dragons, porcelain vases, and beautiful prints. Seeing these "idols," the old woman whom I engaged at first refused to come, saying that if I made people stay among all this ungodliness, I must at least pay them double salary. Obliged to dust the figures daily, she soon got accustomed to them, however, and her son, when the approaching Revolution began to demoralize people, found it profitable to steal small items from my collection. When I reproached him, he began to cry and said that he had a Chinese friend for whom it was such a pleasure to have something from his country that he had not been able to resist the temptation to give him a present. What could one answer to such an elaborate lie? But I was very happy in my new home. I shall never forget those quiet evenings in a comfortable armchair, with an interesting book in my hands, surrounded by the benevolent faces of my innumerable Buddhas. The turmoil of life outside did not intrude in my corner, and until the last moment I thought that life itself would find a way out of the increasing difficulties.

The political situation was becoming more and more complicated; the misunderstandings between government and Duma were growing. The Emperor was not sure what path he must follow. One day he tried to be firm and dissolved the Duma; the next he convoked it again.

I was present at one such convocation. There was a religious service before the opening of the Duma. Unexpectedly, before the service, the Emperor appeared, accompanied by Grand Duke Michael. The Emperor looked haggard. Only his eyes were the same pale blue, with infinite kindness in them. After the service he said a few words, wishing the Duma success, and with the Speaker passed through the assembly room, where the members of the Duma were waiting. Some shouted "hurrah," but there was little enthusiasm in their voices, and the Emperor looked as if he felt like a stranger among the representatives of his people. In the box for distinguished guests sat Natalia Sergeevna, elegant as always. I joined her. Several members of the Duma were also in the box. From the respect they showed her it was obvious she was becoming known in Duma circles. I remained for the beginning of the session. After some formal speeches, the orators of the left began their old attacks on the government. Nothing had changed. All the energy of the Duma was being spent on struggle with the government rather than on constructive work. It is always easier to tear down the policy of others than to build one's own, and the orators in the Duma were successful in destroying the policy of the government without being able to offer an alternative. It left me with a feeling of utter hopelessness.

Meanwhile the government was taking steps of its own that were bound to end in catastrophe. Under the influence of the Empress and Rasputin, Nicholas decided to remove Grand Duke Nicholas[5] as Commander-in-Chief of the army and assume the position himself. Though the Grand Duke had not been particularly successful, he was popular. The soldiers liked him and the public trusted him. He kept aloof from court intrigues and did not listen to suggestions how the War should be conducted. A favorite story among the public was that when Rasputin once announced that he was coming to headquarters to speak with the Grand Duke, the latter had replied: "If you come, I'll hang you." The story may not have been true, but it greatly increased the Grand Duke's popularity. When the Emperor announced his decision to put himself at the head of the army, the whole cabinet and most of his relatives implored him not to do it. But he would not be dissuaded. Grand Duke Nicholas was removed to the Caucasus and the Emperor with the Tsarevich went to Mogilev, the seat of headquarters at that time. This greatly increased the power of the Empress, who remained in Tsarskoe Selo. Her influence became all-pervasive. She wrote long letters to the Emperor persuading him to be firm, and sent him lists of ministers who ought to be removed and names of those who must replace them, citing as chief arguments for such changes the advice of "our old friend," meaning Rasputin. Sometimes, when the Emperor did not act quickly enough, she went to headquarters herself. The influence of Rasputin gave to all her activity a mystical character, as if she were struggling against some evil work of Satan. One could only say: "Poor, doomed Russia!"

Whenever I was free for several days, I would go to Moscow to see my father and in conversation with him regain my faith in the future. People in Moscow could not understand what was happening in the capital, and thinking that I was in a position to know a great deal, asked me how it was possible for a dirty man, half monk and half vagabond, to enter the palace and give advice to the Emperor of all the Russias. I tried to explain it by drawing a parallel with some private family in which a foolish wife—as often happened in old-fashioned merchant families—liked to receive and talk with different

[5] Nikolai Nikolaevich.

[238]

would-be saints, who went from monastery to monastery impressing weak-minded people with their semireligious talk. But there was, of course, a basic difference. In a private family all this foolishness was of no importance; when the same was allowed to happen in the Imperial family, where every word, every movement became an act of state, the results were tragic.

In St. Petersburg there was much less intellectual activity, the bureaucratic atmosphere stifling all but thought of my career. I lived between those two worlds, but as I was on my own outside Moscow, I felt more at home in St. Petersburg, and would have been quite happy in my cozy apartment with my Oriental things had it not been for the foreboding of disaster. But I had learned long ago that man is not master of his own life and that just when he thinks that he has established himself fairly permanently, something unexpected happens and changes everything.

In my case the unexpected came in the form of a request by Krupenskii, our Minister in China, who was being transferred to Japan and asked me to come along as his First Secretary. As I had been in Japan twice, the prospect of seeing it a third time did not excite me, the more so as I had begun to like my life in St. Petersburg very much. Before making a final decision, however, I sought the advice of my chief, Kazakov, who took an interest in my career. He told me that in normal times he would have advised me against going to Japan; I was highly regarded in the Foreign Office and after three or four years in St. Petersburg would be able to claim an independent post. "But we live in abnormal times and are gliding down a precipice; the farther one is away from Russia at such a time the better," he said. "My advice is to accept." Asking for advice, I meant to follow it, and did so against my own wishes. Of all the advice ever given to me, this was unquestionably the best, for it saved my life. After the Revolution almost the whole Foreign Ministry refused to serve the Bolsheviks and was liquidated sooner or later. In my case, in view of my bourgeois origin, it would probably have been sooner than later.

The new Ambassador wanted to leave as soon as possible and I had little time to take care of my belongings. The best things I sent to be stored with my parents, only to be lost during the Revolution, the others were sold. I spent my last Sunday at Gatchina alone with Natalia Sergeevna and the Grand Duke, never guessing the sad fate in store for them. I paid a hurried visit to Moscow. My last recollection of my native city was of Easter night in the Kremlin, with the gorgeous procession round the four cathedrals on the big Palace Place and the ringing of Moscow's thousands of bells. My parting with my parents was sad; I was never to meet them again. I last saw them standing on the platform amidst a group of relatives, seeing me off when I joined the Ambassador on the Siberian express. It was a spring day, the Moscow streets resounded with the noise of carriages, and scattered groups of people bade farewell to travelers to distant regions. Who could have guessed that as they waved good-bye, they waved good-bye to their loved ones and their country forever?

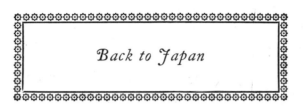

Back to Japan

THERE WAS NOTHING NEW IN THE JOURNEY ACROSS SIBERIA. PERHAPS a little more disorder and more rudeness on the part of the railway guards, but as the Ambassador [Krupenskii] had a special car, we did not notice it a great deal. It was to be the last time that an Ambassador traveled in Russia as a high official. Soon anybody who tried to journey as a high official received only insults; his luggage was thrown out, he himself was affronted, and passengers from the third class filled his carriage. The triumph of democracy had begun. We were spared all that.

As we crossed into Korea we were received with great honors by the Japanese authorities, and were entertained at an elaborate luncheon by the Governor General of Korea, the old Count Terauchi [Masatake]. The old palace was filled with magnificent peonies. Everywhere there seemed to be perfect order, peace, and happiness. Old Korean gentlemen in their white robes smoked small pipes, women worked, children played.

During the night we crossed the sea and in the morning found ourselves in cherry-blossom-covered Japan. Again I had the impression that this was a beautiful and happy country. Only the newspapermen with their silly questions spoiled the general atmosphere. Soon we reached Tokyo, where we were met by the whole Embassy staff, with my friend the gloomy Shchekin at the head. After the usual services in the Embassy church we began our new life. Russia with all its troubles, its conversations and gossip about Rasputin, and its struggle between Emperor and Duma receded into the background. We were surrounded by perfect order and discipline; the Japanese bowed and smiled, and the whole idea of revolution seemed unreal.

It was a happy time for Japan. World War I claimed little from the Japanese. In the first year they destroyed the entire influence of Germany in the Far East; thereafter their war activity was limited to escorting British ships which transported ammunition and food from Australia. The Japanese made huge profits by trading with the allies. Everybody was getting rich and Japanese commerce was gradually replacing British and American commerce in the Far East. The Russian Embassy could not keep apart from the diplomatic world with its endless dinner parties and bridge games, card playing having replaced dancing during the War (there always being accommodations with conscience in diplomatic life). Our new Ambassador was an excellent host, and the dinner parties at the Russian Embassy soon became famous. The fact that the Ambassador invited many Japanese did not add to the gaiety of the dinner parties, because few Japanese and foreigners could communicate with each other and usually just sat around and smiled at each other. But the Japanese seemed to like those receptions. Proud to be the friends and allies of the foreign powers, they tried to imitate them, and Embassy parties served them as lessons in Western behavior.

Tokyo no longer looked like a small village; the city was changing into a magnificent capital with beautiful shops and well-dressed crowds. Foreign ways had penetrated all phases of Japanese life which was full of gaiety, happiness, and lack of concern, but the military remained aloof, working in the barracks and dreaming great dreams. Biding their time, the military did not oppose the people's pursuit of everything foreign, indeed seemed to favor it as the best way of allaying foreign suspicions about Japan's future plans. Furthermore this was a good time to make money and obtain the means for industrial and military power. Thus all foreigners with whom Japan was not at war received a warm welcome. American tourists returned to the United States full of the highest admiration for the Japanese, the few newspapermen who could speak English having assured prominent American visitors that the history of Japanese-American relations proved that the United States and Japan were destined to live in perpetual friendship.

Japan had the best of feelings toward Russia too. Lacking the means for the successful continuation of the War, Russia placed large orders in Japan, and the Japanese government organized a special trust to fill the various orders for ammunition and other goods as quickly as possible. The urgency was such that our Embassy was inundated with telegrams instructing us to ask the Japanese for rifles, guns, and the like. At one time our War Office requested the immediate delivery of one million rifles, and we had to answer that such a number would mean the complete disarmament of the entire Japanese army for our sake. Our former Ambassador [Malevskii-Malevich], who had been of the opinion that an Ambassador must never hurry, had lost his job because he had not been able to satisfy the demands of the War Office quickly enough. The Grand Duke George[1] was sent to persuade the Japanese government to supply us with more ammunition. He was feted everywhere. The whole court, beginning with the Emperor, admired his height and insisted upon standing near him to see the difference. Presents and promises were exchanged.

It was our task also to arrange loans in Japan to pay for our orders. The Japanese were always ready to meet us halfway, and the bankers, who did not think that the Embassy understood much in financial matters and used to tell us how they expected to obtain the most advantageous conditions, had to make great concessions because of the knowledge and obstinacy of Counsellor Shchekin. But in the end nothing came of all those transactions: the Revolution toppled the Russian government and the Soviets refused to pay the old debts.

Before the Revolution our relations with Japan were so good that it was decided to strengthen them further by an alliance, in accordance with which both countries agreed to come to each other's help in the event of attack by a third power. The negotiations took a very short time, and soon after our arrival in Tokyo we plunged into a series of celebrations marking the conclusion of this alliance. The Japanese always followed the same procedure in these celebrations: a luncheon at the Foreign Office with political speeches and "banzai" to the Emperor, a luncheon given by the Tokyo municipality and a lantern pro-

[1] General Prince Georgii Mikhailovich.

[243]

cession of thousands and thousands of Tokyo inhabitants. Such a procession was organized very simply. Anybody who wished to participate received from the police a lantern and twenty-five sen. The result was most effective. At dusk these processions began to move like fire serpents from all sides of the town toward the Embassy. The Ambassador and the staff stood at the gate as thousands of lantern-carrying Japanese passed by and insisted on shaking hands. This lasted for hours, and a newcomer could imagine that he had gained immediate popularity with the inhabitants of Tokyo. Actually, it was merely a matter of a free evening and twenty-five sen.

At that time Marquis Okuma [Shigenobu] was Prime Minister. I always admired the facility with which Okuma could say quite opposite things on different occasions. Addressing members of a temperance society one day, he spoke with great eloquence about the harm of alcohol; talking to a group of wine producers the next day, he held forth with no less eloquence on the joy of drinking. To us he stated that it was a great mistake to think that it was the Americans who had opened Japan to the world; it was the Russians, and he cited the journey of Nikolai Rezanov.[2] Okuma was a jolly old man. As he endeavored to revise the unequal treaties that the Western powers had made with Japan, a patriot who opposed the admittance of foreigners to the country threw a bomb at him [1889]. Though Okuma lost a leg, his energy was not diminished and he used to say that he would live until he was a hundred and twenty. Thus the first year of Krupenskii's service as Ambassador to Japan passed peacefully.

Surrounded by Japanese who were enjoying their success, we thought that our misfortunes would pass away, that the day would come when the Emperor and the Duma would find a common language. It is difficult to be pessimistic when one is young, when the sun shines, and everything around blooms and smiles. Our optimism

[2] The manuscript incorrectly states "Admiral Riazianof." Chamberlain Rezanov negotiated with the Japanese in 1804-05. Russians had visited Japan proper as early as 1739, and had negotiated at some length in 1792-93. But it was Vice Admiral Evfimii Vasilevich Putiatin who most effectively competed with Commodore Matthew C. Perry in the opening of Japan in the 1850's. See G. A. Lensen, *Russia's Japan Expedition of 1852 to 1855* (Gainesville: University of Florida Press, 1955), and Lensen, *The Russian Push Toward Japan: Russo-Japanese Relations, 1697-1875* (Princeton, N.J.: Princeton University Press, 1959).

seemed confirmed by the official dispatches which we received from
our Foreign Office. A government will never confess that it is losing
its grip and the information sent to its representatives abroad is usually designed to encourage them. The Japanese Foreign Office listened to our reports with great skepticism and the wise Foreign Minister Viscount Motono [Ichirō], who had been Japanese Ambassador
to St. Petersburg for over a decade,[3] only shook his head and confessed that according to his information things were much worse in
Russia. He was right. One after another all the decent ministers were
dismissed and replaced by men recommended to the Empress by Rasputin. These persons could not work with the representatives of the
people. Especially hated was Minister of Interior [Aleksandr Dmi-
trievich] Protopopov, who in the presence of the Empress pretended
that he was guided by his faith in the Almighty and did everything to
provoke an uprising, thinking that he would be able to crush it and
thereby put an end to the whole revolutionary movement. The Emperor was sinking deeper and deeper in indifference and fatalism. The
situation was becoming impossible. There were conspiracies to remove
the Emperor and the Empress, but as people did not trust each other
there was no common action, the members of the Imperial family and
the generals, who alone could have carried out such a plan, remaining
too loyal to translate their criticism into action.

Several enthusiastic young men, among them a grand duke [Dmi-
trii Pavlovich], led by the husband of a niece of the Emperor [Prince
Feliks Feliksovich Iusupov], attempted to save Russia by removing
Rasputin, whom they considered its evil spirit. Knowing the monk's
taste for gay suppers, the leader of the conspiracy invited him to his
house. The meal was served in the cellar, a ghastly setting which later
fascinated Hollywood film makers. The sweets and the wine were
poisoned. At first Rasputin refused to eat or drink; eventually he was
persuaded to take some sweets. But to the horror of the host the poison
seemed to have no effect on Rasputin.[4] Going upstairs, the host con-

---

[3] The decade 1906-16.

[4] According to the late Dr. Serge Lensen of the Michigan Department of
Health, to whom this book is dedicated, who for a number of years worked at
the Pasteur Institute in Paris, one of his colleagues there, seeking a scientific
explanation of Rasputin's immunity, found that the particular poison served to
Rasputin in sweets was neutralized by sugar.

ferred with the other conspirators. Suddenly Rasputin, his face livid, appeared at the top of the stairs, crawling on all fours. The sight was so horrid that the conspirators turned to stone, and did not know what to do. Only when Rasputin reached the door and rushed into the garden, did one of them shoot him.

His murder, however welcome, did not remedy the situation. The conspirators were sent into exile, while Rasputin was given a solemn burial by the Imperial couple. Every day the Empress went to attend a requiem at his tomb, and things grew worse than before. Superstitious people began to repeat in half whispers Rasputin's prophecy that his death would usher in the end of Russia.

It was from Viscount Motono that we first heard about the abdication of the Emperor in favor of Grand Duke Michael, but I had scarcely time to realize how close my friend Natalia Sergeevna had come to the throne when the Emperor's abdication was followed by that of the Grand Duke. Later I learned that the abdication of the Emperor in favor of his son had been considered at first, but when the doctor of the Tsarevich had informed the Emperor that the Tsarevich would never be well, he had abdicated both for himself and his son, naming Michael as Tsar. His decision was that of a loving father who did not want to part from his son, but he had no right to abdicate for another person, especially if thereby he broke the straight line of succession. All this was decided in the field headquarters of the Commander-in-Chief, far from the Empress, who would never have allowed the abdication.

As to Grand Duke Michael's abdication, it took place in St. Petersburg. He was also away from his wife, who remained in Gatchina, all communication between Gatchina and the capital having been broken by a railroad strike. Once again the dynasty was plagued by misfortune: at the most decisive moment of his life the Grand Duke was separated from the person on whose decisions he was accustomed to rely. He did conduct himself with great dignity. When members of the provisional government, organized by the Duma in order not to leave the country without any government, called on him to find out whether he would accept the throne, he asked their advice. Notwithstanding their liberal tendencies, several of the ministers declared that he must accept the throne in order to preserve the dynasty, but one of the ministers, the well-known [Aleksandr Feodorovich] Kerenskii, made one of his high-sounding speeches, in which he urged the Grand Duke to leave the decision to the people. Michael asked for a few minutes to think it over, and left the room. When he returned he announced that inasmuch as the ministers were not unanimous, he could not accept the throne, and would await the decision of the Constitutional Assembly whether Russia was to be a monarchy or a republic. Meanwhile he asked that the provisional government rule the country. Kerenskii was in ecstasy and called the Grand Duke the noblest of men, but the fact remained that Michael's decision was the final blow to the [Romanov] dynasty, which had reigned for more than three centuries and had made of Russia one of the greatest countries in the world.

The provisional government, into whose hands governmental authority passed, was an artificial and weak organization. Called "provisional," because it was to convoke a constitutional assembly to decide the question of a new, permanent government for Russia, the provisional government was composed of well-meaning persons of liberal tendencies, who believed in high-sounding phrases but had no idea how to rule a state. As the provisional government promised to continue the war with Germany, a matter of utmost importance to the allies, it received immediate recognition, and all the representatives abroad were perfectly justified in remaining in their posts, obvious as the great difference between the Imperial government which had appointed them and the provisional government was to most of them.

The new government from the beginning carried within itself the seeds of its future destruction. Its members, differing in their degree of liberalism, could not agree, and control slipped into the hands of the people. During a revolution, crowds tend to listen to extreme leftists, and the people, with the help of Bolshevik propaganda, gradually became aware of their power over any government. Instead of following the dictates of great intellects, the government leaders had to cater to the basest elements. I must say, to their credit, that most of our liberals were incapable of doing so. Failing to realize their high ideals, they retired. But in their places stepped ambitious and unscrupulous politicians, who sought to maintain themselves by gaining the good will of the proletariat.

It would be a mistake to think that the Revolution found the Russian proletariat unprepared. The leftist elements were much more prepared for the Revolution than the other classes; the aristocrats and the landlords gave up their posts without even trying to defend them; the liberal-minded middle class which had always considered itself the logical successor to the upper classes in the event of a change in government lacked all organization and real will to rule. The bourgeoisie could be of great help to an existing government, but it was incapable of creating a government of its own—as the short life of the provisional government proved. Only the proletariat was energetic enough to wield the power the monarchy had dropped. The agitators who worked behind the scenes to bring about the Revolution understood this and concentrated all their efforts on the proletariat and on the soldiers, the War having turned many workers into soldiers. When the Revolution took place and the provisional government appeared on the scene, the agitators did not interfere with it at first; they merely organized a Soviet of Worker and Soldier Representatives. The council had no position in the new government and simply voiced opinions, but soon its influence mounted to such an extent that the provisional government could not take any serious step without first assuring itself of the support of the Soviet of Worker and Soldier Representatives. This placed the provisional government in a most awkward position: everyone knew that real power was not in its hands. It was especially difficult to continue the War with the allies whose governments and policies had not changed and who expected that Russia, notwithstanding the Revolution, would remain true to its military commitments. The provisional government could not declare the truth, namely that the Russian army had enough of war, that the soldiers refused to fight and tried to fraternize with the Germans. Instead it said a lot of nonsense, first that the freedom acquired by the Russian people had doubled its energy to continue the War, then, under the influence of the Soviet of Worker and Soldier Representatives, that the character of the War must change, that it must be a war without annexation of territory or compensation. Everybody in Russia started to speak about a war without annexation or compensation, as if a war without greed and ambition were possible; but it was effective propaganda against the continuation of the War. Under the circumstances the position of the provisional government soon became ridiculous; no honest man could remain a member.

The only man who kept his faith in the provisional government until the end was Kerenskii, first because he was the only member who could maintain good relations with the worker and soldier representatives, who wanted to have their man in the provisional government, and second because he found in the provisional government an excellent platform for his exceptional eloquence. When the soldiers refused to advance and began to desert, he persuaded them to advance again. But his success was shortlived, because there was already no discipline in the Russian army, and words can never replace discipline backed up with punishment. At one time it appeared that Kerenskii might succeed in restoring order and saving the country from a worse lot, but alas, Kerenskii was weak and vain. In his speeches he sounded like the savior of Russia but in action he vacillated, and time was lost. I do not wish to be cruel, but I think that Kerenskii was one of the many tragedies which befell Russia in the dark years of her history.

Not only was Kerenskii incapable of resolving the difficulties himself, but by sticking to his position, he prevented others from doing so. Such was the case in his quarrel with General [Lavr Georgievich] Kornilov, the Commander-in-Chief of the army. When it became clear that the provisional government could not do anything, General Kornilov marched with his troops onto the capital to seize power himself. The details of the plot were not clear; there seemed to have been at first some sort of agreement between Kornilov and Kerenskii, who must have seen that things could not be worse and that energetic steps ought to be taken. I knew Kornilov when he was our Military Attaché in Peking; he had a very difficult character. He was a typical soldier, who despised everything civilian. I am sure there could not have been any direct and thorough agreement between Kerenskii and him, and the whole matter was left in the hands of go-betweens, who traveled between St. Petersburg and the General's headquarters. These go-betweens made such a muddle that Kornilov did not know what Kerenskii expected from him and what he in turn could expect from Kerenskii. When Kornilov marched on the capital, Kerenskii became frightened and turned against him and the whole plan fell through. Kornilov was arrested and Kerenskii remained in power, but not for long, because by then others who knew what they wanted were ready to come to the fore. These other people were the Bolsheviks, who had made an earlier, unsuccessful, bid for power; instead of crushing them once and for all, Kerenskii had shown such weakness that the Bolsheviks were able to bide their time and rise again. Their opportunity came with the abortive plot of General Kornilov. This time they were successful: Kerenskii ran away and other members of the provisional government were arrested. Thus the only thing that the provisional government, with all its high-sounding phrases, accomplished was to pave the way for the Bolsheviks.

As long as peace reigned and Russia did not have to cope with the consequences of an unsuccessful war, the activities of the Russian revolutionaries abroad did not present any real danger. The Russian police was very well informed, since many members of the revolutionary organizations were in its pay. The revolutionaries met and discussed their programs, and waited for the opportunity to put them into practice. The most extreme program was that of the Social Democrats, who based their theories on the teachings of Karl Marx. The adherents of this party were known among the Russian revolutionaries as "Bolsheviki" or "Bolsheviks," meaning "those who follow the program of the majority." This was merely a revolutionary nickname; "Russian Marxists" would be equally correct. At the head of the Party stood the famous [Vladimir Ilich] Lenin, and it is to him that the Bolsheviks owe their success.

Born in a provincial town[5] near the Volga River, Lenin was the son of a small bureaucrat by the name of [Ilia Nikolaevich] Ulianov. His eldest brother was hanged for participating in an attempt on the life of Emperor Alexander III. This made a strong impression on young Vladimir who began to show revolutionary tendencies while still in middle school. By the time he became a university student he was a full-fledged revolutionist, became involved in some plot, and was caught and sent to Siberia. But he managed to escape abroad, and there, under the name Lenin, founded the Bolshevik (Communist) Party.

There was something satanic in him. In typical Russian fashion he adopted a theory, that of Karl Marx, and then proceeded to change it into his own theory, with himself as the sole rightful interpreter. He never doubted the truth of his theory and was absolutely indifferent to the number of victims that had to be sacrificed for its sake. It was a true case of *"pereat mundus, fiat justitia,"*[6] with "Lenin" taking

[5] Simbirsk, now Ulianovsk.
[6] "The world perishes, but justice triumphs."

[250]

the place of "*justitia*." While Marx believed that his theory would succeed only in a country with a highly developed industry, where the workers had attained such a state of culture that they could rule the country and continue its evolution, Lenin understood quite well that he could impose his interpretation of Marxism only in such a country as Russia, where but a minority was educated and there could consequently be found enough people to follow his distorted version of Karl Marx's doctrine like a herd of sheep. Cynically, he did not try to hide that he would work with anybody who agreed to submit to him, and when his followers directed his attention to the low morals of some of the Bolsheviks, he retorted that in so big a household as Russia all rubbish could be put to use.

Lenin realized that he could not attain his objective while abroad. The old Russian organization was as yet too strong to be destroyed by a group of revolutionaries. Propaganda alone could not undermine governmental authority. What was needed was an unsuccessful war. The Russo-Japanese War was the opportunity for which Lenin had been waiting. As the whole country protested against it, Lenin and representatives of other revolutionary parties transferred their activity inside Russia. But thanks to the mediation of the President of the United States and the cleverness of Witte, peace was restored and the Revolution crushed. Lenin escaped; other leaders were treated with leniency and exiled to Siberia, whence most of them fled abroad.

Much has been heard about the cruelty with which the Tsarist government fought the revolutionaries; facts prove the contrary. The majority of the most dangerous revolutionaries could easily escape abroad and continue their struggle against Russia, until another war gave them the long awaited opportunity. Successful in his aims, Lenin was clever enough to destroy or, as the Bolsheviks called it, to "liquidate" everybody who tried to oppose him. It is this policy of execution, not their popularity, that explains the persistence of Bolshevik domination.

The horrors of Bolshevism reached the Far Eastern borders only gradually. However, with the movement of troops in Siberia many people succeeded in escaping from Russia, and I had ample opportunity to gain a clear picture of how the Bolsheviks at the time of the provisional government, when Russia was ruled by high ideals and words, penetrated into Russia and using high ideals merely to dupe the gullible, grasped power, and started to wipe out all opposition. The provisional government under Kerenskii did not admit its weakness. In Tokyo we continued to receive dispatches telling us how well the provisional government was getting along, how the first Bolshevik uprising soon after Lenin's arrival from Switzerland via Germany had been put down, and how the revolt of General Kornilov had been crushed. Kerenskii was so sure of himself that following the capture of most Bolshevik leaders (except Lenin, who was hiding in Finland), he did not publish the documents proving that Lenin and his nearest collaborators had come to Russia with the help of the German general staff and were being supported by German money. He set them free, even though Russia was still at war with Germany and they were thus traitors. Three months later Lenin and the Bolsheviks rose again, this time successfully.

✤✤✤

The Christian forgiveness with which the provisional government treated its enemies was reflected in our experiences in Japan. One of the first steps taken by the provisional government was the proclamation of a general amnesty of all political refugees. Most of them wanted to go back to Russia, but had no money for the journey. The provisional government to which they appealed, claiming that an amnesty must be accompanied by funds to make possible their return, assigned a sizable sum of money to our Consul in Yokohama to help the political emigrants traveling from the United States by way of Japan.

Soon Yokohama was filled with refugees, waiting for accommodations to proceed to Vladivostok and beyond across Siberia. They all claimed money from our Consul. Most of them were Jews. Instead of showing their gratitude to the provisional government, they arranged demonstrations before the Consulate at which they openly advocated the overthrow of the provisional government.

We did everything to warn the provisional government that it merely increased its foes by freely bringing to Russia all sorts of emigrants. But our efforts were in vain. Since we belonged to the old regime, our views were dismissed as reactionary. As we refused to submit to these "new elements," they started to denounce us even before returning to Russia. They were especially hostile to our two barons, who could not understand anything that was going on and only repeated all the time, "How terrible! How terrible!" As the Ambassador refused to receive the emigrants, it was my lot to talk to them when they brought their complaints to the Embassy.

Once a deputation of three persons came to complain that the Consul insisted on their traveling through Japan third class. Their argument was strange: they were not accustomed to traveling in the same carriage with Asiatics. My inquiry as to how they expected to travel in Japan without meeting any Asiatics produced no effect on them, and the lady who was the principal speaker did not stop talking, an effeminate-looking young man supporting her tirade. They inundated me with grand phrases about the high ideals to which they had sacrificed their lives, and bemoaned the cruelty with which our Consul was treating them; they were eager to return to their fatherland to work for a new Russia, yet we made their women and children travel like beasts. The third member of the deputation looked like a boxer; he remained silent but clenched his fists. It occurred to me that the deputation had been well chosen: if the charms of the lady and the high ideals of the young man did not persuade me, the fists of the boxer might. As I was no good at exchanging platitudes and even worse at boxing, I began to think about a compromise, and offered that the Embassy would instruct the Consul to buy second-class tickets for women and children. They consented. Had they persisted in their demands, however, the sight of the clenched fists might well have induced me to go as far as getting them a special train. The poor old bureaucrat was no match for these "representatives of New Russia." Once I had promised the second-class accommodations, the conversation became peaceful, and I asked each of the deputies what he had done before in Russia. The lady had tried to shoot a governor but had missed; the young man had taken part in some conspiracy; the silent boxer had been a member of the group which had tossed a bomb into the country house of Prime Minister Stolypin. It was not to the credit of our police that all of them had escaped, had found their way to the United States, and now were returning to Russia—probably to throw bombs at members of the government which paid for their journey back. It is difficult to find a better example of Christian meekness or downright stupidity.

At about this time we were informed that our Ambassador in Washington, [Georgii Petrovich] Bakhmetev, had resigned. In his telegram to the provisional government he said that he had remained at his post, thinking that it would fulfill its promise to the Emperor, who had abdicated on condition that the provisional government convoke without delay a constitutional assembly to determine what sort of government would rule Russia. Confident that given absolute freedom the people would recall the Emperor, Bakhmetev had considered it his duty to remain in his post. But now, he wired, the provisional government invented one delay after another to postpone the convocation of the Assembly, all the while preparing Russia for a republic. He did not wish to participate further in such deceit, and herewith submitted his resignation. The provisional government was furious at the arrogant telegram, and at once appointed a new Ambassador to the United States, an engineer whose name also happened to be Bakhmetev.[7] When the old Bakhmetev was asked whether the new Ambassador were related to him, he is said to have responded that if there was any relationship between George Washington, the President, and George Washington, his Negro cook, the new Bakhmetev could be a relative of his.

On his way to Washington the new Ambassador passed through Japan. It was interesting for us to see what type of diplomat the provisional government sent abroad to represent it. Bakhmetev proved to be a clever and brilliant man, but completely different from our idea of a Russian diplomat. Krupenskii sent our interpreter to meet him at Tsuruga. At the modest station, where he was welcomed by the station master, the chief customs inspector, and two or three other local officials, Bakhmetev assumed a heroic pose and announced that he brought greetings from Free Russia to the people of Japan. As such a statement would have been completely incomprehensible to the Japanese officials, if it could have been rendered in Japanese at all, our interpreter translated the speech in a much simpler form—he said that the Ambassador was very pleased to come to Japan and admire its beautiful landscape. The officials smiled and everybody was pleased.

Bakhmetev was accompanied by some fifty people—representatives of different branches with their wives, their secretaries, and even friends of secretaries—all of them with staggering salaries, unknown in the old diplomatic service. During the long journey through Si-

[7] Boris Aleksandrovich.

beria all of them, especially the ladies, had quarreled with each other, and when, jointly with the representative of the Canadian Pacific Line, I had to arrange places for them on the steamer, it was impossible to find two ladies who would agree to share a cabin. In the end the representative of the company lost his temper and told me that if I did not manage the crowd, he might not be able to control his fists. I appealed to Bakhmetev and he announced that those who did not comply with our cabin arrangements would be sent back to Russia. All bickering ceased at once.

Krupenskii gave a luncheon in honor of Bakhmetev, inviting the Japanese Foreign Minister and several high officials. Bakhmetev made a speech that was so grandiloquent our interpreter could not translate it. After lunch I found myself next to Viscount Motono. To make conversation, I pointed out what clever men the provisional government was sending abroad to represent it. Motono looked at me, then said with a sly expression on his face, "But all that stands on a declining surface and cannot be maintained. It will slip." In the drawing room I saw two members of Bakhmetev's mission show each other ordinary gilded chairs and comment how the old regime had squandered the money of the people, thinking apparently that we of the Embassy sat on chairs of pure gold. We were greatly relieved when this whole crowd left for the United States.

❖❖❖

The position of the Embassy was becoming more and more difficult and the barons were quite right with their "How awful!" It is astonishing how far the microbes of opposition and revolution can travel across land and sea. At this time in Tokyo we had quite a large Russian colony made up of different businessmen, mostly Jews, who came to Tokyo to purchase various supplies which because of the War could not be imported from the West. There were also a number of refugees, who, foreseeing nothing good from developments in Russia, had thought it safer to leave in time. Gradually all these people became increasingly radical and turned more and more against the Embassy. They arranged meetings in a local hotel and insisted that the Embassy staff be present. The Ambassador firmly refused to attend the meetings, but the junior members went. Luckily our gloomy Counsellor Shchekin had a sufficient supply of abusive language to keep the people in line. There was still a certain amount of discipline left and, after all, we lived in Japan under the Japanese and not under the demoralized Russian police.

I could not help but see the humorous side of these meetings. As the Revolution turned political refugees into heroes, we had to have a hero in Tokyo. The only one with any claim to such a role was a Russian who had played an insignificant part in the Revolution of 1905. Escaping to Japan, he had been leading a miserable drunken existence. Found in some slum, he was brought to the meeting and elected president amid enthusiastic applause. He sat there with expressionless eyes, staring at the applauding public, understanding nothing. Then the speeches began—a veritable deluge of grand phrases about the end of slavery, the beginning of freedom, and so forth. As Russia was still at war with Germany, it was decided to collect money for the army and to send a congratulatory telegram wishing complete victory—this at a time when the soldiers already refused to fight and were leaving the front for their villages. There was much discussion about the text of the telegram, to whom to send it, and to whom to hand over the money. In the end the money passed to the president to be never heard of again, and the speeches continued. Suddenly an officer who served under our Military Attaché jumped on a chair and hysterically began to shout that it was all wrong that he saw before him well-dressed people. We must give everything away, he said, and march arm in arm in the streets and, at a loss of words, began to sing the Internationale. Then he fell on the floor crying like a child. A Jew brought him water and tried to console him. It was the last scene I saw of the meeting, which was turning into a madhouse.

The revolutionary microbe was catching. One morning our Military Attaché rushed into the chancery shouting that it was they, the officers of the general staff, who had made the Revolution, and when we looked at him in astonishment, he added, "We always wore a red shirt under our uniforms." When our gloomy Counsellor asked him about his oath, the Attaché responded that in the struggle for freedom the oath was of no value, and stormed out of the chancery. Hearing that his friend had been appointed Minister of War, he soon rushed to St. Petersburg and obtained the position of Vice Minister, but the provisional government was in its last days. When the soldiers started to murder their officers and the high posts became too dangerous, especially when the other Vice Minister was killed by the troops, he hurried back to Tokyo, where he proceeded to agitate among the officers. His true aim was not clear: he had run away from the Bolsheviks, yet once safely in Japan, he played their game, probably remembering his red shirt. Fortunately for us he decided that Japan was too small a field for his activity and left for the United States, where he soon became an active agent of the Soviet government. I believe this was the only case of a real revolt against the Embassy.

The uncertainty continued as long as the provisional government headed Russia. The situation changed with the victory of the Bolsheviks, who ruled with an iron hand.

One morning the Ambassador received a short note from Viscount Motono, informing us that the Foreign Office had received a telegram from the Japanese Embassy in St. Petersburg to the effect that the Bolsheviks had arrested the members of the provisional government. Prime Minister Kerenskii only had escaped; his whereabouts were unknown. As this page of history came to an end, it was clear that Russia was not yet ready to be ruled by high ideals and democratic ideas. After the downfall of the monarchy and several months of shameful lack of statesmanship on the part of the so-called liberal classes, power had passed into the hands of a group of unscrupulous adventurers, with a leader clever enough to realize that Russia could not be ruled without a stick. The blind people who had destroyed the old enlightened tyranny, under which Russia had been making enormous progress and which, after all, had belonged to the family of civilized governments, found themselves under a much worse and inhuman tyranny.

For us at the Embassy the change was tragic. Unless Bolshevism proved transitory and the people in Russia rejected its power and principles, so contrary to the Russian character and creed, our careers were finished and we would be thrown into the street without fatherland, family, or money. The evening we received the bad news I went to the station to see off some countrymen who were returning to Russia not knowing what they would find there. Walking back, I was so absorbed in my gloomy thoughts that I did not notice the car behind me. Suddenly I was blinded by strong light and knocked down.

Some Japanese picked me up. I was all right, but I wondered whether being killed on the spot might not have been the best way out of all the troubles I saw before me.

In the morning my energy returned. I realized that I could continue to exist, that the world was large, and that somewhere I was bound to find a place. As our Counsellor, appointed by the provisional government in its last days as Minister to Persia, had left some time ago for St. Petersburg, I assumed his responsibilities. Meanwhile the Ambassador sounded out the Japanese Foreign Secretary about the attitude of the Japanese government toward events in Russia and dispatched telegrams to our Russian ambassadors abroad to determine their course of action. Soon the general picture was clear. Nobody trusted the new government; few expected that it would last. As Siberia was still non-Bolshevik, the Japanese government wanted us to remain in our position. Our representatives in Europe thought likewise, and it was decided to keep the diplomatic offices functioning as long as possible, the Ambassador in Paris acting as our senior representative. But we no longer received any financial support from the Russian government. I do not know what means of existence were found in Europe; in the Far East the question was resolved simply. Our Legation in Peking informed us that China had agreed to continue making the Boxer indemnity payments to the Russo-Asiatic Bank and the Bank was willing to support the Russian representatives in China and Japan. Thus our Embassy and all our Consulates continued to function as if nothing had happened and Krupenskii even remained in the position of Dean of the Diplomatic Corps. I believe it was the only case in history when an Embassy functioned without the government it represented. When asked whom we did represent, I replied that we represented the glorious past and the hope of a more glorious future.

❖❖❖

We soon discovered that we had plenty to do. Siberia, after the first moments of uncertainty, began to fight against the Bolsheviks, so did Manchuria. The Russian Embassy in Tokyo, theoretically representing the whole country, tried to support, insofar as possible, every local movement against the Bolsheviks, giving advice to all the inexperienced organizations and, if they deserved it, recommending them to the attention of the foreign powers who, as the war with Germany still continued, were very anxious about developments in Siberia. Since a great number of German and Austrian prisoners were interned in Siberia, it was feared in Europe and in America that with the help of the Soviet government a new enemy front could be created there. It was the chief reason for the foreign intervention in the Russian Far East. During this period the old Russian Embassy was the center for everything connected with Russian interests and we had far more to do than in normal times. I must mention here that our Ambassador, with his wonderful tact and abundant common sense, enjoyed the esteem of all foreign representatives as well as of the Japanese government. I never knew him to waver from his anti-Bolshevik attitude. He fully maintained the dignity of the old Russian Embassy, and when he had to leave for Europe I tried to live up to the same tradition and, without undue conceit, must say that our efforts deserved greater success.

$$9$$

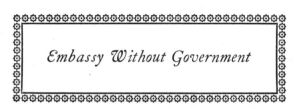

FROM NOVEMBER 7, 1917, ON, THE EMBASSY WAS AN EMBASSY WITHOUT a government. We tried to keep closely in touch with our fellow representatives in Europe, but the great distances and the high cost of exchanging telegrams made this extremely difficult, and gradually we became quite independent in our handling of Far Eastern affairs. We joined the Council of Ambassadors, which was formed in Europe with Ambassador Giers, our oldest Ambassador, and then our Ambassador to Rome, at the head. The Council's center of activity was Paris, where the position of our Embassy was not clear, because the last legal Ambassador, the former Minister of Foreign Affairs [Sazonov] had retired, while his successor, the noted Russian lawyer and member of the Duma [Vasilii Alekseevich] Maklakov, had not had time to present his credentials when the provisional government had fallen and the French government refused to recognize him. To improve matters Giers left his post in Italy and went to Paris, for he was well known there and commanded greater prestige than Maklakov. But though the Council did its best to acquire the right to speak for the old Russian government, the ally of France and England in the war against Germany, a right that it possessed in its own imagination, it failed to persuade the foreign powers that it could represent something that had ceased to exist.

Under the circumstances our Council could not play an important part; all it could do was to present empty protests every time the Bol-

sheviks were treated as the legal government of Russia. Much was
said about the ingratitude of France, which had forgotten that Russia,
at the beginning of the War, had sacrificed its best troops to save Paris,
but considering what a terrible blow the defection of Russia in 1917
was to France, her feelings were understandable. After all, gratitude
never plays a serious role in politics.

We had no such complications in Japan. Japanese patriotism had
never been touched by the war with Germany. The Japanese fulfilled
their obligations toward their English ally, took Germany's Far Eastern possessions, and made a lot of money; the rest did not interest
them very much. They needed our presence in Tokyo, because the
admission of Bolshevik representatives was out of the question, and
we got along well in regard to various Manchurian and Chinese problems. We did not feel the slightest difference in our position. The
same was true with respect to our relations with the foreign representatives in Tokyo. Our Ambassador remained the Dean of the entire
Diplomatic Corps, and every new foreign ambassador or minister had
to call first of all on Krupenskii. I was aware of the fact that unless
the struggle in Russia ended with the triumph of the White cause,
our position was that of a fool's paradise, but then if Providence sends
one to such a paradise, why not make the best of it? After all, better a
fool's paradise than the Bolshevik hell.

Our information about events in Russia was confined to reports
from the Japanese Foreign Minister and to telegrams from Paris.
News conveyed by the Japanese Embassy, which still remained in St.
Petersburg, left no doubt that the Bolsheviks, under the leadership of
Lenin, lost no time in effecting their program and destroying every
vestige of Old Russia. By the confiscation of all bank deposits, the new
government with the stroke of a pen ruined everyone who had anything to lose; by confining everyone to a small part of his house and
by filling the rest with people from the street, the Bolsheviks undermined the whole concept of private property. No longer masters of
their own house, many preferred to move out rather than be insulted
by beggars who had become the real masters of their belongings.
Worst of all, people who disagreed with the new rulers were liquidated without justice or pity, and such a state of fear was created that
people were silenced and all opposition disappeared.

I was often asked by foreigners who did not want to believe all the horrors attributed to the Bolsheviks and who persisted in seeing in them democratic elements which had replaced the old reactionary forces, how it was possible in such a short time to ruin millions of people. My answer was: study the first decrees of the Bolsheviks once they were in power, and you will understand the whole picture. The confiscation of all bank deposits alone had sufficed to make paupers of all millionaires. I cite the example of my parents, who had been rich by Russian standards. My father had retired from business and had been living comfortably on the money kept in the banks and on the income from different shares. When the Bolsheviks confiscated all deposits and declared all factories state property, he was deprived of everything—and not only he and the other rich people, but everybody who owned anything and was considered by the Bolsheviks a member of the bourgeoisie, the class which created goods without which the population could not exist.

The news from our representatives in Paris was not without hope. We were told that the Bolsheviks experienced great difficulties, that opposition was growing, that when [Leon] Trotskii, who had become Commissar for Foreign Affairs, paid his first visit to the Foreign Office he found it empty, because none of the officials were willing to work with the Bolsheviks. The same was rumored true in other departments. We heard that more moderate representatives of Russian radicals, the so-called Mensheviks, tried to persuade British and French statesmen that if the allies would modify their peace terms with Germany so as to bring about an immediate end to the War, the Bolshevik cause would collapse.

All this sounded extremely foolish to us. It was true that most of the clerks in the Foreign Office had refused to work for the Bolsheviks, but the worst elements remained and the new rulers, once in control of the central administrative apparatus and thus the source of all favors and punishments, had no difficulty in finding new personnel. They had at their disposal the great mass of Jews, who, because of the great restrictions under which they had had to live in Old Russia, were with few exceptions imbued with the revolutionary spirit. Among the political emigrants there had always been many Jews, and without doubt the majority of the Bolshevik leadership at first consisted of Jews. Many went so far as to say that the whole Bolshevik movement was the creation of the Jews, who always wanted to dominate the world. There was even the myth that there existed a secret organization of Jewish wise men, who periodically met to decide how to influence the policy of the world in order to bring about Jewish domination.

To be sure, the world's Jewry had enormous power because of its unity and immense capital, but to think that everything in the world is done in accordance with the decisions of some mysterious old Jewish sages is utterly fantastic. Tempting as it might be to shift all responsibility for what has happened in Russia onto the Jews, neither Lenin nor Stalin was a Jew and to suppose that we Russians were so weakminded that a few Jews could have led us would be humiliating. It would be more correct to say simply that Lenin accepted anybody ready to work for him, be he Jew, Christian, Georgian, or Rumanian. At first the great majority who worked with him were Jews, but with time their number diminished. If the Jews had expected to fare well under Bolshevism, they were greatly disappointed. Lenin, as well as Stalin, took from the Jews what the Jews had to give to promote their ideas. Jews who did not conform were liquidated like anyone else. Bolshevism did not permit independent thinking.

✠✠✠

Toward the end of November we received the first communication from the new government in the form of a telegram signed by Commissar for Foreign Affairs Trotskii. Demanding that we reply at once whether we were willing to serve the new government, and stating that those who were not must at once leave their posts, passing them on to those next in rank, the wire warned that refusal to obey the order and continuation of the old policy would be considered a serious crime against the state and punished accordingly. The Ambassador called together the Embassy staff, read the telegram, and asked for everybody's reaction. He added that those who agreed to obey the order of Trotskii must leave the Embassy forthwith, since the Bolshevik government was not recognized in Japan and the Embassy therefore, could not house Soviet functionaries. The same question was directed to all Consular officials. Everyone refused to serve the new government. The attitude of all the Russian Embassies, Legations, and Consulates throughout the whole world was the same. With the single exception of a baron who was so delighted that the Soviet government had decided to start peace negotiations with Germany that he sent an enthusiastic affirmation reply in answer to the telegram of the Soviet Commissar, all Russian diplomats ignored Trotskii's peremptory demand and remained on their posts. The Soviet government did not renew its pretentions on our loyalty and henceforth the old Russian Embassy in Japan cut all ties with St. Petersburg. When our Ambassador showed Trotskii's telegram to the Japanese Foreign Office, he was told that the Japanese government did not recognize the Soviet government and continued to regard him as the Russian Ambassador, no Soviet agent to be admitted to Japan. Inasmuch as Bolshevism was completely alien to the principles on which the Japanese Empire had been founded, any compromise between the two states seemed quite impossible and, for the time being, the Embassy could consider itself quite safe from any Soviet efforts to undermine its status.

In this respect we were in a much better position than our fellow representatives in Europe, where the Bolsheviks from the very beginning had begun their intrigues to prevent a complete break with England and France. Their policy was clever, and though the powers at first had tried to help the White movement, which fought against the Bolsheviks in the south and north of Russia, they gave more thought to the danger of an alliance between the Bolsheviks and the Germans than to the future of Russia, their efforts remaining half-hearted, and when Germany was crushed, they recalled their forces and their promises remained unfulfilled. Many statesman, the very powerful British Prime Minister [David] Lloyd George, for example, gave thought to keeping Russia weak and trading with the Bolsheviks.

More and more ignored, our representatives in Europe tried to persuade our former allies of the necessity of admitting some representatives of Old Russia to the Paris Peace Conference; instead, they were told to meet with Bolshevik representatives on Princess Island near Constantinople to effect a reconciliation, a fantastic proposal turned down by both sides. It became increasingly clear that European interest in Russia, once she failed to meet her obligations toward the allies, waned and was replaced by plans for the disposition of the huge inheritance the dying colossus was expected to leave. Russia was not admitted to the Peace Conference and no one sought her opinion about the postwar settlement of European affairs.

The Big Three at the Peace Conference had different ideas as to what was to be done with Russia. President Wilson with his ideals believed in self-determination. He did not take into consideration that it was not always high ideals that play the leading role in self-determination; furthermore, as an American he thought that what was good for Americans must be good for all peoples. Lloyd George, who in his own country struggled against all hereditary rights, had the greatest contempt for such rights in other countries too. Thus his sympathies must have been with the Bolsheviks; furthermore, being an Englishman, he saw that the chief source of a nation's might lay in trade. Believing that one can trade even with cannibals, he planned to enter into commercial relations with the new rulers of Russia. As for [Georges] Clemenceau, he exerted all his energy to oppose the adoption of Wilson's principle of self-determination where it affected French interests. Though she had saved France at the beginning of the war, Russia had played out her part and no longer interested France.

Nobody thought of the future; nobody listened to those who pointed to the special nature of Bolshevism, which was working, as Lenin himself was openly proclaiming, for the destruction of capitalism and for world revolution. Victory breeds conceit, and conceit breeds blindness.

Thus Russia, after hopelessly knocking at the doors of the nations, tried to organize her own defense against the Bolsheviks. The south of Russia became the center of operations against the "Reds." In Kiev, Hetman [Pavel Petrovich] Skoropadskii with the help of German troops prevented the Bolsheviks from spreading their power further south, while remnants of the old Russian army, unable to reconcile themselves to the Bolshevik regime, were gathering in the Cossack region. At the head of these forces stood General [Anton Ivanovich] Denikin, with General Kornilov at his side. As long as the War lasted, these forces received a certain amount of support from England and France.

The great weakness of the movement lay in the fact that notwithstanding all the disasters of the past, it continued to be torn asunder by different parties and personalities, that the White forces had to act in hostile surroundings, because the peasants did not realize the harm which Bolshevism would bring them and did not trust the

[265]

White forces, and above all that the commanders of the old Russian army units in St. Petersburg deemed it more important to preserve the army than to fight Lenin, whose ability to maintain himself for long they doubted.

Appointed Commissar of War, Trotskii was able to use these forces to counteract the drive from the south, so that the Civil War saw two parts of the old Russian army—the Whites and the Reds—decimating each other. At first the Whites were very successful. As they approached Moscow and St. Petersburg, the end of Bolshevism seemed near, but somehow at the most critical moment the Bolsheviks were always saved by some unexpected turn of events. The White forces in their quick advance outran their supply lines and the ammunition promised by England did not come. Whether this was accidental or whether the restoration of Old Russia did not enter into the plans of Lloyd George, the White forces had to retreat. After a last heroic stand in the Crimea, under the command of Baron [Petr Nikolaevich] Wrangel, the White cause vanished in smoke. The remnants of the White army were evacuated to Constantinople and gradually dispersed throughout the whole world. Thus began the Golgotha of the Russian refugees, which continues yet except for those fortunate enough to have made their way to the United States.

Short and unsatisfactory as the above description of the struggle against the Bolsheviks in the West may be, it is necessary to understand the similar struggle in the Far East. The role which the Russian Embassy in Tokyo played permits me to describe it with some authority.

Once it was settled that our Embassy would continue functioning, we resumed the usual diplomatic life with its dinner parties, bridge, and golf. Senseless as these activities seemed under the circumstances, we had no choice. We were regarded as diplomats and as such had to conform with diplomatic customs.

As mentioned before, Viscount Motono was Foreign Minister. He had been Japanese Ambassador in St. Petersburg for more than ten years; he and his wife had been extremely popular, and were sincerely attached to Russia. The Revolution held no mysteries for him, and he had few illusions as to what it would bring to Russia. Motono remained sympathetic toward Old Russia. He assured our Ambassador that instructions had been given to the Japanese Ambassador in

St. Petersburg to avoid all steps which could be interpreted as recognition of the Bolshevik regime. He said there could be no question of recognition; the Japanese government did not consider the group of traitors who had temporarily seized power in St. Petersburg as representing all of Russia and did not hold the Russian people as a whole responsible for the action of the band of Bolsheviks. The old Russian Embassy continued to function as a true Embassy, spoke in the name of Russia, and was treated accordingly by the Japanese. Much has changed since then, but I consider it my duty to underline the loyal attitude which the Japanese government displayed toward Old Russia as long as there was hope that its power might be restored.

Our Ambassador in Paris communicated to us that the allies had informed their representatives in St. Petersburg that they would democratize their war aims when Russia had a government recognized by the whole country. This was typical of the attitude of the allies toward the Bolsheviks. They refuse to recognize their government, yet at the same time with vague promises tried to make them co-operate with the allies in the continuation of the war against Germany. Their thinly veiled attempts to woo the Bolsheviks, whom they regarded as no better than bandits, greatly strengthened the latter, indeed, furnished Lenin with a trump card that he skillfully used in his game with the allies at the time when the Bolsheviks were so weak that firm allied opposition could easily have led to their downfall.

Our representatives in Europe reported that there were signs that the struggle against the Bolsheviks would intensify and that there was speculation concerning Japan's attitude in such a struggle. Some foreign papers even stated that the Japanese were sending forces to Vladivostok. Krupenskii telegraphed our Embassy in Paris that there was absolutely no foundation to such rumors, that nobody in Japan thought of an active intervention, and that to provoke Japan to such a step would be dangerous. It would be of no practical value in weakening the Bolsheviks, and could only create the ambition in Japanese military circles to further Japanese aims at the expense of Russia. After discussing the matter with Motono, Krupenskii could telegraph our representatives in Paris, Washington, and London, that the dispatch of troops to Vladivostok had not even been discussed by the Japanese government. Steps of this sort, Motono had said, could be taken only if Japanese interests were violated: if, for instance

Japanese subjects were attacked, which did not seem likely. Bolshevik seizure of Vladivostok or the Siberian railway would not precipitate Japanese intervention unless the allies considered such an intervention desirable. Adding that Japan did not wish to turn the Russian people against herself, Motono had agreed with Krupenskii that if the occupation of Vladivostok became necessary, it must be preceded by the solemn pledge that the occupation would be only temporary, would not be tantamount to the seizure of Russian territory, and would be undertaken in order to help the local Russian authorities.

Notwithstanding the correct attitude of Viscount Motono we fully realized that the collapse of Russia in the Far East was in the interest of Japan, whose secret hope it was that the allies, preoccupied with the War in Europe, would not be able to send troops to the Far East and would invest Japan with the mandate to keep order in that part of the world.

The military clique deemed it its duty to use every opportunity to increase Japan's might. Because of Japan's isolation during the Tokugawa period,[1] the military had arrived on the world scene too late to participate in the distribution of colonies in the Far East; by the time they had started their active policy almost everything had been parceled out, and their eyes had fallen on the enormous territories of China and Russia.

We at the Embassy had little doubt that the chaos in Russia would prompt the Japanese militarists to take the next step in their march toward a greater Japan, however much the Minister of War, General Tanaka [Giichi], who at the beginning of his career had been attached to one of the Russian guard regiments and spoke Russian, assured our Ambassador of his friendship. As he put it, he had drunk so much vodka with Russian officers during his service in Russia that nothing could destroy the ties. But none of this prevented Tanaka from leaving a testament in which he posthumously tried to persuade his countrymen of the necessity of pursuing a most aggressive policy.[2] Considering the general state of affairs, however, one cannot accuse Japan of perfidy in choosing this moment to satisfy the aspirations of her military

[1] The Tokugawa period lasted from about 1600 to 1868; Japan's seclusion from 1639 to 1854.

[2] The so-called Tanaka Memorial may have been spurious, but the continental ambitions set down in it were held to varying degrees by Tanaka and the military.

leaders. After all, the Russian Revolution gave rise to ambitious plans elsewhere, and it is a great question what steps the European powers would have taken in the dismemberment of the Russian Empire, had they not been absorbed in war. It is a strange historical paradox that the War which was the chief cause of the appearance of the Bolsheviks in Russia saved Russia from dismemberment.

As an Embassy without a government, our Embassy in Tokyo was in no position to forestall these disastrous consequences. All it could do was to try, if a foreign intervention became inevitable, to prevent Japan from being left in sole charge of such an intervention. From the point of view of blocking Bolshevik penetration in the Far East, an international expeditionary force may not have been as effective as the army of one strong power like Japan, but unilateral action by one country posed a greater danger of territorial annexation than if several powers, with their mutual suspicious, were on the spot. Thus whenever there was a rumor of Japanese plans to send troops to Vladivostok, Krupenskii informed our representatives in Paris and Washington thereof, pointing to the importance of not letting Japan carry out such an enterprise alone.

Meanwhile Bolshevism spread in Siberia. At Khabarovsk a meeting of local soldier and worker representatives adopted decisions of a Bolshevik character. As a countermove the representative of the former provisional government handed over his authority to a gathering of moderate elements. Rumors reached us from Vladivostok that local extremists, acting jointly with the Bolsheviks, had taken the commercial port, the telegraph, post offices, and the banks; and Motono informed our Embassy that the Japanese government had decided to send a cruiser there. Word was received from Paris that the English government was sending a warship from Hong Kong, and shortly the American government followed suit by dispatching the cruiser *Brooklyn*. Thus a regular intervention was in the making and we were not alone in our struggle against Bolshevik penetration of the Far East.

At the same time we learned from Paris that the dismemberment of the old Russian Empire had begun, the French government recognizing the independence of Finland. Separatist movements swept through Russia from the Caucasus to Siberia, until every small province wanted to declare its independence. I think this separatist tendency was due to the fact that various groups of leaders were known only in a limited area and in order to retain their power had to make the territory in which they expected to play a prominent role as small as possible. During every revolution the interim period between the fall of the old government and the establishment of the new provides ample opportunity for ambitious men who put personal interests above patriotism. In Siberia a score of organizations whose leaders would not admit that anybody but they could save Russia from the Bolsheviks passed before our eyes. Whenever a stronger and possibly more effective organization appeared on the scene, the self-styled saviors who headed the weaker groups would not, as a rule, submit and join forces against their common foe; instead, they squandered their energy intriguing against the other groups until the Bolsheviks came and crushed them all.

Bolshevik successes undermined the influence of anti-Bolshevik Russians, who sought to advise the different European governments on dealing with Russia. Thrown back upon their own counsels, the foreign powers did not exclude contact with the new rulers. In Tokyo we received countless telegrams, in which our representatives informed us of various steps they had suggested to the respective governments for coping with the Bolsheviks, but we never heard the outcomes of their proposals. Years later, many of their suggestions proved to have been quite sound, but by then it was too late.

In Tokyo our position was much stronger and less humiliating. Japan as yet had no wish to have anything to do with the Bolsheviks. The genial General Tanaka did not openly oppose Viscount Motono, who with his knowledge of Russia was always on our side, and every time some Russian organization in Harbin or Vladivostok made any suggestion to the Japanese authorities we were the first to know about it. But rumors that the sending of troops to Siberia was being discussed in Europe and America began to alarm Motono, and he hinted to Krupenskii that Japan opposed such an expedition and, if necessary, would act independently. Knowing that Japan could not protest if her European allies decided to intervene, Krupenskii nevertheless reported the conversation to Paris, warning against allowing Japan to act alone in Siberia. Gradually the question of sending troops to Siberia gave rise to a "polite disagreement" between Japan and the United States, the Japanese Prime Minister [Terauchi Masatake] declaring at the opening of Parliament, that the situation in Siberia might force Japan to send troops there, the American Ambassador [Roland S.] Morris countering in a verbal statement that active steps in Siberia were not desirable.

❖❖❖

Meanwhile we learned from our Minister in Peking that in Manchuria, in the railway zone near the Russian frontier, a young Cossack officer by the name of [Grigorii] Semenov had started to muster Cossacks and Buryats to fight the approaching Bolsheviks. His movement was popular with the local inhabitants, and the foreign military attachés grew interested in it, and after visiting Semenov advised their governments to supply him with money and ammunition. Our Minister added that it also would be useful to interest the Japanese in this enterprise. Krupenskii duly conferred with Motono and as a result the Japanese general staff sent an officer to the headquarters of Semenov.

In such a way Ataman Semenov appeared on the scene. He began in an atmosphere of general sympathy and support, but as often happens with young and ignorant officers, his early success and general support went to his head, he imagined himself a great leader and even began to imitate Napoleon. As heroes of this sort cannot do without romance, a Gypsy woman assumed the role of Josephine. A number of shady characters attached themselves to Semenov and persuaded him, in order to acquire the means necessary for his enterprise, illegally to confiscate railway cargo under the pretext that its owners were Jews and Bolshevik sympathizers. Thus the movement, which had once promised success and could have been the beginning of a true struggle against Bolshevism, gradually degenerated.

At first the Embassy tried to help Semenov, because he undoubtedly had something that attracted people to him and rendered him popular with the Cossacks, Mongols, and different adventurers who constituted the bulk of his army. Many former Russian officers joined him, among them the famous "Mad Baron" [Ungern-Sternberg] who displayed such cruelty in exterminating everybody whom he regarded as Bolshevik that he was feared throughout Manchuria and Inner Mongolia and ultimately was killed by his own men. But from the beginning the Embassy refused to become involved in Semenov's

[271]

financial transactions and he dealt directly with the Japanese through special representatives in Tokyo. These representatives were usually naïve and ignorant Cossack officers who had never seen anything outside the provincial towns of Siberia. For them Tokyo was like Paris; they stayed in the best hotel and spent a lot of money. They treated the Embassy with great respect, however.

After the collapse of his enterprise Semenov decided to go to the United States. When he arrived in New York he was met at the station by a crowd of people who tried to pin bits of paper on his coat. Thinking that they were his admirers presenting him with laudatory addresses, Semenov was about to make a suitable speech when he discovered that the persons were creditors and were summoning him to court for the confiscation of their goods in Manchuria. He was jailed, but after some time was released and allowed to go back to the Far East, where he tried to play a prominent part among the Russian refugees in Manchuria. As before, the Japanese supported him and expected to make use of him in their projected expedition into Russian territory. Though nothing came of this, the Japanese, who remained faithful to people who worked for them, continued to support him until the last. He stayed near Dairen and till the end was full of different projects. Many Russian refugees believed in him and I heard in Tokyo that when everything was lost, Semenov was still organizing a Russian government-to-be and distributing ministerial posts. When Soviet troops occupied Manchuria and entered Dairen, Semenov did not escape in time. In vain he tried to persuade the Bolsheviks that he had always sympathized with them. He was arrested, taken to Moscow with a group of former White leaders, and after the usual confession of errors liquidated.

I saw Semenov only once. He did not impress me as a heroic figure. He was fat and did not sound very clever. Vanity and love of food, wine, and women prevented him from making a substantial contribution to the White cause. He was not without his good points; at a time when millions passed through his hands and many of his lieutenants retired with considerable sums, he himself had nothing but debts at the end of his career. But what can never be forgiven him is that when such a noble leader as Admiral [Aleksandr Vasil'evich] Kolchak assumed command of the White movement and gave it at last a serious character, Semenov did not recognize the leadership of a better man and join forces with him, but actively opposed him and to a large measure contributed to his downfall.

❖·❖·❖

The anarchy in Siberia was growing. In every small town there appeared some sort of organization which pretended to be the real government of Siberia, willing to continue the war with Germany and prevent Bolshevik penetration in Siberia. Usually such an organization would begin by sending a telegram, signed by completely unknown names, to the Embassy in Tokyo, asking that it insist on recognition of the organization by the Japanese government. Such a telegram was normally followed by one from another organization, warning us not to trust the former organization, half of whose members were Bolsheviks. Although theoretically ready to collaborate with any organization willing to fight the Bolsheviks, the Embassy could not discern in this chaos which organization deserved its support and could do nothing but wait for the appearance of a really serious organization, capable of doing something.

Our attention was concentrated on Harbin, the main city of the Chinese Eastern Railway zone, which was not yet contaminated by Bolshevik propaganda and was becoming more and more a refuge of White elements escaping from Russia. Though these spent most of their time quarreling, it seemed likely that they could be welded into something more serious than those accidental organizations of unknown elements, half conservative, half Bolshevik, which appeared in Siberia from day to day and clamored for support. At the head of the Chinese Eastern Railway there was still the old General [Dmitrii Leonidovich] Horvat, who was very well known in the Far East and kept his position by trying to reconcile the various factions which tried to play a political role in Harbin.

The Embassy did its best to support General Horvat and referred requests which continued to come from different organizations to the General. But unification of the movement under Horvat remained wishful thinking. Every general in Harbin seemed to have his own organization, and did not want to submit to Horvat or to anybody else. All the generals did was talk, so that Ataman Semenov seemed to be the only man who did any fighting against the Bolsheviks, but supported by the Japanese, he increasingly became their agent and ignored developments in Harbin.

Meanwhile a group of people who called themselves the representatives of the Siberian government, organized in Tomsk, arrived in Harbin. At the head of this group was a Jew by the name of Petr Derber, who called himself Prime Minister of the Siberian government. The group seemed to consist of radical elements, and General Horvat refused to have anything to do with them. They telegraphed the Embassy, demanding that all Japanese support for the anti-Bolshevik movement be given to them. We referred them to General Horvat and had no more to do with this Siberian government. Then another group of representatives of a Siberian government appeared, and charged that the earlier representatives had been impostors. This group seemed to be more serious, and I shall speak about our relations with it later. But the most important event during this period was the arrival in the Far East of Admiral Kolchak, the future supreme ruler and head of the Omsk government, which together with the White movement of General Denikin in European Russia, presented the most serious attempt to smash the power of the Bolsheviks.

Admiral Kolchak was well-known in Russia. During the World War he had been Commander-in-Chief of the Black Sea Fleet and had battled German and Turkish forces with remarkable success. Upon the outbreak of the Revolution he had to contend with disorders among his own sailors. For a long time he maintained his popularity among his men, but as the provisional government was absolutely incapable of supporting the heads of the army and navy in their struggle with Bolshevik propaganda, Kolchak's hold weakened and he was in danger of being killed by his own sailors. To save the Admiral the provisional government recalled him to St. Petersburg and then dispatched him to the United States in connection with some military orders placed there.

When Admiral Kolchak heard about the inception of an anti-Bolshevik movement in Siberia, he at once proceeded to the Far East and offered his services to our Peking Legation. Kolchak was sent to Harbin to assist General Horvat in organizing the military units that were to take the field against the Reds in Siberia.

Our Minister in Peking [Prince Nikolai Aleksandrovich Kuda-

shev] sent the First Secretary of the Legation to Tokyo to inform
us of the plans, worked out in Peking, and to obtain assurance of
Japanese support. From the Secretary we learned quite by chance
that General Nakajima [Masatake], the Harbin representative of
the Japanese Minister of War, had promised General Horvat
ammunition and money, a promise which had greatly strengthened Horvat's position. When our Ambassador, who had not heard
of such a pledge, asked Viscount Motono how much truth there
was in the report, Motono replied that Nakajima had no authority to make such promises and that Japan could not give such aid
without previous agreement with the allies. Here was our first indi-
cation of Japanese double-dealing with regard to Russian efforts to
organize a Russian movement against the Bolsheviks.

As far as the Embassy could determine, actual Japanese support
of the Russian anti-Bolshevik forces was confined to the modest
help given Ataman Semenov. This help only demoralized Semenov,
who began to act in such a way that it was difficult to distinguish
whether he was playing the part of a popular leader against the Reds
or of a highway robber.

It was such an atmosphere of intrigue and mistrust that faced
Kolchak, a man of unblemished honesty, devoted to saving his country
from utter ruin. Arriving in Harbin, he summoned the various
military leaders who were supposed to be subordinate to him. Ataman
Semenov, whose detachment was the only one capable of combatting
the Reds, refused to come or to recognize Kolchak's authority. Wishing to unite rather than to divide further, Kolchak went to Semenov's
headquarters to discuss the matter, but Semenov refused to see him.
General Nakajima, who was usually under the influence of alcohol,
openly supported Semenov, and once when Kolchak was inspecting
the military forces of Harbin, he made fun of Kolchak. This provoked
a quarrel between the two, and Kolchak telegraphed us that as long
as Nakajima was in Harbin, he could not fulfill his mission. The
Embassy did all it could to smooth out the matter. All our sympathies
were with Kolchak, but we realized that we were not in a position to
do anything without the support of Japan. We could not demand
the recall of General Nakajima, and had to rest satisfied with the
promise that he would receive special instructions. In the end Nakajima was recalled, but not before he had created for Kolchak the

reputation of a Japanophobe, the story being spread that Kolchak had publicly asserted in Peking that one cannot trust the Japanese. Kolchak denied this, and said that he understood very well that Japan was the only country in the Far East which could help the White cause.

The question was whether Japan really wanted to help us. I doubt it very much. If the Foreign Office assured us of Japan's willingness to help us, it was not to recreate the Old Russia but to organize an autonomous Far Eastern buffer state, weak enough to be dependent on Japan. It was clear that Japanese aid would not extend farther than the maritime region, that Japanese troops would not push beyond Lake Baikal.

Japan never really supported Admiral Kolchak because it realized that his activity in the Far East was only a stepping-stone for the liberation of all Russia; it preferred to work with Ataman Semenov, who belonged to the Far East and would rather play an important role in a buffer state than a minor one in a restored Russia. Kolchak understood this well, but I do not think that he would have given vent to his mistrust of Japan when there was no one else on whom he could lean. It was in the interest of the Japanese to compromise Admiral Kolchak, and General Nakajima, who during his stay as Military Attaché in St. Petersburg had acquired a good knowledge of the Russian character, was the right man for the job. It was the usual story of how a sly, unscrupulous person can undermine and even render harmful the most unselfish noble work. This is what happened to Kolchak in Harbin. He came to bring unity and real patriotism to the White movement, which lacked both; instead, disunity and selfishness increased, partly due to the work of Japanese agents. General Horvat, who was supposed to be at the head of the Harbin organization, was willing to help Admiral Kolchak, but he tried to reconcile the irreconcilable with the usual result that he not only did not render any real assistance to Kolchak, but lost the little authority he had. Horvat finally hinted to the Embassy that it might be useful to invite Kolchak to Tokyo to report on the situation in Harbin and become acquainted with the leaders of the Japanese police.

We took the hint, and invited Kolchak. His whole personality was impressive, but one could see immediately that he was a sick man, in the state of highest nervous tension. I shall never forget his small, trim, typical naval figure, pacing on the lawn before our chancery, smoking endless cigarettes and talking about his plans, about the impossible situation in Harbin, and about the incomprehensible behavior of the Japanese. His indignation was well founded, but there was nothing the Embassy could do. No one could deny the many shortcomings of the White movement, especially in the Far East—its lack of heroic figures, its provincial atmosphere, its selfishness, its envy and intrigues—shortcomings on which the Japanese played as an artist plays his instrument, but such was reality and no authority could countermand it. The Bolsheviks meanwhile were in a different position: from the outset they took hold of the central administrative apparatus. Thus they had an enormous advantage over the Whites, who had to start from scratch, without proper leaders and resources, in an atmosphere of distrust and disunity, working with purely theoretical parties that pulled in different directions. Only a man with a strong and imperturbable character and the cleverness and slyness of a serpent could have dealt with such a situation. With nobility of thought and character at a discount, one's own nobility became a drawback, I thought, as I listened to Kolchak.

The Admiral lived too much in the past, when the might of the whole Empire had stood behind him; he could not reconcile himself to the fact that Harbin harbored only the intrigues and selfish aims of second-rate personalities. In his report to the Ambassador he drew a picture of general disorganization; he spoke of the utter unwillingness of the various detachments to obey orders and of Japanese and Russian intrigues in the railway zone. "Not having any personal aims except the desire to work among those who put the interests and welfare of the fatherland first," he concluded, "I accepted the post of commander of the Russian forces in the Chinese Eastern Railway zone, fully aware that to succeed I would have to work hand in hand with the chivalrous Japanese. I sincerely desired such collaboration, never expecting that the Japanese military mission in Harbin would respond with such humiliating and hopeless conditions." Though Kolchak tried to explain the Japanese attitude in terms of Nakajima's personal hostility toward him, Kolchak's own personality probably was responsible to a large degree, for the Japanese do not appreciate open-heartedness and nobility of character. Lacking these features, they do not like to see them in others; they suspect that they are merely a mask for more sinister

[277]

feelings. Even if the Japanese had been sincere in their desire to help the White Russians, which they were not, they would have wanted their help to be accepted with gratitude and flattery, but Admiral Kolchak was the last person to flatter anybody.

Krupenskii did everything to ameliorate the relations between Kolchak and the Japanese military. But though he took Kolchak to see Minister of War General Tanaka and the latter made his usual declarations of love for the old Russian army and gave the usual dinner with geishas and sake, the meeting did not rise above generalities. Our Naval Attaché tried hard to give the Admiral a good rest and make him forget about Harbin, but Kolchak would not be calmed. Ever excited, he constantly returned to the futile subject of organizing something in Harbin. He was an active man and could not sit around with folded arms waiting for better times. As the war with Germany was still in progress, he asked the British government through its Ambassador to be attached to some British regiment on active duty. Informed eventually that he could proceed to Syria and there join the British forces as a common soldier, Kolchak accepted the offer without hesitation, and soon left Japan.

❖❖❖

Meanwhile the chaos in Harbin continued. Semenov, after initial successes in the border region, began to retreat, all the while confiscating goods and admitting of no authority or law other than his own. Various organizations in Harbin pleaded for Japanese help. In Vladivostok authority passed into the hands of the local *zemstvo*, the majority of which did not distinguish themselves from Bolsheviks, and only the presence of local troops and foreign cruisers forestalled the excesses with which the Bolsheviks usually began to rule in the localities under their occupation.

About this time there appeared the first detachment of Czechoslovaks, who were destined to play a part in the struggle against the Reds in Siberia. Inducted into the Austrian army during the War, these Czechoslovaks had shown no desire to fight against the Russians and had surrendered by the thousands. They were interned in the prisoner camps, but because of their friendliness were allowed a certain freedom. At the time of the provisional government they were suffered to form special detachments under the leadership of Russian officers.

There appeared special Czechoslovak organizations, connected with similar organizations in Europe, which under the leadership of [Thomas Garrigue] Masaryk were working for the independence of Czechoslovakia. When the Bolsheviks came to power, they eyed these organizations with suspicion and as the civil war began, ordered the disarmament of the Czechoslovak detachments. The Czechoslovaks refused to surrender their arms and decided to fight their way to Siberia, to Vladivostok, with the hope of sailing from there to their country.[3]

The Bolsheviks were not yet strong enough to cope with the Czechoslovaks, and the latter easily reached Siberia. On the way they were joined by White Russian detachments and by the time they reached the Volga River the group already formed a serious anti-Bolshevik force. But they were little interested in the Russian struggle against Bolshevism; their chief aim was to return to their own country. Nevertheless they indirectly helped different Russian organizations to start an anti-Bolshevik movement in the Volga region. Unlike the Czechoslovak soldiers, the Russians remained disorganized. Unable to agree, would-be leaders telegraphed our Embassy in Tokyo, so that in addition to the wires from different organizations in Siberia we began to receive messages from Samara, Ufa, and other points from various organizations, each claiming to be the real thing.

As the Czechoslovaks pushed through Siberia, their vanguard reaching Vladivostok, success turned their heads, and they began to behave like conquerors in an enemy country, looting and carrying with them objects which had nothing to do with a military expedition—furniture, pictures, even pianos. They occupied trains whenever they needed them and thought nothing of leaving behind Russian refugees, who were trying to escape from the advancing Bolsheviks. Their conduct not only compromised the Czechoslovak cause but contributed to the victory of Bolshevism: suffering a great deal at the hands of different foreigners who rode high during the intervention, the ignorant masses developed a preference for life under native tyrants to the tyranny of aliens.

Except for occasional telegrams we knew little about events in Siberia. Some of the Czechoslovak leaders made their way to Tokyo and

[3] Actually, the Czechoslovaks wished to join the allied Western Front to continue the war against Germany.

called on the Ambassador. They realized the difficulty of transporting nearly eighty thousand Czechoslovaks from Vladivostok to Europe, but though they expressed the opinion that it would be better to leave them for a while in Siberia to assist in the defense of the region against the Bolsheviks, they admitted that the majority were determined to return home and that it would be difficult to restrain them. We learned that the Czechoslovaks were under the protection of France and that a French general [Maurice Janine] was to come to Siberia and assume supreme command over all the Czechoslovaks.

As the Bolsheviks made a humiliating separate peace with Germany,[4] the allies began to take a greater interest in the various White Russian organizations in Siberia as well. The problems in Europe during and after the War were many, however, and efforts to help the White Russians remained half-hearted and only brought disillusionment to these Russians, who perhaps expected more than they had a right to expect. The empty assertion that the war with Germany had been fought "to make the world safe for democracy" played into the hands of the Bolsheviks, whose propaganda pictured them as nearer to democratic ideals than the Whites, many of whom dreamed of the restoration of the monarchy. The Bolsheviks so hypnotized the world's democratic elements that years passed before the true nature of Bolshevism became clear to the majority of reasonable people. By then it was too late to crush Bolshevism.

This ideological chaos pervaded even the Siberian organizations, which grew like mushrooms after a spring rain. Such ideological differences could not be reconciled. Consequently there were two Siberian governments in Vladivostok. One consisted of well-meaning but vague and powerless democratic elements; it left local administration in the hands of the Bolshevik-dominated *zemstvo* and real power in the hands of the Czechoslovaks. The other was the government of General Horvat, who with the support of conservative elements in Harbin had proclaimed himself a dictator and had also moved to Vladivostok. Not allowed to enter the city, Horvat remained on his train, which stood not far from that of the other Siberian government, both so-called governments ignoring each other.

The appearance of the Czechoslovaks in Vladivostok brought the question of foreign intervention to a head. When England, France,

[4] The Treaty of Brest-Litovsk, March 3, 1918.

and the United States decided to send troops to Vladivostok under the pretext of helping the Czechoslovaks, the Japanese at once sent a large contingent of their own troops. While most of the foreign troops remained in Vladivostok, the Japanese pushed into the interior and quickly occupied the greater part of the maritime region. Here they found the forces of Ataman Semenov, with whom they were closely affiliated. With Japanese help Semenov occupied Chita. Making it his headquarters, he controlled railway transportation between the interior of Siberia and Vladivostok.

The Japanese made little distinction between the Bolsheviks and the local population. When they occupied a village, they claimed provisions from the peasants and treated them roughly. As a result the local populace began to hate the Japanese more than they did the Bolsheviks. The suffering of the common people seemed without end —first war, then revolution and the exactions of Reds, Whites, and foreigners.

❖❖❖

The Russian Embassy in Tokyo, willing as it was to help every White movement that was really supported by the population, could not distinguish from afar between the different organizations asking for its support. When a telegram was received from yet another organization, the Directory of Five, formed in Ufa and claiming to represent a fusion of anti-Bolshevik organizations in the Volga region and Siberia, the Ambassador decided to send someone to Vladivostok to find out which of the innumerable White organizations represented the most promising and really serious anti-Bolshevik effort. The thankless mission fell on me.

I proceeded to Tsuruga, and from there by steamer to Vladivostok. The boat was full of refugees from abroad who were returning to Russia in the hope of rising high by working with the Bolsheviks. Most of them were Jews. One of them, a huge Jew, already considered himself a great leader and made arrogant speeches about his future activity in Russia. In the evening as I was going to the bathroom in a Japanese kimono, he stopped me and scolded me for wearing what he called a disgraceful dress of the yellow race. Not wishing to start a quarrel, I answered with a laugh that, without pretending to be a democrat, I seemed to be more democratic in the matter of racial equality than he with all his grand talk about creating a new world.

When we arrived in Vladivostok a group of untidy and arrogant young people in school uniforms came aboard and summoned all passengers to the dining room. They were the representatives of the local *zemstvo*, and had come to check passports. My Embassy passport created a great commotion, and they began to whisper. The big Jew joined them, and probably reported that he had seen me wearing a kimono. It was my only experience with the half-Bolshevik elements, and I was afraid that they would drag me somewhere for further interrogation. Fortunately at that moment the former representative of our Foreign Office in the maritime region came to meet me. He seemed to have some authority with the *zemstvo* representatives and obtained permission for me to land.

My colleague, whom I knew from China, told me that the town was absolutely full since the arrival of the foreign missions and that with difficulty he had found a room for me in the house of a local lawyer. A bed had been set up for me in the lawyer's study, and when we arrived, the lawyer's wife told me at once that they were having a party to celebrate the name day of their daughter, and invited me to join the festivities. It seemed not right to me to start my mission to find the future government of Russia by joining a party of absolute strangers and I refused, saying that I was too tired after my journey. But I was not left alone, and soon the desk of the lawyer was covered with dishes apparently prepared for the party, which, judging by the noise, must have been very gay. People shouted, laughed, and danced, hopping across the rooms in lively mazurkas. It was very different from the picture I had of life in Vladivostok. With great difficulty I fell asleep, only to have nightmares about the big Jew, who appeared even more ferocious than on the boat.

In the morning my colleague came to take me to the different "governments," which tried to rule Russia from their railway carriages. I first called on General Horvat, whom I knew from before, and whom I would understand more easily. After a long walk along the railroad tracks we came to a lonely train, far from the center of town. To my great astonishment the train was guarded by Chinese, dressed as Russian Cossacks. It seemed humorous to me that a dictator could not find enough real Cossacks and had to dress up Chinese as such.

The old General with his magnificent beard, known throughout

China, was in one of the carriages which he had used when he had headed the Chinese Eastern Railway. His charming and ambitious wife was with him. With his usual geniality he told me that as the arrival of the Czechoslovaks and the foreign military missions had made Vladivostok the center of the White movement, his supporters had persuaded him to move his organization here. He had planned, of course, to come with his troops, but the foreign missions did not allow military forces to enter Vladivostok, and so he sat with his ministers in the train and did not know what to do. His approach to the foreign missions, which, he had thought, would have been interested in organizing an anti-Bolshevik movement, was rebuffed; he was told that unless he and the Siberian government came to an agreement, both would be ignored by the foreign powers, because the latter would deal with only one Russian government and not with different organizations. But how, General Horvat exclaimed with great indignation, could he agree with the Siberian government, which consisted mostly of Socialists, who in his eyes did not differ much from Bolsheviks? He concluded sarcastically that it was easy to give advice from Tokyo, where Japanese ministers mouthed their sympathy, while Japanese agents on the spot did everything to hinder any serious effort to create a movement against the Bolsheviks, supporting only Ataman Semenov, whose actions merely compromised the White movement. The General spoke the truth. Nevertheless, as I pointed out, only the Bolsheviks stood to gain from the quarrels among ourselves, and there was really nothing left for him to do but to follow the advice of the foreign missions and conclude an agreement with the Siberian government, which did seem to be connected with the anti-Bolshevik movement that had started in Siberia. General Horvat asked me to convey to the Ambassador that he was quite ready to come to an agreement with the Siberian government; he did express doubt about the value of such an agreement. It was one thing to agree on paper, quite another thing to put the agreement into effect.

Before I left, Horvat introduced me to his cabinet which consisted mostly of old employees of the Chinese Eastern Railway. All of them wanted to know whether Japan would help them. I had to answer that Japan would help only herself, that I strongly doubted that she was interested in the restoration of a strong Russia, and that we could rely on no one but ourselves. As I left the train I had the impression that all those servants of the old regime were useful only so long as they had behind them the whole might of Old Russia; once they were faced with the necessity of creating something from nothing, they were lost and hoped that somebody would come to help them.

Next I visited the Siberian government. Again I had to jump over railroad ties. It began to snow when I reached the desolate little station near which the train of the Siberian government stood. I was asked to wait, since Prime Minister [P. V.] Vologodskii was busy, and walked up and down the empty platform. The snowfall increased. Suddenly a tall, strange figure with the hat rakishly placed on the curly head and the overcoat loosely hanging from the shoulders, looking like the monument of the poet [Aleksandr Sergeevich] Pushkin on Tver Square in Moscow, approached me. It turned out to be the Minister of Foreign Affairs of the Siberian government. He invited me to a dirty restaurant car, where we drank tea and engaged in a political conversation full of high-sounding words and phrases. He had just returned from Peking, where the Minister, Prince Kudashev, had feted him with a grand reception and they had come to a complete agreement regarding the policy to be followed by the Siberian government. Expounding the policy, all the time repeating that "he and the Prince had decided" this and that, he abandoned himself to a dream which had absolutely no relation to the real state of affairs. When he concluded with the hope that Japan would agree to play the part expected from her, i.e., the part of a chivalrous country ready to help her neighbor in distress, I could only reply, as I had to the ministers of General Horvat, that Japan would do solely what suited her own interests and that at the moment, inexperienced as yet in dealing with the Bolsheviks, her policy seemed to be the creation in the Far East of a Japanese-dominated buffer state. The Minister seemed displeased with my pessimism, but just then I was summoned to the head of the Siberian government, and escaped further useless discussion of a political situation which existed only in his imagination.

Mr. Vologodskii was a modest and sensible man, who recognized the uncertainty of his position. When I asked him what he thought of the latest events in Siberia and of the new organization which seemed to have been formed at Ufa, he confessed that since his arrival in Vladivostok he had not been in touch with events in Siberia. He was not in full agreement with the program of the new organization, but his advice was not to discourage the Ufa organization by ignoring it, but to await further developments before cooperating. He said that he did not see what he could do in Vladivostok where the foreign missions had taken matters into their own hands, ignoring, it seemed, any Russian effort of creating an anti-Bolshevik movement, and that he seriously thought of returning to Siberia. It was a relief not to hear the grand phrases behind which the so-called leaders of the anti-Bolshevik movement usually hid their lack of power and sound policy. Yet the conversation with Vologodskii left me greatly depressed, and I returned to town to see first the leaders of the Czechoslovaks, then the responsible persons in the foreign missions.

The Czechoslovaks made no pretense of amiability. As far as one could understand, their only desire was to return to their country and the difficulties that they encountered in doing so, especially the wishes of the allies to make them stay in Siberia to help the White Russians in their struggle against the Bolsheviks, only made them furious with the White Russians. As they had nothing to fear from the Bolsheviks, their attitude toward them was changing. The general praise which they received for their struggle for the freedom and independence of their country turned their heads, and they viewed the fight of the White Russians against the Bolsheviks as a struggle of reaction against freedom. It seemed to me absolutely hopeless to expect any real help from the Czechoslovaks.

The representatives of the foreign missions, whom I saw also, did not seem to understand the general situation. Confused by the Russian leaders, every one of whom praised his own cause and ran down that of his rivals, they declared that unless the different organizations came to an agreement among themselves, none of them could hope to get any support from the allies. At the same time they showed the greatest anxiety about the Japanese, who, pretending to be in Siberia for the same reason as the other allies, acted independently from them.

Exhausted and depressed, I returned to my room in the house of the lawyer, and passed the first part of the evening in writing and ciphering a telegram to the Ambassador in Tokyo. I could not find anything encouraging to tell him. I reported that in my opinion not a single organization with which I had talked had any real power or future, least of all the dictatorship of General Horvat, that no real support could be expected from the Czechoslovaks, and that the allies had no clear idea why they had come to Siberia. All we could do was hope that something really serious would come from the purely Russian movement in western Siberia, about which there were but the vaguest rumors. I could not say anything about the Japanese, as I was almost certain that they had broken our code. The rest of the evening I passed with my host and his family, drinking countless glasses of weak tea with lemon.

✣✣✣

The next day I decided to become acquainted with the city and its atmosphere. Vladivostok was beautiful: with its magnificent port and scenic view and curtain of hills it deserved the name "Rule the East." It was a fine, sunny day and the main street was filled with smartly dressed foreign officers and soldiers who attracted the attention of young and fresh-looking local beauties. As the latter walked in groups, visibly excited at the sight of so many young men in uniform, I felt somewhat ashamed that my compatriots, especially the women, could not show more restraint.

The restaurant where a colleague took me was packed with officers of different nationalities. Vodka, caviar, and other Russian delicacies filled the tables; nobody seemed to think about the tragedy of Russia. An old friend from Tokyo, the interpreter of the Italian Embassy, sent to follow events on the spot, rushed up to me with joyful praise of Vladivostok, complaining only that he had lived in Japan for nearly thirty years without realizing that such a paradise existed some thirty hours from Tokyo. I was astonished at his exaggeration, but my colleague explained that the Italian spent all his evenings in the local club, playing poker and winning thousands and thousands of rubles. No wonder he saw everything in such a rosy light.

After two days of such a life, I was longing to return to Japan. The sight of the foreigners, feasting on the misfortunes of my country, caused me to reflect sadly on the cynical selfishness of political friendships. After a second visit to the venerable General Horvat, who was thinking of returning to Harbin where every street urchin knew him and where he was considered a great political figure, I passed through another inspection of the suspicious local *zemstvo* representatives, and took the boat back to Japan.

❖❖❖

I was delighted to get back to the Embassy, where we continued to live among the recollections of old grandeurs, deluding ourselves that not everything was lost. I made my report to the Ambassador, who confessed that it did not astonish him; the gloomy Counsellor was delighted that all his predictions had proven correct. I tried to inject a note of optimism by holding out the possibility that something would come of the movement in the interior of Siberia. As a matter of fact, news which we began to receive from this new center of anti-Bolshevik activity did look somewhat promising. The so-called Dictatorship of Five, which had emerged from the agreement at Ufa, moved to Omsk in western Siberia and there tried to work jointly with the Siberian Duma, which had been created in Tomsk.

The Directory of Five had the great advantage of large resources. When the anti-Bolshevik forces, appearing in the Volga region in the wake of the triumphal march of the Czechoslovaks through Russia, had captured Kazan they found in the local branch of the Russian State Bank part of the gold reserve the Imperial government had sent there when the German advance had threatened St. Petersburg. Taken to Omsk, this money was now used by the Omsk government, as the Directory of Five came to be known. For the first time an anti-Bolshevik organization commanded considerable funds. Soon Omsk became the center of all anti-Bolshevik forces in Siberia.

At that time the local government consisted mostly of Socialist Revolutionaries, members of the party to which Kerenskii had belonged; they continued the policy of the provisional government, a policy which had resulted in the triumph of Bolshevism. But there lived in Omsk also a large number of old army officers who had escaped from the Bolsheviks and hunger to Siberia, which as yet was a country of plenty. To them Kerenskii and everything connected with him were anathema, as they held him chiefly responsible for the downfall of Russia. Lacking all discipline, these officers became the most turbulent element; they did not hide their discontent with the Omsk government and tried to conspire against it.

Under the circumstances it was decided to strengthen the government by including a well-known military figure, capable of controlling the military elements without whom no anti-Bolshevik army could be created. The only such man in the East was Admiral Kolchak. Though he was already in Singapore, on his way to Syria to join the British army, he was located through the efforts of the Legation in Peking and the Embassy in Tokyo, and invited to join the Omsk government as Minister of War. Assured that he would work far away from the rotten atmosphere of the extreme Far East, where the Japanese had undermined his earlier efforts, Kolchak accepted the offer and rushed back to Siberia.

With Kolchak's arrival in Omsk, events moved quickly. The military displayed their great enthusiasm for him by staging a coup d'état. Without consulting Kolchak, they arrested the most radical members of the Omsk government, and proclaimed the Admiral Supreme Ruler of the anti-Bolshevik movement in Siberia. This change in government transpired quickly and without bloodshed. Kolchak accepted the new position, and the arrested members of the government were supplied with funds to go abroad. Though this was done on condition that they would not agitate against Kolchak, no sooner were they out of Siberia than the deposed officials began to abuse Kolchak and tell how much better they could organize a movement against the Bolsheviks. Fortunately they did not stay in Japan long, but proceeded to Paris, where they joined the group of Socialist revolutionaries who never learned any lesson, still do not admit any of their faults, and in the person of Kerenskii, their most prominent member,[5] continue in an attempt to persuade the world that everybody else was responsible for the downfall of Old Russia. Yet Kerenskii at one time had such influence in Russia that the course of the Revolution practically depended on him. It was he who used his authority, albeit honorably and unconsciously, to pave the way for the Bolsheviks.

The first steps of Admiral Kolchak were very successful. He cleared eastern Siberia of Bolsheviks, occupied Ekaterinburg, and was preparing to join the forces of General Denikin, who was moving on Moscow. Both Denikin and General [Nikolai Nikolaevich] Iudenich, who was approaching St. Petersburg, recognized Admiral Kolchak as

[5] Now a resident of the United States.

supreme ruler of the entire White movement. Only Ataman Semenov, who was in Chita, between Omsk and Vladivostok, refused to recognize Kolchak, and even sent him an ultimatum when Kolchak was proclaimed supreme ruler. Nothing came of the ultimatum, but Semenov controlled the lines of communication with Vladivostok and prevented any goods from reaching Omsk. When Kolchak sent several million gold rubles to Tokyo to pay for ammunition ordered from Japanese factories at the time of the provisional government, Semenov simply confiscated the gold, and the ammunition urgently needed by Kolchak's armed forces never reached its destination.

It may be that left to himself, Semenov would not have dared to act in such a way, but the Japanese agents who surrounded him urged him to disobey Kolchak. Kolchak thought only of a united Russia, while Japan desired the creation of a buffer state under her influence. Kolchak worked for a strong Russia, but a strong Russia, capable of playing an important part in the Far East, was counter to the interests of the Japanese, who even then were dreaming of an exclusive sphere of interest in that area. To this must be added their old hostility to Kolchak, dating back to his activity in Manchuria.

Our Ambassador had several conversations both with the Foreign Minister and the Minister of War, in which he asked them to instruct their agents in Siberia not to support Semenov in his hostile attitude toward Kolchak. As always, the Japanese assured him that they were not interested in supporting Semenov, and the Minister of War even showed him the text of his telegrams to Japan's representatives in Chita, instructing them to advise Semenov to modify his attitude toward Kolchak. Apparently the Japanese had a way of telegraphing instructions in such a manner that the person to whom they were addressed understood them in quite the opposite sense of the text, because nothing was changed and poor Kolchak wasted half of his energy and temper in trying to settle his relations with Semenov. The leftist elements also hindered Kolchak; they regarded the saving of Russia as their own monopoly, and, I think, would have preferred the subjugation of Russia by the Bolsheviks to a rightist victory. The Czechoslovaks, who wanted to leave Siberia, supported Kolchak only half-heartedly and were ready to listen to the leftist criticism of Kolchak. No wonder that Kolchak was in a state of perpetual nervous

[289]

tension and lacked the necessary calm to deal with such conflicting elements.

❖❖❖

When the White forces took Ekaterinburg, the place where the Emperor and his whole family had been murdered, Kolchak set up a special commission to find out the details of the crime. The White forces had advanced too quickly for the Reds to destroy all traces of their crime, and the commission found enough material to recreate the whole ghastly scene. The Emperor, the Empress, the Tsarevich, and the four daughters had been exiled by the provisional government to Tobolsk. From there they had been moved to Ekaterinburg, to the house of a local merchant. The Bolsheviks, who continued their confinement, assigned a special commissar with a special guard to watch the Imperial family closely, afraid, it seemed, of a White conspiracy to free the Emperor. The Emperor himself showed an extraordinary lack of self-assertion since his abdication and arrest by the provisional government, and suffered the privations and humiliations with the meekness of a saint. Those who had to guard him usually began by treating him very rudely, but ended by admiring and pitying him. Even Kerenskii, who considered Nicholas II responsible for all the misfortunes which had befallen Russia, could not deny in his memoirs the nobility of his character when under arrest. Only such utterly inhuman creatures as the Bolsheviks could remain blind and indifferent to the suffering of the Imperial famliy.

When the forces of Kolchak were approaching Ekaterinburg the commissar received instructions to liquidate the Imperial family. Taking a few guards whom he could trust, the commissar in the evening went to the rooms where the Emperor and his family were confined and ordered them to descend into the cellar. There they were stood against the wall and heartlessly mowed down. As the Emperor, the Empress, the angelic-looking Tsarevich, and the four beautiful girls, who were just on the threshold of life, fell on the stone floor in pools of blood, some of them were only wounded and continued to moan until the executioners finished them off with bayonets. In the night the corpses were taken into a wood, drenched with gasoline, and burned to hide all traces of the crime. The central authorities denied their participation in the execution of the Imperial family, insisting that it was done by local Bolsheviks, but during the investigation a telegram from the Central Executive Committee was found, authorizing the local Bolsheviks to carry out the execution. The investigating commission interrogated the witnesses who were still in Ekaterinburg, found traces of the assassination in the cellar and bones and bits of jewelry, which the members of the Imperial family had been hiding in their dresses, on the spot where the bodies had been burned.

Thus perished the last Tsar of Russia (if one does not count Grand Duke Michael, in whose favor Nicholas abdicated but who never accepted the throne). Poor Nicholas, dominated by his abnormal wife, had never been fit to rule a great empire. His only crime, if it can be called a crime, was that he had believed the monarchy to be sacred, and that he felt that what had been good for his father was good for him. Unlike his father, however, he had been too weak to live by his creed, making concessions at times of crisis, going back on his word once the crisis had passed. Acting not from selfish motives but from misplaced love for Russia, he would have made a model private citizen; but he ought never to have ruled. He had expiated his faults by his dignified suffering and tragic death, and I am sure that if Old Russia with its intense religious feeling could be restored, the Russian Church, freed from the tyranny of the Bolsheviks, would as one of its first acts proclaim Nicholas II an Orthodox saint.

The commission set up by Kolchak discovered also the fate of the other members of the Imperial family, who had been exiled to Siberia after the Revolution. They had been shot at the edge of an abandoned coal pit, so that their corpses had fallen into the pit. The commission found the place and recovered the bodies. It was evident that several of them had not been dead when they had fallen into the pit. Among them was the Empress' sister, the Grand Duchess Elizabeth, who after the assassination of her husband, the Grand Duke Serge, by a terrorist some time before the Revolution, had entered a monastery and had led a life of great probity. She had tried several times to persuade her sister, the Empress, to send the infamous Rasputin away from the court. Her body is now buried in the Russian temple in Jerusalem. The only body which could not be found was that of the Grand Duke Michael. The Bolsheviks at the beginning of their rule had sent him to Perm, near the Siberian frontier, with his faithful secretary, Johnson, who had refused to leave him. Interned in some furnished rooms, they were awakened one night by some strangers posing as friends, and, it is supposed, taken to an adjoining wood and shot. No trace was found of their bodies.

Of all the victims of Bolshevik bestiality, the figure of Grand Duke Michael stands out most clearly in my memory. I recall the afternoon in Gatchina, when I remained with him alone, and he complained that fate had made him a member of the Imperial family, while all he wanted was to live quietly with his wife and son far away from all political turmoil. Against his will he had to decide one of the most critical questions in Russian history; he had to pay with his life for having been born a brother of the Emperor. Alas, the taking of Ekaterinburg was the only triumph of Kolchak in his campaign against the Reds.

✤✤✤

Disunity among Kolchak's professed supporters, the dwindling enthusiasm of the Czechoslovaks, and the indifference of the population, which had not yet experienced all the horrors of Bolshevik life, undermined Kolchak's efforts, and he began to retreat to Siberia under the pressure of Red forces. The White armies in European Russia also fell back after initial successes. The causes were the same: disunity of the anti-Bolsheviks and mistrust of the White forces by the peasants, who feared the return of the landlords and the loss of advantages which they had gained at the beginning of the Revolution. It has been held against Kolchak that when his forces were near St. Petersburg and he could have obtained Finnish help in exchange for the promise to grant Finland full independence, Kolchak declared that such a question could be decided only by the pan-Russian Assembly which would be convoked after the liberation of Russia from the Bolsheviks. From a purely political point of view Kolchak may have made a mistake, but it was not in his nature as an ardent patriot, working always for the glory of the Empire, to take upon himself the responsibility of dismembering Russia.

At the time both England and France more or less recognized the Omsk government and sent their Tokyo ambassadors as representatives. Both Sir Charles Eliot and M. Reignaut greatly admired Kolchak and were in favor of aiding him, but after the failure in south Russia, where the forces sent to help had been quickly demoralized by

Bolshevik propaganda, nobody in Europe wanted to start another war in far-off Siberia.

The American Ambassador [Roland S. Morris], who came from Tokyo to Omsk to acquaint himself with the Omsk government, also was very sympathetic to Kolchak and even asked for a detailed list of items which the United States could supply, promising to support these demands in his report to the President. For a time the hopes of the Omsk government were sustained by this, but nothing happened. Upon his return to Tokyo the American Ambassador modified his opinion about the Omsk government, and I heard him express the view that the entire historical development of Russia had been quite wrong and that it would be best for Russia to begin her history all over again. The whole country must disintegrate into small communities, and these must gradually join together, bringing into being a central government. When I modestly asked who, during this process which would take centuries to complete, would protect Russia from greedy neighbors, the Ambassador grandly announced that we would be defended by the word of the President of the United States, who would proclaim a "hands off Russia" policy, but he changed the subject when I remarked that with every new President American policy was subject to change. Here was a glaring example of the firm belief of the United States in the miraculous efficacy of democracy even in a country in whose development it had not played any significant part.

The Japanese kept aloof from the activities of the Omsk government. They sent an Ambassador to Omsk, but he seemed to have absolutely no influence in Tokyo, and the Japanese military continued their intrigues with their puppet Semenov. When Kolchak, as no help was forthcoming from the West, in desperation turned to the Japanese government through our Embassy and asked for two divisions of Japanese troops, the Japanese replied as before: they could not send any troops beyond Lake Baikal.

The situation in Omsk was getting desperate, and everyone who could fled the sinking ship. Most people headed for Harbin, which was becoming more and more a city in which Russian refugees could find everything to which they had been accustomed: a Russian atmosphere, good food, and endless political debate. Notwithstanding the tragedy which had befallen their country and themselves and in spite of the fact that most of them arrived penniless, they refused to

[293]

be pessimistic. Harbin had the gaiety of a colonial town, where the Russian refugees, far away from everything, soon forgot the horrors through which they had passed and joined in the local merry-go-round. No wonder that many of the new arrivals remained in Harbin and later, when Harbin fell under Japanese domination, moved to Shanghai and there recreated a new Harbin in the French concession.

❖❖❖

Comparatively few Russians came to Japan, partly because entry into Japan was more difficult, partly because Russians, though I do not know why, generally feel more at home in China. Most of the Russians in Japan at that time were those waiting for passage to the United States. Among them were some who played a prominent part in Old Russia. Thus we had a visit from Prince [Georgii Evgenevich] Lvov, who had been head of the provisional government. We were greatly interested to see what manner of man had headed the government at the time of revolutionary upheaval. Our disillusion was complete. Instead of a strong man who could if not stop, at any rate try to stop, the approaching disaster, we saw a mild old man. Listening to such men there was no doubt left that all these kind-hearted theorists never had a chance against such unscrupulous leaders as Lenin, Trotskii, and Stalin, whose actions were rooted in the basest and most primitive instincts of the Russian people. Prince Lvov was going to the United States and Europe to support the cause of Admiral Kolchak, but it was clear that this tired and soft old man could not support any cause.

The greatest blow to the Omsk government was the departure of the remaining Czechoslovak forces. These, according to Russians who succeeded to reach Vladivostok, occupied all available trains, kicking off Russian refugees fleeing from the Bolsheviks and leaving them on the platforms without food and shelter, while it was between twenty and thirty below zero Réaumur [between −77 and −99 degrees Fahrenheit]. Only God knows what became of them.

Kolchak remained until the last moment. Only when all the foreign representatives and most of his ministers had left, did he follow suit with Prime Minister V. Pepeliaev. A car with the remaining gold was attached to his train. The flags of the allied nations were hoisted on his carriage, as he put himself under the protection of a Czechoslovak detachment. Slowly moving east, the train was stopped at the small town of Nizhneudinsk[6] just before Irkutsk; a revolt had taken place in Irkutsk and the rebels, acting under Bolshevik instructions, were demanding the surrender of Kolchak. The Czechoslovaks under whose protection Kolchak had put himself sought instructions from Janine, the French general under whose overall command the Czechoslovak forces in Siberia had been placed. Janine faintheartedly ordered them to surrender Kolchak to the revolutionary government in Irkutsk. Kolchak and his Prime Minister were taken to Irkutsk and handed over to the rebels, who promptly showed that they were tools of the Soviet government. A tribunal was set up to try Kolchak and Pepeliaev; they were condemned to death and shot without delay. The protocols of the tribunal, obtained and published by the Hoover Library in Palo Alto [California], show the nobility with which Kolchak conducted himself before the Red tribunal. The few witnesses testified to the great courage Kolchak displayed during the execution. He died as he had lived—a great man. His last act before being surrendered was to send a telegram to Ataman Semenov, transferring to him the leadership of the anti-Bolshevik movement in Siberia.

Semenov used the telegram to boost his own importance and with Japanese support laid claim to the authority he felt the Kolchak government had possessed. As for fighting the Bolsheviks, there was nothing heroic in his efforts. As mentioned, he held out in Chita for a while, but as soon as real danger approached, escaped to Manchuria. There he tried to cut an important figure among Russian refugees, but when Soviet troops occupied the town, he was taken prisoner and hauled off to Moscow, where he was hanged or shot.

Deprived of a real supreme commander by the demise of Kolchak, each general tried to save his own soldiers by escaping to Manchuria. Marching through the frozen Siberian wilderness without food or proper clothing, the men experienced a frightful ordeal. General Kappel, who laid down his life in leading his soldiers out of Siberia, stood out in particular and became a legendary figure.

The Embassy followed the debacle with despair, but could do nothing. The Japanese did not hide that they had lost all hope for a

---

[6] The manuscript mistakenly states Verkhneudinsk.

White triumph, and intrigued with leftist elements in eastern Siberia to create a buffer state in the form of a Far Eastern Republic. Once looked upon as saviors, the Japanese with their harsh treatment of the populace only aroused hatred. The other foreigners abandoned Siberia. The departure of the American troops was the final blow. The Americans, before leaving, addressed a stiff note to the Japanese; they accused them of ignoring the decisions made by the allies at the beginning of the Siberian intervention and of pursuing their own selfish interests. But the Japanese paid no heed, and were glad to be left alone in Siberia. The country was full of partisans whom the Japanese had to fight. One group of partisans, under the command of a half-mad commissar, attacked the town of Nikolaevsk and killed half the population, including the Japanese Consul and most of the Japanese inhabitants. The Japanese were indignant and erected a special monument with the figure of Justice, eyes covered and scales in hand, and the inscription that they would never forget the murder of their compatriots in Nikolaevsk, but did nothing else.

✜✜✜

Great changes occurred in our Embassy. One morning Counsellor Shchekin complained of a pain in his chest. As he and I returned from work he commented that old age was not a pleasure. These were his last words to me. Half an hour later I received a message that he was dead. I rushed from the club to his modest house and found him on the floor. The days that followed were sad. The doctor, the undertaker, the clergyman all crowded in the small house. The undertaker dressed the body in a white kimono and as the coffin was being closed, his old Japanese servant shoved several cigars inside, saying that the deceased liked so much to smoke cigars. One of our barons, ready to joke at every occasion, commented that at least it would be easy to find our Counsellor on Judgment Day among the crowd of resurrected: one would merely have to look for a man in a white kimono, a cigar in hand. In the evening the coffin was carried into our cathedral. I was the only one present at the first service, the public service being the following day. The church was dark. As I listened to the monotonous voice of the priest, I realized that all of us were probably fated to die in a foreign country, away from family and relations. We did not even know if our relations were still alive. Once we had been happy;

now we were reduced to utter loneliness in an absolutely strange country, not knowing what was in store for us. Was fate kinder to those who had always been discontented?

Soon a change occurred in the entire position of our Embassy. The Japanese were expecting a visit from the Prince of Wales, and Baron Hayashi [Gonsuke] the Japanese Ambassador to England, came to Tokyo to make the necessary preparations. He was greatly astonished to find not only that the old Russian Embassy existed, but that the Russian Ambassador continued to be the Dean of the Diplomatic Corps. Baron Hayashi explained that in London the Russian Embassy had been closed and that it would be awkward if the usual welcome speech of the Diplomatic Corps were given by the Russian Ambassador, whose government no longer existed. The Foreign Office agreed, but showing great consideration sent a high official to the Ambassador to explain the situation. The official declared that the Foreign Office had no intention of stopping the activity of our Embassy or of desiring the resignation of our Ambassador, but that it could not continue to recognize him as Dean of the Diplomatic Corps and invite him to court functions. He conveyed the hope of the Foreign Office that the Ambassador would remain in Japan, where he and all the personnel of our Embassy would continue to enjoy the privileges of foreign representatives. The Ambassador, who had already concluded that he could be of no further use to the White cause, replied that he personally did not want to stay in the modified position, but that he would pass on the Embassy to me, second in rank since the death of Shchekin, and that he hoped the Foreign Office would recognize me as Russian Chargé d'Affaires and treat me with the same consideration as they had treated him. The Foreign Office seemed relieved and gave all the assurances about my position, the foreign representatives being duly informed. After a farewell dinner by the Russian colony and a speech in which he tried to persuade the emigrés not to quarrel among themselves, Krupenskii departed for Europe. I remained at the head of the Embassy.

❖❖❖

My ambition had been fulfilled. I had achieved a top position in the diplomatic service. But I realized that all this was the result of extremely artificial circumstances and could not last long. After all,

[297]

there was no government to support me, and the appearance of a government which I could recognize was very problematical. After the downfall of Kolchak nothing serious could be expected from the White movement in Siberia. The only consolation I had was that the Embassy still enjoyed a measure of prestige and that I could consider myself as a captain who stays with his ship till it sinks.

The Japanese lived up to their promises and all the time that I headed the Embassy, for nearly four years, treated me as a full-fledged Russian representative. The foreign diplomats treated me as their colleague and my relations with the Russian colony were good. Life in Japan continued to be agreeable; there was as yet no visible sign that the country was preparing to dominate the Far East. The cherry blossoms were blooming, the population, which during the War had become very prosperous, was growing more and more Europeanized and was indulging in pleasures imported from Europe and America. Thus I could continue to live in my fool's paradise.

After the downfall of the Omsk government, White activity was centered around Vladivostok, where many Russian military men, supporters of Kolchak, were struggling against ever-increasing leftist elements. The only ones who stood between Vladivostok and the surrounding country were the Japanese, and many Russians sought to promote their fortunes by trying to win the good will of the latter. For a while the White organizations were headed by M. K. Dietrichs,[7] a worthy Russian general who at one time had been connected with the Czechoslovaks. He was unable to bring about unity between the troops and the town authorities and soon left for Shanghai. Following him, a local merchant by the name of [S. D.] Merkulov, assumed leadership with Japanese help. As long as the Japanese were in Vladivostok, the government of Merkulov tried to play the part of a real government, sending telegrams to the Embassy, full of grand phrases concerning its future. When, in connection with its request that the Japanese remain in Vladivostok longer, I called on Matsudaira, the Chief of the Russian Section in the Foreign Office, who had recently returned from Vladivostok, I found him ill-tempered and extremely pessimistic. He said that the White cause in Siberia was irrevocably lost and informed me that the Japanese government had decided to recall its troops. As for the government of Merkulov, nobody took it

[7] Mikhail Diterikhs. See *Morskiia Zapiski*, Vol. XIII, 4 (New York, 1955), 74.

seriously. I duly informed Merkulov of the Japanese government's decision, but a man who is doomed would rather believe a favorable falsehood than the disagreeable truth, and Merkulov listened to low-ranking Japanese, who came to Vladivostok in large numbers to make money by deals with local speculators on the vast supplies which had piled up and were rotting in Vladivostok, Japanese who were interested in keeping alive the illusion that Japanese soldiers would remain in Vladivostok.

Merkulov even sent a special mission to Tokyo to ask the Japanese Foreign Office not to recall the troops. I do not think that the mission thought much of me, because all I could do was to repeat that the decision to withdraw the soldiers had already been made, even the date for the recall fixed. When I called on the delegates in their hotel, they showed me a dirty, unshaven Japanese, wandering down the corridors, and mysteriously told me that he was the old tutor of the Minister of War and that through him they were trying to persuade the Minister not to recall the troops. What could I say to these people who believed that the decision of the government could be countermanded by a decrepit old man who pretended to be a former tutor of one of the Ministers? The mission returned full of hopes, but when the fixed date arrived, the Japanese soldiers left Vladivostok and sailed home. With the departure of the Japanese troops the Reds lifted their heads and a regular advance against Vladivostok began. The tide was turning and the Merkulov government decided to flee while fleeing was good. Some of its members made their way to Harbin; Merkulov himself came to Japan and after some time left for Canada, where he lived in Victoria, fondly thinking back to the glorious days when he had been head of state.

A group of Socialist Revolutionaries who had struggled against Merkulov proclaimed a new government following his departure, but the Bolsheviks were already at the gates of the city, and all the Socialist Revolutionaries could do was to issue the proclamation that they were taking power in their hands, board a Japanese steamer, and flee to Japan. When I saw these people in Tokyo I could not refrain from telling them that I did not understand their logic. When it had been possible to do something, they had only quarreled with each other and had refused to cooperate; when it had become too late to do anything, they had issued a high-sounding proclamation about their readiness to fight against the Bolsheviks and had immediately left Russia on the same boat as the members of the other anti-Bolshevik governments.

As the Bolsheviks approached, Vladivostok was gripped by panic. Till the last moment many residents had thought that somebody would prevent Bolshevik occupation of the city. Now they rushed to the port, where Admiral [Iu. K.] Stark was preparing to leave with the remainder of the former Russian fleet in Vladivostok, so that the vessels would not fall into the hands of the Bolsheviks. The Admiral could not refuse asylum to the crowd of women and children, including pupils of the military schools, earlier evacuated from Omsk, and the ships were laden to such an extent that they could barely move. The Admiral planned to drop the refugees at the nearest Korean port, then, if necessary, proceed further, but when the fleet arrived at Genzan the local authorities, on instructions from Tokyo, categorically refused to let the refugees land or the fleet to remain in port. As Admiral Stark lacked coal to undertake a long journey and could not do so anyway with all the women and children on board without any accommodations whatever, he refused to move unless the refugees were allowed on shore and sent telegrams to the Embassy and the Naval Attaché, asking them to arrange the matter with the Japanese government.

I rushed to the Foreign Office where I was met by Mr. Matsudaira. He was furious, and at once began to shout that the Japanese had never asked the refugees to come and refused to do anything for them. As the Bolshevik commander had promised not to take any retaliatory measures against the inhabitants of Vladivostok, there had been absolutely no need for them to run away and they had done it on their own responsibility and could not claim any help from the Japanese government. The local authorities had instructions to furnish supplies to Admiral Stark, and he must leave Genzan forthwith. As Matsudaira gave vent to his indignation, his sympathies suddenly seemed on the side of the Reds. I replied that recriminations would not get us anywhere. He knew perfectly well that as long as the refugees remained on board, Stark could not leave Genzan; if he stayed, famine would shortly break out among the women and children; epidemics would follow. Soon the whole world would hear that Russian refugees on vessels in a Japanese port were dying because the Japanese refused to let them land for fear of irritating their new friends, the Bolsheviks. I told him that it gave me little pleasure to come and beg for help, but the Russian refugee problem was a world problem and if such small countries as Serbia and Czechoslovakia had opened their doors to the refugees, surely Japan could allow several hundred to land temporarily. But my arguments only made Matsudaira angrier, and he continued to repeat that the Japanese had not invited them. Rebuffed, I went to see the American Ambassador.

Mr. [Charles Beecher] Warren received me at once. I told him the whole story and said that without his help I could not do anything. Mr. Warren asked me to give him five minutes to think it over. When the five minutes were up, he flew into action: rang for the Secretary, ordered him to arrange an interview with the Minister of Foreign Affairs, summoned by telephone the editor of the American newspaper, and sent for Dr. Teusler of the American Red Cross. The editor received instructions to publish in the next issue a strong article about the miseries of the Russian refugees and the refusal of the Japanese to do something for them; the doctor was asked to arrange an expedition of Red Cross nurses from the local American hospital to Genzan to see what could be done for the women and children. After giving all these instructions, the Ambassador went to see the Minister. I returned home full of admiration for his efficiency. I was especially impressed by the discipline. No one argued with the Ambassador, and the only answer to what he said was "Yes, sir."

The next day I was summoned by the Vice Minister, who informed me that an order had gone to Genzan to allow the Russian refugees to land. They would be put up in empty barracks, and the Japanese Red Cross was sending doctors and nurses to look after them. After receiving the necessary coal, Admiral Stark must leave Genzan. As for the refugees, they could not stay on for long; gradually they would be sent to Harbin or Shanghai. Thanks to the intervention of the American Embassy, the whole matter of the Russian refugees in Genzan was arranged satisfactorily.

Supplied with coal, Admiral Stark proceeded to Shanghai. Here he encountered the same difficulties, the Chinese refusing to let the ships remain. Realizing that they might ultimately surrender the fleet to the Bolsheviks, Stark left for Manila, where his fleet would not run the risk of being handed over to the Reds. On the way to the Philippines the fleet ran into a storm and several old vessels perished with many people aboard. How cruel that they should have escaped death at the hand of the Bolsheviks only to meet it at the bottom of the sea! In Manila the ships which reached port were interned. Some of the crew found employment, but the majority, including Admiral Stark, after some time moved to the United States.

Japan, meanwhile, was seeking to conclude an agreement with the Far Eastern Republic.[8] Notwithstanding the latter's ties with the Soviet government, Japan still hoped to create a buffer state. Several unofficial meetings were held with representatives of the Republic. But when Matsudaira proceeded to Changchun to conclude a final agreement, he found as the representative of the Far Eastern Republic the prominent Soviet diplomat [Adolf Abramovich] Ioffe. The curtain had lifted and Moscow stood in plain view. There was nothing for the Japanese to do but enter into direct negotiations with the Soviet government, and soon the myth of a Far Eastern Republic was forgotten.[9]

The first attempt of Japan to reach an understanding with the Soviet government was unsuccessful. The Japanese came to Changchun thinking that they could dictate their conditions to the Bolsheviks and began by demanding an apology and compensation for the murder of the Japanese inhabitants and Consul at Nikolaevsk. The Bolsheviks refused even to discuss the question on the grounds that the deed had been done by partisans and the Soviet government was not responsible. But the crime was still too fresh in the memory of the Japanese for them to return to Japan without obtaining any indemnity. The negotiations collapsed and our Embassy got another lease on life.

❖❖❖

I often marveled at our position in Tokyo. The diplomatic list referred to our Embassy as "the old Russian Embassy." We were no longer invited to the official functions at court, but otherwise retained all diplomatic privileges, and whenever I wanted to discuss something

[8] Ostensibly an independent democratic republic, the Far Eastern Republic was in fact the first "people's democracy," the Communists taking over and annexing the transitory buffer between Russia and Japan to the Soviet Union upon the withdrawal of the Japanese from Vladivostok.

[9] The Far Eastern Republic existed from 1920-22.

concerning my countrymen in Japan I was always received at the Foreign Office as a Russian representative. I enjoyed all the agreeable sides of diplomatic life without having to satisfy any superiors. The other diplomats treated me as if I were still a Russian representative. Without any effort or special desire on my part I continued to participate in the diplomatic merry-go-round. When the Prince of Wales came to Tokyo, I was introduced to him as the Old Russian representative, and was touched by his expression of sorrow concerning the misfortunes of my country. He thereby gained my lasting sympathy, and I was sorry for the tragedy which befell him later; I say "tragedy," for to me it seemed tragic to discard a throne for love, ambition being always stronger than love in my case.

What I appreciated most in my life in Tokyo was my friendship with the family of the Belgian Ambassador, Baron [Albert de] Bassompièrre, which remained in Tokyo for nearly fifteen years and replaced for me my own family, lost in the Revolution. During my years in Tokyo I saw the Bassompièrre children grow up, the daughters marry, and the third generation come into the world. The Baron read me his reports and we had endless political discussions. The Baroness arranged weekly bridge parties for me, excusing my fits of bad temper whenever I was losing.

Other friends who made my life easier were the Batys. He was in the employ of the Japanese Foreign Office as an adviser in international law. Every Christmas they gave a party, to which they invited all their bachelor friends to remind them of Christmas with its turkey and plum pudding. The number of these guests gradually diminished until only two of us, a Japanese lady and I, attended regularly. Every year the Japanese lady would tell me the same story from a Japanese legend, how two stars would meet only once a year, then disappear into space until the next meeting. The Batys reminded me of characters out of Dickens. They never thought of leaving Japan, and built a summer house near Lake Chuzenji, in the mountains above Nikko. Every summer they invited me to come and stay with them, and as I watched the gorgeous sunsets or relaxed in a sailboat, I forgot all my misfortunes and lived only in the present. I shall always remember those evenings when Miss Baty and I played solitaire, Dr. Baty dozing with two cats on his lap. All that is now past. Miss Baty died during the Second World War, her strong patriotism and love for Japan entwined in tragic conflict. Dr. Baty, who had been so absorbed in his international law that he did not notice how the War came and could not look on the Japanese as his enemies, remained in their service, though knowing his disapproval of any war, they never asked his advice. After the War the British authorities accused him of being a traitor and deprived him of the protection of the British Embassy. I thought it very unfair and cruel, and at every opportunity defended my friend, saying that there was nothing of a traitor in him, his only fault having been in living in an artificial world created by his own idealism and kindness of heart, where there was no room for hate and hostility.

Surrounded by so much friendship, I did not feel the uselessness of my existence. To be sure I did my best to explain to anybody who would listen the real nature and danger of Bolshevism, but few people paid heed. I came to the conclusion that in this cynical world success justifies everything. As long as the foreigners thought that the Bolsheviks would not last, they gave half-hearted support to the White movement; when they saw that the Bolsheviks were firmly entrenched, they lost interest in the White cause, and forgetting all the crimes committed by the Bolsheviks, began to approach the rulers of Russia through special agents. To justify their action, they created a theory about the evolution of Bolshevism. Lenin, who himself had not believed at first that the Bolsheviks could remain in power, was quick to take advantage of the change in the attitude of the foreign powers, and restored a semblance of free trade, though openly admitting with his usual cynicism that he took this step backward only in order to jump forward at the first opportunity. Without ever losing sight of his objective, Lenin did not contradict the foreign powers when they chose to see things not as they were but as they wanted them to be.

The question of how to deal with Soviet Russia was complicated by the attitude of Germany, which after her defeat in World War I, gave thought to restoring her position by an alliance with Soviet Russia, something that England tried to prevent. I remember that there were repercussions of this even in Tokyo. After the end of the War, the German government had sent there as Ambassador Dr. [Wilhelm] Solf, a member of Cabinet at the time of the Kaiser. Dr. Solf's chief aim was to restore Germany's position in the Far East. The Japanese called him the most popular Ambassador in Tokyo, and even the English elected him president of their Asiatic Society. I knew Dr. Solf favored Japanese recognition of the Soviet government. Once he called on me and after some insignificant conversation asked why I did not recognize the Soviet regime. When he saw my astonishment, he cited his own example—he too had served the last Emperor, but this had not prevented him for patriotic reasons from recognizing and serving the Socialist government which had succeeded the monarchy. I retorted that he did not seem to be aware of the great difference between the German Socialists and the Russian Bolsheviks. We too had recognized the provisional government which had succeeded the Russian monarchy, but I would never dare to ask him if he would consent to serve the German Spartakists, should they seize power in Germany. Dr. Solf made no reply and never reverted to the topic, but when Japan recognized Soviet Russia and its first representative appeared in Tokyo, Solf guided his first steps.

I scarcely had time to assume my new position as representative of a nonexistent government, when the Japanese made their second attempt to enter into an agreement with the Soviet government. This time the initiative came from Viscount Goto [Shimpei], a prominent Japanese official who had always considered himself a promoter of Russo-Japanese friendship. After the War, when the Japanese obtained the southern part of the Chinese Eastern Railway and created the South Manchurian Railway, a gold mine for Japanese officials, Goto became its chief administrator. When the Japanese began to plan a Russo-Japanese understanding, Goto, then vice president of the Russo-Japanese Society, suddenly remembered his pro-Russian leanings and, ignoring the fact that there was nothing in common between the old Russian and the Soviet governments, began to promote the idea of recognizing the Soviet government. In speeches and written articles he asserted that friendship with Russia was the favorite idea of Emperor Meiji, and that he considered it his duty to fulfill the will of the late Emperor. But the Russia of Emperor Meiji's days had been a monarchy, not ruled by a band of revolutionaries whose ideas were poison to all normal states. The Foreign Office was opposed to Goto's propaganda, but Goto ignored its opposition and invited Ioffe to Tokyo as his personal guest to explore the possibility of an understanding between the two countries. By this invitation Goto forced the hand of the Foreign Office, which had to make the best of the invitation and appointed one of its officials for the negotiations with Ioffe.

The behavior of Ioffe toward the Japanese was arrogant. He declared himself ill and received the representatives of the Foreign Office lying in bed. He was even photographed in such a pose, the Japanese sitting modestly before a fat Jew in a nightshirt in bed. All former Russian diplomats must have turned in their graves. Reading about this in the local press, I was sure that the end of our Embassy was approaching, and kept asking myself what I should do when my fool's paradise would end. My fears proved premature. Once again the negotiations foundered over the question of compensation for the Nikolaevsk massacre. The Japanese wanted to obtain concessions for the exploitation of oil and coal in northern Sakhalin, but the Soviets refused to discuss compensation. As long as the monument of blindfolded Justice stood opposite Kudan,[10] the great temple where the souls of fallen heroes were supposed to dwell, the Japanese could not be expected to modify their demands. Thus Ioffe was carried to the station and left for Shanghai to help the Soviet mission implant the principles of Bolshevism in the minds of Chinese revolutionaries. Our Embassy had another lease on life.

This time the lease was much longer than anybody could have expected. Nineteen twenty-three was the year of the great earthquake, which proved so disastrous that for a long time thereafter the Japanese government could think only of rebuilding the destroyed towns and restoring normal life. The question of an agreement with the Soviet government was postponed indefinitely. Some of the Japanese statesmen probably understood the danger of admitting Soviet representatives with their inevitable propaganda at a time when the populace was still under the impression of the great disaster.

❖❖❖

Earthquakes were a frequent occurrence in Japan, but usually they were mild and brief. Japanese scientists had been trying to determine the causes of earthquakes and the possibility of predicting their occurrence, but with little success. A few days before the earthquake of September 1, 1923, a certain Professor Oyama, who was considered the greatest expert on earthquakes, gave a lecture in which he stated that there was no reason to expect an earthquake. It is said that the

[10] The famous Yasukuni Shrine for the war dead, situated at Kudan.

old man was so upset by his loss of face when the great earthquake shattered his prophecy that he fell ill and died within a week.

I myself was not in Tokyo at the moment of the earthquake. Our Military Attaché had invited me to spend the weekend in Nikko. Nikko was far from the center of the earthquake, but that Saturday at noon, as we were walking among the huge cypresses which surrounded the temples, we had the strange feeling that the earth was beginning to rock under our feet, and the still, majestic cypresses began to move. The sight was uncanny. The pilgrims around us stopped with frightened faces. One did not know what to expect. The movement repeated itself three times; then everything was quiet. People said that such a regular movement of the earth indicated that a big earthquake had occurred somewhere, but Saturday passed without our hearing anything. At five o'clock in the morning I was aroused by the servant who told me that during the night the Emperor, who was spending the summer in Nikko, had been informed that half of Tokyo had been destroyed by the earthquake and was burning.

Considering it my duty to be in Tokyo, I hastened to the station to find out if there was a train to the capital. I was told that there was no communication with Tokyo, but that a train would be sent, though it was not known how far it would be able to go. The train was waiting for the Minister of the Imperial Household. When he appeared, I asked whether we would reach Tokyo. Count Makino [Nobuaki] solemnly replied that if we kept our heads we might reach Tokyo toward evening.

It was a terrible journey. The train was packed, with many people sitting on the roof. Instead of the usual three hours, it took about ten to reach the suburbs of Tokyo. Approaching a river some twenty miles from the capital, we discovered that part of the bridge had fallen into the river, the rails, with the ties still attached to them, hanging in the air. Crossing the bridge I felt like a movie hero who had to perform daring stunts. What gave me courage was that the old Minister, supported by two men, was doing the same stunts.

On the other side of the river we found a special train which took us a little closer to Tokyo. Here we saw the magnitude of the disaster. The city was burning, and the sky was covered with black clouds. The stations were jammed with people who had fled from Tokyo; stunned they lay on the platforms, their meager belongings beside them. I saw a foreigner, apparently a German. When I asked him what was happening in Tokyo, he replied that the entire city was "kaput." Continuing with Count Makino I got as far as a little station about ten miles from Tokyo; the train could go no further. I took leave of Count Makino and started walking. As I neared the city the signs of destruction increased, while tremors continued to shake the restless earth. The fires were dreadful.

Toward evening I reached Ueno Park, near the train terminal. The Park was filled with refugees preparing to spend the night in the open. As always, once the initial panic had passed, the Japanese accepted things calmly, even cracked jokes. When I came to the end of the Park, whence the streets of Tokyo could be seen, a ghastly sight greeted my eyes: one side of the large street which led to the center of town had been reduced to smoldering ruins; the other side was still burning. The flames, like some enormous monster, devoured building after building. No resistance was possible.

To reach the center of town I had to walk in the opposite direction from the crowd. Impossible as it seemed at first, it proved not so difficult. The first things that the Japanese tried to save were their soft *futon* or thick blankets between which they slept, and I found it easy to squeeze through. Soon I reached the main street, the pride of Tokyo, where the best shops were situated and where thousands of Japanese walked in the afternoons. The whole street had burned. Flames still devoured luxury articles in the big department stores; astonishingly nobody tried to steal anything.

Having covered all these miles without seeing a single house that had escaped the fire, I lost all hope of finding the Embassy standing. With a feeling of despair I crossed Hibiya Park, not far from which our Embassy was located. This Park too was full of refugees who had installed themselves for the night. As I stepped from the Park, my hopes revived. I could see the House of Parliament standing, and behind it in an open place our Embassy, slightly damaged but also standing. Entering the compound I was met by a crowd of Russians who had left their houses to find asylum in the Embassy. The two Bishops were among them. The earthquake had toppled the bell tower onto the Cathedral, crushing the main building, the subsequent fire destroying the entire surrounding part of the city. The Bishops had barely escaped, street after street being blocked by fire.

The earthquake had occurred at twelve o'clock, when people in every house were cooking their meals. The wooden dwellings fell like matchboxes on the burning charcoal and fire spread at once. The movement of the earth had displaced the water pipes and there was no way of putting out the fire. Thus different quarters of Tokyo burned until there was nothing left or until the wind shifted and the fire turned. The Embassy had been saved in such a way.

I was touched that everybody seemed glad to see me, and the Bishop exclaimed that now that the master was back, everything would be all right. There was nothing I could do about the tremors which continued to shake the ground from time to time, but I did stop the quarreling which had already started among my countrymen. The argument had broken out when somebody had ordered the Japanese servants to bring him beer from the Embassy cellar. The servants refused, saying that the cellar was empty. This some of the Russians could not believe. I offered to show them the empty cellar, warning, however, that I would not be responsible if we were buried by a renewed earthquake. Only one man had the courage to make the inspection and to substantiate sadly the existence of an Embassy without either beer or wine.

The continuing tremors made sleeping indoors out of the question, and I ordered the servants to bring carpets from the house and to arrange a general dormitory on the lawn before the Embassy. I found it very comical that the chief boy, who was directing the arrangement, followed the protocol for an official dinner party in assigning places. Thus I was put between the two Bishops. Luckily it did not rain and the night was warm. It would have been quite agreeable to sleep outside, if only one of the Bishops had not snored so loudly.

After three days I had enough of camping outdoors and moved back into the Embassy. I did have my bed carried to my study downstairs, and slept near the open door in case of another earthquake. Only once later, in January, did another earthquake shake the house. Meanwhile somebody spread the rumor that the Koreans had taken advantage of the general disorder, had revolted, and were killing the Japanese. This proved to be a complete fabrication, but people went about armed and I too bought a revolver and slept with it under my pillow, though I knew quite well that I would never use it.

The toll in life and property claimed by the earthquake was enormous. In one place nearly sixty thousand persons perished. Surrounded by fire, they had gathered at an open spot, but the flames had not spared them, had drawn near enough to ignite their clothes and blankets, burning sixty thousand alive. At every step one heard ghastly stories. Many Russians perished in Yokohama, where the earthquake had been even worse than in Tokyo. When railway communication was restored, I went there with the Bishop and we held services on the spots where Russians, who had probably been killed, had once lived. It was a sad sight: the whole town in ruins, the Bishop, the Embassy priest and I wandering among the piles of stones and burned wood, trying to locate the former houses under the ruins of which our compatriots had perished.

It was a beautiful day, and without anything to obstruct the view, one could see how magnificently Yokohama was situated: on one side the endless sea, on the other receding hills. The population, stunned by the earthquake, was slowly reviving. Every morning one could see an incessant stream of humanity pass before the Embassy in a cloud of dust as the owners of houses and shops in the burned part of the city returned from their refuge for a daily search among the ruins for the remnants of their former treasures.

Soon they were joined by Russians who came from Kobe, where most of the foreign inhabitants of Yokohama had been taken by a Vancouver-bound Canadian ship when they had fled panic-stricken to the water. Some of the Russians now returned to search for gold, which they suspected their countrymen, especially friends of Ataman Semenov, mistrustful of banks, to have been hiding in their apartments. Opposed though I was to their strange vocation, I could not deny them the hospitality of the Embassy. Every morning the "gold diggers" left with shovels and other instruments to pass the day in Yokohama, returning to the Embassy late in the evening, exhausted and dirty, to the horror of one of our barons, who was afraid that these people would either kill us or bring some dreadful disease. He was especially afraid of a fierce-looking Abyssinian, whom one of the Russian generals had brought as an orderly. One evening this Abyssinian came to my bedroom and proudly showed me his master's golden sword, which he had dug from the ruins of the house where he had lived.

The Americans were of the greatest help to the foreigners stranded in Tokyo. The Japanese had enough to do to help their own people. The Americans took it upon themselves to care for the foreigners, and the American Ambassador and most of his staff rushed to Tokyo from Karuizawa, where they had been spending the summer. Finding their own Embassy burned down, they simply rented the entire Imperial Hotel and offered to pay for the meals of foreigners. Consequently the hotel became the meeting place for all foreigners. Our Russians, who ordinarily could never have afforded the luxury of Imperial Hotel meals, made regular trips to the place. They called it "to feast on the President's account."

Once a Russian lady came to me to complain that the Americans had refused to serve a Japanese student friend whom she had brought to such a meal. When I tried to explain to her that the Americans could not feed the entire Japanese population, she countered that the student was a nice boy; then came back another time to assure me that her relations with the student were strictly platonic; she simply wanted to show him how foreigners eat. An American cruiser, summoned by the Embassy, came from Manila with provisions and clothes. I must confess that never before had I had such a supply of excellent oranges. Sometimes the Americans were even too efficient. They posted on the door of their office a list of persons supposedly lost. Some had simply been stranded in the country, and were slow in reaching Tokyo; finding their names on the list of dead persons, they naturally protested. This did not upset the clerk in the least; he simply took a pencil and scratched their names out. I admired the quickness with which people were killed and resurrected.

Then millions began pouring from the United States, millions thanks to which the Russian refugees could leave the country. A special commission was organized in Kobe to help the foreigners leave Japan. A strict English captain headed the Russian section. When I met him later, he told me that he had never met a more peculiar people than the Russians. Many could not decide where to go; their desires changed constantly. Several ladies sold their tickets and used the money to buy cosmetics. When the captain had been angry, as they had returned to ask for another ticket, they had accused him of not being a gentleman, of trying to make them go to Shanghai dressed like frumps! Another lady, offered passage to Mexico, put as a condition the opportunity to visit Harbin weekends. I am sure that many of the Russians, had they had time to think, would have preferred to remain in Japan, where they had enjoyed good times until the earthquake. I did nothing to stop them, since most were refugees in the true sense of the word, former generals, high officials, and other people who had seen better times. For them there were absolutely no prospects in Japan and I trembled at the thought of what would become of them when the Japanese recognized the Soviets. From this point of view, the earthquake was a blessing in disguise, especially because the refugees who came to Japan after the earthquake were quite different in character: they were former soldiers, workers, and peasants who following the remnants of Kolchak's forces, found their way to Manchuria, China, and Japan. They adapted themselves much better to the new circumstances, found ways to make money, and with few exceptions were not dependent on outside help.

As I have said, an unexpected result of the earthquake was the postponement of the question of Japanese recognition of the Soviet government. Our diplomatic existence was prolonged for another two years. But most of the members of the Embassy left for Europe or the United States. The Commercial Attaché [Miller] departed first; this was natural because there was no commerce between Russia and Japan. He was followed by the Military Attaché [Col. Podtiagin] with his family. The last years they had shared the Embassy building with me. After the earthquake they had installed themselves in the large ballroom, deeming it the safest place in the Embassy, and with the aid of screens had converted it into an apartment. I remember how they rehearsed what to do in the event of a repetition of the earthquake, how one would jump through the window and the other hand out the children. I am afraid that a real earthquake would not have given them time for all these ceremonies. The Naval Attaché [Rear Admiral Boris Petrovich Dudorov] with his numerous family was next to leave Tokyo.

I remained alone with our interpreter.

✤✤✤

Once I had a rather awkward experience. The Bolsheviks had imprisoned some Japanese in Vladivostok. A protest meeting was organized in Tokyo and as usual inflammatory speeches drove the crowd half-mad. Looking for an object on which to vent their indignation, they remembered that there was a Russian Embassy in Tokyo. I was sitting quietly in the chancery when I was told that a mob was approaching the Embassy, ready to attack it. We hardly had time to close the gates, when the crowd, armed with sticks and stones, surrounded the compound. I had all the trouble in the world to persuade the mob that ours was a White Embassy and not a Red Embassy, that my sympathies were completely with them, and that I was quite willing to protest with them. I also telephoned the Foreign Office and police were sent to disperse the overzealous crowd.

Notwithstanding the uncertainty of my position, life in Tokyo continued to be agreeable. I even took up golf, though I had to hide this from my modest compatriots, who would never have admitted that a grown-up person could spend hours in trying to send a ball into a hole without falling into a second childhood, a reputation I could not afford if I wanted to retain a modicum of prestige in the Russian colony. I found golf extremely soothing. Placing yourself in a position where you forget everything except how many strokes it takes you to put the ball into the hole may be childish, but it helps to develop a certain equanimity necessary in meeting the blows which fate may send your way.

✛✛✛

With the passage of time the disastrous effects of the earthquake began to disappear. The Japanese displayed astonishing energy in rebuilding their capital. Millions were spent on widening streets and on the construction of modern five- to six-story concrete buildings, and the whole of Tokyo acquired a much more European character. The entire atmosphere changed. People discovered the advantage of cafés and small eating places, and the new Ginza overflowed with tea houses. There came into being what people called a "café civilization." The relation between the sexes became closer. The innumerable café and dancing girls became the objects of flirtation. Romance which had been hidden in Old Japan came into the open. The young men and girls began to model their life and conduct after the characters they saw in American movies. Love, kissing, sex—words which some

[313]

twenty years before were rarely heard in Japan—became the chief concern of Japanese youth, and as it was felt that a higher civilization must have gangsters and sex crimes, both appeared on the Japanese scene and Japanese newspapers bulged with stories of the most sordid crimes.

Policemen, who had played the role of chief protectors of decency, vice being confined to strictly regulated special quarters, did not know what measures to take against this new freedom. They made mothers responsible for the behavior of their daughters, obliging them to accompany the latter if they worked in dance halls in order to prevent their falling into the hand of unscrupulous persons. Foreigners were considered especially dangerous, and every dance hall had to keep special spies to watch over their flirtations with Japanese girls. For the first time, sex relations became a source of blackmail in Japan.

In a word, the earthquake of 1923 cracked the moral foundations of Japanese life, and the worst features of European civilization penetrated through these cracks into the inner soul of Japan. It is not astonishing that old and decent Japanese were apprehensive and that later the military were able to cloak their own ambitions in a drive to rid their country of the pernicious influence of European civilization and restore Japan's old civilization, "the Way of the Gods."

The sight of their countrymen falling under the influence of European civilization provoked the ire of various reactionaries, notably an influential old man by the name of Toyama Mitsuru, whose misplaced patriotism made him the evil genius of Japan. Toyama dominated the Black Dragon Society, which sought to remove officials whose influence it considered undesirable. Soon after the earthquake, Toyama began to take issue with the trend toward Westernization, civil admiration for liberalism diminishing the authority of the Emperor. Toyama's championship of Imperial authority versus liberalism, political parties and rights of Parliament, showed that his activity became more and more connected with militarists, who kept outside of party politics.

It was easy for the military to avoid being drawn into political strife without losing authority, because the Japanese constitution left the nomination of the ministers of war and navy not to the Prime Minister but directly to the Emperor. If the candidates, who had to be regular army or navy men, refused to serve in the government, no cabinet could be formed.[11] The Emperor, though he theoretically had the power to make a general accept the post, would not overrule the orders of the army. Thus the military clique, when it wished, could dominate the government. As a rule the militarists did not use their power openly, but arranged things behind the scenes. The Elder Statesman[12] would not recommend to the Emperor as prime minister a person unwilling to compromise with the military and thus unacceptable to the latter. Only before a war do the militarists come into the open and assume full power. All these manipulations we experienced in the years preceding the Second World War. At first the hand of the military clique was not seen. Political parties seemed in control of the government and people spoke of the progress Japan was making in the development of constitutionalism. Then came the period when the military deemed it necessary to give a new direction to public opinion and different reactionary organizations went into action, first with speeches, then with threats and assassinations. The role of the militarists became increasingly apparent, but they continued to operate through parliament and the political parties, which degenerated into mere tools, until all pretense seemed unnecessary and General Tojo [Hideki] appeared on the scene.

I was most interested in the attitude of the militarists toward the Bolsheviks. When the struggle against Bolshevism began, the Japanese were undoubtedly more staunchly anti-Bolshevik than any other participants in the Siberian intervention. Gradually they became less concerned with fighting Bolshevism than with turning the fight against Bolshevism to their own advantage, so much so that White Russian leaders began to wonder whether the Japanese might not be more dangerous than the Bolsheviks. When the anti-Bolshevik movement collapsed, the Japanese military remained strongly anti-Bolshevik at

[11] It was not the Constitution but the Imperial Ordinance of 1900, issued when General Yamagata was premier, that gave the military "a life-and-death hold over all subsequent cabinets" by providing that only generals and lieutenant-generals and admirals and vice admirals on active duty could be appointed Minister of War and Minister of the Navy, respectively. (See Hugh Borton, *Japan's Modern Century* [New York, 1955], p. 146.)

[12] The Elder Statesmen, or *genro*, were an extraconstitutional group of statesmen who had affected the restoration of the Imperial government and dominated the shaping of modern Japan.

home, but abroad were ready to make the common mistake of trying to render the Bolsheviks harmless by recognizing them and by establishing normal relations with them.

I hoped that while Japan slowly reverted to normal, something would happen to open Japanese eyes to the danger of recognizing the Soviet government. But, thanks to Japanese energy, the country was rebuilt much sooner than expected, and by the end of 1924 the Japanese government took steps to renew talks with the Soviets. This time negotiations took place in Peking, where the Japanese Minister Yoshizawa [Kenkichi] received instructions to approach the Soviet representative [Lev Mikhailovich] Karakhan. This time the Japanese did not insist on an apology or compensation for the Nikolaevsk massacre, and the negotiations proceeded quickly. Hence all the grand phrases pronounced after the murder of their subjects suffered the fate of all grand phrases—they remained empty words, and even the blindfolded figure of Justice erected as a reminder of the tragedy was discreetly moved behind the temple of Kudan so as not to offend the eyes of the new friends.

❖❖❖

Certain that the negotiations would not falter again, the Foreign Office invited me and asked me the fatal question, what I intended to do with the Embassy and the rest of the property of the former Russian government. To this my answer had long been ready. I declared that I would never hand over the Embassy and the rest of the property to the Soviet government, because I did not consider it the rightful successor to the old government, adding, fond as we Russians are of grand phrases, "over my dead body." The Vice Minister looked astonished; surely I must realize, he said, that upon Japan's recognition of the Soviet government, the latter would be considered the legal Russian government and its representatives would have the right to occupy the old Embassy. I explained that I would be willing to surrender the Embassy to the Japanese government, providing I was permitted to declare in writing that I did not recognize the Embassy and that the whole matter was so arranged as to avoid my being placed face to face with the Soviet representative. To my surprise the Vice Minister consented. He promised that I would be given advance notice when negotiations entered their final stage and that provision would be made for a time lapse of two weeks between my surrender of the Embassy to the Foreign Office and the arrival of Soviet officials. I thanked the Vice Minister for this arrangement; while it did not alter the fact that the Embassy would fall into Bolshevik hands, it at least saved me from the humiliation of a formal surrender.

I returned to the Embassy and began to prepare myself for the final act in my diplomatic career. I instructed the Consulates to arrange with local authorities for the transfer to them of the property of the old Russian government. I added that I would not deem it possible for any of the officials to enter Soviet service; if they wanted to leave Japan, their passage to Europe or America would be paid. I must say that all of them remained loyal to the former Russian government and not a single one went over to the Soviets. Then I spent many days going through the archives, considering it my duty not to leave any letters or documents which could compromise those who had struggled against the Bolsheviks in Siberia and had not been able to escape. Many nights of hard work went on this, but had the Bolsheviks found their names in the Embassy files the position of many Russians could have become tragic.

My most important task was to settle with the Japanese Foreign Office the status of the White Russian refugees in Japan following the recognition of Soviet Russia, specifically whether the Soviet authorities would have any rights over them. I wrote the Foreign Office in this connection several times and even presented a memorandum outlining my views on the matter, insisting that the Japanese government must not withdraw its protection from the refugees. The Japanese postponed their answer until the last moment and even then did not commit themselves in a formal document. They handed me a piece of paper which stated that the Russian refugees would be considered stateless and as such would be under Japanese protection as long as they tried to earn a living in an honest way and did not mix in political strife. Aware though I was that the piece of paper was not truly a Japanese commitment, I knew the Japanese well enough to realize that this was the best I could get. I must say that the Japanese never refused their protection to the Russian refugees and the question of their submission to Soviet authority never arose. When the Soviet Embassy opened in Japan, it announced that Russian refugees had three months in which to register as Soviet citizens or lose Russian citizenship. As far as I know only one or two registered. The rest preferred to forfeit their Russian citizenship.

At last the fatal day arrived and an official from the Foreign Office came to receive the Embassy and all that it contained. Though he was extremely amiable and accepted everything without any formality, it was a sad day for me. The ten years which I had spent in Tokyo had been happy years for me personally, notwithstanding the torments of my country. Selfish as it may sound, the tragic events had occurred far away, consideration and friendship sweetening our life in Japan. I would be very ungrateful if I did not give the Japanese credit for this.[13]

The Embassy had employed many Japanese servants, who had numerous relatives living with them. I had been astonished to learn during the census that, counting women and children, some one hundred Japanese lived in our compound. Before leaving the Embassy I gave every servant three months' salary as severance pay, explaining that thereby ended my duty toward them, and it was up to the Foreign Office to decide how long they could remain in their houses in the Embassy compound. I asked what they intended to do, and was horrified to learn that all of them with only one exception intended to stay until the new Ambassador arrived and even asked me to recommend them to him. Such a lack of understanding of the change in the position of the Embassy saddened me. Here were people who should have known through what tragedy the Embassy was passing, but for them everything was reduced to a mere change in ambassadors. I was disgusted and told them that there could be no question of my recommending them and that I did not wish to see them anymore. I realized that I was not fair; after all, to them

---

[13] At this point the manuscript contains seven lines, fairly thoroughly crossed out. With some effort the general meaning can be reconstructed, however, and does seem worthy of mention. Abrikossow recalls that after passing with the Japanese official from room to room, they came to the small Embassy church. "I could not help expressing regret at having to leave all these sacred things to such anti-religious people as the Bolsheviks, who will only ridicule and destroy them. To my astonishment the official asked why then I left them. I took the hint, and the following day all holy images and sacred things were sent to the Orthodox Cathedral in Tokyo."

as Japanese it mattered little who paid their salary. The only man who refused to work for the Reds after serving the Whites was our chancery servant [Sayama]. To recompense him for his fidelity I asked him and his family to share my fate as long as I remained in Japan, an offer I never regretted. His presence near me and his understanding of my position made my life in Japan easier, and I was sorry to part with him when I left the country.

On the day of my departure from the Embassy, Foreign Minister [Shidehara Kijuro] received me in a farewell audience. He assured me that it was not love for the Bolsheviks that had induced Japan to recognize Soviet Russia, but Russia was her close neighbor and unless she recognized the Soviet government she had no one to whom to address her claims and protests and could not avoid the constant violation of her interests. Now she could at least discuss the different questions which kept arising between the two neighboring states. When I expressed doubt that recognition would facilitate matters, because it would give the Soviets free entry into Japan and direct access to the Japanese public, the Minister acknowledged that the Japanese understood this very well and had obtained from the Bolsheviks the promise to abstain from spreading any propaganda in Japan, agreeing in turn not to allow any White activity in the country. It was obvious that Soviet-Japanese relations were not beginning in a particularly friendly atmosphere, but at the time the powers still believed in the sanctity of international promises; they did not realize that the Soviet rulers had introduced a system which respected the sanctity of treaty obligations only as long as it was to their advantage to do so.

The Foreign Minister repeated his promise that the White Russian refugees in Japan would enjoy the protection of the Japanese government and that nobody would be obliged to submit to the Soviet authorities, but warned that they must abstain from anti-Bolshevik activity. When I told the Foreign Minister that I intended to remain in Japan to help my compatriots to adapt themselves to the new situation, the Minister to my surprise expressed full approval and assured me that I would continue to receive from the Japanese authorities all possible help as long as I did not claim any official position. Thus we parted as good friends, and every time I met Baron Shidehara he treated me with great amity.

✥✥✥

On the evening of February 15, 1925, I left the Embassy. How fortunate that no newspapermen witnessed the humiliating sight, how the last representative of the powerful Russian Empire slipped through a side door and accompanied by a rickshaw laden with his personal belongings walked through the dark, narrow streets to his new dwelling. The house to which I moved consisted of four rooms—two downstairs for the servant and his family, two upstairs for me. It had paper windows, no heating, and a solitary lamp, which could not disperse the gloom of the oncoming night. I felt tired and miserable.

Sitting in the armchair I closed my eyes and reflected on my situation. It was easy to pity myself. I had begun my life brilliantly; now I was reduced to the lonely life of a refugee without country, family, or future. This state of mind did not last long, however. There is some sense in making others pity one, but to pity oneself is useless; it merely increases the surrounding gloom. I remember how my father had consoled us whenever something disagreeable had happened to us by saying that things could be much worse. Now I thought in what dreadful predicament I would be, were I still in Russia. Instead, I was beyond the reach of the Bolsheviks and was responsible only for myself; there was no real cause for despair. It is the privilege of a healthy and sensible man to have enough optimism to fight the misfortunes which beset him. I ordered a hot bath and went to bed under several Japanese *futon* and fell asleep, not even thinking about the difference between my miserable garret and the lofty bedroom in which I had slept the night before. The next morning my garret was full of sun, my servant prepared for me an ambassadorial breakfast, and I started my new life in high spirits.

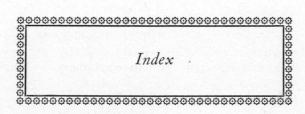

Index